Microsoft

Access 2002

Complete Concepts and Techniques

Gary B. Shelly
Thomas J. Cashman
Philip J. Pratt
Mary Z. Last

D0573302

COURSE
TECHNOLOGY ™

THOMSON LEARNING

COURSE TECHNOLOGY
25 THOMSON PLACE
BOSTON MA 02210

SHELLY
CASHMAN
SERIES®

Australia • Canada • Denmark • Japan • Mexico • New Zealand • Philippines • Puerto Rico • Singapore
South Africa • Spain • United Kingdom • United States

COURSE TECHNOLOGY

THOMSON LEARNING

COPYRIGHT © 2002 Course Technology, a division of Thomson Learning.
Printed in the United States of America

Asia (excluding Japan)
Thomson Learning
60 Albert Street, #15-01
Albert Complex
Singapore 189969

Japan
Thomson Learning
Palaceside Building 5F
1-1-1 Hitotsubashi, Chiyoda-ku
Tokyo 100 0003 Japan

Australia/New Zealand
Nelson/Thomson Learning
102 Dodds Street
South Melbourne, Victoria 3205
Australia

Latin America
Thomson Learning
Seneca, 53
Colonia Polanco
11560 Mexico D.F. Mexico

South Africa
Thomson Learning
Zonnebloem Building,
Constantia Square
526 Sixteenth Road
P.O. Box 2459
Halfway House, 1685
South Africa

Canada
Nelson/Thomson Learning
1120 Birchmount Road
Scarborough, Ontario
Canada M1K 5G4

UK/Europe/Middle East
Thomson Learning
Berkshire House
168-173 High Holborn
London, WC1V 7AA United Kingdom

Spain
Thomson Learning
Calle Magallanes, 25
28015-MADRID
ESPANA

APPROVED COURSEWARE

"Microsoft and the Microsoft Office User Specialist Logo are registered trademarks of Microsoft Corporation in the United States and other countries. Course Technology is an independent entity from Microsoft Corporation, and not affiliated with Microsoft Corporation in any manner. This textbook may be used in assisting students to prepare for a Microsoft Office User Specialist Exam. Neither Microsoft Corporation, its designated review company, nor Course Technology warrants that use of this textbook will ensure passing the relevant Exam.

"Use of the Microsoft Office User Specialist Approved Courseware Logo on this product signifies that it has been independently reviewed and approved in complying with the following standards: 'Acceptable coverage of all content related to the Microsoft Office Exam entitled "Microsoft Access 2002 Core Exam," and sufficient performance-based exercises that relate closely to all required content, based on sampling of text.'"

PHOTO CREDITS: Microsoft Access 2002 *Project 1, pages A 1.04-05* Trojan horse, Trojan horse fresco, Courtesy of ArtToday; adults helping child with headset, silhouettes, Courtesy of Dynamic Graphics; adult and child reading, teacher and students at computers, Courtesy of PhotoDisc, Inc.; *Project 2, pages A 2.02-03* Father holding baby, globe artwork, Courtesy of Nova Development, child's portrait, Courtesy of PhotoDisc, Inc.; *Project 4, pages A 4.02-03* World, cellular telephone, man on cellular telephone, computer monitor, and keyboard, Courtesy of PhotoDisc, Inc.; Compass, road signs, road, man with map, books, satellite, people at sign, and globe, Courtesy of ArtToday; *Project 5 A 5.02-03* Fingerprints, Courtesy of ArtToday; CD-ROM, buildings, keyboards, people on stairway, and railroad tracks, Courtesy of PhotoDisc, Inc.; Man on telephone, man working at computer, and building with columns, Courtesy of PhotoDisc, Inc.

ISBN 0-7895-6281-2

2 3 4 5 6 7 8 9 10   BC   06 05 04 03 02

Microsoft
Access 2002
Complete Concepts and Techniques

Contents

■ APPENDIX A

MICROSOFT ACCESS HELP SYSTEM

■ APPENDIX B

SPEECH AND HANDWRITING RECOGNITION

■ APPENDIX C

PUBLISHING OFFICE WEB PAGES TO A WEB SERVER

■ APPENDIX D

RESETTING THE ACCESS TOOLBARS AND MENUS   A D.01

■ APPENDIX E

MICROSOFT OFFICE USER SPECIALIST CERTIFICATION PROGRAM

Preface

The Shelly Cashman Series® offers the finest textbooks in computer education. We are proud of the fact that our series of Microsoft Office 4.3, Microsoft Office 95, Microsoft Office 97, and Microsoft Office 2000 textbooks have been the most widely used books in education. With each new edition of our Office books, we have made improvements based on the software and comments made by the instructors and students. The *Microsoft Office XP* books continue with the innovation, quality, and reliability that you have come to expect from the Shelly Cashman Series.

In this *Microsoft Access 2002* book, you will find an educationally sound and easy-to-follow pedagogy that combines a step-by-step approach with corresponding screens. All projects and exercises in this book are designed to take full advantage of the Access 2002 enhancements. The popular Other Ways and More About features offer in-depth knowledge of Access 2002. The new Learn It Online page presents a wealth of additional exercises to ensure your students have all the reinforcement they need. The project openers provide a fascinating perspective of the subject covered in the project. The project material is developed carefully to ensure that students will see the importance of learning Access for future coursework.

Objectives of This Textbook

Microsoft Access 2002: Complete Concepts and Techniques is intended for a two-unit course that presents Microsoft Access 2002. No experience with a computer is assumed, and no mathematics beyond the high school freshman level is required. The objectives of this book are:

- To teach the fundamentals of Access 2002
- To expose students to practical examples of the computer as a useful tool
- To acquaint students with the proper procedures to create databases suitable for course work, professional purposes, and personal use
- To develop an exercise-oriented approach that allows learning by doing
- To introduce students to new input technologies
- To encourage independent study, and help those who are working alone
- To assist students preparing to take the Microsoft Office User Specialist examination for Microsoft Access Core level

Approved by Microsoft as Courseware for the Microsoft Office User Specialist Program Core Level

This book has been approved by Microsoft as courseware for the Microsoft Office User Specialist (MOUS) program. After completing the projects and exercises in this book, students will be prepared to take the Core level Microsoft Office User Specialist Exam for Microsoft Access 2002. By passing the certification exam for a Microsoft software program, students demonstrate their proficiency in that program to employers. This exam is offered at participating centers, participating corporations, and participating employment agencies. See Appendix E for additional information on the MOUS program and a table that includes the Access 2002 MOUS skill sets and corresponding page numbers on which a skill is discussed in the book or visit the Web site mous.net. To purchase a Microsoft Office User Specialist certification exam, visit desktopiq.com.

The Shelly Cashman Series Microsoft Office User Specialist Center Web page (Figure 1) has more than fifteen Web pages you can visit to obtain additional information on the MOUS program. The Web page scsite.com.offxp/cert.htm includes links to general information on certification, choosing an application for certification, preparing for the certification exam, and taking and passing the certification exam.

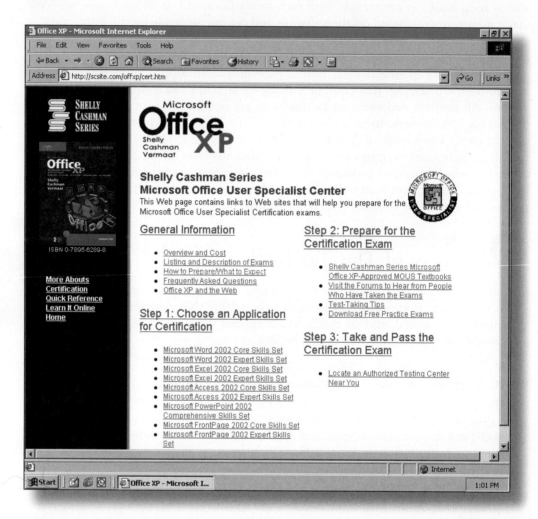

FIGURE 1   The Shelly Cashman Series Microsoft Office User Specialist Center Web Page

The Shelly Cashman Approach

Features of the Shelly Cashman Series *Microsoft Access 2002* books include:

- **Project Orientation:** Each project in the book presents a practical problem and complete solution in an easy-to-understand approach.
- **Step-by-Step, Screen-by-Screen Instructions:** Each of the tasks required to complete a project is identified throughout the project. Full-color screens accompany the steps.
- **Thoroughly Tested Projects:** Every screen in the book is correct because it is produced by the author only after performing a step, resulting in unprecedented quality.

- Other Ways Boxes and Quick Reference Summary: The Other Ways boxes displayed at the end of most of the step-by-step sequences specify the other ways to do the task completed in the steps. Thus, the steps and the Other Ways box make a comprehensive reference unit.
- More About Feature: These marginal annotations provide background information and tips that complement the topics covered, adding depth and perspective.
- Integration of the World Wide Web: The World Wide Web is integrated into the Access 2002 learning experience by (1) More About annotations that send students to Web sites for up-to-date information and alternative approaches to tasks; (2) a MOUS information Web page so students can prepare for the MOUS Certification examinations; (3) an Access 2002 Quick Reference Summary Web page that summarizes the ways to complete tasks (mouse, menu, shortcut menu, and keyboard); and (4) the Learn It Online page at the end of each project, which has project reinforcement exercises, learning games, and other types of student activities.

Organization of This Textbook

Microsoft Access 2002: Complete Concepts and Techniques provides detailed instruction on how to use Access 2002. The material is divided into six projects, a Web Feature, an Integration Feature, five appendices, and a Quick Reference Summary.

Project 1 – Creating a Database Using Design and Datasheet Views In Project 1, students are introduced to the concept of a database and shown how to use Access 2002 to create a database. Topics include creating a database; creating a table; defining the fields in a table; opening a table; adding records to a table; closing a table; and previewing and printing the contents of a table. Other topics in this project include using a form to view data; using the Report Wizard to create a report; and using Access Help. Students also learn how to design a database to eliminate redundancy.

Project 2 – Querying a Database Using the Select Query Window In Project 2, students learn to use queries to obtain information from the data in their databases. Topics include creating queries, running queries, and printing the results. Specific query topics include displaying only selected fields; using character data in criteria; using wildcards; using numeric data in criteria; using various comparison operators; and creating compound criteria. Other related topics include sorting, joining tables, and restricting records in a join. Students also use calculated fields, statistics, and grouping.

Project 3 – Maintaining a Database Using the Design and Update Features of Access 2002 In Project 3, students learn the crucial skills involved in maintaining a database. Topics include using Datasheet view and Form view to add new records, change existing records, and delete records, and to locate and filter records. Students also learn the processes of changing the structure of a table; adding additional fields; changing characteristics of existing fields; creating a variety of validation rules; and specifying referential integrity. Students perform mass changes and deletions using queries; create single-field and multiple-field indexes; and use subdatasheets to view related data.

Other Ways

1. Select form, click Open button on Database toolbar
2. Double-click form
3. In Voice Command mode, select form, say "Open"

More About

Date Fields in Queries: Using Expressions

Expressions have a special meaning in date fields in queries. Numbers that appear in expressions represent numbers of days. The expression <Date()-30 for Start Date finds drivers who started anytime up to 30 days before the day on which you run the query.

Web Feature – Publishing to the Internet Using Data Access Pages In this Web Feature, students learn to create a data access page to enable users to access the data in a database via the Internet. Topics include creating a data access page using the Page Wizard, previewing a data access page from within Access 2002, and using a data access page.

Project 4 – Reports, Forms, and Combo Boxes In Project 4, students learn to create custom reports and forms. Topics include creating queries for reports; using the Report Wizard; modifying a report design; saving a report; printing a report; creating a report with groups and subtotals; removing totals from a report; and changing the characteristics of items on a report. Other topics include creating an initial form using the Form Wizard; modifying a form design; moving fields; and adding calculated fields and combo boxes. Students learn how to change a variety of field characteristics such as font styles, formats, and colors.

Project 5 – Enhancing Forms with OLE Fields, Hyperlinks, and Subforms In Project 5, students learn to use date, memo, OLE, and hyperlink fields. Topics include incorporating these fields in the structure of a database; updating the data in these fields and changing table properties; creating a form that uses a subform to incorporate a one-to-many relationship between tables; manipulating subforms on a main form; incorporating date, memo, OLE, and hyperlink fields in forms; and incorporating various visual effects in forms. Students also learn to use the hyperlink fields to access Web pages and to use date and memo fields in a query.

Project 6 – Creating an Application System Using Macros, Wizards, and the Switchboard Manager In Project 6, students learn how to create a switchboard system, which is a system that allows users easily to access tables, forms, and reports simply by clicking buttons. Topics include creating and running macros; creating and using Lookup Wizard fields; using the Input Mask wizard; and creating and using a switchboard system.

Integration Feature – Sharing Data among Applications In the Integration Feature, students learn how to embed an Excel worksheet in an Access database and how to link a worksheet to a database. Students also learn how to prepare Access data for use in other applications. Topics include embedding worksheets; linking worksheets; using the resulting tables; using the Export command to export database data to an Excel worksheet; using drag-and-drop to export data to a Word document; and using the Export command to create a snapshot of a report.

Appendices The book includes five appendices. Appendix A presents an introduction to the Microsoft Access Help system. Appendix B describes how to use the speech and handwriting recognition capabilities of Access 2002. Appendix C explains how to publish Web pages to a Web server. Appendix D shows how to reset the menus and toolbars. Appendix E introduces students to the Microsoft Office User Specialist (MOUS) Certification program.

Quick Reference Summary In Microsoft Access 2002, you can accomplish a task in a number of ways, such as using the mouse, menu, shortcut menu, and keyboard. The Quick Reference Summary at the back of the book provides a quick reference to each task presented.

End-of-Project Student Activities

A notable strength of the Shelly Cashman Series *Microsoft Access 2002* books is the extensive student activities at the end of each project. Well-structured student activities can make the difference between students merely participating in a class and students retaining the information they learn. The activities in the Shelly Cashman Series *Microsoft Access 2002* books include the following.

- **What You Should Know** A listing of the tasks completed within a project together with the pages on which the step-by-step, screen-by-screen explanations appear.
- **Learn It Online** Every project features a Learn It Online page comprised of ten exercises. These exercises include True/False, Multiple Choice, Short Answer, Flash Cards, Practice Test, Learning Games, Tips and Tricks, Newsgroup usage, Expanding Your Horizons, and Search Sleuth.
- **Apply Your Knowledge** This exercise usually requires students to open and manipulate a file on the Data Disk. To obtain a copy of the Data Disk, follow the instructions on the inside back cover of this textbook.
- **In the Lab** Three in-depth assignments per project require students to apply the knowledge gained in the project to solve problems on a computer.
- **Cases and Places** Up to seven unique real-world case-study situations.

Shelly Cashman Series Teaching Tools

The three ancillaries that accompany this textbook are: Teaching Tools (ISBN 0-7895-6323-1), Course Presenter (ISBN 0-7895-6466-1), and MyCourse.com. These ancillaries are available to adopters through your Course Technology representative or by calling one of the following telephone numbers: Colleges and Universities, 1-800-648-7450; High Schools, 1-800-824-5179; Private Career Colleges, 1-800-477-3692; Canada, 1-800-268-2222; and Corporations and Government Agencies, 1-800-340-7450.

Teaching Tools

The contents of the Teaching Tools CD-ROM are listed below.

- **Instructor's Manual** The Instructor's Manual includes the following for each project: project objectives; project overview; detailed lesson plans with page number references; teacher notes and activities; answers to the end-of-project exercises; a test bank of 110 questions for every project (25 multiple-choice, 50 true/false, and 35 fill-in-the-blank) with page number references; and transparency references. The transparencies are available through the Figures in the Book. The test bank questions are the same as in ExamView and Course Test Manager.
- **Figures in the Book** Illustrations for every screen and table in the textbook are available in electronic form. Use this ancillary to present a slide show in lecture or to print transparencies for use in lecture with an overhead projector.

- ExamView ExamView is a state-of-the-art test builder that is easy to use. With ExamView, you quickly can create printed tests, Internet tests, and computer (LAN-based) tests. You can enter your own test questions or use the test bank that accompanies ExamView. The test bank is the same as the one described in the Instructor's Manual section. Instructors who want to continue to use our earlier generation test builder, Course Test Manager, rather than ExamView, can call Customer Service at 1-800-648-7450 for a copy of the Course Test Manager database for this book.
- Course Syllabus Any instructor who has been assigned a course at the last minute knows how difficult it is to come up with a course syllabus. For this reason, sample syllabi are included that can be customized easily to a course.
- Lecture Success System Lecture Success System files are used to explain and illustrate the step-by-step, screen-by-screen development of a project in the textbook without entering large amounts of data.
- Instructor's Lab Solutions Solutions and required files for all the In the Lab assignments at the end of each project are available. Solutions also are available for any Cases and Places assignment that supplies data.
- Lab Tests/Test Outs Tests that parallel the In the Lab assignments are supplied for the purpose of testing students in the laboratory on the material covered in the project or testing students out of the course.
- Project Reinforcement True/false, multiple choice, and short answer questions.
- Student Files All the files that are required by students to complete the Apply Your Knowledge exercises are included.
- Interactive Labs Eighteen completely updated, hands-on Interactive Labs that take students from ten to fifteen minutes each to step through help solidify and reinforce mouse and keyboard usage and computer concepts. Student assessment is available.

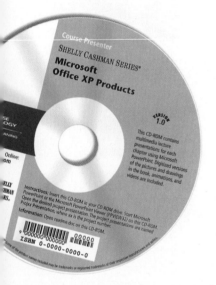

Course Presenter

Course Presenter is a lecture presentation system that provides PowerPoint slides for each project. Presentations are based on the projects' objectives. Use this presentation system to present well-organized lectures that are both interesting and knowledge-based. Course Presenter provides consistent coverage at schools that use multiple lecturers in their applications courses.

MyCourse.com

MyCourse.com offers instructors and students an opportunity to supplement classroom learning with additional course content. You can use MyCourse.com to expand on traditional learning by completing readings, tests, and other assignments through the customized, comprehensive Web site. For additional information, visit MyCourse.com and click the Help button.

SAM XP

SAM XP is a powerful skills-based testing and reporting tool that measures your students' proficiency in Microsoft Office applications through real-world, performance-based questions. SAM XP is available for a minimal cost.

Shelly Cashman Online

Shelly Cashman Online (Figure 2) is a World Wide Web service available to instructors and students of computer education. Visit Shelly Cashman Online at scseries.com. Shelly Cashman Online is divided into four areas:

- **Series Information** Information on the Shelly Cashman Series products.
- **Teaching Resources** This area includes password-protected data, course outlines, teaching tips, and ancillaries such as ExamView.
- **Community** Opportunities to discuss your course and your ideas with instructors in your field and with the Shelly Cashman Series team.
- **Student Center** Dedicated to students learning about computers with Shelly Cashman Series textbooks and software. This area includes cool links and much more.

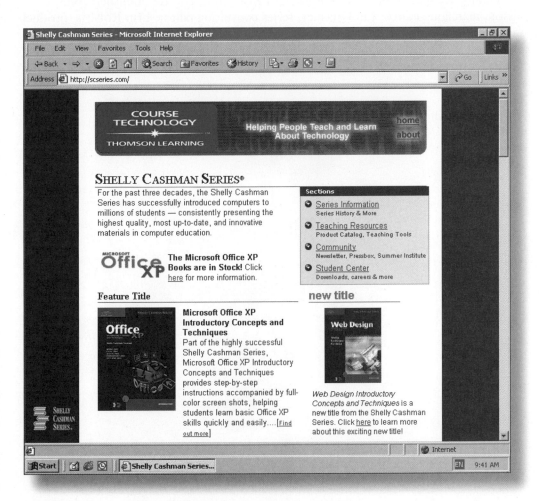

FIGURE 2 Shelly Cashman Online

Acknowledgments

The Shelly Cashman Series would not be the leading computer education series without the contributions of outstanding publishing professionals. First, and foremost, among them is Becky Herrington, director of production and designer. She is the heart and soul of the Shelly Cashman Series, and it is only through her leadership, dedication, and tireless efforts that superior products are made possible.

Under Becky's direction, the following individuals made significant contributions to these books: Doug Cowley, production manager; Ginny Harvey, series specialist and developmental editor; Ken Russo, senior Web and graphic designer; Mike Bodnar, associate production manager; Mark Norton, Web designer; Betty Hopkins and Richard Herrera, interior design; Meena Moest, product review manager; Bruce Greene, multimedia product manager; Michelle Linder, Christy Otten, Stephanie Nance, Kenny Tran, Chris Schneider, Sharon Lee Nelson, Sarah Boger, Amanda Lotter, Ryan Ung, and Michael Greco, graphic artists; Jeanne Black, Betty Hopkins, and Kellee LaVars, Quark layout artists; Lyn Markowicz, Nancy Lamm, Kim Kosmatka, Pam Baxter, Eva Kandarpa, and Marilyn Martin, copy editors/ proofreaders; Cristina Haley, proofreader/indexer; Sarah Evertson of Image Quest, photo researcher; Ginny Harvey, Rich Hansberger, Kim Clark, and Nancy Smith, contributing writers; and Richard Herrera, cover design.

Finally, we would like to thank Richard Keaveny, associate publisher; John Sisson, managing editor; Jim Quasney, series consulting editor; Erin Roberts, product manager; Erin Runyon, associate product manager; Francis Schurgot and Marc Ouellette, Web product managers; Rachel VanKirk, marketing manager; and Reed Cotter, editorial assistant.

Gary B. Shelly
Thomas J. Cashman
Philip J. Pratt
Mary Z. Last

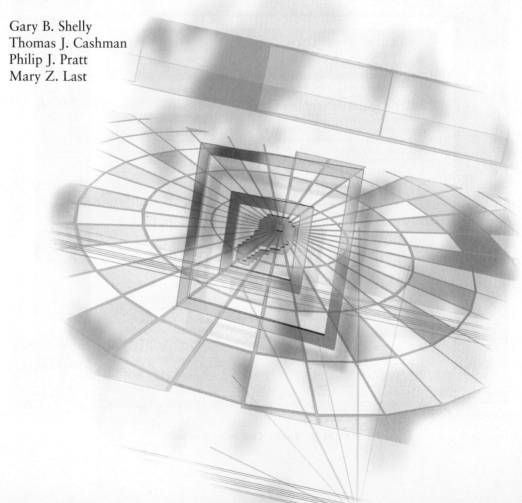

Shelly Cashman Series – Traditionally Bound Textbooks

The Shelly Cashman Series presents the following computer subjects in a variety of traditionally bound textbooks. For more information, see your Course Technology representative or call 1-800-648-7450. For Shelly Cashman Series information, visit Shelly Cashman Online at **scseries.com**

COMPUTERS	
Computers	Discovering Computers 2002: Concepts for a Digital World, Web Enhanced, Complete Edition
	Discovering Computers 2002: Concepts for a Digital World, Web Enhanced, Introductory Edition
	Discovering Computers 2002: Concepts for a Digital World, Web Enhanced, Brief Edition
	Teachers Discovering Computers: Integrating Technology in the Classroom 2e
	Exploring Computers: A Record of Discovery 4e
	Study Guide for Discovering Computers 2002: Concepts for a Digital World, Web Enhanced
	Essential Introduction to Computers 4e (32-page)

WINDOWS APPLICATIONS	
Microsoft Office	Microsoft Office XP: Essential Concepts and Techniques (5 projects)
	Microsoft Office XP: Brief Concepts and Techniques (9 projects)
	Microsoft Office XP: Introductory Concepts and Techniques (15 projects)
	Microsoft Office XP: Advanced Concepts and Techniques (11 projects)
	Microsoft Office XP: Post Advanced Concepts and Techniques (11 projects)
	Microsoft Office 2000: Essential Concepts and Techniques (5 projects)
	Microsoft Office 2000: Brief Concepts and Techniques (9 projects)
	Microsoft Office 2000: Introductory Concepts and Techniques, Enhanced Edition (15 projects)
	Microsoft Office 2000: Advanced Concepts and Techniques (11 projects)
	Microsoft Office 2000: Post Advanced Concepts and Techniques (11 projects)
Integration	Integrating Microsoft Office XP Applications and the World Wide Web: Essential Concepts and Techniques
PIM	Microsoft Outlook 2002: Essential Concepts and Techniques
Microsoft Works	Microsoft Works 6: Complete Concepts and Techniques[1] • Microsoft Works 2000: Complete Concepts and Techniques[1] • Microsoft Works 4.5[1]
Microsoft Windows	Microsoft Windows 2000: Complete Concepts and Techniques (6 projects)[2]
	Microsoft Windows 2000: Brief Concepts and Techniques (2 projects)
	Microsoft Windows 98: Essential Concepts and Techniques (2 projects)
	Microsoft Windows 98: Complete Concepts and Techniques (6 projects)[2]
	Introduction to Microsoft Windows NT Workstation 4
	Microsoft Windows 95: Complete Concepts and Techniques[1]
Word Processing	Microsoft Word 2002[2] • Microsoft Word 2000[2] • Microsoft Word 97[1] • Microsoft Word 7[1]
Spreadsheets	Microsoft Excel 2002[2] • Microsoft Excel 2000[2] • Microsoft Excel 97[1] • Microsoft Excel 7[1] Microsoft Excel 5[1]
Database	Microsoft Access 2002[2] • Microsoft Access 2000[2] • Microsoft Access 97[1] • Microsoft Access 7[1]
Presentation Graphics	Microsoft PowerPoint 2002[2] • Microsoft PowerPoint 2000[2] • Microsoft PowerPoint 97[1] Microsoft PowerPoint 7[1]
Desktop Publishing	Microsoft Publisher 2002[1] • Microsoft Publisher 2000[1]

PROGRAMMING	
Programming	Microsoft Visual Basic 6: Complete Concepts and Techniques[1] • Programming in QBasic
	Java Programming: Complete Concepts and Techniques[1] • Structured COBOL Programming 2e

INTERNET	
Browser	Microsoft Internet Explorer 5: An Introduction • Microsoft Internet Explorer 4: An Introduction
	Netscape Navigator 6: An Introduction • Netscape Navigator 4: An Introduction
Web Page Creation and Design	Web Design: Introductory Concepts and Techniques • HTML: Complete Concepts and Techniques[1]
	Microsoft FrontPage 2002: Essential Concepts and Techniques • Microsoft FrontPage 2002[2]
	Microsoft FrontPage 2000[1] • JavaScript: Complete Concepts and Techniques[1]

SYSTEMS ANALYSIS	
Systems Analysis	Systems Analysis and Design 4e

DATA COMMUNICATIONS	
Data Communications	Business Data Communications: Introductory Concepts and Techniques 3e

[1]Also available as an Introductory Edition, which is a shortened version of the complete book
[2]Also available as an Introductory Edition, which is a shortened version of the complete book and also as a Comprehensive Edition, which is an extended version of the complete book

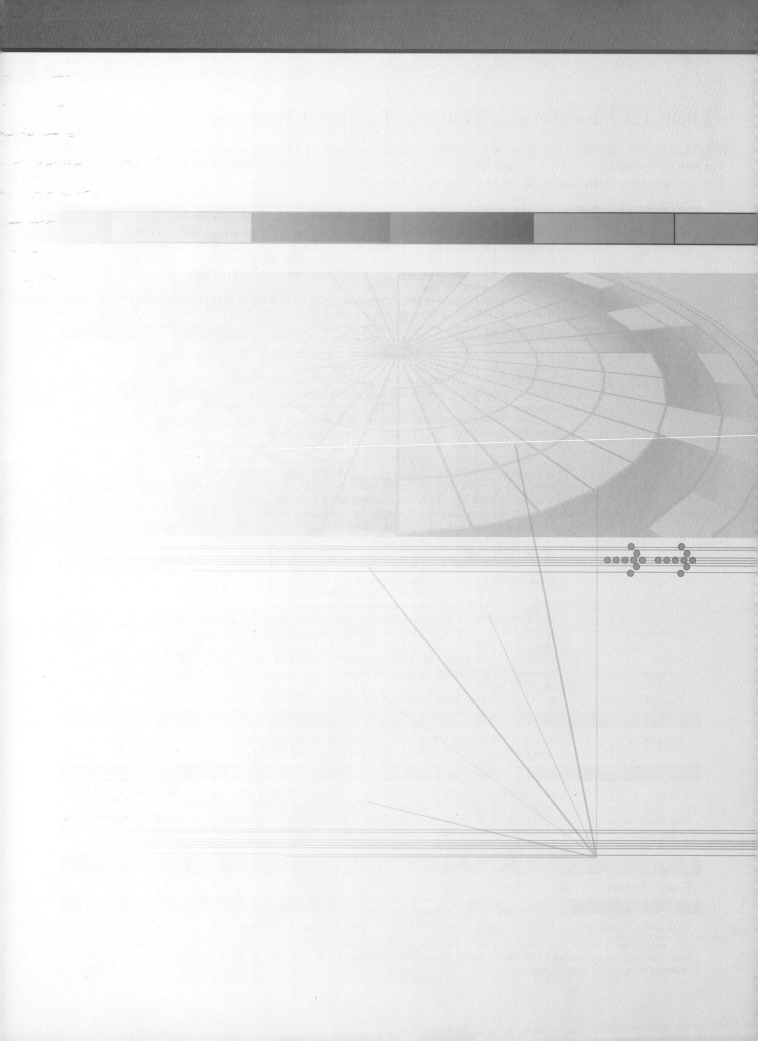

Microsoft

ACCESS

Microsoft Access 2002

Creating a Database Using Design and Datasheet Views

You will have mastered the material in this project when you can:

OBJECTIVES

- Describe databases and database management systems
- Describe the speech recognition capabilities of Access
- Start Access
- Describe the features of the Access desktop
- Create a database
- Create a table and define the fields in a table
- Open a table
- Add records to a table
- Close a table
- Close a database and quit Access
- Open a database
- Print the contents of a table
- Use a form to view data
- Create a custom report
- Use the Access Help system to answer your questions
- Design a database to eliminate redundancy

Education and Mentoring

Enriching the Learning Experience

Advocates of educational reform are making a difference in the learning experience. They work in partnership with educators, students, community members, and financial supporters. Their goal is to enhance student learning, deliver a common message to the education system, align priorities, encourage collaboration at every level, document successful outcomes from a variety of programs, and work toward long-term systemic change. They strive to improve the quality of education, reduce classroom sizes, integrate technology, and strengthen relationships among the partners.

One effective way of enriching the learning process is to involve various groups in education. College students, for example, who qualify for the Federal Work-Study Community Service Program work off campus helping students in kindergarten through ninth grade in the America Reads Program, whose goal is to ensure that every child can read well and independently by the end of the third grade and the America Counts Program, whose purpose is to help students through the ninth grade in developing and building strong mathematical skills.

More than 6,600 schools serving 1,600 communities have received grants and participate in the 21st Century Community Learning Centers program, which is a key component in the U.S. Department of Education Administration's efforts to keep children safe and provide academic development and other recreational and enrichment opportunities.

Building Databases

The International Telementor Center, hosted by the Center for Science, Mathematics & Technology Education (CSMATE) at Colorado State University, assists telementoring relationships between professional adults and students worldwide. The goal of telementoring, which combines mentoring with electronic communication, is to help students in the important subject areas of math, science, engineering, communications, and career and education planning.

In mythology, Mentor advised Odysseus, who led the Greeks in the Trojan War. Today, mentors instruct and lead others in need of guidance and direction. Common partnerships in the computer field bring together network experts with culturally diverse school districts to network classrooms within the region; technology buffs to develop distance education programs for students in remote areas; and software experts to install programs in computer labs and then train teachers.

Building these partnerships requires superb technological and organizational skills, strong marketing, and dedicated staff members. The nation's largest nonprofit computerization assistance center, CompuMentor, is one of these successful partnering organizations. CompuMentor has linked its staff with more than 23,000 schools and other nonprofit organizations since 1987.

The heart of its success is matching computer experts with the appropriate school or organization. Some mentors volunteer long term, while others agree to work intensively for a few days, particularly in telecommunications areas. Potential mentors complete an application at CompuMentor's Web site (www.compumentor.org) by entering specific information in boxes, called fields, pertaining to their knowledge of operating systems, networking, and hardware repair. They give additional information about their available working hours, training experience, and special skills in office and accounting applications, databases, and desktop publishing.

This information structures records in the CompuMentor database. The staff then can search these records to find a volunteer whose skills match the school's or organization's needs. Similarly in Project 1, you will use the Access database management system to enter records in the Alisa Vending Services database so the staff can match drivers with vendors whose machines require replenishing, maintenance, and repairs.

Uniting schools with appropriate experts increases awareness of educational issues and ultimately improves the learning process. For more information on building mentoring relationships, visit the U.S. Department of Education Web site (www.ed.gov) or call 1-800-USA-LEARN.

Microsoft Access 2002

Creating a Database Using Design and Datasheet Views

CASE PERSPECTIVE

Alisa Vending Services is a company that places vending machines in its customers' facilities. In return for the privilege of placing the vending machine, Alisa pays each customer a share of the profits from the machine. Payments are made quarterly. Alisa must track the amount already paid to each customer this year. It also must track the amount due to each customer for the current quarter.

Alisa employs drivers to service its customers. Each customer is assigned to a specific driver. The driver replenishes the food and beverage items in the machine, collects the money, and performs routine maintenance and simple repairs.

To ensure operations run smoothly, Alisa Vending Services needs to maintain data on its drivers and their assigned customers. Rather than using a manual system, Alisa wants to organize the data in a database, managed by a database management system such as Access. In this way, Alisa can keep its data current and accurate while management can analyze the data for trends and produce a variety of useful reports. Your task is to help Alisa Vending Services in creating and using their database.

What Is Microsoft Access?

Microsoft Access is a powerful database management system (DBMS) that functions in the Windows environment and allows you to create and process data in a database. Some of the key features are:

▶ **Data entry and update**   Access provides easy mechanisms for adding, changing, and deleting data, including the ability to make mass changes in a single operation.

▶ **Queries (questions)**   Using Access, it is easy to ask complex questions concerning the data in the database and receive instant answers.

▶ **Forms**   In Access, you can produce attractive and useful forms for viewing and updating data.

▶ **Reports**   Access contains a feature to create sophisticated reports easily for presenting your data.

▶ **Web Support**   Access allows you to save objects, reports, and tables in HTML format so they can be viewed using a browser. You also can create data access pages to allow real-time access to data in the database via the Internet.

Project One — Alisa Vending Services

Creating, storing, sorting, and retrieving data are important tasks. In their personal lives, many people keep a variety of records such as names, addresses, and telephone numbers of friends and business associates, records of investments, records of expenses for tax purposes, and so on. These records must be arranged for quick access. Businesses also must be able to store and access information quickly and easily. Personnel and inventory records, payroll information, client records, order data, and accounts receivable information all are crucial and must be available readily.

The term **database** describes a collection of data organized in a manner that allows access, retrieval, and use of that data. A database management system, such as Access, allows you to use a computer to create a database; add, change, and delete data in the database; sort the data in the database; retrieve data in the database; and create forms and reports using the data in the database.

In Access, a database consists of a collection of tables. Figure 1-1 shows a sample database for Alisa Vending Services, which consists of two tables. The Customer table contains information about the customers to whom Alisa Vending Services provides services. Each customer is assigned to a specific driver. The Driver table contains information about the drivers to whom these customers are assigned.

The rows in the tables are called **records**. A record contains information about a given person, product, or event. A row in the Customer table, for example, contains information about a specific customer.

The columns in the tables are called fields. A **field** contains a specific piece of information within a record. In the Customer table, for example, the fourth field, City, contains the city where the customer is located.

More About

Databases in Access

In some DBMSs, every table, query, form, or report is stored in a separate file. This is not the case in Access, in which a database is stored in a single file on disk. The file contains all the tables, queries, forms, reports, and programs that you create for this database.

fields

customers of driver Larissa Tuttle

Customer table

CUSTOMER NUMBER	NAME	ADDRESS	CITY	STATE	ZIP CODE	AMOUNT PAID	CURRENT DUE	DRIVER NUMBER
BA95	Bayside Hotel	287 Riley	Hansen	FL	38513	$21,876.00	$892.50	30
BR46	Baldwin-Reed	267 Howard	Fernwood	FL	37023	$26,512.00	$2,672.00	60
CN21	Century North	1562 Butler	Hansen	FL	38513	$8,725.00	$0.00	60
FR28	Friend's Movies	871 Adams	Westport	FL	37070	$4,256.00	$1,202.00	75
GN62	Grand Nelson	7821 Oak	Wood Key	FL	36828	$8,287.50	$925.50	30
GS29	Great Screens	572 Lee	Hansen	FL	38513	$21,625.00	$0.00	60
LM22	Lenger Mason	274 Johnson	Westport	FL	37070	$0.00	$0.00	60
ME93	Merks College	561 Fairhill	Bayville	FL	38734	$24,761.00	$1,572.00	30
RI78	Riter University	26 Grove	Fernwood	FL	37023	$11,682.25	$2,827.50	75
TU20	Turner Hotel	8672 Quincy	Palmview	FL	36114	$8,521.50	$0.00	60

records

Driver table

DRIVER NUMBER	LAST NAME	FIRST NAME	ADDRESS	CITY	STATE	ZIP CODE	HOURLY RATE	YTD EARNINGS
30	Tuttle	Larissa	7562 Hickory	Laton Springs	FL	37891	$16.00	$21,145.25
60	Powers	Frank	57 Ravenwood	Gillmore	FL	37572	$15.00	$19,893.50
75	Ortiz	Jose	341 Pierce	Douglas	FL	37613	$17.00	$23,417.00

driver Larissa Tuttle

FIGURE 1-1

The first field in the Customer table is the Customer Number. This is a code assigned by Alisa Vending Services to each customer. Similar to many organizations, Alisa Vending Services calls it a *number* although it actually contains letters. The customer numbers have a special format. They consist of two uppercase letters followed by a two-digit number.

These numbers are unique; that is, no two customers will be assigned the same number. Such a field can be used as a **unique identifier**. This simply means that a given customer number will display only in a single record in the table. Only one record exists, for example, in which the customer number is CN21. A unique identifier also is called a **primary key**. Thus, the Customer Number field is the primary key for the Customer table.

The next seven fields in the Customer table are Name, Address, City, State, Zip Code, Amount Paid, and Current Due. The Amount Paid field contains the amount that Alisa has paid already to the customer this year. The Current Due field contains the amount due from Alisa to the customer for the current period, but not yet paid.

For example, customer BA95 is Bayside Hotel. It is located at 287 Riley in Hansen, Florida. The zip code is 38513. The customer has been paid $21,876.00 so far this year and is due to be paid $892.50 for the current period.

Each customer is assigned to a single driver. The last field in the Customer table, Driver Number, gives the number of the customer's driver.

The first field in the Driver table, Driver Number, is the number assigned by Alisa Vending Services to the driver. These numbers are unique, so Driver Number is the primary key of the Driver table.

The other fields in the Driver table are Last Name, First Name, Address, City, State, Zip Code, Hourly Rate, and YTD Earnings. The Hourly Rate field gives the driver's hourly billing rate, and the YTD Earnings field contains the total amount that has been paid to the driver for services so far this year.

For example, driver 30 is Larissa Tuttle. She lives at 7562 Hickory in Laton Springs, Florida. Her zip code is 37891. Her hourly billing rate is $16.00 and her YTD earnings are $21,145.25.

The driver number displays in both the Customer table and the Driver table. It is used to relate customers and drivers. For example, in the Customer table, you see that the driver number for customer BA95 is 30. To find the name of this driver, look for the row in the Driver table that contains 30 in the Driver Number field. Once you have found it, you know the customer is assigned to Larissa Tuttle. To find all the customers assigned to Larissa Tuttle, on the other hand, look through the Customer table for all the customers that contain 30 in the Driver Number field. Her customers are BA95 (Bayside Hotel), GN62 (Grand Nelson), and ME93 (Merks College).

Together with the management of Alisa Vending Services, you have determined the data that must be maintained in the database is that shown in Figure 1-1 on the previous page. You first must create the database and the tables it contains. In the process, you must define the fields included in the two tables, as well as the type of data each field will contain. You then must add the appropriate records to the tables. You also must print the contents of the tables. Finally, you must create a report with the Customer Number, Name, Amount Paid, and Current Due fields for each customer served by Alisa Vending Services. Other reports and requirements for the database at Alisa Vending Services will be addressed with the Alisa Vending Services management in the future.

More *About*

The Access Help System

Need Help? It is no further than the Ask a Question box in the upper-right corner of the window. Click the box that contains the text Type a question for help (Figure 1-3), type help and then press the ENTER key. Access will respond with a list of items you can click to learn about obtaining help on any Access-related topic. To find out what is new in Access 2002, type what's new in Access in the Ask a Question box.

Starting Access

To start Access, Windows must be running. Perform the following steps to start Access.

Steps **To Start Access**

---

1 **Click the Start button on the Windows taskbar, point to Programs on the Start menu, and then point to Microsoft Access on the Programs submenu.**

The commands on the Start menu display above the Start button and the Programs submenu displays (Figure 1-2). If the Office Voice Recognition software is installed on your computer, then the Language bar may display somewhere on the desktop.

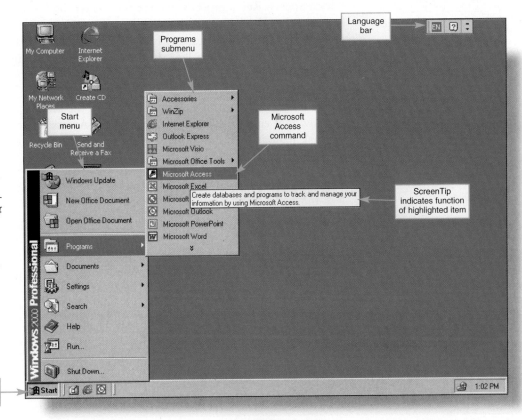

FIGURE 1-2

2 **Click Microsoft Access.**

Access starts. After several seconds, the Access window displays (Figure 1-3). If the Language bar displayed on the desktop when you started Access, then it expands to display additional buttons.

3 **If the Access window is not maximized, double-click its title bar to maximize it.**

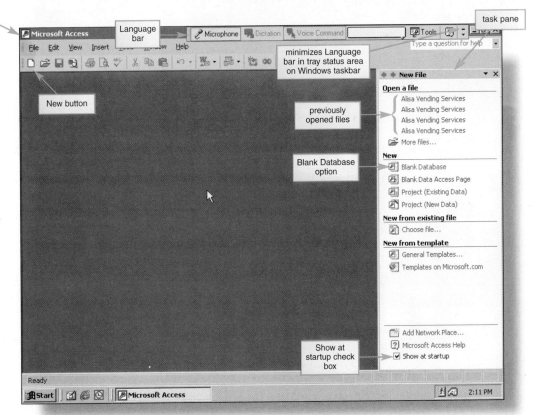

FIGURE 1-3

Task Panes

When you first start Access, a small window called a task pane may display docked on the right side of the screen. You can drag a task pane title bar to float the pane in your work area or dock it on either the left or right side of a screen, depending on your personal preference.

The screen in Figure 1-3 on the previous page shows how the Access window looks the first time you start Access after installation on most computers. If the Office Speech Recognition software is installed on your system, then when you start Access either the Language bar displays somewhere on the desktop (shown at the top of Figure 1-3) or the Language Indicator button displays on the right side of the Windows taskbar (Figure 1-5). In this book, the Language bar will be kept minimized until it is used. For additional information about the Language bar, see Appendix B on page A B.01.

Notice also that a task pane displays on the screen. A **task pane** is a separate window that enables users to carry out some Access tasks more efficiently. In this book, the task pane is used only to create a new database and then it should not display.

Speech Recognition

When you begin working in Access, if you have the **Office Speech Recognition software** installed and a microphone, you can speak the names of toolbar buttons, menus, menu commands, list items, alerts, and dialog box controls, such as OK and Cancel. You also can dictate field entries, such as text and numbers. To indicate whether you want to speak commands or dictate field entries, you use the **Language bar** (Figure 1-4a). You can display the Language bar in two ways: (1) click the Language Indicator button in the tray status area on the Windows taskbar by the clock, and then click Show the Language bar on the menu (Figure 1-4b), or (2) point to the **Speech command** on the **Tools menu** and then click the **Speech Recognition command** on the **Speech submenu**.

If the Language Indicator button does not display in the tray status area, and if the Speech command is unavailable (dimmed) on the Tools menu, the Office Speech Recognition software is not installed. To install the software, you first must start Word and then click Speech on the Tools menu.

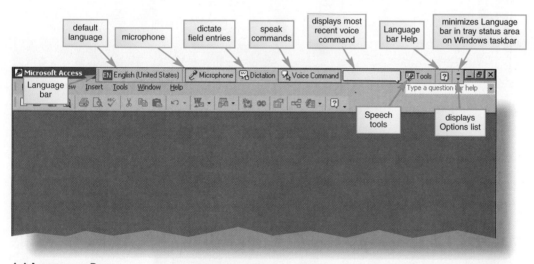

(a) Language Bar

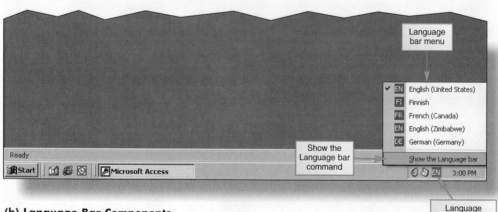

(b) Language Bar Components

FIGURE 1-4

If you have speakers, you can instruct the computer to read a document to you. By selecting the appropriate option, you can have the document read in a male or female voice.

Additional information on the Office speech and handwriting recognition capabilities is available in Appendix B.

Creating a New Database

In Access, all the tables, reports, forms, and queries that you create are stored in a single file called a database. Thus, before creating any of these objects, you first must create the database that will hold them. You use the Blank Database option in the task pane to create a new database. To allow the full Access window to display when you work with a database, you should close the task pane after creating a new database. Perform the following steps to create a new database and save the database on a floppy disk in drive A.

More About

Creating a Database: The Database Wizard

Access includes a Database Wizard that can guide you by suggesting some commonly used databases. To use the Database Wizard, click New on the Database toolbar, and then click General Templates in the New File task pane. When the Templates dialog box displays, click the Databases tab, and then click the database that is most appropriate for your needs. Follow the instructions in the Database Wizard dialog boxes to create the database.

Steps **To Create a New Database**

1 If the Language bar displays, click its Minimize button. If a dialog box displays, click the OK button. If necessary, click the New button on the Database toolbar to display the task pane. Click the Blank Database option in the task pane (see Figure 1-3 on page A 1.09), and then click the Save in box arrow. Point to 3½ Floppy (A:).

The Save in List displays in the File New Database dialog box (Figure 1-5). Your file name text box may display db1.mdb.

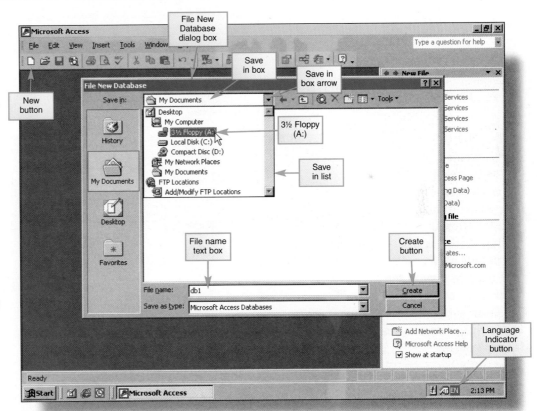

FIGURE 1-5

2 Click 3½ Floppy (A:). Click the File name text box. Repeatedly press the BACKSPACE key to delete db1 and then type Alisa Vending Services as the file name. Point to the Create button.

The file name is changed to Alisa Vending Services (Figure 1-6).

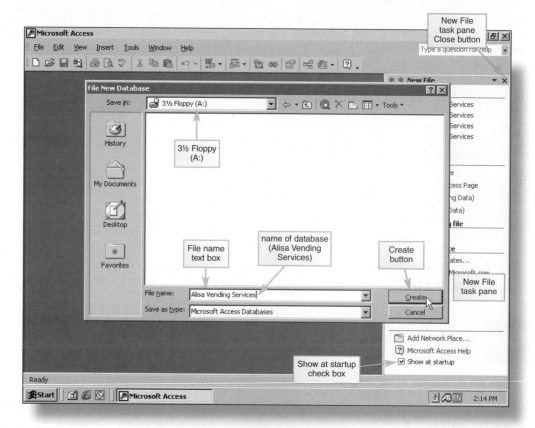

FIGURE 1-6

3 Click the Create button to create the database. If the task pane displays, click the Show at startup check box at the bottom of the task pane to remove the check mark and then click the Close button in the upper-right corner to close the task pane.

The Alisa Vending Services database is created. The Alisa Vending Services : Database window displays on the desktop (Figure 1-7). The New File task pane does not display.

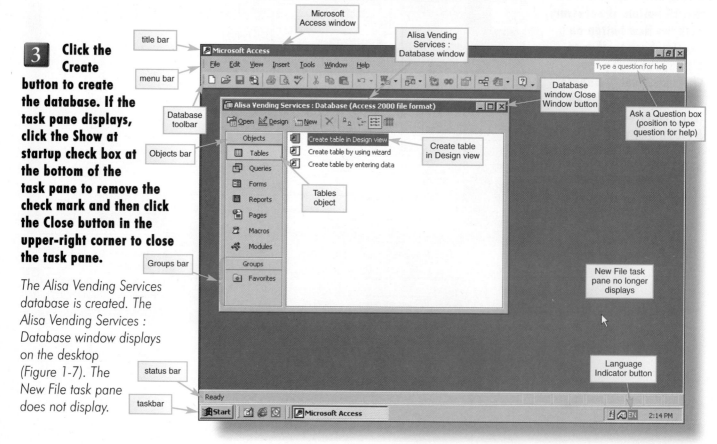

FIGURE 1-7

The Access Desktop and the Database Window

The first bar on the desktop (Figure 1-7) is the **title bar**. It displays the title of the product, Microsoft Access. The button on the right is the **Close button**. Clicking the Close button closes the window.

The second bar is the **menu bar**. It contains a list of menu names. To open a menu from the menu bar, click the menu name. Initially a personalized version of the menu, a short menu that consists of commands you have selected most recently, displays. After a few seconds, the full menu displays. If the command you wish to select is on the short menu, you can select it immediately. If not, wait a few seconds to view the full menu. (The menus shown throughout this book are the full menus, the ones that display after a few seconds.)

The third bar is the **Database toolbar**. The Database toolbar contains buttons that allow you to perform certain tasks more quickly than using the menu bar. Each button contains a picture, or **icon**, depicting its function. The specific toolbar or toolbars that display will vary, depending on the task on which you are working.

The **taskbar** at the bottom of the screen displays the Start button, any active windows, and the current time.

Immediately above the Windows taskbar is the **status bar** (Figure 1-7). It contains special information that is appropriate for the task on which you are working. Currently, it contains the word, Ready, which means Access is ready to accept commands.

The **Database window**, referred to in Figure 1-7 as the Alisa Vending Services : Database window, is a special window that allows you to access easily and rapidly a variety of objects such as tables, queries, forms, and reports. To do so, you will use the various components of the window.

Creating a Table

An Access database consists of a collection of tables. Once you have created the database, you must create each of the tables within it. In this project, for example, you must create both the Customer and Driver tables shown in Figure 1-1 on page A 1.07.

To create a table, you describe the **structure** of the table to Access by describing the fields within the table. For each field, you indicate the following:

1. **Field name** — Each field in the table must have a unique name. In the Customer table (Figure 1-8 on the next page), for example, the field names are Customer Number, Name, Address, City, State, Zip Code, Amount Paid, Current Due, and Driver Number.

2. **Data type** — Data type indicates to Access the type of data the field will contain. Some fields can contain only numbers. Others, such as Amount Paid and Current Due, can contain numbers and dollar signs. Still others, such as Name and Address, can contain letters.

3. **Description** — Access allows you to enter a detailed description of the field.

You also can assign field widths to text fields (fields whose data type is Text). This indicates the maximum number of characters that can be stored in the field. If you do not assign a width to such a field, Access assumes the width is 50.

More About

Toolbars

Normally, the correct Access toolbar automatically will display. If it does not, click View on the menu bar, and then click Toolbars. Click the toolbar for the activity in which you are engaged and then click the Close button. See Appendix D for additional details.

More About

Access File Formats

By default, Access creates a new database in Access 2000 format. A file in Access 2000 file format can be opened in both Access 2000 and Access 2002. This allows you to share your database with users who do not have Access 2002. You can open a file in Access 2002 format only in Access 2002. Certain features of Access 2002 are not available if the database is in Access 2000 file format.

More About

Creating a Table: The Table Wizard

Access includes a Table Wizard that guides you by suggesting some commonly used tables and fields. To use the Table Wizard, click the Tables object in the Database window. Right-click Create table by using wizard and then click Open on the shortcut menu. Follow the directions in the Table Wizard dialog boxes. After you create the table, you can modify it at any time by opening the table in Design view.

Structure of Customer table

FIELD NAME	DATA TYPE	FIELD SIZE	PRIMARY KEY?	DESCRIPTION
Customer Number	Text	4	Yes	Customer Number (Primary Key)
Name	Text	20		Customer Name
Address	Text	15		Street Address
City	Text	15		City
State	Text	2		State (Two-Character Abbreviation)
Zip Code	Text	5		Zip Code (Five-Character Version)
Amount Paid	Currency			Amount Paid to Customer This Year
Current Due	Currency			Amount Due to Customer This Period
Driver Number	Text	2		Number of Customer's Driver

Data for Customer table

CUSTOMER NUMBER	NAME	ADDRESS	CITY	STATE	ZIP CODE	AMOUNT PAID	CURRENT DUE	DRIVER NUMBER
BA95	Bayside Hotel	287 Riley	Hansen	FL	38513	$21,876.00	$892.50	30
BR46	Baldwin-Reed	267 Howard	Fernwood	FL	37023	$26,512.00	$2,672.00	60
CN21	Century North	1562 Butler	Hansen	FL	38513	$8,725.00	$0.00	60
FR28	Friend's Movies	871 Adams	Westport	FL	37070	$4,256.00	$1,202.00	75
GN62	Grand Nelson	7821 Oak	Wood Key	FL	36828	$8,287.50	$925.50	30
GS29	Great Screens	572 Lee	Hansen	FL	38513	$21,625.00	$0.00	60
LM22	Lenger Mason	274 Johnson	Westport	FL	37070	$0.00	$0.00	60
ME93	Merks College	561 Fairhill	Bayville	FL	38734	$24,761.00	$1,572.002	30
RI78	Riter University	26 Grove	Fernwood	FL	37023	$11,682.25	$2,827.50	75
TU20	Turner Hotel	8672 Quincy	Palmview	FL	36114	$8,521.50	$0.00	60

FIGURE 1-8

You also must indicate which field or fields make up the **primary key**; that is, the unique identifier, for the table. In the sample database, the Customer Number field is the primary key of the Customer table and the Driver Number field is the primary key of the Driver table.

The rules for field names are:

1. Names can be up to 64 characters in length.
2. Names can contain letters, digits, and spaces, as well as most of the punctuation symbols.
3. Names cannot contain periods, exclamation points (!), accent graves (`), or square brackets ([ ]).
4. The same name cannot be used for two different fields in the same table.

Data Types (General)

Different database management systems have different available data types. Even data types that are essentially the same can have different names. The Access Text data type, for example, is referred to as Character in some systems and Alpha in others.

a type. This indicates the type of data that can be stored in ... you will use in this project are:

... can contain any characters.

... eld can contain only numbers. The numbers either can be ...ve. Fields are assigned this type so they can be used in arith-... Fields that contain numbers but will not be used for arith-... usually are assigned a data type of Text. The Driver Number ..., is a text field because the driver numbers will not be ...rithmetic.

3. **Currency** — The field can contain only dollar amounts. The values will be displayed with dollar signs, commas, decimal points, and with two digits following the decimal point. Like numeric fields, you can use currency fields in arithmetic operations. Access assigns a size to currency fields automatically.

The field names, data types, field widths, primary key information, and descriptions for the Customer table are shown in Figure 1-8. With this information, you are ready to begin creating the table. To create the table, use the following steps.

Data Types (Access)

Access offers a wide variety of data types, some of which have special options associated with them. For more information on data types, visit the Access 2002 More About Web page (scsite.com/ac2002/more.htm) and then click Data Types.

Steps **To Create a Table**

1 **Right-click Create table in Design view and then point to Open on the shortcut menu.**

The shortcut menu for creating a table in Design view displays (Figure 1-9).

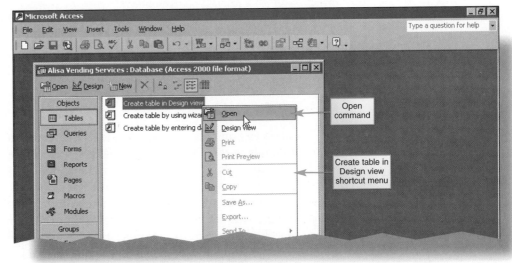

FIGURE 1-9

2 **Click Open and then point to the Maximize button for the Table1 : Table window.**

The Table1 : Table window displays (Figure 1-10).

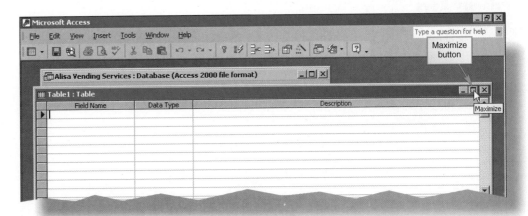

FIGURE 1-10

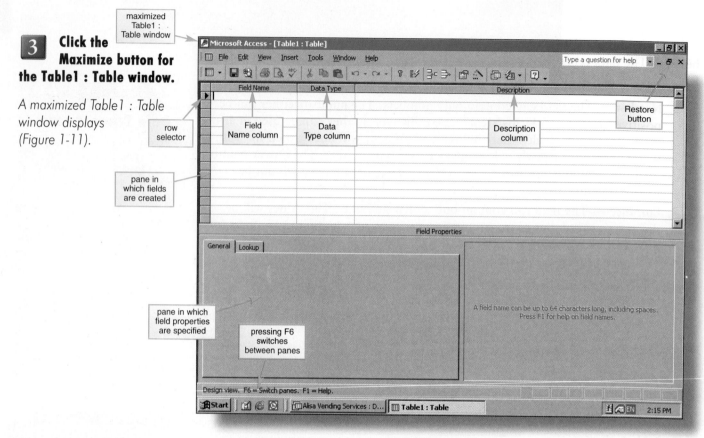

FIGURE 1-11

3 **Click the Maximize button for the Table1 : Table window.**

A maximized Table1 : Table window displays (Figure 1-11).

Defining the Fields

The next step in creating the table is to define the fields by specifying the required details in the Table window. Make entries in the Field Name, Data Type, and Description columns. Enter additional information in the Field Properties box in the lower portion of the Table window. Press the F6 key to move from the upper **pane** (portion of the screen), the one where you define the fields, to the lower pane, the one where you define field properties. Enter the appropriate field size and then press the F6 key to return to the upper pane. As you define the fields, the **row selector** (Figure 1-11), the small box or bar that, when clicked, selects the entire row, indicates the field you currently are describing. It is positioned on the first field, indicating Access is ready for you to enter the name of the first field in the Field Name column.

Perform the following steps to define the fields in the table.

Steps: To Define the Fields in a Table

1 **Type** Customer Number **(the name of the first field) in the Field Name column and then press the TAB key.**

The words, Customer Number, display in the Field Name column and the insertion point advances to the Data Type column, indicating you can enter the data type (Figure 1-12). The word, Text, one of the possible data types, currently displays. The arrow indicates a list of data types is available by clicking the arrow. The field properties for the Customer Number field display in the lower pane.

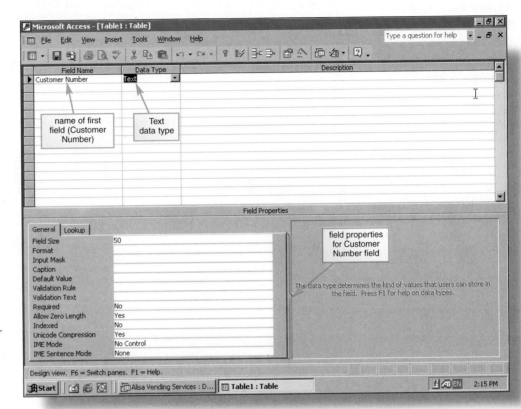

FIGURE 1-12

2 **Because Text is the correct data type, press the TAB key to move the insertion point to the Description column, type** Customer Number (Primary Key) **as the description and then point to the Primary Key button on the Table Design toolbar.**

A *ScreenTip*, which is a description of the button, displays partially obscuring the description of the first field (Figure 1-13).

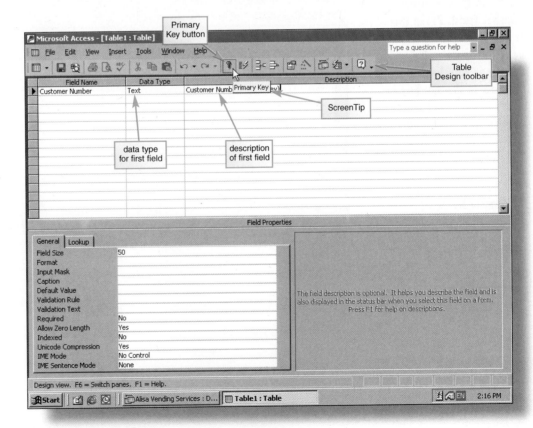

FIGURE 1-13

3 **Click the Primary Key button to make Customer Number the primary key and then press the F6 key to move the insertion point to the Field Size property box.**

The Customer Number field is the primary key as indicated by the key symbol that displays in the row selector (Figure 1-14). The current entry in the Field Size property box (50) is selected.

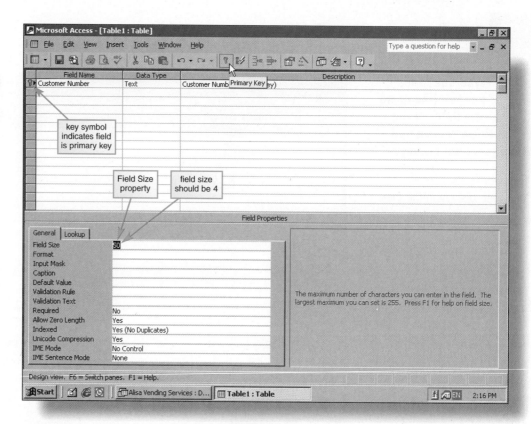

FIGURE 1-14

4 **Type 4 as the size of the Customer Number field. Press the F6 key to return to the Description column for the Customer Number field and then press the TAB key to move to the Field Name column in the second row.**

The insertion point moves to the second row just below the field name Customer Number (Figure 1-15).

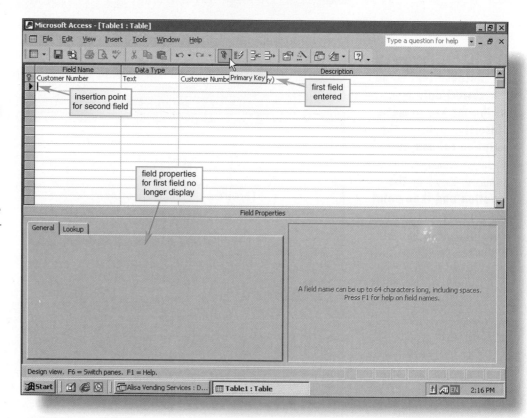

FIGURE 1-15

5 Use the techniques illustrated in Steps 1 through 4 to make the entries from the Customer table structure shown in Figure 1-8 on page A 1.14 up through and including the name of the Amount Paid field. Click the Data Type box arrow and then point to Currency.

The additional fields are entered (Figure 1-16). A list of available data types displays in the Data Type column for the Amount Paid field.

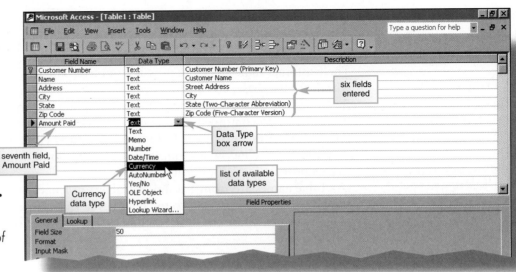

FIGURE 1-16

6 Click Currency and then press the TAB key. Make the remaining entries from the Customer table structure shown in Figure 1-8.

The fields are all entered (Figure 1-17).

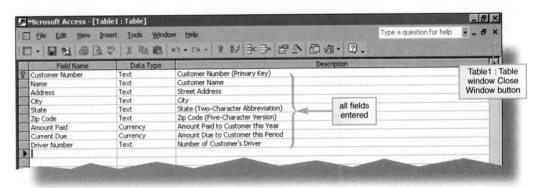

FIGURE 1-17

Correcting Errors in the Structure

When creating a table, check the entries carefully to ensure they are correct. If you make a mistake and discover it before you press the TAB key, you can correct the error by repeatedly pressing the BACKSPACE key until the incorrect characters are removed. Then, type the correct characters. If you do not discover a mistake until later, you can click the entry, type the correct value, and then press the ENTER key.

If you accidentally add an extra field to the structure, select the field by clicking the row selector (the leftmost column on the row that contains the field to be deleted). Once you have selected the field, press the DELETE key. This will remove the field from the structure.

If you forget a field, select the field that will follow the field you wish to add by clicking the row selector, and then press the INSERT key. The remaining fields move down one row, making room for the missing field. Make the entries for the new field in the usual manner.

If you made the wrong field a primary key field, click the correct primary key entry for the field and then click the Primary Key button on the Table Design toolbar.

As an alternative to these steps, you may want to start over. To do so, click the Close Window button for the Table1 : Table window and then click No. The original desktop displays and you can repeat the process you used earlier.

More About

Correcting Errors

Even after you have entered data, it still is possible to correct errors in the structure. Access will make all the necessary adjustments to the structure of the table as well as to the data within it. (It is simplest to make the correction, however, before any data is entered.)

More *About*

Adding Records

As soon as you have entered or modified a record and moved to another record, the original record is saved. This is different from other tools. The rows entered in a spreadsheet, for example, are not saved until the entire spreadsheet is saved.

Saving and Closing a Table

The Customer table structure now is complete. The final step is to save the table within the database. At this time, you should give the table a name. Once you save the table structure, you can continue working in the Table window or you can close the window. To continue working in the Table Design window, click the Save button on the Table Design toolbar. To save the table and close the Table Design window, click the Close Window button. If you close the Table window without saving first, Access provides an opportunity to do so.

Table names are from 1 to 64 characters in length and can contain letters, numbers, and spaces. The two table names in this project are Customer and Driver.

To save and close the table, complete the following steps.

Steps **To Save and Close a Table**

1 Click the Close Window button for the Table1 : Table window (see Figure 1-17 on the previous page). (Be sure not to click the Close button on the Microsoft Access title bar, because this would close Microsoft Access.) Point to the Yes button in the Microsoft Access dialog box.

The Microsoft Access dialog box displays (Figure 1-18).

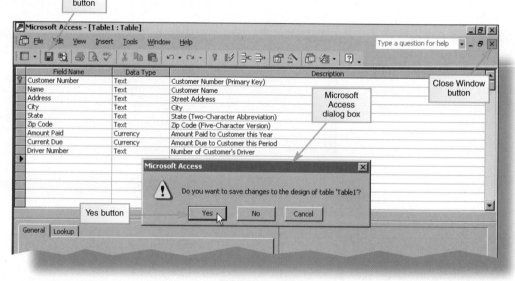

FIGURE 1-18

2 Click the Yes button in the Microsoft Access dialog box and then type Customer as the name of the table. Point to the OK button.

The Save As dialog box displays (Figure 1-19). The table name is entered.

3 Click the OK button in the Save As dialog box.

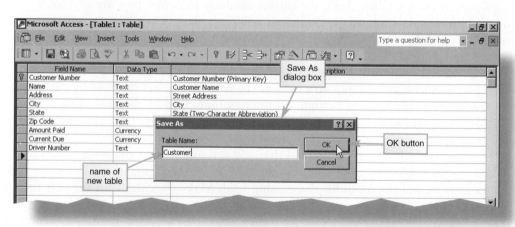

FIGURE 1-19

The table is saved. The window containing the table design no longer displays.

Adding Records to a Table

Creating a table by building the structure and saving the table is the first step in a two-step process. The second step is to add records to the table. To add records to a table, the table must be open. To open a table, right-click the table in the Database window and then click Open on the shortcut menu. The table displays in Datasheet view. In **Datasheet view**, the table is represented as a collection of rows and columns called a **datasheet**. It looks very much like the tables shown in Figure 1-1 on page A 1.07.

You often add records in phases. You may, for example, not have enough time to add all the records in one session. To illustrate this process, this project begins by adding the first two records in the Customer table (Figure 1-20). The remaining records are added later.

Customer table (first 2 records)								
CUSTOMER NUMBER	NAME	ADDRESS	CITY	STATE	ZIP CODE	AMOUNT PAID	CURRENT DUE	DRIVER NUMBER
BA95	Bayside Hotel	287 Riley	Hansen	FL	38513	$21,876.00	$892.50	30
BR46	Baldwin-Reed	267 Howard	Fernwood	FL	37023	$26,512.00	$2,672.00	60

FIGURE 1-20

To open the Customer table and then add records, perform the following steps.

Steps **To Add Records to a Table**

1 **Right-click the Customer table in the Alisa Vending Services : Database window and then point to Open on the shortcut menu.**

The shortcut menu for the Customer table displays (Figure 1-21). The Alisa Vending Services : Database window is maximized because the previous window, the Customer : Table window, was maximized. (If you wanted to restore the Database window to its original size, you would click the Restore Window button.)

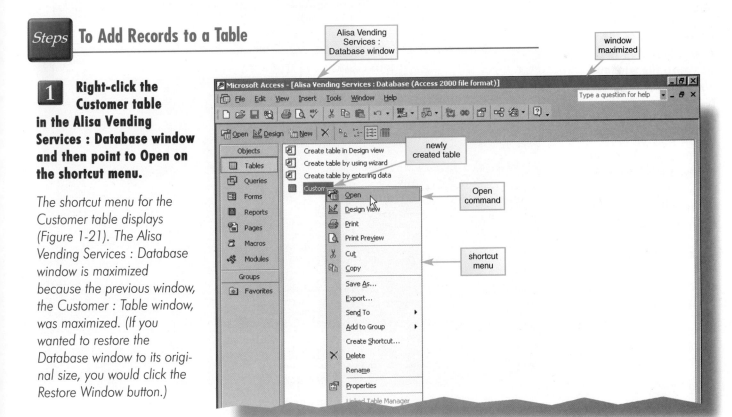

FIGURE 1-21

2 **Click Open on the shortcut menu.**

The Customer : Table window displays (Figure 1-22). The window contains the Datasheet view for the Customer table. The **record selector,** the small box or bar that, when clicked, selects the entire record, is positioned on the first record. The status bar at the bottom of the window also indicates that the record selector is positioned on record 1.

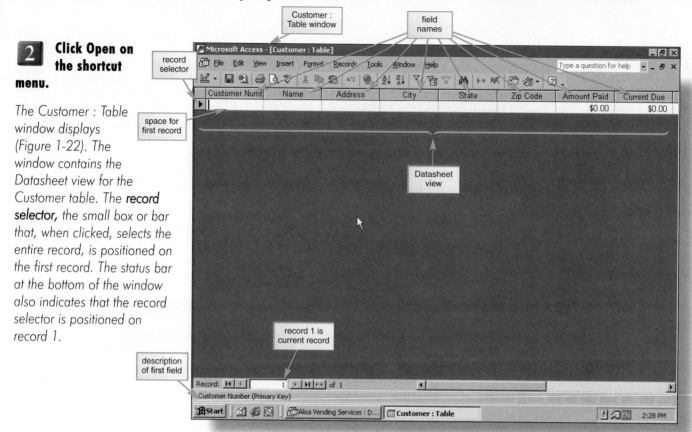

FIGURE 1-22

3 **If your window is not already maximized, click the Maximize button to maximize the window containing the table. Type** BA95 **as the first customer number (see Figure 1-20 on the previous page). Be sure you type the letters in uppercase, because that is the way they are to be entered in the database.**

The customer number is entered, but the insertion point is still in the Customer Number field (Figure 1-23).

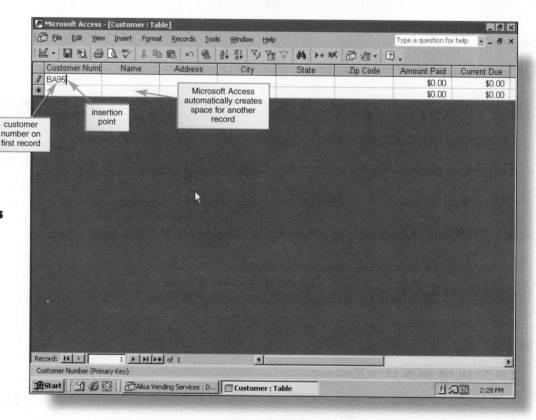

FIGURE 1-23

4 **Press the TAB key to complete the entry for the Customer Number field. Type the following entries, pressing the TAB key after each one:**
Bayside Hotel **as the name,** 287 Riley **as the address,** Hansen **as the city,** FL **as the state, and** 38513 **as the zip code.**

The Name, Address, City, State, and Zip Code fields are entered (Figure 1-24).

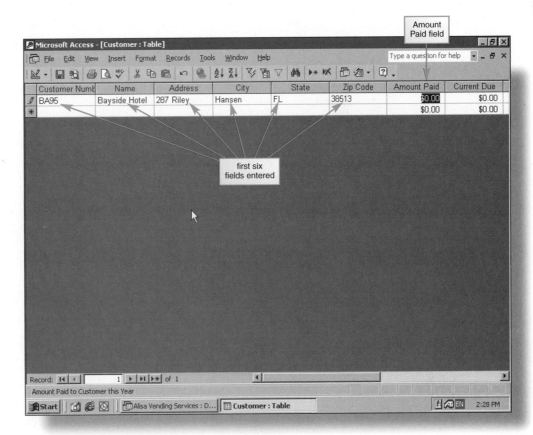

FIGURE 1-24

5 **Type** 21876 **as the amount paid amount and then press the TAB key. (You do not need to type dollar signs or commas. In addition, because the digits to the right of the decimal point were both zeros, you did not need to type either the decimal point or the zeros.) Type** 892.50 **as the current due amount and then press the TAB key. Type** 30 **as the driver number to complete the record.**

The fields have shifted to the left (Figure 1-25). The amount paid and current due values display with dollar signs and decimal points. The insertion point is positioned in the Driver Number field.

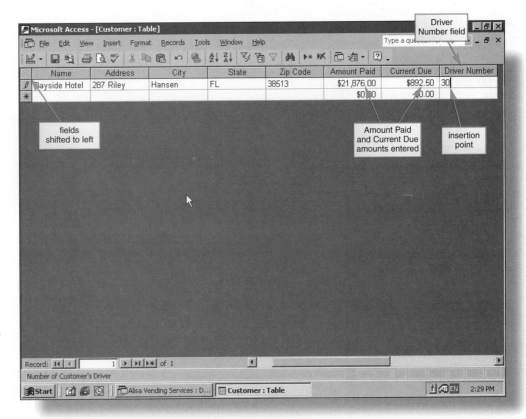

FIGURE 1-25

6 **Press the TAB key.**

The fields shift back to the right, the record is saved, and the insertion point moves to the customer number on the second row (Figure 1-26).

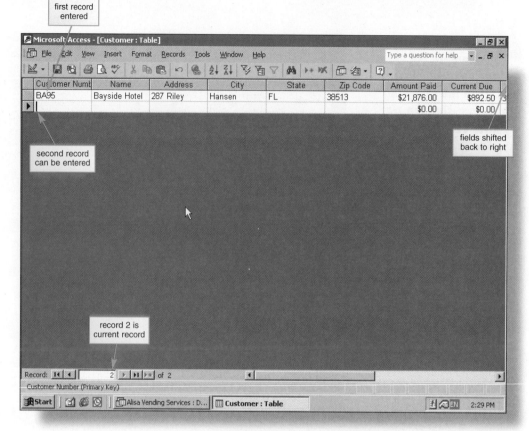

FIGURE 1-26

7 **Use the techniques shown in Steps 3 through 6 to add the data for the second record in Figure 1-20 on page A 1.21. Point to the Close Window button.**

The second record is added and the insertion point moves to the customer number on the third row (Figure 1-27).

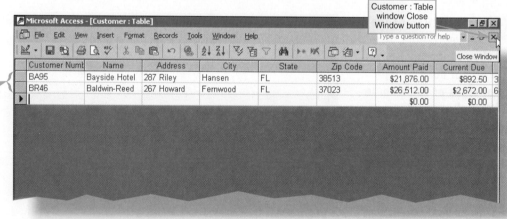

FIGURE 1-27

Closing a Table and Database

It is a good idea to close a table as soon as you have finished working with it. It keeps the screen from getting cluttered and prevents you from making accidental changes to the data in the table. Assuming that these two records are the only records you plan to add during this session, perform the following steps to close the table and the database. If you no longer will work with the database, you should close the database as well.

Steps To Close a Table and Database

1 **Click the Close Window button for the Customer : Table window (see Figure 1-27). Point to the Close Window button for the Alisa Vending Services : Database window.**

The datasheet for the Customer table no longer displays (Figure 1-28).

2 **Click the Close Window button for the Alisa Vending Services : Database window.**

The Alisa Vending Services : Database window no longer displays.

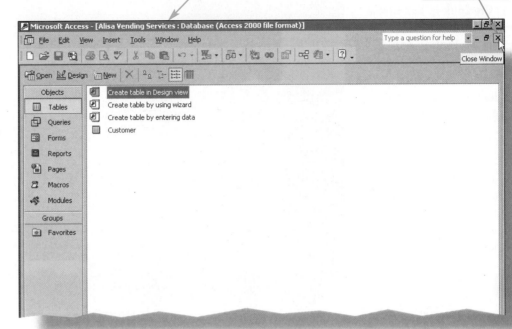

FIGURE 1-28

Opening a Database

To work with any of the tables, reports, or forms in a database, the database must be open. To open a database from within Access, click Open on the Database toolbar. To resume adding records to the Customer table, open the database by performing the following steps.

Steps To Open a Database

1 **Point to the Open button on the Database toolbar (Figure 1-29).**

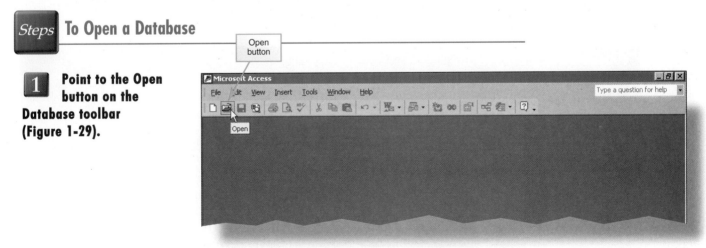

FIGURE 1-29

2 Click the Open button. If necessary, click the Look in box arrow and then click 3½ Floppy (A:) in the Look in box. If it is not selected already, click the Alisa Vending Services database name. Point to the Open button.

The Open dialog box displays (Figure 1-30). The 3½ Floppy (A:) folder displays in the Look in box and the files on the floppy disk in drive A display. (Your list may be different.)

3 Click the Open button.

The database opens and the Alisa Vending Services : Database window displays.

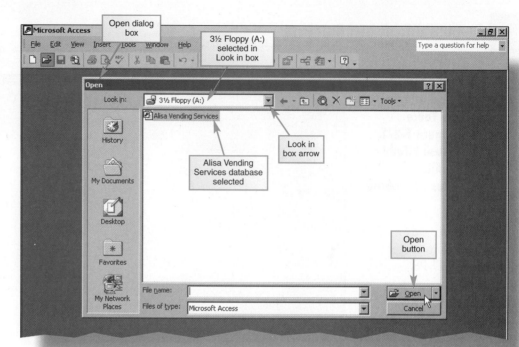

FIGURE 1-30

Table 1-1	Navigation Buttons in Datasheet View
BUTTON	**PURPOSE**
First Record	Moves to the first record in the table
Previous Record	Moves to the previous record
Next Record	Moves to the next record
Last Record	Moves to the last record in the table
New Record	Moves to the end of the table to a position for entering a new record

Adding Additional Records

You can add records to a table that already contains data using a process almost identical to that used to add records to an empty table. The only difference is that you place the insertion point after the last data record before you enter the additional data. To do so, use the **Navigation buttons** found near the lower-left corner of the screen. The purpose of each of the Navigation buttons is described in Table 1-1.

Complete the following steps to add the remaining records (Figure 1-31) to the Customer table.

Customer table (last 8 records)

CUSTOMER NUMBER	NAME	ADDRESS	CITY	STATE	ZIP CODE	AMOUNT PAID	CURRENT DUE	DRIVER NUMBER
CN21	Century North	1562 Butler	Hansen	FL	38513	$8,725.00	$0.00	60
FR28	Friend's Movies	871 Adams	Westport	FL	37070	$4,256.00	$1,202.00	75
GN62	Grand Nelson	7821 Oak	Wood Key	FL	36828	$8,287.50	$925.50	30
GS29	Great Screens	572 Lee	Hansen	FL	38513	$21,625.00	$0.00	60
LM22	Lenger Mason	274 Johnson	Westport	FL	37070	$0.00	$0.00	60
ME93	Merks College	561 Fairhill	Bayville	FL	38734	$24,761.00	$1,572.00	30
RI78	Riter University	26 Grove	Fernwood	FL	37023	$11,682.25	$2,827.50	75
TU20	Turner Hotel	8672 Quincy	Palmview	FL	36114	$8,521.50	$0.00	60

FIGURE 1-31

Steps **To Add Additional Records to a Table**

1 Right-click the Customer table in the Alisa Vending Services : Database window and then click Open on the shortcut menu. When the Customer table displays, maximize the window by clicking the Maximize button. Point to the New Record button.

The datasheet displays (Figure 1-32).

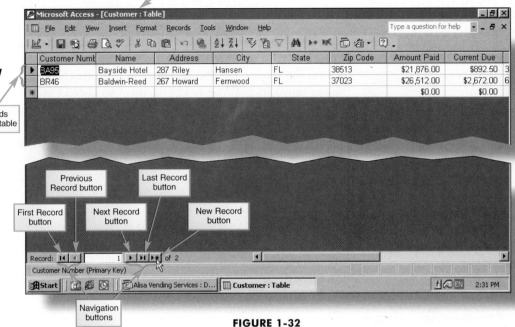

FIGURE 1-32

2 Click the New Record button.

Access places the insertion point in position to enter a new record (Figure 1-33).

FIGURE 1-33

3 Add the remaining records from Figure 1-31 using the same techniques you used to add the first two records. Point to the Close Window button.

The additional records are added (Figure 1-34).

FIGURE 1-34

4 Click the Close Window button.

The window containing the table closes and the Alisa Vending Services : Database window displays.

Other Ways

1. Click New Record button on Table Datasheet toolbar
2. In Voice Command mode, say "New Record"

More About

Printing the Contents of a Table

You can change the paper size, paper source, or the printer that will be used to print the report. To change any of these, select the Page sheet in the Page Setup dialog box, click the appropriate down arrow, and then select the desired option. You can change the margins by selecting the Margins sheet in the Page Setup dialog box.

Correcting Errors in the Data

Check your entries carefully to ensure they are correct. If you make a mistake and discover it before you press the TAB key, correct it by pressing the BACKSPACE key until the incorrect characters are removed and then typing the correct characters.

If you discover an incorrect entry later, correct the error by clicking the incorrect entry and then making the appropriate correction. If the record you must correct is not on the screen, use the Navigation buttons (Next Record, Previous Record, and so on) to move to it. If the field you want to correct is not visible on the screen, use the horizontal scroll bar along the bottom of the screen to shift all the fields until the one you want displays. Then make the correction.

If you add an extra record accidentally, select the record by clicking the record selector that immediately precedes the record. Then, press the DELETE key. This will remove the record from the table. If you forget a record, add it using the same procedure as for all the other records. Access will place it in the correct location in the table automatically.

If you cannot determine how to correct the data, you are, in effect, stuck on the record. Access neither allows you to move to any other record until you have made the correction, nor allows you to close the table. If you encounter this situation, simply press the ESC key. Pressing the ESC key will remove from the screen the record you are trying to add. You then can move to any other record, close the table, or take any other action you desire.

Previewing and Printing the Contents of a Table

When working with a database, you often will need to print a copy of the table contents. Figure 1-35 shows a printed copy of the contents of the Customer table. (Yours may look slightly different, depending on your printer.) Because the Customer table is wider substantially than the screen, it also will be wider than the normal printed page in portrait orientation. **Portrait orientation** means the printout is across the width of the page. **Landscape orientation** means the printout is across the length of the page. Thus, to print the wide database table, use landscape orientation. If you are printing the contents of a table that fits on the screen, you will not need landscape orientation. A convenient way to change to landscape orientation is to **preview** what the printed copy will look like by using Print Preview. This allows you to determine whether landscape orientation is necessary and, if it is, to change easily the orientation to landscape. In addition, you also can use Print Preview to determine whether any adjustments are necessary to the page margins.

Customer   9/8/2003

Customer Num	Name	Address	City	State	Zip Code	Amount Paid	Current Due	Driver Number
BA95	Bayside Hotel	287 Riley	Hansen	FL	38513	$21,876.00	$892.50	30
BR46	Baldwin-Reed	267 Howard	Fernwood	FL	37023	$26,512.00	$2,672.00	60
CN21	Century North	1562 Butler	Hansen	FL	38513	$8,725.00	$0.00	60
FR28	Friend's Movies	871 Adams	Westport	FL	37070	$4,256.00	$1,202.00	75
GN62	Grand Nelson	7821 Oak	Wood Key	FL	36828	$8,287.50	$925.50	30
GS29	Great Screens	572 Lee	Hansen	FL	38513	$21,625.00	$0.00	60
LM22	Lenger Mason	274 Johnson	Westport	FL	37070	$0.00	$0.00	60
ME93	Merks College	561 Fairhill	Bayville	FL	38734	$24,761.00	$1,572.00	30
RI78	Riter University	26 Grove	Fernwood	FL	37023	$11,682.25	$2,827.50	75
TU20	Turner Hotel	8672 Quincy	Palmview	FL	36114	$8,521.50	$0.00	60

FIGURE 1-35

Perform the following steps to use Print Preview to preview and then print the Customer table.

 Steps **To Preview and Print the Contents of a Table**

1 **Right-click the Customer table and then point to Print Preview on the shortcut menu.**

The shortcut menu for the Customer table displays (Figure 1-36).

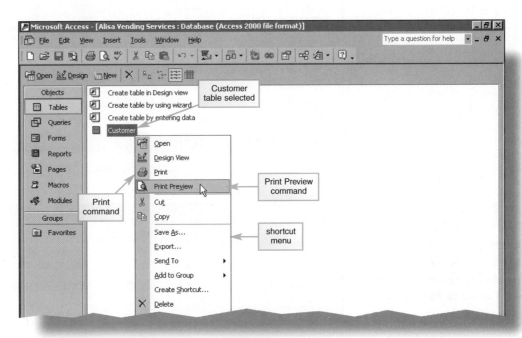

FIGURE 1-36

2 **Click Print Preview on the shortcut menu. Point to the approximate position shown in Figure 1-37.**

The preview of the report displays. The mouse pointer shape changes to a magnifying glass, indicating you can magnify a portion of the report.

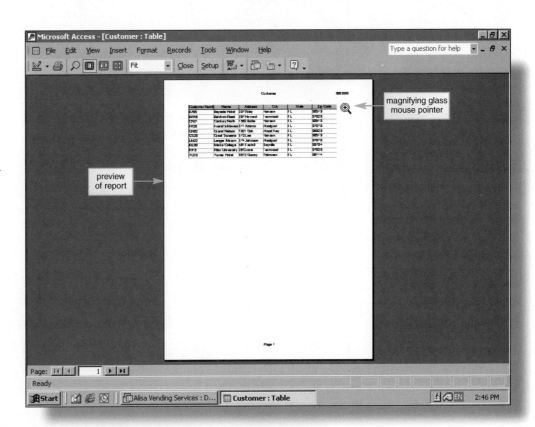

FIGURE 1-37

3 Click the magnifying glass mouse pointer in the approximate position shown in Figure 1-37 on the previous page.

The portion surrounding the mouse pointer is magnified (Figure 1-38). The last field that displays is the Zip Code field. The Amount Paid, Current Due, and Driver Number fields do not display. To display the additional fields, you will need to switch to landscape orientation.

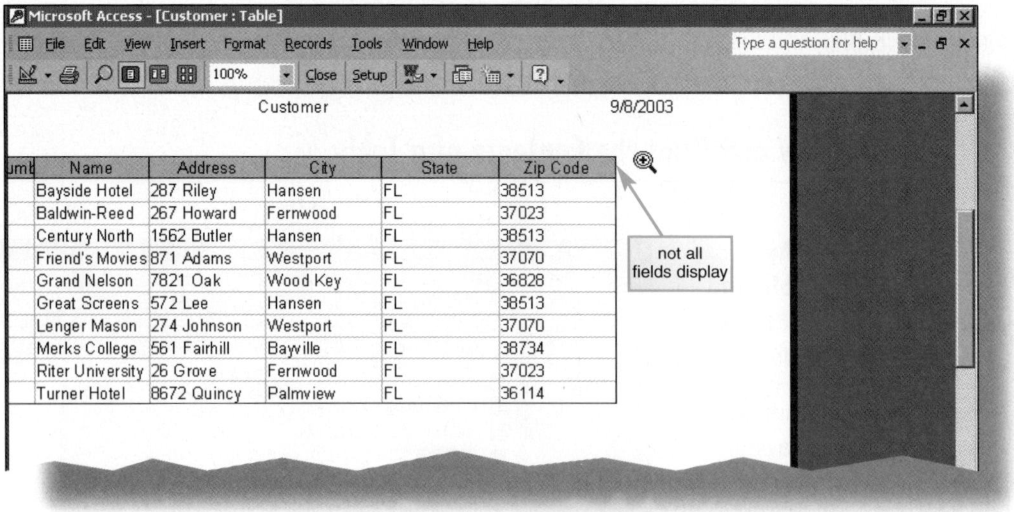

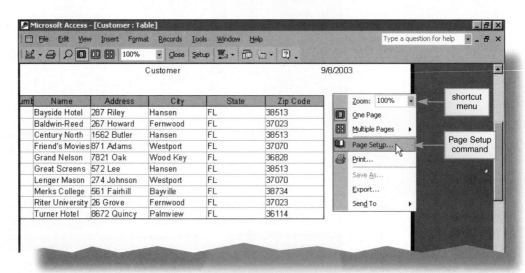

FIGURE 1-38

4 With the mouse pointer in the approximate position shown in Figure 1-38, right-click the report and then point to Page Setup.

The shortcut menu displays (Figure 1-39).

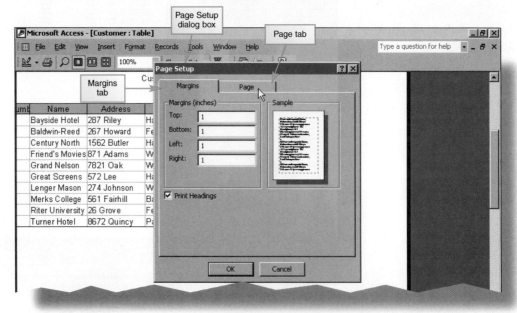

FIGURE 1-39

5 Click Page Setup and then point to the Page tab.

The Page Setup dialog box displays (Figure 1-40).

FIGURE 1-40

6 Click the Page tab and then point to the Landscape option button.

The Page sheet displays (Figure 1-41). The Portrait option button currently is selected. (*Option button* refers to the round button that indicates choice in a dialog box. When the corresponding option is selected, the button contains within it a solid circle. Clicking an option button selects it, and deselects all others.)

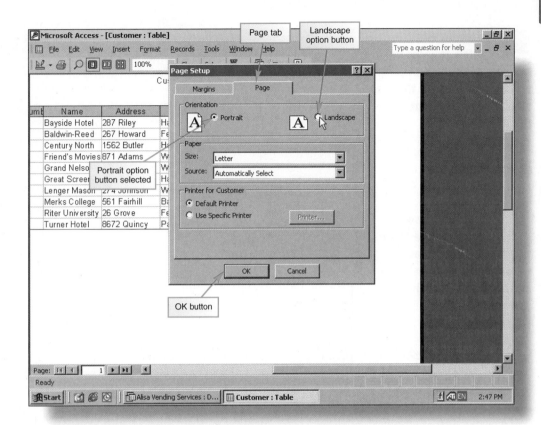

FIGURE 1-41

7 Click Landscape and then click the OK button. Point to the Print button on the Print Preview toolbar.

The orientation is changed to landscape as shown by the report that displays on the screen (Figure 1-42). The last field that displays is the Driver Number field, so all fields currently display. If they did not, you could decrease the left and right margins; that is, the amount of space left by Access on the left and right edges of the report.

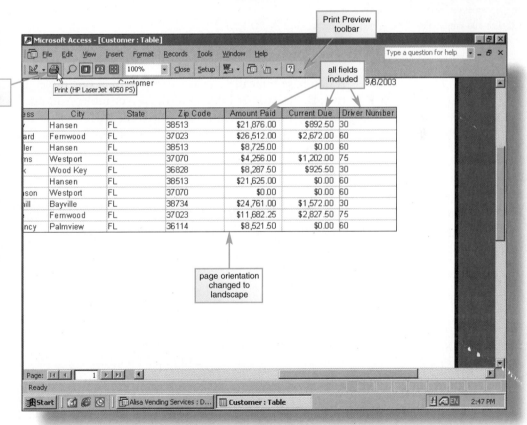

FIGURE 1-42

Microsoft Access 2002

8 **Click the Print button to print the report and then point to the Close button on the Print Preview toolbar (Figure 1-43).**

The report prints. It looks like the report shown in Figure 1-35 on page A 1.28.

9 **Click the Close button on the Print Preview toolbar when the report has been printed to close the Print Preview window.**

The Print Preview window closes and the Alisa Vending Services : Database window displays.

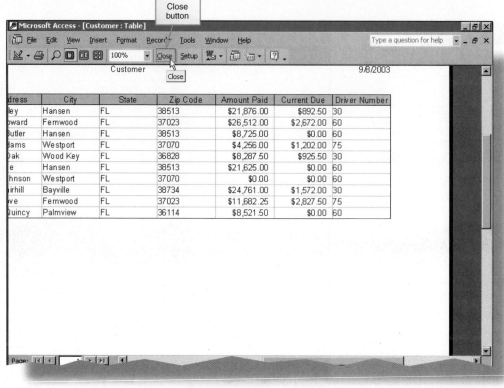

FIGURE 1-43

Creating Additional Tables

A database typically consists of more than one table. The sample database contains two, the Customer table and the Driver table. You need to repeat the process of creating a table and adding records for each table in the database. In the sample database, you need to create and add records to the Driver table. The structure for the table is given in Figure 1-44a and the data for the table is given in Figure 1-44b. The steps to create the table follow.

Structure of Driver table

FIELD NAME	DATA TYPE	FIELD SIZE	PRIMARY KEY?	DESCRIPTION
Driver Number	Text	2	Yes	Driver Number (Primary key)
Last Name	Text	10		Last Name of Driver
First Name	Text	8		First Name of Driver
Address	Text	15		Street Address
City	Text	15		City
State	Text	2		State (Two-Character Abbreviation)
Zip Code	Text	5		Zip Code (Five-Character Version)
Hourly Rate	Currency			Hourly Rate of Driver
YTD Earnings	Currency			YTD Earnings of Driver

FIGURE 1-44a

Data for Driver table								
DRIVER NUMBER	LAST NAME	FIRST NAME	ADDRESS	CITY	STATE	ZIP CODE	HOURLY RATE	YTD EARNINGS
30	Tuttle	Larissa	7562 Hickory	Laton Springs	FL	37891	$16.00	$21,145.25
60	Powers	Frank	57 Ravenwood	Gillmore	FL	37572	$15.00	$19,893.50
75	Ortiz	Jose	341 Pierce	Douglas	FL	37613	$17.00	$23,417.00

FIGURE 1-44b

Steps To Create an Additional Table

1 Make sure the Alisa Vending Services database is open. Right-click Create table in Design view and then click Open on the shortcut menu. Enter the data for the fields for the Driver table from Figure 1-44a. Be sure to click the Primary Key button when you enter the Driver Number field. Point to the Close Window button for the Table1 : Table window after you have entered all the fields.

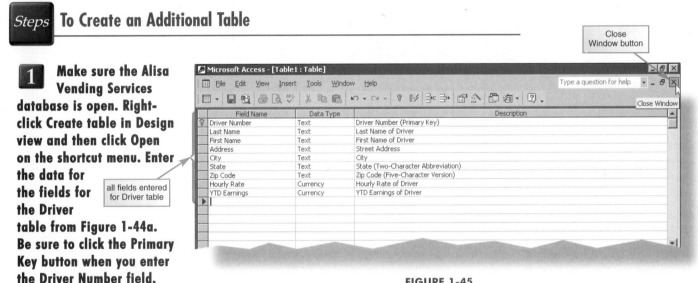

FIGURE 1-45

The entries display (Figure 1-45).

2 Click the Close Window button, click the Yes button in the Microsoft Access dialog box when asked if you want to save the changes, type Driver as the name of the table, and then point to the OK button in the Save As dialog box.

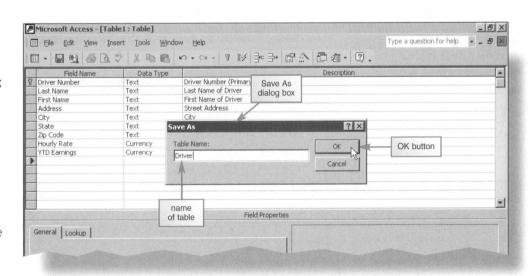

The Save As dialog box displays (Figure 1-46). The table name is entered.

3 Click the OK button.

FIGURE 1-46

The table is saved in the Alisa Vending Services database. The window containing the table structure no longer displays.

Adding Records to the Additional Table

Now that you have created the Driver table, use the following steps to add records to it.

Steps **To Add Records to an Additional Table**

1 **Right-click the Driver table and point to Open on the shortcut menu.**

The shortcut menu for the Driver table displays (Figure 1-47).

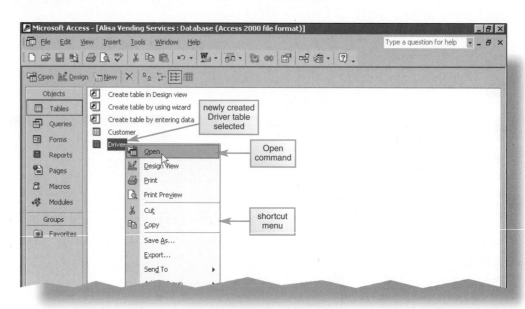

FIGURE 1-47

2 **Click Open on the shortcut menu and then enter the Driver data from Figure 1-44b on the previous page into the Driver table. Point to the Close Window button.**

The datasheet displays with three records entered (Figure 1-48).

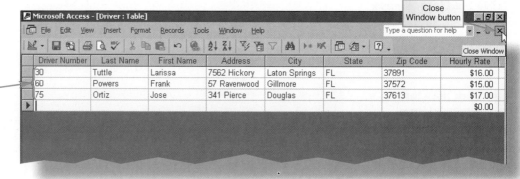

Driver Number	Last Name	First Name	Address	City	State	Zip Code	Hourly Rate
30	Tuttle	Larissa	7562 Hickory	Laton Springs	FL	37891	$16.00
60	Powers	Frank	57 Ravenwood	Gillmore	FL	37572	$15.00
75	Ortiz	Jose	341 Pierce	Douglas	FL	37613	$17.00
							$0.00

FIGURE 1-48

3 **Click the Close Window button for the Driver : Table window.**

Access closes the table and removes the datasheet from the screen.

Using a Form to View Data

In creating tables, you have used Datasheet view; that is, the data on the screen displayed as a table. You also can use **Form view**, in which you see a single record at a time.

The advantage with Datasheet view is you can see multiple records at once. It has the disadvantage that, unless you have few fields in the table, you cannot see all the fields at the same time. With Form view, you see only a single record, but you can see all the fields in the record. The view you choose is a matter of personal preference.

More About

Forms

Attractive and functional forms can improve greatly the data entry process. Forms are not restricted to data from a single table, but can incorporate data from multiple tables as well as special types of data like pictures and sounds. A good DBMS like Access furnishes an easy way to create sophisticated forms.

Creating a Form

To use Form view, you first must create a form. The simplest way to create a form is to use the New Object: AutoForm button on the Database toolbar. To do so, first select the table for which the form is to be created in the Database window and then click the New Object: AutoForm button. A list of available objects displays. Click AutoForm in the list to select it.

Perform the following steps using the New Object: AutoForm button to create a form for the Customer table.

Steps To Use the New Object: AutoForm Button to Create a Form

1 Make sure the Alisa Vending Services database is open, the Database window displays, and the Customer table is selected. Point to the New Object: AutoForm button arrow on the Database toolbar (Figure 1-49).

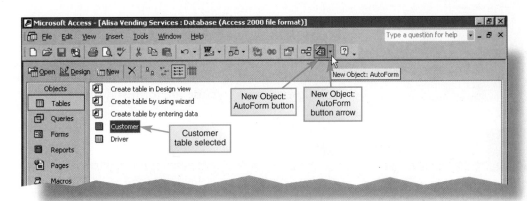

FIGURE 1-49

2 Click the New Object: AutoForm button arrow and then point to AutoForm.

A list of objects that can be created displays (Figure 1-50).

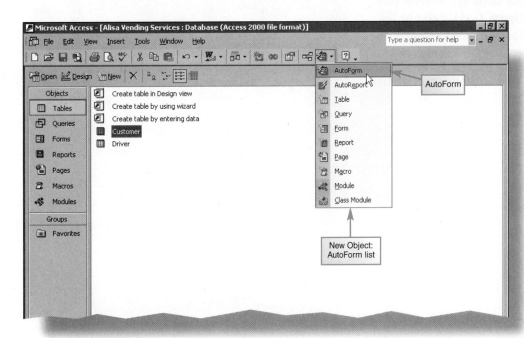

FIGURE 1-50

3 Click AutoForm in the New Object: AutoForm list.

After a brief delay, the form displays (Figure 1-51). If you do not move the mouse pointer after clicking AutoForm, the ScreenTip for the Database Window button may display when the form opens. An additional toolbar, the Formatting toolbar, also displays. (When you close the form, this toolbar no longer displays.)

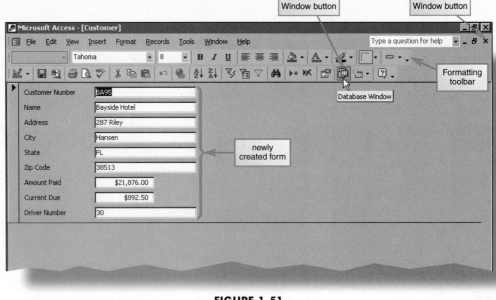

FIGURE 1-51

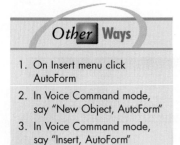

Other Ways

1. On Insert menu click AutoForm

2. In Voice Command mode, say "New Object, AutoForm"

3. In Voice Command mode, say "Insert, AutoForm"

Closing and Saving the Form

Closing a form is similar to closing a table. The only difference is that you will be asked if you want to save the form unless you previously have saved it. Perform the following steps to close the form and save it as Customer.

Steps **To Close and Save a Form**

1 Click the Close Window button for the Customer window (see Figure 1-51). Point to the Yes button in the Microsoft Access dialog box.

The Microsoft Access dialog box displays (Figure 1-52).

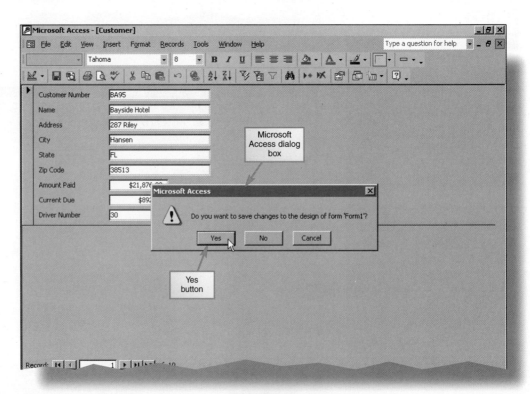

FIGURE 1-52

2 **Click the Yes button and then point to the OK button in the Save As dialog box.**

The Save As dialog box displays (Figure 1-53). The name of the table (Customer) becomes the name of the form automatically. This name could be changed, if desired.

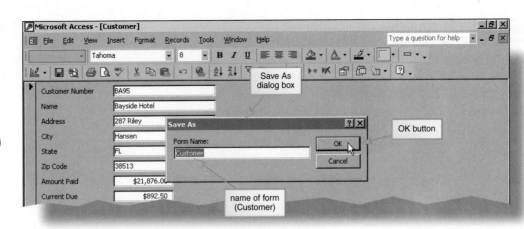

FIGURE 1-53

3 **Click the OK button.**

The form is saved as part of the database and the form closes. The Alisa Vending Services : Database window again displays.

Opening the Saved Form

Once you have saved a form, you can use it at any time in the future by opening it. Opening a form is similar to opening a table; that is, make sure the form to be opened is selected, right-click, and then click Open on the shortcut menu. Before opening the form, however, the Forms object, rather than the Tables object, must be selected.

Perform the following steps to open the Customer form.

Other **Ways**

1. Double-click Control-menu icon on title bar for window
2. On File menu click Close
3. In Voice Command mode, say "File, Close"

Steps **To Open a Form**

1 **With the Alisa Vending Services database open and the Database window on the screen, point to Forms on the Objects bar (Figure 1-54).**

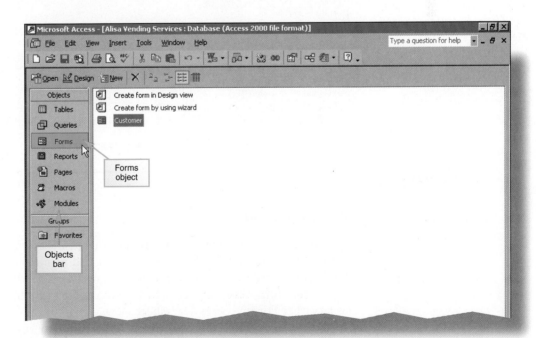

FIGURE 1-54

2 Click Forms, right-click the Customer form, and then point to Open on the shortcut menu.

The Forms object is selected and the list of available forms displays (Figure 1-55). Currently, the Customer form is the only form. The shortcut menu for the Customer form displays.

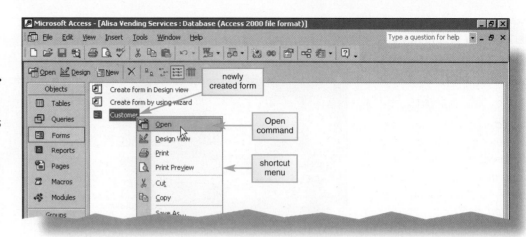

FIGURE 1-55

3 Click Open on the shortcut menu and then point to the Next Record button in preparation for the next task.

The Customer form displays (Figure 1-56).

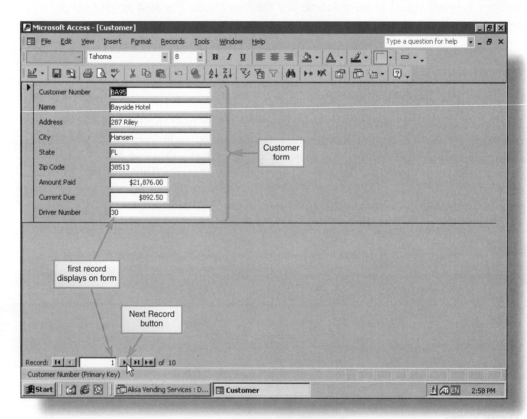

FIGURE 1-56

Other Ways

1. Click Forms object, double-click desired form
2. Click Forms object, click desired form, click Open button
3. Click Forms object, click desired form, press ALT+O
4. In Voice Command mode, say "Forms, [click desired form], Open"

Using the Form

You can use the form just as you used Datasheet view. You use the Navigation buttons to move between records. You can add new records or change existing ones. To delete the record displayed on the screen, after selecting the record by clicking its record selector, press the DELETE key. Thus, you can perform database operations using either Form view or Datasheet view.

Because you can see only one record at a time in Form view, to see a different record, such as the fifth record, use the Navigation buttons to move to it. To move from record to record in Form view, perform the following step.

Steps: To Use a Form

1 **Click the Next Record button four times.**

The fifth record displays on the form (Figure 1-57).

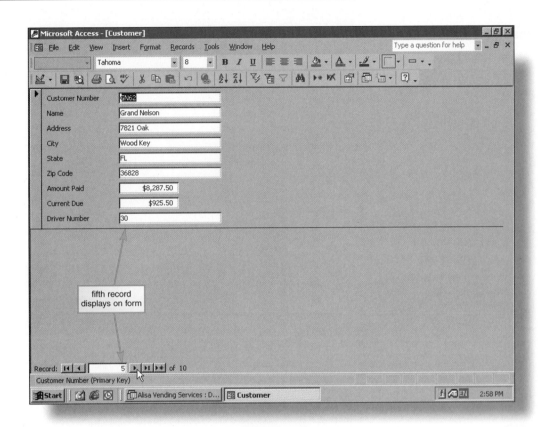

fifth record displays on form

FIGURE 1-57

Switching Between Form View and Datasheet View

In some cases, once you have seen a record in Form view, you will want to move to Datasheet view to again see a collection of records. To do so, click the View button arrow on the Form View toolbar and then click Datasheet View in the list that displays.

Perform the following steps to switch from Form view to Datasheet view.

Steps: To Switch from Form View to Datasheet View

1 **Point to the View button arrow on the Form View toolbar (Figure 1-58).**

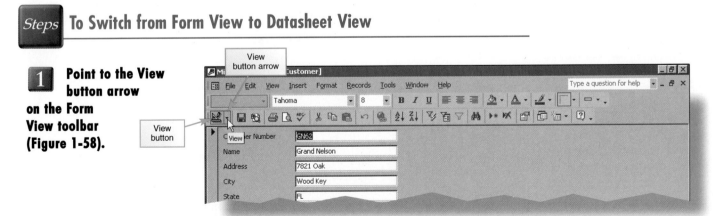

View button arrow

View button

FIGURE 1-58

2 **Click the View button arrow and then point to Datasheet View.**

The list of available views displays (Figure 1-59).

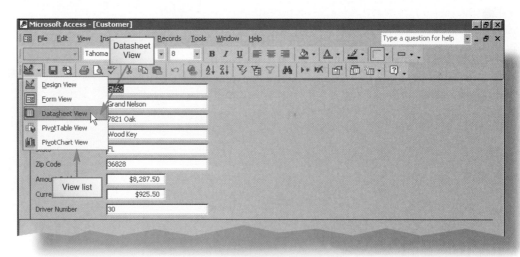

FIGURE 1-59

3 **Click Datasheet View and then point to the Close Window button.**

The table displays in Datasheet view (Figure 1-60). The record selector is positioned on the fifth record.

4 **Click the Close Window button.**

The Customer window closes and the datasheet no longer displays.

Customer Numt	Name	Address	City	State	Zip Code	Amount Paid	Current Due	
BA95	Bayside Hotel	287 Riley	Hansen	FL	38513	$21,876.00	$892.50	3
BR46	Baldwin-Reed	267 Howard	Fernwood	FL	37023	$26,512.00	$2,672.00	6
CN21	Century North	1562 Butler	Hansen	FL	38513	$8,725.00	$0.00	6
FR28	Friend's Movies	871 Adams	Westport	FL	37070	$4,256.00	$1,202.00	7
GN62	Grand Nelson	7821 Oak	Wood Key	FL	36828	$8,287.50	$925.50	3
GS29	Great Screens	572 Lee	Hansen	FL	38513	$21,625.00	$0.00	6
LM22	Lenger Mason	274 Johnson	Westport	FL	37070	$0.00	$0.00	6
ME93	Merks College	561 Fairhill	Bayville	FL	38734	$24,761.00	$1,572.00	3
RI78	Riter University	26 Grove	Fernwood	FL	37023	$11,682.25	$2,827.50	7
TU20	Turner Hotel	8672 Quincy	Palmview	FL	36114	$8,521.50	$0.00	6
*						$0.00	$0.00	

Record: 5 of 10

Customer Number (Primary Key)

FIGURE 1-60

Other Ways

1. On View menu click Datasheet View
2. In Voice Command mode, say "View, Datasheet View"

Creating a Report

Earlier in this project, you printed a table using the Print button. The report you produced was shown in Figure 1-35 on page A 1.28. While this type of report presented the data in an organized manner, the format is very rigid. You cannot select the fields to display, for example; the report automatically includes all the fields and they display in precisely the same order as in the table. There is no way to change the title, which will automatically be the same as the name of the table.

In this section, you will create the report shown in Figure 1-61. This report features significant differences from the one in Figure 1-35 The portion at the top of the report in Figure 1-61, called a **page header**, contains a custom title. The contents of this page header display at the top of each page. The **detail lines**, which are the lines that are printed for each record, contain only those fields you specify and in the order you specify.

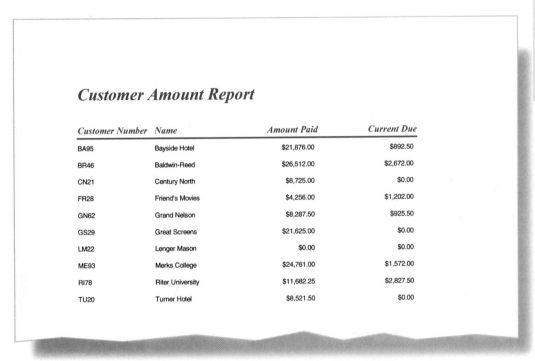

Customer Amount Report

Customer Number	Name	Amount Paid	Current Due
BA95	Bayside Hotel	$21,876.00	$892.50
BR46	Baldwin-Reed	$26,512.00	$2,672.00
CN21	Century North	$8,725.00	$0.00
FR28	Friend's Movies	$4,256.00	$1,202.00
GN62	Grand Nelson	$8,287.50	$925.50
GS29	Great Screens	$21,625.00	$0.00
LM22	Lenger Mason	$0.00	$0.00
ME93	Merks College	$24,761.00	$1,572.00
RI78	Riter University	$11,682.25	$2,827.50
TU20	Turner Hotel	$8,521.50	$0.00

FIGURE 1-61

Perform the following steps to create the report in Figure 1-61.

Steps To Create a Report

1 **Click Tables on the Objects bar. Make sure the Customer table is selected. Click the New Object: AutoForm button arrow on the Database toolbar and then point to Report.**

The list of available objects displays (Figure 1-62).

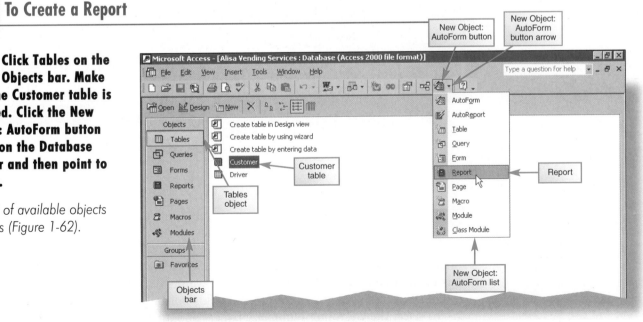

FIGURE 1-62

2 **Click Report and then point to Report Wizard.**

The New Report dialog box displays (Figure 1-63).

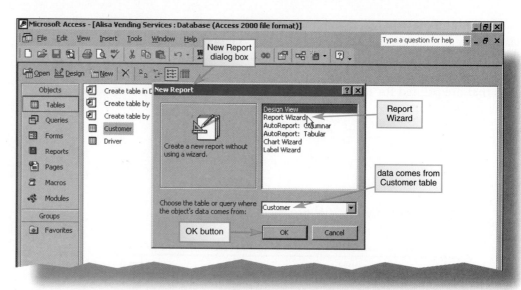

FIGURE 1-63

3 **Click Report Wizard and then click the OK button. Point to the Add Field button.**

The Report Wizard dialog box displays (Figure 1-64).

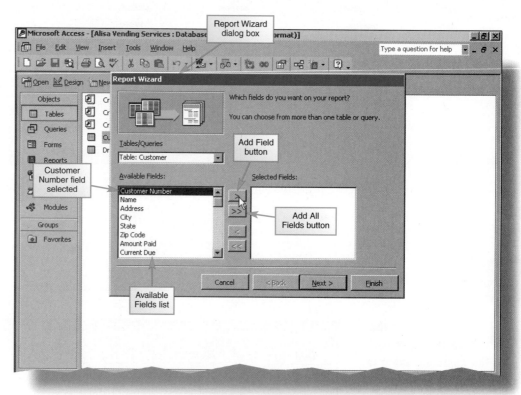

FIGURE 1-64

Selecting the Fields for the Report

To select a field for the report, that is, to indicate the field is to be included in the report, click the field in the Available Fields list. Next, click the Add Field button. This will move the field from the Available Fields box to the Selected Fields box, thus including the field in the report. If you wanted to select all fields, a shortcut is available simply by clicking the Add All Fields button.

To select the Customer Number, Name, Amount Paid, and Current Due fields for the report, perform the following steps.

Steps | To Select the Fields for a Report

1 **Click the Add Field button to add the Customer Number field. Add the Name field by clicking it and then clicking the Add Field button. Add the Amount Paid and Current Due fields just as you added the Customer Number and Name fields. Point to the Next button.**

The fields for the report display in the Selected Fields box (Figure 1-65).

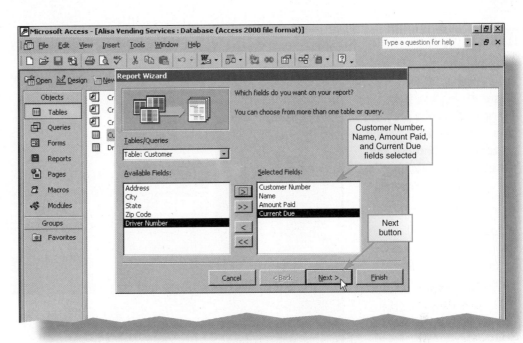

FIGURE 1-65

2 **Click the Next button.**

The Report Wizard dialog box displays (Figure 1-66).

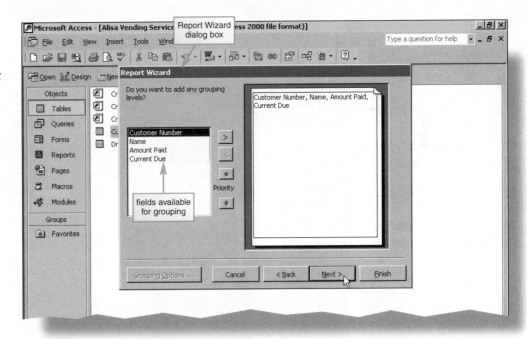

FIGURE 1-66

Other Ways

1. Double-click field

Completing the Report

Several additional steps are involved in completing the report. With the exception of changing the title, the Access selections are acceptable, so you simply will click the Next button.

Perform the steps on the next page to complete the report.

Steps **To Complete a Report**

1   **Because you will not specify any grouping, click the Next button in the Report Wizard dialog box (see Figure 1-66 on the previous page. Click the Next button a second time because you will not need to change the sort order for the records.**

The Report Wizard dialog box displays (Figure 1-67). In this dialog box, you can change the layout or orientation of the report.

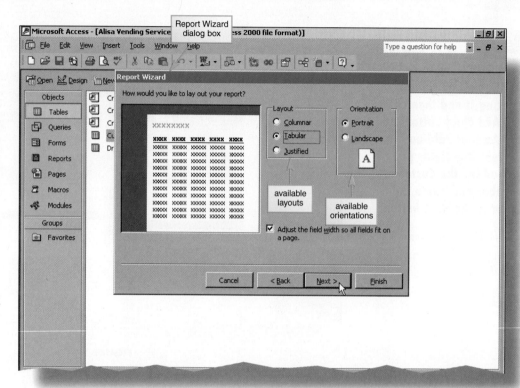

FIGURE 1-67

2   **Make sure that Tabular is selected as the layout and Portrait is selected as the orientation and then click the Next button.**

The Report Wizard dialog box displays (Figure 1-68). In this dialog box, you can select a style for the report.

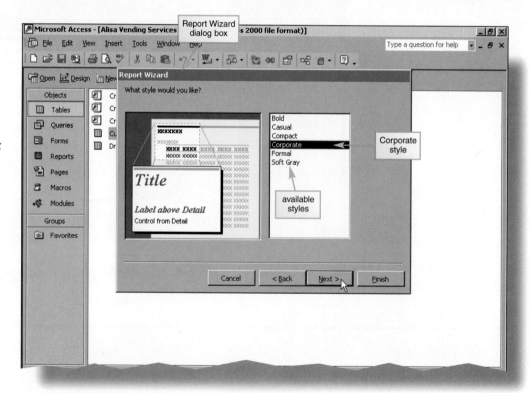

FIGURE 1-68

<table>
<tr><td>

3 **Be sure that the Corporate style is selected, click the Next button, type** Customer Amount Report **as the new title, and then point to the Finish button.**

The Report Wizard dialog box displays (Figure 1-69). The title is typed.

</td><td>

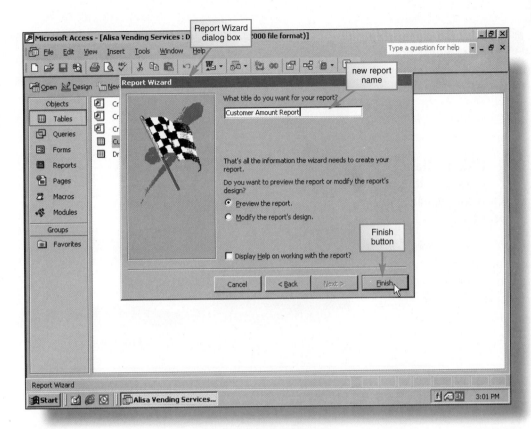

</td></tr>
</table>

FIGURE 1-69

<table>
<tr><td>

4 **Click the Finish button.**

A preview of the report displays (Figure 1-70). Yours may look slightly different, depending on your printer.

</td><td>

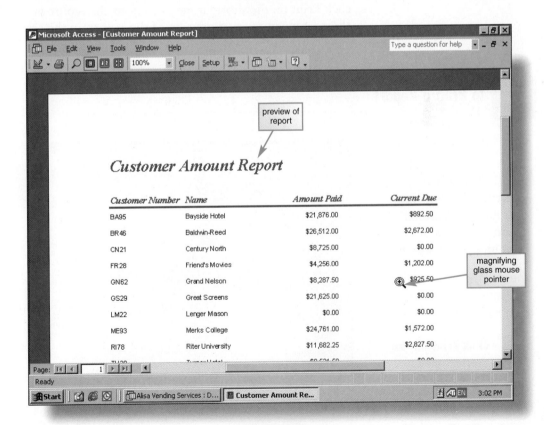

</td></tr>
</table>

FIGURE 1-70

5 Click the magnifying glass mouse pointer anywhere within the report to see the entire report.

The entire report displays (Figure 1-71).

6 Click the Close Window button in the Customer Amount Report window.

The report no longer displays. It has been saved automatically using the name Customer Amount Report.

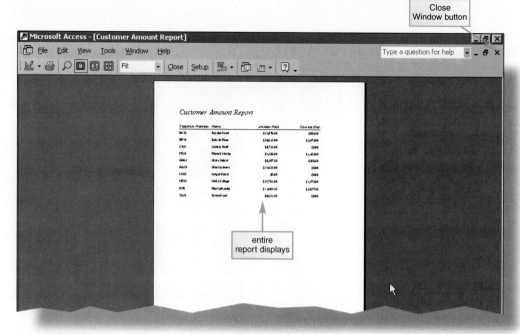

FIGURE 1-71

Printing the Report

To print a report from the Database window, first right-click the report. Then click Print on the shortcut menu to print the report or click Print Preview on the shortcut menu to see a preview of the report on the screen.

Perform the following steps to print the report.

Steps **To Print a Report**

1 If necessary, click Reports on the Objects bar in the Database window, right-click the Customer Amount Report, and then point to Print on the shortcut menu.

The shortcut menu for the Customer Amount Report displays (Figure 1-72).

2 Click Print on the shortcut menu.

The report prints. It should look similar to the one shown in Figure 1-61 on page A 1.41.

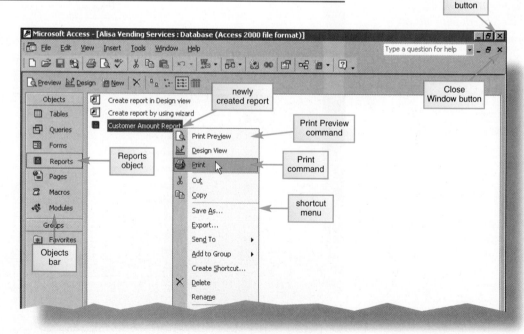

FIGURE 1-72

Closing the Database

Once you have finished working with a database, you should close it. The following step closes the database by closing its Database window.

TO CLOSE A DATABASE

1 Click the Close Window button for the Alisa Vending Services : Database window.

Access Help System

At any time while you are using Access, you can get answers to questions by using the Access Help system. Used properly, this form of online assistance can increase your productivity and reduce your frustrations by minimizing the time you spend learning how to use Access.

The following section shows how to get answers to your questions using the Ask a Question box. For additional information on using the Access Help system, see Appendix A on page A A.01 and Table 1-2 on page A 1.49.

Obtaining Help Using the Ask a Question Box on the Menu Bar

The **Ask a Question box** on the right side of the menu bar lets you type in free-form questions, such as *how do I save* or *how do I create a Web page*, or you can type in terms, such as *copy*, *save*, or *formatting*. Access responds by displaying a list of topics related to what you entered. The following steps show how to use the Ask a Question box to obtain information on removing a primary key.

More *About*

Quick Reference

For a table that lists how to complete tasks covered in this book using the mouse, menu, shortcut menu, and keyboard, see the Quick Reference Summary at the back of this book or visit the Shelly Cashman Series Office XP Web page (scsite.com/offxp/qr.htm) and then click Microsoft Access 2002.

More *About*

The Access Help System

The best way to become familiar with the Access Help system is to use it. Appendix A includes detailed information on the Access Help system and exercises that will help you gain confidence in using it.

Steps **To Obtain Help Using the Ask a Question Box**

1 **Click the Ask a Question box on the right side of the menu bar. Type** how do I remove a primary key **in the box (Figure 1-73).**

FIGURE 1-73

2 **Press the ENTER key.**

A list of topics displays relating to the question, "how do I remove a primary key" (Figure 1-74).

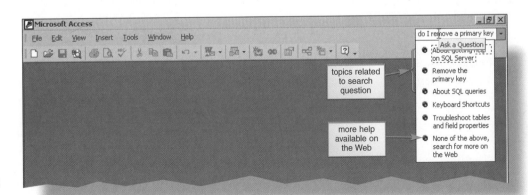

FIGURE 1-74

3 **Point to the Remove the primary key topic.**

The mouse pointer changes to a hand indicating it is pointing to a link (Figure 1-75).

FIGURE 1-75

4 **Click Remove the primary key.**

Access displays a Microsoft Access Help window that provides Help information about removing the primary key (Figure 1-76).

5 **Click the Close button on the Microsoft Access Help window title bar.**

The Microsoft Access Help window closes.

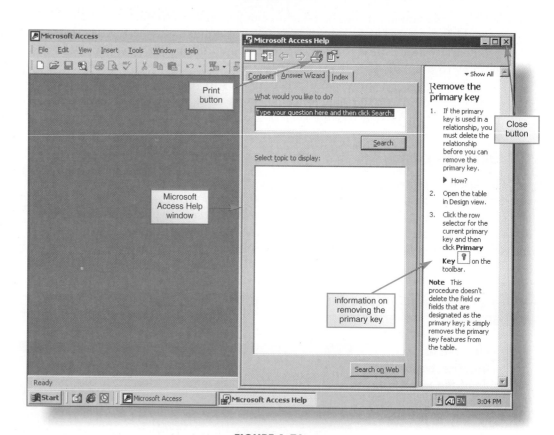

FIGURE 1-76

Other **Ways**

1. Click Microsoft Access Help button on toolbar
2. On Help menu click Microsoft Access Help
3. In Voice Command mode, say "Help, Microsoft Access Help"

Use the buttons in the upper-left corner of the Microsoft Access Help window (Figure 1-76) to navigate through the Help system, change the display, and print the contents of the window.

As you enter questions and terms in the Ask a Question box, Access adds them to its list. Thus, if you click the Ask a Question box arrow, a list of previously asked questions and terms will display.

Table 1-2 summarizes the 10 categories of Help available to you. Because of the way the Access Help system works, be sure to review the rightmost column of Table 1-2 if you have difficulties activating the desired category of Help. Additional information on using the Access Help system is available in Appendix A.

Table 1-2 Access Help System

TYPE	DESCRIPTION	HOW TO ACTIVATE
Answer Wizard	Answers questions or searches for terms that you type in your own words.	Click the Microsoft Access Help button on the Database window toolbar. Click the Answer Wizard tab.
Ask a Question box	Answers questions or searches for terms that you type in your own words.	Type a question or term in the Ask a Question box on the menu bar and then press the ENTER key.
Contents sheet	Groups Help topics by general categories. Use when you know only the general category of the topic in question.	Click the Microsoft Access Help button on the Database window toolbar. Click the Contents tab.
Detect and Repair	Automatically finds and fixes errors in the application.	Click Detect and Repair on the Help menu.
Hardware and Software Information	Shows Product ID and allows access to system information and technical support information.	Click About Microsoft Access on the Help menu and then click the appropriate button.
Index sheet	Similar to an index in a book. Use when you know exactly what you want.	Click the Microsoft Access Help button on the Database window toolbar. If necessary, maximize the Help window by double-clicking its title bar. Click the Index tab.
Office Assistant	Similar to the Ask a Question box in that the Office Assistant answers questions that you type in your own words, offers tips, and provides help for a variety of Access features.	Click the Office Assistant icon. If the Office Assistant does not display, click Show the Office Assistant on the Help menu.
Office on the Web	Used to access technical resources and download free product enhancements on the Web.	Click Office on the Web on the Help menu.
Question Mark button	Used to identify unfamiliar items in a dialog box.	Click the Question Mark button on the title bar in a dialog box and then click an item in the dialog box.
What's This? command	Used to identify unfamiliar items on the screen.	Click What's This? on the Help menu and then click an item on the screen.

You can use the Office Assistant to search for Help on any topic concerning Access. For additional information on using the Access Help system, see Appendix A.

Quitting Access

After you close a database, you can open another database, create a new database, or simply quit Access and return to the Windows desktop. The following step quits Access.

TO QUIT ACCESS

1 Click the Close button in the Microsoft Access window (see Figure 1-72 on page A 1.46).

Designing a Database

Database design refers to the arrangement of data into tables and fields. In the example in this project, the design is specified, but in many cases, you will have to determine the design based on what you want the system to accomplish.

With large, complex databases, the database design process can be extensive. Major sections of advanced database textbooks are devoted to this topic. Often, however, you should be able to design a database effectively by keeping one simple principle in mind: Design to remove redundancy. **Redundancy** means storing the same fact in more than one place.

To illustrate, you need to maintain the following information shown in Figure 1-77. In the figure, all the data is contained in a single table. Notice that the data for a given driver (number, name, address, and so on) occurs on more than one record.

Customer table

CUSTOMER NUMBER	NAME	ADDRESS	CITY	STATE	ZIP CODE	AMOUNT PAID	CURRENT DUE	DRIVER NUMBER	LAST NAME	FIRST NAME	ADDRESS
BA95	Bayside Hotel	287 Riley	Hansen	FL	38513	$21,876.00	$892.50	30	Tuttle	Larissa	7562 Hickory
BR46	Baldwin-Reed	267 Howard	Fernwood	FL	37023	$26,512.00	$2,672.00	60	Powers	Frank	57 Ravenwood
CN21	Century North	1562 Butler	Hansen	FL	38513	$8,725.00	$0.00	60	Powers	Frank	57 Ravenwood
FR28	Friend's Movies	871 Adams	Westport	FL	37070	$4,256.00	$1,202.00	75	Ortiz	Jose	341 Pierce
GN62	Grand Nelson	7821 Oak	Wood Key	FL	36828	$8,287.50	$925.50	30	Tuttle	Larissa	7562 Hickory
GS29	Great Screens	572 Lee	Hansen	FL	38513	$21,625.00	$0.00	60	Powers	Frank	57 Ravenwood
LM22	Lenger Mason	274 Johnson	Westport	FL	37070	$0.00	$0.00	60	Powers	Frank	57 Ravenwood
ME93	Merks College	561 Fairhill	Bayville	FL	38734	$24,761.00	$1,572.00	30	Tuttle	Larissa	7562 Hickory
RI78	Riter University	26 Grove	Fernwood	FL	37023	$11,682.25	$2,827.50	75	Ortiz	Jose	341 Pierce
TU20	Turner Hotel	8672 Quincy	Palmview	FL	36114	$8,521.50	$0.00	60	Powers	Frank	57 Ravenwood

FIGURE 1-77

duplicate driver names

MoreAbout

Database Design (Normalization)

A special technique for identifying and eliminating redundancy is called normalization. For more information on normalization, visit the Access 2002 More About Web page (scsite.com/ac2002/more.htm) and then click Normalization.

Storing this data on multiple records is an example of redundancy, which causes several problems, including:

1. Redundancy wastes space on the disk. The address of driver 30 (Larissa Tuttle), for example, should be stored only once. Storing this fact several times is wasteful.
2. Redundancy makes updating the database more difficult. If, for example, Larissa Tuttle moves, her address would need to be changed in several different places.
3. A possibility of inconsistent data exists. Suppose, for example, that you change the address of Larissa Tuttle on customer GN62's record to 146 Valley, but do not change it on customer BA95's record. In both cases, the driver number is 30, but the addresses are different. In other words, the data is inconsistent.

The solution to the problem is to place the redundant data in a separate table, one in which the data will no longer be redundant. If, for example, you place the data for drivers in a separate table (Figure 1-78), the data for each driver will display only once.

Notice that you need to have the driver number in both tables. Without it, no way exists to tell which driver is associated with which customer. All the other driver data, however, was removed from the Customer table and placed in the Driver table. This new arrangement corrects the problems of redundancy in the following ways:

1. Because the data for each driver is stored only once, space is not wasted.
2. Changing the address of a driver is easy. You have only to change one row in the Driver table.
3. Because the data for a driver is stored only once, inconsistent data cannot occur.

MoreAbout

Database Design (Design Method)

A variety of methods have been developed for designing complex databases given a set of input and output requirements. For more information on database design methods, visit the Access 2002 More About Web page (scsite.com/ac2002/more.htm) and then click Database Design.

driver data is in separate table

Driver table

DRIVER NUMBER	LAST NAME	FIRST NAME	ADDRESS	CITY	STATE	ZIP CODE	HOURLY RATE	YTD EARNINGS
30	Tuttle	Larissa	7562 Hickory	Laton Springs	FL	37891	$16.00	$21,145.25
60	Powers	Frank	57 Ravenwood	Gillmore	FL	37572	$15.00	$19,893.50
75	Ortiz	Jose	341 Pierce	Douglas	FL	37613	$17.00	$23,417.00

Customer table

CUSTOMER NUMBER	NAME	ADDRESS	CITY	STATE	ZIP CODE	AMOUNT PAID	CURRENT DUE	DRIVER NUMBER
BA95	Bayside Hotel	287 Riley	Hansen	FL	38513	$21,876.00	$892.50	30
BR46	Baldwin-Reed	267 Howard	Fernwood	FL	37023	$26,512.00	$2,672.00	60
CN21	Century North	1562 Butler	Hansen	FL	38513	$8,725.00	$0.00	60
FR28	Friend's Movies	871 Adams	Westport	FL	37070	$4,256.00	$1,202.00	75
GN62	Grand Nelson	7821 Oak	Wood Key	FL	36828	$8,287.50	$925.50	30
GS29	Great Screens	572 Lee	Hansen	FL	38513	$21,625.00	$0.00	60
LM22	Lenger Mason	274 Johnson	Westport	FL	37070	$0.00	$0.00	60
ME93	Merks College	561 Fairhill	Bayville	FL	38734	$24,761.00	$1,572.00	30
RI78	Riter University	26 Grove	Fernwood	FL	37023	$11,682.25	$2,827.50	75
TU20	Turner Hotel	8672 Quincy	Palmview	FL	36114	$8,521.50	$0.00	60

FIGURE 1-78

Designing to omit redundancy will help you to produce good and valid database designs.

CASE PERSPECTIVE SUMMARY

In Project 1, you assisted Alisa Vending Services in their efforts to place their data in a database. You created the database that Alisa will use. Within the Alisa Vending Services database, you created the Customer and Driver tables by defining the fields within them. You then added records to these tables. Once you created the tables, you printed the contents of the tables. You also used a form to view the data in the table. Finally, you used the Report Wizard to create a report containing the Customer Number, Name, Amount Paid, and Current Due fields for each customer served by Alisa Vending Services.

Project Summary

In Project 1, you learned about databases and database management systems. You learned how to create a database and how to create the tables within a database. You saw how to define the fields in a table by specifying the characteristics of the fields. You learned how to open a table, how to add records to it, and how to close it. You also printed the contents of a table. You created a form to view data on the screen and also created a custom report. You learned how to use Microsoft Access Help. Finally, you learned how to design a database to eliminate redundancy.

What You Should Know

Having completed this project, you now should be able to perform the following tasks:

- Add Additional Records to a Table (*A 1.27*)
- Add Records to a Table (*A 1.21*)
- Add Records to an Additional Table (*A 1.34*)
- Close a Database (*A 1.47*)
- Close a Table and Database (*A 1.25*)
- Close and Save a Form (*A 1.36*)
- Complete a Report (*A 1.44*)
- Create a New Database (A 1.11)
- Create a Report (*A 1.41*)
- Create a Table (*A 1.15*)
- Create an Additional Table (*A 1.33*)
- Define the Fields in a Table (*A 1.17*)
- Obtain Help Using the Ask a Question Box (*A 1.47*)
- Open a Database (*A 1.25*)
- Open a Form (*A 1.37*)
- Preview and Print the Contents of a Table (*A 1.29*)
- Print a Report (*A 1.46*)
- Quit Access (A 1.47)
- Save and Close a Table (A 1.20)
- Select the Fields for a Report (*A 1.43*)
- Start Access (*A 1.09*)
- Switch from Form View to Datasheet View (*A 1.39*)
- Use a Form (*A 1.39*)
- Use the New Object: AutoForm Button to Create a Form (*A 1.35*)

More About

Microsoft Certification

The Microsoft Office User Specialist (MOUS) Certification program provides an opportunity for you to obtain a valuable industry credential — proof that you have the Access 2002 skills required by employers. For more information, see Appendix E or visit the Shelly Cashman Series MOUS Web page at scsite.com/offxp/cert.htm.

Learn It Online

Instructions: To complete the Learn It Online exercises, start your browser, click the Address bar, and then enter scsite.com/offxp/exs.htm. When the Office XP Learn It Online page displays, follow the instructions in the exercises below.

1 Project Reinforcement TF, MC, and SA

Below Access Project 1, click the Project Reinforcement link. Print the quiz by clicking Print on the File menu. Answer each question. Write your first and last name at the top of each page, and then hand in the printout to your instructor.

2 Flash Cards

Below Access Project 1, click the Flash Cards link. When Flash Cards displays, read the instructions. Type 20 (or a number specified by your instructor) in the Number of Playing Cards text box, type your name in the Name text box, and then click the Flip Card button. When the flash card displays, read the question and then click the Answer box arrow to select an answer. Flip through Flash Cards. Click Print on the File menu to print the last flash card if your score is 15 (75%) correct or greater and then hand it in to your instructor. If your score is less than 15 (75%) correct, then redo this exercise by clicking the Replay button.

3 Practice Test

Below Access Project 1, click the Practice Test link. Answer each question, enter your first and last name at the bottom of the page, and then click the Grade Test button. When the graded practice test displays on your screen, click Print on the File menu to print a hard copy. Continue to take practice tests until you score 80% or better. Hand in a printout of the final practice test to your instructor.

4 Who Wants to Be a Computer Genius?

Below Access Project 1, click the Computer Genius link. Read the instructions, enter your first and last name at the bottom of the page, and then click the Play button. Hand in your score to your instructor.

5 Wheel of Terms

Below Access Project 1, click the Wheel of Terms link. Read the instructions, and then enter your first and last name and your school name. Click the Play button. Hand in your score to your instructor.

6 Crossword Puzzle Challenge

Below Access Project 1, click the Crossword Puzzle Challenge link. Read the instructions, and then enter your first and last name. Click the Play button. Work the crossword puzzle. When you are finished, click the Submit button. When the crossword puzzle redisplays, click the Print button. Hand in the printout.

7 Tips and Tricks

Below Access Project 1, click the Tips and Tricks link. Click a topic that pertains to Project 1. Right-click the information and then click Print on the shortcut menu. Construct a brief example of what the information relates to in Access to confirm you understand how to use the tip or trick. Hand in the example and printed information.

8 Newsgroups

Below Access Project 1, click the Newsgroups link. Click a topic that pertains to Project 1. Print three comments. Hand in the comments to your instructor.

9 Expanding Your Horizons

Below Access Project 1, click the Articles for Microsoft Access link. Click a topic that pertains to Project 1. Print the information. Construct a brief example of what the information relates to in Access to confirm you understand the contents of the article. Hand in the example and printed information to your instructor.

10 Search Sleuth

Below Access Project 1, click the Search Sleuth link. To search for a term that pertains to this project, select a term below the Project 1 title and then use the Google search engine at google.com (or any major search engine) to display and print two Web pages that present information on the term. Hand in the printouts to your instructor.

online

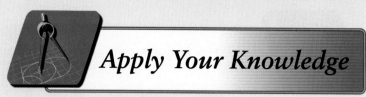

Apply Your Knowledge

1 Changing Data and Creating Reports

Instructions: Start Access. Open the database Beyond Clean from the Data Disk. See the inside back cover of this book for instructions for downloading the Data Disk or see your instructor for information on accessing the files required in this book. Beyond Clean is a company that specializes in cleaning and light custodial work for commercial businesses. Beyond Clean has a database that keeps track of its custodians and clients. The database has two tables. The Client table contains data on the clients who use the services of Beyond Clean. The Custodian table contains data on the individuals employed by Beyond Clean. The structure and data are shown for the Client table in Figure 1-79 and for the Custodian table in Figure 1-80.

Structure of Client table

FIELD NAME	DATA TYPE	FIELD SIZE	PRIMARY KEY?	DESCRIPTION
Client Number	Text	4	Yes	Client Number (Primary Key)
Name	Text	20		Client Name
Address	Text	15		Street Address
City	Text	15		City
State	Text	2		Sate (Two-Character Abbreviation)
Zip Code	Text	5		Zip Code (Five-Character Version)
Telephone Number	Text	12		Telephone Number (999-999-9999 Version)
Balance	Currency			Amount Owed by Client
Custodian Id	Text	3		Id of Client's Custodian

Data for Client table

CLIENT NUMBER	NAME	ADDRESS	CITY	STATE	ZIP CODE	TELEPHONE NUMBER	BALANCE	CUSTODIAN ID
AD23	Adder Cleaners	407 Mallery	Anders	TX	31501	512-555-4070	$105.00	002
AR76	The Artshop	200 Wymberly	Liberty Estates	TX	31499	510-555-0200	$80.00	009
BE29	Beacher's	224 Harbor Oak	Liberty Estates	TX	31499	510-555-2024	$70.00	009
CR67	Cricket Store	506 Mallery	Anders	TX	31501	512-555-6050	$0.00	002
DL61	Del Sol	123 Village	Kingston	TX	31534	513-555-1231	$135.00	013
GR36	Great Foods	1345 Frederic	Kingston	TX	31534	513-555-5431	$104.00	013
HA09	Halyards Mfg	5689 Demerre	Anders	TX	31501	512-555-6895	$145.00	009
ME17	Merry Café	879 Vinca	Kingston	TX	31534	513-555-9780	$168.00	013
RO45	Royal Palms	678 Liatris	Anders	TX	31501	512-555-4567	$0.00	002
ST21	Steed's	809 Lantana	Liberty Estates	TX	31499	510-555-9080	$123.00	009

FIGURE 1-79

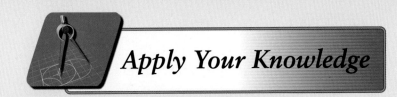

Apply Your Knowledge

Structure of Custodian table

FIELD NAME	DATA TYPE	FIELD SIZE	PRIMARY KEY?	DESCRIPTION
Custodian Id	Text	3	Yes	Custodian Identification Number (Primary Key)
Last Name	Text	12		Last Name of Custodian
First Name	Text	8		First Name of Custodian
Address	Text	15		Street Address
City	Text	15		City
State	Text	2		State (Two-Character Abbreviation)
Zip Code	Text	5		Zip Code (Five-Character Version)
Pay Rate	Currency			Hourly Pay Rate

Data for Custodian table

CUSTODIAN ID	LAST NAME	FIRST NAME	ADDRESS	CITY	STATE	ZIP CODE	PAY RATE
002	Deakle	Terry	764 Hubbard	Anders	TX	31501	$9.50
009	Lee	Michelle	78 Dunlop	Liberty Estates	TX	31499	$9.75
013	Torres	Juan	345 Red Poppy	Anders	TX	31501	$9.65

FIGURE 1-80

Perform the following tasks.

1. Open the Custodian table in Datasheet view and add the following record to the table: Close the Custodian table.

CUSTODIAN ID	LAST NAME	FIRST NAME	ADDRESS	CITY	STATE	ZIP CODE	PAY RATE
011	Meeder	Pat	113 Lantana	Liberty Estates	TX	31499	$9.50

2. Open the Custodian table again. Notice that the record you just added has been moved. It is no longer at the end of the table. The records are in order by the primary key, Custodian Id.
3. Print the Custodian table. PREVIEW.
4. Open the Client table.
5. Change the Custodian Id for client BE29 to 011.
6. Print the Client table.
7. Create the report shown in Figure 1-81 for the Client table.
8. Print the report.

Balance Due Report

Client Number	Name	Balance
AD23	Adder Cleaners	$105.00
AR76	The Artshop	$80.00
BE29	Beacher's	$70.00
CR67	Cricket Store	$0.00
DL61	Del Sol	$135.00
GR36	Great Foods	$104.00
HA09	Halyards Mfg	$145.00
ME17	Merry Café	$168.00
RO45	Royal Palms	$0.00
ST21	Steed's	$123.00

FIGURE 1-81

In the Lab

1 Creating the Wooden Crafts Database

Problem: Jan Merchant is an enterprising business person who has a small kiosk in a shopping mall that sells handcrafted wooden items for children, such as trains, tractors, and puzzles. Jan purchases products from individuals that make wooden products by hand. The database consists of two tables. The Product table contains information on products available for sale. The Supplier table contains information on the individuals that supply the products.

Instructions: Perform the following tasks.

1. Create a new database in which to store all the objects related to the merchandise data. Call the database Wooden Crafts.
2. Create the Product table using the structure shown in Figure 1-82. Use the name Product for the table.
3. Add the data shown in Figure 1-82 to the Product table.
4. Print the Product table.
5. Create the Supplier table using the structure shown in Figure 1-83. Use the name Supplier for the table.
6. Add the data shown in Figure 1-83 to the Supplier table.
7. Print the Supplier table.
8. Create a form for the Product table. Use the name Product for the form.

Structure of Product table

FIELD NAME	DATA TYPE	FIELD SIZE	PRIMARY KEY?	DESCRIPTION
Product Id	Text	4	Yes	Product Id Number (Primary Key)
Description	Text	20		Description of Product
On Hand	Number			Number of Units On Hand
Cost	Currency			Cost of Product
Selling Price	Currency			Selling Price of Product
Supplier Code	Text	2		Code of Product Supplier

Data for Product table

PRODUCT ID	DESCRIPTION	ON HAND	COST	SELLING PRICE	SUPPLIER CODE
BF01	Barnyard Friends	3	$54.00	$60.00	PL
BL23	Blocks in Box	5	$29.00	$32.00	AP
CC14	Coal Car	8	$14.00	$18.00	BH
FT05	Fire Truck	7	$9.00	$12.00	AP
LB34	Lacing Bear	4	$12.00	$16.00	AP
MR06	Midget Railroad	3	$31.00	$34.00	BH
PJ12	Pets Jigsaw	10	$8.00	$12.00	PL
RB02	Railway Bridge	1	$17.00	$20.00	BH
SK10	Skyscraper	6	$25.00	$30.00	PL
UM09	USA Map	12	$14.00	$18.00	AP

FIGURE 1-82

In the Lab

Structure for Supplier table

FIELD NAME	DATA TYPE	FIELD SIZE	PRIMARY KEY?	DESCRIPTION
Supplier Code	Text	2	Yes	Supplier Code (Primary Key)
First Name	Text	10		First Name of Supplier
Last Name	Text	15		Last Name of Supplier
Address	Text	20		Street Address
City	Text	20		City
State	Text	2		State (Two-Character Abbreviation)
Zip Code	Text	5		Zip Code (Five-Character Version)
Telephone Number	Text	12		Telephone Number (999-999-9999 Version)

Data for Supplier table

SUPPLIER CODE	FIRST NAME	LAST NAME	ADDRESS	CITY	STATE	ZIP CODE	TELEPHONE NUMBER
AP	Antonio	Patino	34 Fourth	Bastrop	NM	75123	505-555-1111
BH	Bert	Huntington	67 Beafort	Richford	CA	95418	707-555-3334
PL	Ping	Luang	12 Crestview	Mockington	AZ	85165	602-555-9990

FIGURE 1-83

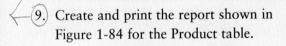

9. Create and print the report shown in Figure 1-84 for the Product table.

2 Creating the Restaurant Supply Database

Problem: A distributor supplies local restaurants with non-food supplies such as napkins, paper towels, and cleaning supplies. The distributor employs sales representatives who receive a base salary as well as a commission on sales. The database consists of two tables. The Customer table contains information on the restaurants that buy supplies from the distributor. The Sales Rep table contains information on the sales representative assigned to the restaurant account.

Inventory Report

Product Id	Description	On Hand	Cost
BF01	Barnyard Friends	3	$54.00
BL23	Blocks in Box	5	$29.00
CC14	Coal Car	8	$14.00
FT05	Fire Truck	7	$9.00
LB34	Lacing Bear	4	$12.00
MR06	Midget Railroad	3	$31.00
PJ12	Pets Jigsaw	10	$8.00
RB02	Railway Bridge	1	$17.00
SK10	Skyscraper	6	$25.00
UM09	USA Map	12	$14.00

FIGURE 1-84

(continued)

In the Lab

Creating the Restaurant Supply Database *(continued)*

Instructions: Perform the following tasks.

1. Create a new database in which to store all the objects related to the restaurant data. Call the database Restaurant Supply.
2. Create the Customer table using the structure shown in Figure 1-85. Use the name Customer for the table.
3. Add the data shown in Figure 1-85 to the Customer table.
4. Print the Customer table.
5. Create the Sales Rep table using the structure shown in Figure 1-86. To change the field size for the Comm Rate field, click the row selector for the field, and then click the Field Size property box. Click the Field Size property box arrow, and then click Double in the list. Use the name Sales Rep for the table.

Structure of Customer table

DATA FIELD NAME	DATA TYPE	FIELD SIZE	PRIMARY KEY?	DESCRIPTION
Customer Number	Text	4	Yes	Customer Number (Primary Key)
Name	Text	20		Name of Customer
Address	Text	15		Street Address
Telephone	Text	8		Telephone (999-9999 Version)
Balance	Currency			Amount Currently Due
Amount Paid	Currency			Amount Paid Year-to-Date
Sales Rep Number	Text	2		Number of Sales Representative

Data for Customer table

CUSTOMER NUMBER	NAME	ADDRESS	TELEPHONE	BALANCE	AMOUNT PAID	SALES REP NUMBER
AM23	American Pie	223 Johnson	555-2150	$95.00	$1,595.00	44
BB34	Bob's Café	1939 Jackson	555-1939	$50.00	$0.00	51
BI15	Bavarian Inn	3294 Devon	555-7510	$445.00	$1,250.00	49
CB12	China Buffet	1632 Clark	555-0804	$45.00	$610.00	49
CM09	Curry and More	3140 Halsted	555-0604	$195.00	$980.00	51
EG07	El Gallo	1805 Broadway	555-1404	$0.00	$1,600.00	44
JS34	Joe's Seafood	2200 Lawrence	555-0313	$260.00	$600.00	49
LV20	Little Venice	13 Devon	555-5161	$100.00	$1,150.00	49
NC25	New Crete	1027 Wells	555-4210	$140.00	$450.00	44
RD03	Reuben's Deli	787 Monroe	555-7657	$0.00	$875.00	51
VG21	Veggie Gourmet	1939 Congress	555-6554	$60.00	$625.00	44

FIGURE 1-85

6. Add the data shown in Figure 1-86 to the Sales Rep table.
7. Print the Sales Rep table.
8. Create a form for the Customer table. Use the name Customer for the form.

In the Lab

Structure of Sales Rep table

FIELD NAME	DATA TYPE	FIELD SIZE	PRIMARY KEY?	DESCRIPTION
Sales Rep Number	Text	2	Yes	Sales Rep Number (Primary Key)
Last Name	Text	15		Last Name of Sales Rep
First Name	Text	10		First Name of Sales Rep
Address	Text	15		Street Address
City	Text	15		City
State	Text	2		State (Two-Character Abbreviation)
Zip Code	Text	5		Zip Code (Five-Character Version)
Salary	Currency			Annual Base Salary
Comm Rate	Number	Double		Commission Rate
Commission	Currency			Year-to-Date Total Commissions

Data for Sales Rep table

SALES REP NUMBER	LAST NAME	FIRST NAME	ADDRESS	CITY	STATE	ZIP CODE	SALARY	COMM RATE	COMMISSION
44	Charles	Pat	43 Fourth	Lawncrest	WA	67845	$19,000.00	0.05	$213.50
49	Gupta	Pinn	678 Hillcrest	Manton	OR	68923	$20,000.00	0.06	$216.60
51	Ortiz	Jose	982 Victoria	Lawncrest	WA	67845	$18,500.00	0.05	$92.75

FIGURE 1-86

9. Open the form you created and change the address for customer number EG07 to 185 Broad.
10. Change to Datasheet view and delete the record for customer number BB34.
11. Print the Customer table.
12. Create and print the report shown in Figure 1-87 for the Customer table.

Customer Status Report

Customer Number	Name	Balance	Amount Paid
AM23	American Pie	$95.00	$1,595.00
BI15	Bavarian Inn	$445.00	$1,250.00
CB12	China Buffet	$45.00	$610.00
CM09	Curry and More	$195.00	$980.00
EG07	El Gallo	$0.00	$1,600.00
JS34	Joe's Seafood	$260.00	$600.00
LV20	Little Venice	$100.00	$1,150.00
NC25	New Crete	$140.00	$450.00
RD03	Reuben's Deli	$0.00	$875.00
VG21	Veggie Gourmet	$60.00	$625.00

FIGURE 1-87

In the Lab

3 Creating the Condo Management Database

Problem: A condo management company located in a ski resort community provides a rental service for condo owners who want to rent their units. The company rents the condos by the week to ski vacationers. The database consists of two tables. The Condo table contains information on the units available for rent. The Owner table contains information on the owners of the rental units.

Instructions: Perform the following tasks.

1. Create a new database in which to store all the objects related to the rental data. Call the database Condo Management.

2. Create the Condo table using the structure shown in Figure 1-88. Use the name Condo for the table. Note that the table uses a new data type, Yes/No for the Powder Room and Linens fields. The Yes/No data type stores data that has one of two values. A Powder Room is a half-bathroom; that is, there is a sink and a toilet but no shower or tub.

3. Add the data shown in Figure 1-88 to the Condo table. To add a Yes value to the Powder Room and Linens fields, click the check box that displays in each field.

Structure of Condo table

FIELD NAME	DATA TYPE	FIELD SIZE	PRIMARY KEY?	DESCRIPTION
Unit Number	Text	3	Yes	Condo Unit Number (Primary Key)
Bedrooms	Number			Number of Bedrooms
Bathrooms	Number			Number of Bathrooms
Sleeps	Number			Maximum Number that can sleep in rental unit
Powder Room	Yes/No			Does the condo have a powder room?
Linens	Yes/No			Are linens (sheets and towels) furnished?
Weekly Rate	Currency			Weekly Rental Rate
Owner Id	Text	4		Id of Condo Unit's Owner

Data for Condo table

UNIT NUMBER	BEDROOMS	BATHROOMS	SLEEPS	POWDER ROOM	LINENS	WEEKLY RATE	OWNER ID
101	1	1	2			$675.00	HJ05
108	2	1	3		Y	$1,050.00	AB10
202	3	2	8	Y	Y	$1,400.00	BR18
204	2	2	6	Y		$1,100.00	BR18
206	2	2	5		Y	$950.00	GM50
308	2	2	6	Y	Y	$950.00	GM50
403	1	1	2			$700.00	HJ05
405	1	1	3			$750.00	AB10
500	3	3	8	Y	Y	$1,100.00	AB10
510	2	1	4	Y	Y	$825.00	BR18

FIGURE 1-88

In the Lab

Structure of Owner table

FIELD NAME	DATA TYPE	FIELD SIZE	PRIMARY KEY?	DESCRIPTION
Owner Id	Text	4	Yes	Owner Id (Primary Key)
Last Name	Text	15		Last Name of Owner
First Name	Text	10		First Name of Owner
Address	Text	15		Street Address
City	Text	15		City
State	Text	2		State (Two-Character Abbreviation)
Zip Code	Text	5		Zip Code (Five-Character Version)
Telephone	Text	12		Telephone Number (999-999-9999 Version)

4. Use Microsoft Access Help to learn how to resize column widths in Datasheet view and then reduce the size of the Unit Number, Bedrooms, Bathrooms, Sleeps, Powder Room, and Linens columns. Be sure to save the changes to the layout of the table.
5. Print the Condo table.
6. Create the Owner table using the structure shown in Figure 1-89. Use the name Owner for the table.
7. Add the data shown in Figure 1-89 to the Owner table.
8. Print the Owner table.
9. Create a form for the Condo table. Use the name Condo for the form.
10. Open the form you created and change the weekly rate for Unit Number 206 to $925.00.
11. Print the Condo table.
12. Create and print the report shown in Figure 1-90 for the Condo table.

Data for Owner table

OWNER ID	LAST NAME	FIRST NAME	ADDRESS	CITY	STATE	ZIP CODE	TELEPHONE
AB10	Alonso	Bonita	281 Robin	Whitehall	OK	45241	405-555-6543
BR18	Beerne	Renee	39 Oak	Pearton	WI	48326	715-555-7373
GM50	Graty	Mark	21 West 8th	Greenview	KS	31904	913-555-2225
HJ05	Heulbert	John	314 Central	Munkton	MI	49611	616-555-3333

FIGURE 1-89

Available Condo Rentals Report

Unit Number	Bedrooms	Bathrooms	Weekly Rate	Owner Id
101	1	1	$675.00	HJ05
108	2	1	$1,050.00	AB10
202	3	2	$1,400.00	BR18
204	2	2	$1,100.00	BR18
206	2	2	$925.00	GM50
308	2	2	$950.00	GM50
403	1	1	$700.00	HJ05
405	1	1	$750.00	AB10
500	3	3	$1,100.00	AB10
510	2	1	$825.00	BR18

FIGURE 1-90

Cases and Places

The difficulty of these case studies varies:
◗ are the least difficult; ◗◗ are more difficult; and ◗◗◗ are the most difficult.

1

◗   To help finance your college education, you and two of your friends have formed a small business. You provide help to organizations in need of computer expertise. You have established a small clientele and realize that you need to computerize your business. You gather the information shown in Figure 1-91.

Design and create a database to store the data related to your business. Then create the necessary tables, enter the data from Figure 1-91, and print the tables. To personalize this database, replace Jan Smith's name with your own name.

CUSTOMER NUMBER	NAME	ADDRESS	TELEPHONE NUMBER	BALANCE	HELPER ID	HELPER LAST NAME	HELPER FIRST NAME	HOURLY RATE
AL35	Alores Gifts	12 Thistle	555-1222	$145.00	89	Smith	Jan	$12.50
AR43	Arsan Co.	34 Green	555-3434	$180.00	82	Ortega	Javier	$12.45
BK18	Byrd's Kites	56 Pampas	555-5678	$0.00	82	Ortega	Javier	$12.45
CJ78	Cee J's	24 Thistle	555-4242	$170.00	78	Chang	Pinn	$12.35
CL45	Class Act	89 Lime	555-9876	$129.00	89	Smith	Jan	$12.50
LB42	Le Boutique	12 Lemon	555-9012	$160.00	82	Ortega	Javier	$12.45
LK23	Learn n Kids	44 Apple	555-4004	$0.00	78	Chang	Pinn	$12.35
ME30	Meeker Co.	789 Poppy	555-0987	$195.00	89	Smith	Jan	$12.50
RE20	Ready Eats	90 Orange	555-9123	$0.00	78	Chang	Pinn	$12.35
SR34	Shoe Repair	62 Lime	555-4378	$140.00	89	Smith	Jan	$12.50

FIGURE 1-91

Cases and Places

2 ▶ After lengthy negotiations, your town now has a minor league baseball team. The team owners and the town government are vigorously promoting the benefits of the new team. As part of their marketing strategy, they are selling items with the new team logo. The marketing team has asked you to create and update a database that they can use to keep track of their inventory and suppliers. The current inventory is shown in Figure 1-92.

Design and create a database to store the team's inventory. Then create the necessary tables, enter the data from Figure 1-92, and print the tables.

ITEM ID	DESCRIPTION	UNITS ON HAND	COST	SELLING PRICE	SUPPLIER CODE	SUPPLIER NAME	SUPPLIER TELEPHONE
3663	Baseball Cap	30	$10.15	$18.95	LG	Logo Goods	517-555-3853
3683	Coasters (4)	12	$7.45	$9.00	BH	Beverage Holders	317-555-4747
4563	Coffee Mug	20	$1.85	$4.75	BH	Beverage Holders	317-555-4747
4593	Glasses (4)	8	$8.20	$10.75	BH	Beverage Holders	317-555-4747
5923	Jacket	12	$44.75	$54.95	LG	Logo Goods	517-555-3853
5953	Shorts	10	$14.95	$19.95	AC	Al's Clothes	616-555-9228
6189	Sports Towel	24	$3.25	$6.75	LG	Logo Goods	517-555-3853
6343	Sweatshirt	9	$27.45	$34.95	AC	Al's Clothes	616-555-9228
7810	Tee Shirt	32	$9.50	$14.95	AC	Al's Clothes	616-555-9228
7930	Travel Mug	11	$2.90	$3.25	BH	Beverage Holders	317-555-4747

FIGURE 1-92

3 ▶▶ The tourism director of your town has asked you to create a database of local attractions. She wants to keep track of the type of attraction, for example, museums, historic homes, zoo, botanical gardens, nature trails, hike/bike paths, or public parks. She also needs to know the address of the attraction, days and times it is open, whether or not there is a cost associated with the attraction, and a telephone number for more information.

Design and create a database to meet the tourism director's needs. Create the necessary tables, enter some sample data, and print the tables to show the director. *Note*: Type of attraction is really a category into which the attraction fits. Use the Table Wizard and select the Category table to create this table. If you want, you can rename the fields in the table. (*Hint*: See More About Creating a Table: The Table Wizard on page A 1.13.)

Cases and Places

4 ▶▶ The high school Math club has started a tutoring program. Math club members are tutoring elementary students in basic math concepts. Each math club member is assigned one or more students to tutor. The elementary students who participate can earn points that can be redeemed for prizes donated by local merchants. Club members who participate keep track of the hours they spend tutoring. The state has promised to reward the high school club with the most number of tutoring hours. The club must keep track of the elementary students including each student's name, school the student attends, year in school, identity of the high school student tutor, and hours tutored. The club also must keep track of the high school students recording such information as name, year in school, and total number of hours spent tutoring.

Design and create a database to meet the Math club's needs.

5 ▶▶▶ As a hobby, many people collect items such as baseball cards, ceramic frogs, model trains, and ships in a bottle. Sometimes, they also trade items with other collectors. What do you collect? Create a database that can store data related to a particular hobby collection.

Determine the type of data you will need, then design and create a database to meet those needs. Create the necessary tables, enter some sample data, and print the tables.

6 ▶▶▶ You are getting ready to look for a job and realize you will need to plan your job search carefully. The Database Wizard includes a Contact Management template that can create a database that will help you keep track of your job contacts.

Create the Contact Management database using the Database Wizard. (*Hint*: See More About Creating a Database: The Database Wizard on page A 1.11.) Determine whether or not you need any extra fields, such as home telephone. Use the form that the wizard creates to enter some sample data. Then, print the report that the wizard created with the sample data.

Microsoft Access 2002

PROJECT

2

Querying a Database Using the Select Query Window

You will have mastered the material in this project when you can:

O B J E C T I V E S

- State the purpose of queries
- Create a new query
- Use a query to display all records and all fields
- Run a query
- Print the answer to a query
- Close a query
- Clear a query
- Use a query to display selected fields
- Use text data and wildcards in criteria in a query
- Use numeric data and comparison operators in criteria
- Use compound criteria
- Sort the answer to a query
- Join tables in a query and restrict the records in a join
- Use calculated fields in a query
- Calculate statistics in a query
- Save a query and use a saved query

The Search for Missing Youngsters

National Database to the Rescue

Each year, more than one million children are reported lost, injured, or otherwise missing or abducted. Thousands of these youngsters are kidnapped by an ex-spouse, some run away, and others are victims of foul play. All parents fear the loss of a child no matter the circumstances. When this unfortunate situation occurs, everyone should help in any way possible.

The National Center for Missing and Exploited Children (NCMEC) maintains a database that includes records of thousands of these missing children. Through this organization, although the youth may be missing physically from their families, they appear in photo images on its Internet site, milk cartons, and other forms of publicity.

NCMEC was created in 1984 as a public and private partnership to help the public search for missing children. Since the nonprofit center opened, more than 1.3 million calls have been channeled through its national hotline (1-800-THE-LOST). In addition, NCMEC has partnered with the U.S. Department of Justice's Office

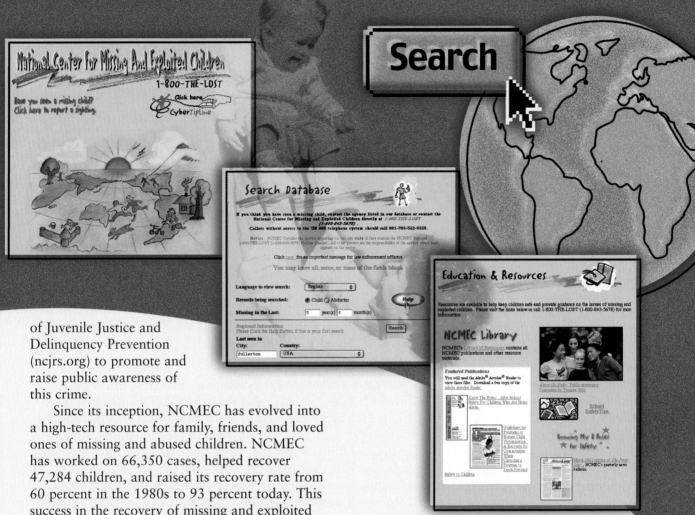

Search

of Juvenile Justice and Delinquency Prevention (ncjrs.org) to promote and raise public awareness of this crime.

Since its inception, NCMEC has evolved into a high-tech resource for family, friends, and loved ones of missing and abused children. NCMEC has worked on 66,350 cases, helped recover 47,284 children, and raised its recovery rate from 60 percent in the 1980s to 93 percent today. This success in the recovery of missing and exploited youth worldwide is attributed to human resources, technological advancements, training workshops, program development, and research and evaluation. Through consistent private, community, and public partnerships, including relationships with Intel, IBM, and Tektronix, NCMEC has grown into a solid force for solving child cases.

One example of the advanced technology utilized by NCMEC is a database that contains photographs of missing children. Investigators and Web users are able to open the database and create a precise query based on such fields as the child's name, age, eye color, and weight. Then they run the query, and within a matter of seconds they have answers to the requested information. You can create queries and view some of these images at the NCMEC Web site (ncmec.org). Similarly, you will query the Alisa Vending Services database in this project to obtain answers to questions regarding customer names and locations, current balances, and driver names.

Moreover, NCMEC's imaging specialists can alter a child's photograph to show how he or she might appear many years after disappearing. Subsequently, these images are stored in corresponding fields in the computerized imaging database. Many children who may not have been located otherwise have been found using this enhancement technology.

The Multimedia Kiosk Program, which IBM donated to NCMEC, placed 50 kiosks in high pedestrian traffic areas such as LaGuardia Airport in New York and in large shopping malls throughout the country. They provide a functional database for the general public to learn about missing children and a means to transfer information quickly to affected friends and family.

Through the efforts of NCMEC, the nation now has a solid weapon and resource for the fight against child endangerment.

Microsoft Access 2002

Querying a Database Using the Select Query Window

PROJECT

2

CASE PERSPECTIVE

With the database consisting of customer and driver data created, the management and staff of Alisa Vending Services expect to obtain the benefits they anticipated when they set up the database. One of the more important benefits is the capability of easily asking questions concerning the data in the database and rapidly getting the answers. Among the questions they want answered are the following:

1. What are the amount paid and current due amount for customer FR28?
2. Which customers' names begin with Gr?
3. Which customers are located in Hansen?
4. What is the total amount (amount paid plus current due amount) for each customer?
5. Which customers of driver 60 have amounts paid of greater than $20,000?

Your task is to assist the management of Alisa Vending Services in obtaining answers to these questions as well as any other questions they deem important.

Introduction

A database management system such as Access offers many useful features, among them the capability of answering questions such as those posed by the management of Alisa Vending Services (Figure 2-1). The answers to these questions, and many more, are found in the database, and Access can find the answers quickly. When you pose a question to Access, or any other database management system, the question is called a query. A **query** is simply a question represented in a way that Access can understand.

Thus, to find the answer to a question, you first create a corresponding query using the techniques illustrated in this project. Once you have created the query, you instruct Access to run the query; that is, to perform the steps necessary to obtain the answer. Access then will display the answer in Datasheet view.

Project Two — Querying the Alisa Vending Services Database

You must obtain answers to the questions posed by the management of Alisa Vending Services. These include the questions shown in Figure 2-1, as well as any other questions that management deems important.

What are the amount paid and current due amounts for customer FR28?

Which customers' names begin with Gr?

Which customers are located in Hansen?

What is the total amount (amount paid + current due amount) for each customer?

Which customers of driver 60 have amounts paid of greater than $20,000.00?

Customer table

CUSTOMER NUMBER	NAME	ADDRESS	CITY	STATE	ZIP CODE	AMOUNT PAID	CURRENT DUE	DRIVER NUMBER
BA95	Bayside Hotel	287 Riley	Hansen	FL	38513	$21,876.00	$892.50	30
BR46	Baldwin-Reed	267 Howard	Fernwood	FL	37023	$26,512.00	$2,672.00	60
CN21	Century North	1562 Butler	Hansen	FL	38513	$8,725.00	$0.00	60
FR28	Friend's Movies	871 Adams	Westport	FL	37070	$4,256.00	$1,202.00	75
GN62	Grand Nelson	7821 Oak	Wood Key	FL	36828	$8,287.50	$925.50	30
GS29	Great Screens	572 Lee	Hansen	FL	38513	$21,625.00	$0.00	60
LM22	Lenger Mason	274 Johnson	Westport	FL	37070	$0.00	$0.00	60
ME93	Merks College	561 Fairhill	Bayville	FL	38734	$24,761.00	$1,572.00	30
RI78	Riter University	26 Grove	Fernwood	FL	37023	$11,682.25	$2,827.50	75
TU20	Turner Hotel	8672 Quincy	Palmview	FL	36114	$8,521.50	$0.00	60

CUSTOMER NUMBER	NAME
GN62	Grand Nelson
GS29	Great Screens

CUSTOMER NUMBER	NAME
BR46	Baldwin-Reed
GS29	Great Screens

CUSTOMER NUMBER	NAME	ADDRESS
BA95	Bayside Hotel	287 Riley
CN21	Century North	1562 Butler
GS29	Great Screens	572 Lee

CUSTOMER NUMBER	NAME	TOTAL AMOUNT
BA95	Bayside Hotel	$22,768.50
BR46	Baldwin-Reed	$29,184.00
CN21	Century North	$8,725.00
FR28	Friend's Movies	$5,458.00
GN62	Grand Nelson	$9,213.00
GS29	Great Screens	$21,625.00
LM22	Lenger Mason	$0.00
ME93	Merks College	$26,333.00
RI78	Riter University	$14,509.75
TU20	Turner Hotel	$8,521.50

CUSTOMER NUMBER	NAME	AMOUNT PAID	CURRENT DUE
FR28	Friend's Movies	$4,256.00	$1,202.00

FIGURE 2-1

More About

Queries: Query Languages

Prior to the advent of query languages in the mid 1970s, obtaining answers to questions concerning data in a database was very difficult, requiring that someone write lengthy (several hundred line) programs in languages like COBOL.

More About

Queries: The Simple Query Wizard

The Simple Query Wizard creates select queries that retrieve data from the fields you specify in one or more tables. To use the Simple Query Wizard, click the New Object: AutoForm button arrow and then click Query on the list that displays. When the New Query dialog box displays, click Simple Query Wizard. Follow the directions in the Simple Query Wizard dialog boxes.

Opening the Database

Before creating queries, first you must open the database. The following steps summarize the procedure to complete this task.

TO OPEN A DATABASE

1 Click the Start button, click Programs on the Start menu, and then click Microsoft Access on the Programs submenu.

2 Click Open on the Database toolbar and then click 3½ Floppy (A:) in the Look in box. Make sure the database called Alisa Vending Services is selected.

3 Click the Open button in the Open dialog box. If the Tables object is not already selected, click Tables on the Objects bar.

The database is open and the Alisa Vending Services : Database window displays.

Creating a New Query

You create a query by making entries in a special window called a **Select Query window**. Once the database is open, the first step in creating a query is to select the table for which you are creating a query in the Database window. Next, using the New Object: AutoForm button, you will design the new query. The Select Query window will display. It typically is easier to work with the Select Query window if it is maximized. Thus, as a standard practice, maximize the Select Query window as soon as you have created it. In addition, it often is useful to resize both panes within the window. This enables you to resize the field list that displays in the upper pane so more fields display.

Perform the following steps to begin creating a query.

Steps To Create a Query

1 **Be sure the Alisa Vending Services database is open, the Tables object is selected, and the Customer table is selected. Click the New Object: AutoForm button arrow on the Database toolbar and point to Query on the list that displays.**

The list of available objects displays (Figure 2-2).

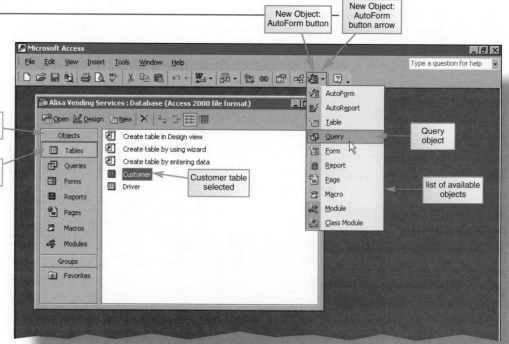

FIGURE 2-2

2 Click Query and point to the OK button.

The New Query dialog box displays (Figure 2-3).

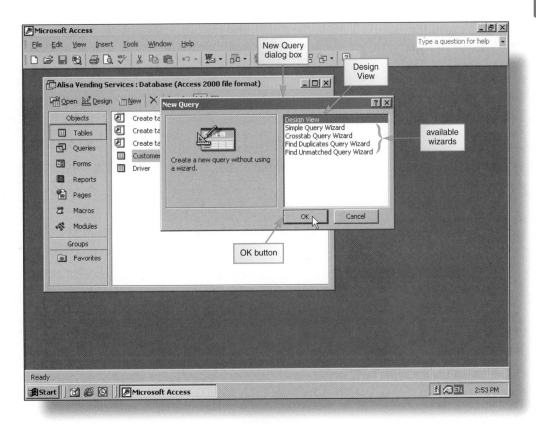

FIGURE 2-3

3 With Design View selected, click the OK button and then point to the Maximize button for the Query1 : Select Query window.

The Query1 : Select Query window displays (Figure 2-4).

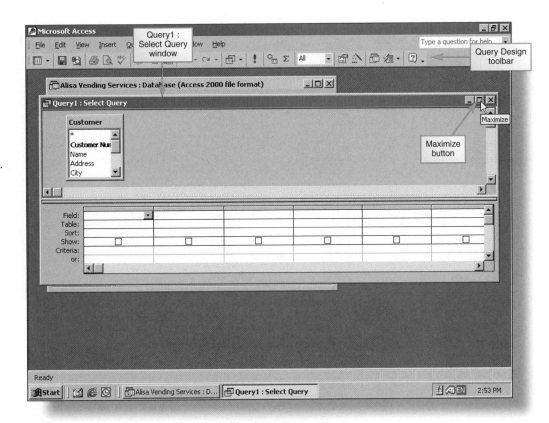

FIGURE 2-4

4 Maximize the Query1 : Select Query window by clicking its Maximize button, and then point to the dividing line that separates the upper and lower panes of the window. The mouse pointer will change shape to a two-headed arrow with a horizontal bar.

The Query1 : Select Query window is maximized (Figure 2-5). The upper pane contains a field list for the Customer table. The lower pane contains the **design grid**, which is the area where you specify fields to be included, sort order, and the criteria the records you are looking for must satisfy.

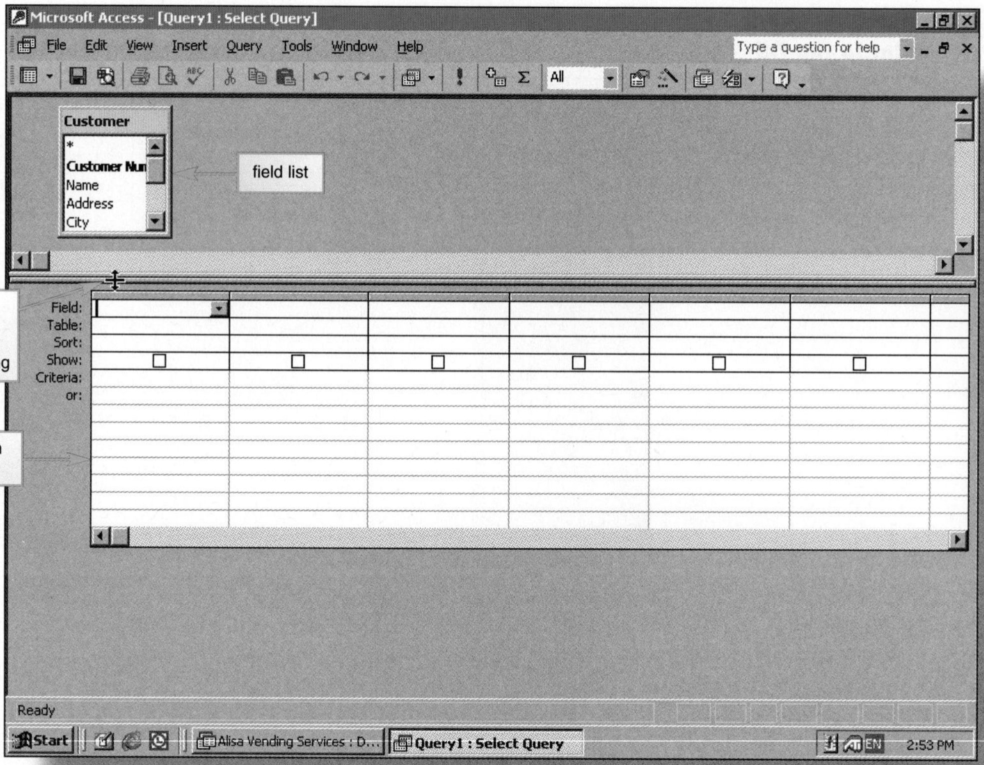

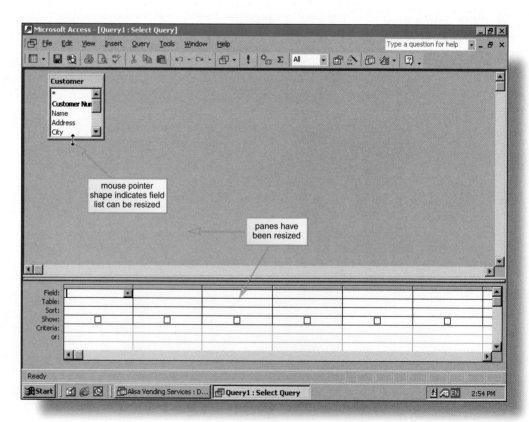

FIGURE 2-5

5 Drag the line down to the approximate position shown in Figure 2-6 and then move the mouse pointer to the lower edge of the field list so it changes shape to a two-headed arrow.

FIGURE 2-6

6 Drag the lower edge of the field list down far enough so all fields in the Customer table are visible.

All fields in the Customer table display (Figure 2-7).

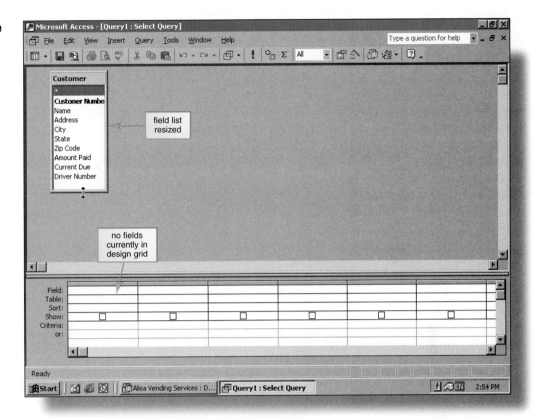

FIGURE 2-7

Using the Select Query Window

Once you have created a new Select Query window, you are ready to create the actual query by making entries in the design grid in the lower pane of the window. You enter the names of the fields you want included in the Field row in the grid. You also can enter criteria, such as the fact that the customer number must be FR28, in the Criteria row of the grid. When you do so, only the record or records that match the criterion will be included in the answer.

Displaying Selected Fields in a Query

Only the fields that appear in the design grid will be included in the results of the query. Thus, to display only certain fields, place only these fields in the grid, and no others. If you place the wrong field in the grid inadvertently, click Edit on the menu bar and then click Delete to remove it. Alternatively, you could click Clear Grid on the Edit menu to clear the entire design grid and then start over.

The steps on the next page create a query to show the customer number, name, and driver number for all customers by including only those fields in the design grid.

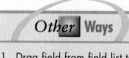

Steps To Include Fields in the Design Grid

1 Make sure you have a maximized Query1 : Select Query window containing a field list for the Customer table in the upper pane of the window and an empty design grid in the lower pane. Point to the Customer Number field in the field list (Figure 2-8).

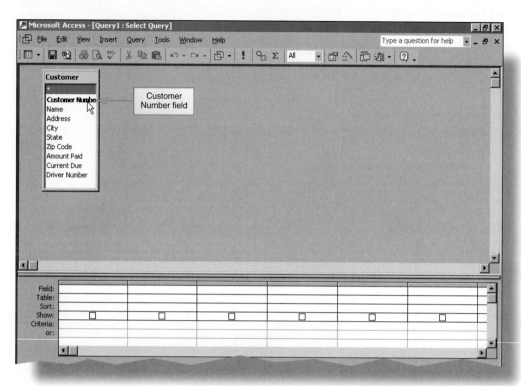

FIGURE 2-8

2 Double-click the Customer Number field to include it in the query. Point to, and then double-click, the Name field to include it in the query. Include the Driver Number field using the same technique. Point to the Run button on the Query Design toolbar.

The Customer Number, Name, and Driver Number fields are included in the query (Figure 2-9).

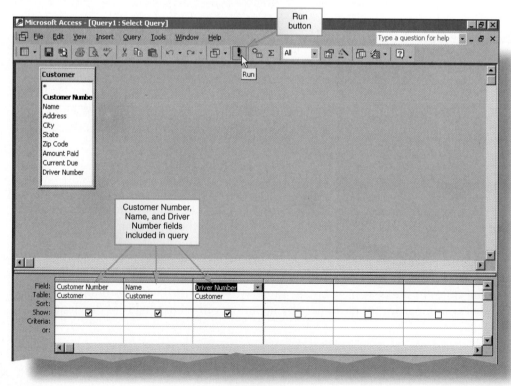

FIGURE 2-9

Other Ways

1. Drag field from field list to design grid
2. Click column in grid, click arrow, click field

Running a Query

Once you have created the query, you need to run the query to produce the results. To do so, click the Run button. Access then will perform the steps necessary to obtain and display the answer. The set of records that makes up the answer will be displayed in Datasheet view. Although it looks like a table that is stored on your disk, it really is not. The records are constructed from data in the existing Customer table. If you were to change the data in the Customer table and then rerun this same query, the results would reflect the changes. Perform the following step to run the query.

Steps **To Run the Query**

1 **Click the Run button on the Query Design toolbar.**

The query is executed and the results display (Figure 2-10).

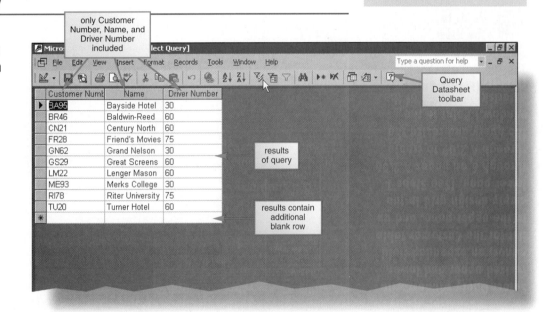

FIGURE 2-10

Printing the Results of a Query

To print the results of a query, use the same techniques you learned in Project 1 on page A 1.29 to print the data in the table. Complete the following steps to print the query results that currently display on the screen.

TO PRINT THE RESULTS OF A QUERY

1 Point to the Print button on the Query Datasheet toolbar (Figure 2-11).

2 Click the Print button.

The results print.

If the results of a query require landscape orientation, switch to landscape orientation before you click the Print button as indicated in Project 1 on page A 1.29.

Other Ways

1. On Query menu click Run
2. In Voice Command mode, say "Run"

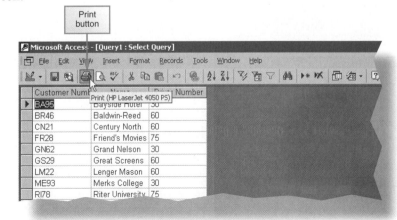

FIGURE 2-11

Returning to the Select Query Window

You can examine the results of a query on your screen to see the answer to your question. You can scroll through the records, if necessary, just as you scroll through the records of any other table. You also can print a copy of the table. In any case, once you are finished working with the results, you can return to the Select Query window to ask another question. To do so, use the View button arrow on the Query Datasheet toolbar as shown in the following steps.

 To Return to the Select Query Window

 **1** Point to the View button arrow on the Query Datasheet toolbar (Figure 2-12).

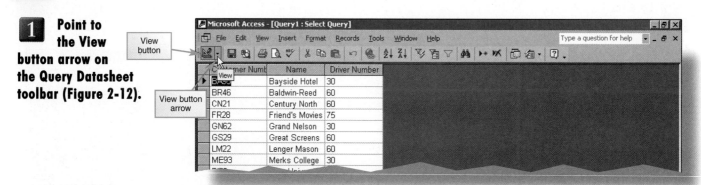

FIGURE 2-12

 **2** Click the View button arrow and then point to Design View.

The Query View list displays (Figure 2-13).

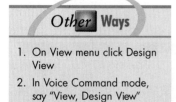 **3** Click Design View.

The Query1 : Select Query window again displays.

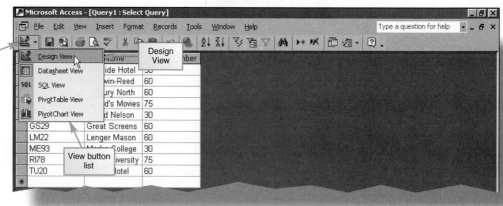

FIGURE 2-13

Other Ways

1. On View menu click Design View
2. In Voice Command mode, say "View, Design View"

Because Design View is the first command on the View button list, you do not have to click the View button arrow and then click Design View. You simply can click the View button itself.

Closing a Query

To close a query, close the Select Query window. When you do so, Access displays the Microsoft dialog box asking if you want to save your query for future use. If you think you will need to create the same exact query often, you should save the query. For now, you will not save any queries. You will see how to save them later in the project. The following steps close a query without saving it.

 To Close the Query

1 Point to the Close Window button for the Query1 : Select Query window (Figure 2-14).

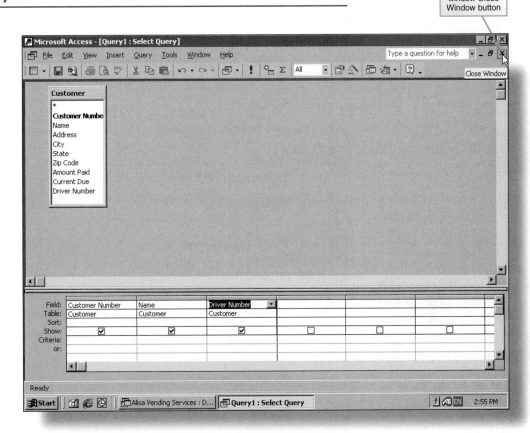

FIGURE 2-14

2 Click the Close Window button for the Query1 : Select Query window and then point to the No button.

The Microsoft Access dialog box displays (Figure 2-15). Clicking the Yes button saves the query and clicking the No button closes the query without saving.

3 Click the No button in the Microsoft Access dialog box.

The Query1 : Select Query window closes and no longer displays. The query is not saved.

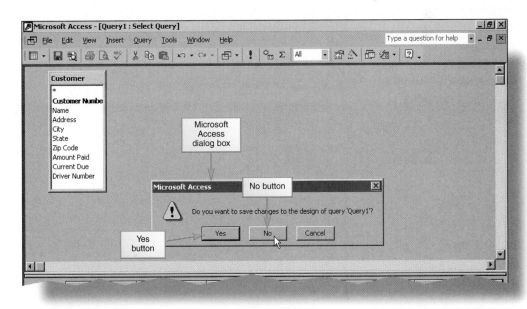

FIGURE 2-15

Other Ways

1. On File menu click Close
2. In Voice Command mode, say "File, Close"

Including All Fields in a Query

If you want to include all fields in a query, you could select each field individually. There is a simpler way to include all fields, however. By selecting the **asterisk** (*) in the field list, you are indicating that all fields are to be included. Complete the following steps to use the asterisk to include all fields.

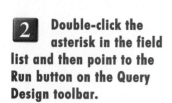

To Include All Fields in a Query

1 Be sure you have a maximized Query1 : Select Query window with resized upper and lower panes, an expanded field list for the Customer table in the upper pane, and an empty design grid in the lower pane. (See Steps 1 through 6 on pages A 2.06 through A 2.09 to create the query and resize the window.) Point to the asterisk at the top of the field list.

A maximized Query1 : Select Query window displays (Figure 2-16). The two panes have been resized.

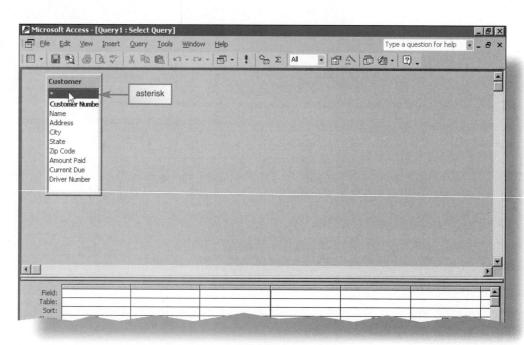

FIGURE 2-16

2 Double-click the asterisk in the field list and then point to the Run button on the Query Design toolbar.

The table name, Customer, followed by a period and an asterisk is added to the design grid (Figure 2-17), indicating all fields are included.

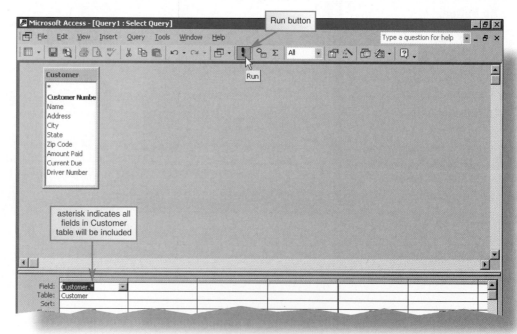

FIGURE 2-17

3 Click the Run button.

The results display and all fields in the Customer table are included (Figure 2-18).

View button

4 Click the View button on the Query Datasheet toolbar to return to the Query1 : Select Query window.

The Query1 : Select Query window replaces the datasheet.

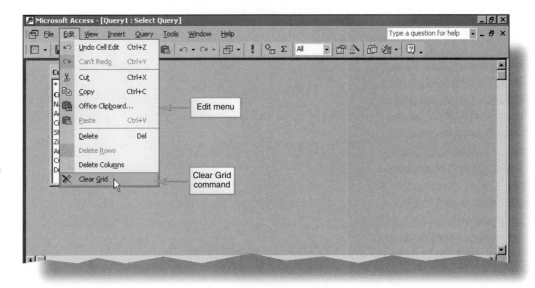

Customer Numb	Name	Address	City	State	Zip Code	Amount Paid	Current Due
BA95	Bayside Hotel	287 Riley	Hansen	FL	38513	$21,876.00	$892.50
BR46	Baldwin-Reed	267 Howard	Fernwood	FL	37023	$26,512.00	$2,672.00
CN21	Century North	1562 Butler	Hansen	FL	38513	$8,725.00	$0.00
FR28	Friend's Movies	871 Adams	Westport	FL	37070	$4,256.00	$1,202.00
GN62	Grand Nelson	7821 Oak	Wood Key	FL	36828	$8,287.50	$925.50
GS29	Great Screens	572 Lee	Hansen	FL	38513	$21,625.00	$0.00
LM22	Lenger Mason	274 Johnson	Westport	FL	37070	$0.00	$0.00
ME93	Merks College	561 Fairhill	Bayville	FL	38734	$24,761.00	$1,572.00
RI78	Riter University	26 Grove	Fernwood	FL	37023	$11,682.25	$2,827.50
TU20	Turner Hotel	8672 Quincy	Palmview	FL	36114	$8,521.50	$0.00
*						$0.00	$0.00

all fields included

FIGURE 2-18

Clearing the Design Grid

If you make mistakes as you are creating a query, you can fix each one individually. Alternatively, you simply may want to **clear the query**; that is, clear out the entries in the design grid and start over. One way to clear out the entries is to close the Select Query window and then start a new query just as you did earlier. A simpler approach, however, is to click Clear Grid on the Edit menu. Perform the following steps to clear a query.

Steps To Clear a Query

1 Click Edit on the menu bar and then point to Clear Grid on the Edit menu.

The Edit menu displays (Figure 2-19). If the Clear Grid command does not display immediately, wait a few seconds for the full menu to display.

2 Click Clear Grid.

Access clears the design grid so you can enter your next query.

Edit menu

Clear Grid command

FIGURE 2-19

The Access Help System

Need Help? It is no further than the Ask a Question box in the upper-right corner of the window. Click the box that contains the text, Type a question for help (Figure 2-20), type help, and then press the ENTER key. Access will respond with a list of items you can click to learn about obtaining help on any Access-related topic. To find out what is new in Access 2002, type what's new in Access in the Ask a Question box.

Entering Criteria

When you use queries, usually you are looking for those records that satisfy some criterion. You might want the name, amount paid, and current due amounts of the customer whose number is FR28, for example, or of those customers whose names start with the letters, Gr. To enter criteria, enter them in the Criteria row in the design grid below the field name to which the criterion applies. For example, to indicate that the customer number must be FR28, you first must add the Customer Number field to the design grid. You then would type FR28 in the Criteria row below the Customer Number field.

The next examples illustrate the types of criteria that are available.

Using Text Data in Criteria

To use **text data** (data in a field whose data type is Text) in criteria, simply type the text in the Criteria row below the corresponding field name. The following steps query the Customer table and display the customer number, name, amount paid, and current due amount of customer FR28.

 To Use Text Data in a Criterion

1 One by one, double-click the Customer Number, Name, Amount Paid, and Current Due fields to add them to the query. Point to the Criteria row for the first field in the design grid.

The Customer Number, Name, Amount Paid, and Current Due fields are added to the design grid (Figure 2-20). The mouse pointer on the Criteria entry for the first field (Customer Number) has changed shape to an I-beam.

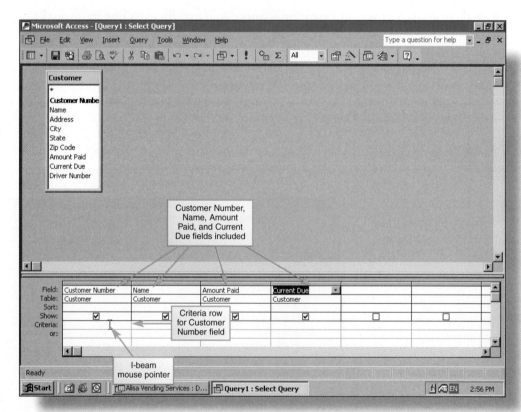

FIGURE 2-20

2 **Click the Criteria row, type** FR28 **as the criterion for the Customer Number field and then point to the Run button on the Query Design toolbar.**

The criterion is entered (Figure 2-21).

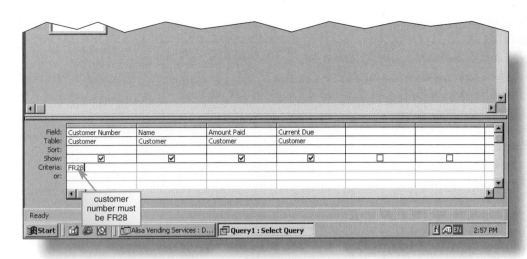

FIGURE 2-21

3 **Click the Run button to run the query.**

The results display (Figure 2-22). Only customer FR28 is included. (The extra blank row contains $0.00 in the Amount Paid and Current Due fields. Unlike text fields, which are left blank, number and currency fields in the extra row contain 0. Because the Amount Paid and Current Due fields are currency fields, the values display as $0.00.)

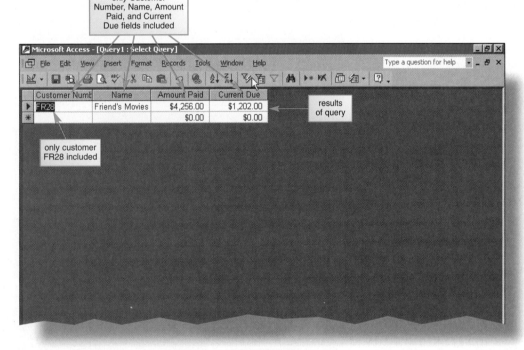

FIGURE 2-22

Using Wildcards

Two special wildcards are available in Microsoft Access. **Wildcards** are symbols that represent any character or combination of characters. The first of the two wildcards, the **asterisk** (*), represents any collection of characters. Thus Gr* represents the letters, Gr, followed by any collection of characters. The other wildcard symbol is the **question mark** (?), which represents any individual character. Thus t?m represents the letter, T, followed by any single character followed by the letter, m, such as Tim or Tom.

The steps on the next page use a wildcard to find the number, name, and address of those customers whose names begin with Gr. Because you do not know how many characters will follow the Gr, the asterisk is appropriate.

Using Text Data in Criteria

Some database systems require that text data must be enclosed in quotation marks. For example, to find customers in Texas, TX would be entered as the criterion for the State field. In Access this is not necessary, because Access will insert the quotation marks automatically.

Steps **To Use a Wildcard**

1 **Click the View button on the Query Datasheet toolbar to return to the Query1 : Select Query window. If necessary, click the Criteria row under the Customer Number field. Use the DELETE or BACKSPACE key to delete the current entry ("FR28"). Click the Criteria row under the Name field. Type Gr* as the entry and point to the Run button on the Query Design toolbar.**

The criterion is entered (Figure 2-23).

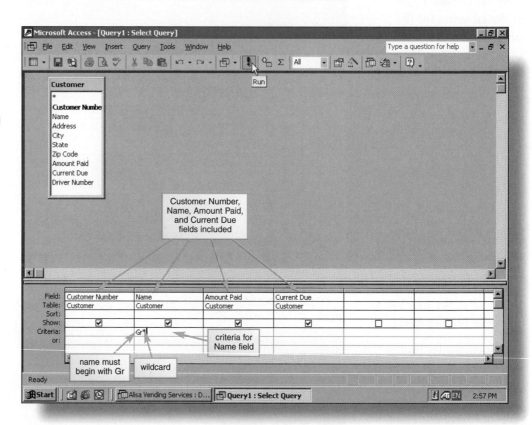

FIGURE 2-23

2 **Click the Run button to run the query.**

The results display (Figure 2-24). Only the customers whose names start with Gr are included.

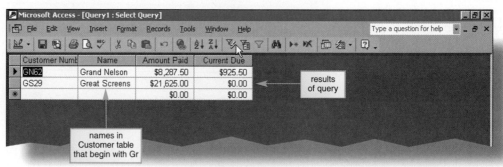

FIGURE 2-24

Criteria for a Field Not in the Result

In some cases, you may have criteria for a particular field that should not appear in the results of the query. For example, you may wish to see the customer number, name, address, and amount paid for all customers located in Hansen. The criterion involves the City field, which is not one of the fields to be included in the results.

To enter a criterion for the City field, it must be included in the design grid. Normally, this also would mean it would appear in the results. To prevent this from happening, remove the check mark from its Show check box in the Show row of the grid. The following steps illustrate the process by displaying the customer number, name, and amount paid for customers located in Hansen.

Steps **To Use Criteria for a Field Not Included in the Results**

1 **Click the View button on the Query Datasheet toolbar to return to the Query1 : Select Query window. On the Edit menu, click Clear Grid.**

Access clears the design grid so you can enter the next query.

2 **Include the Customer Number, Name, Address, Amount Paid, and City fields in the query. Type** Hansen **as the criterion for the City field and then point to the City field's Show check box.**

The fields are included in the grid, and the criterion for the City field is entered (Figure 2-25).

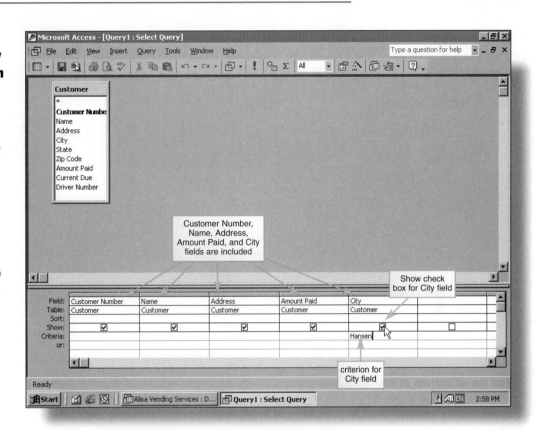

FIGURE 2-25

3 **Click the Show check box to remove the check mark and then point to the Run button on the Query Design toolbar.**

The check mark is removed from the Show check box for the City field (Figure 2-26), indicating it will not show in the result. Because the City field is a text field, Access has added quotation marks before and after Hansen automatically.

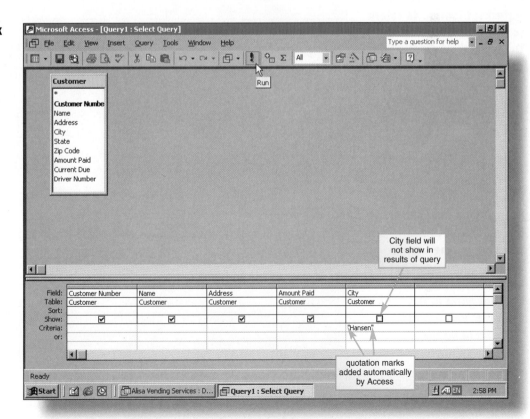

FIGURE 2-26

4 Click the Run button to run the query.

The results display (Figure 2-27). The City field does not display. The only customers included are those located in Hansen.

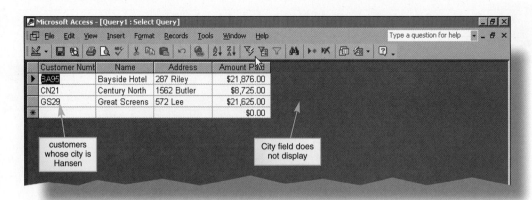

FIGURE 2-27

Using Numeric Data in Criteria

To enter a number in a criterion, type the number without any dollar signs or commas. Complete the following steps to display all customers whose current due amount is $0.00. To do so, you will need to type a 0 (zero) as the criterion for the Current Due field.

Steps **To Use a Number in a Criterion**

1 Click the View button on the Query Datasheet toolbar to return to the Query1 : Select Query window. On the Edit menu, click Clear Grid.

Access clears the design grid so you can enter the next query.

2 Include the Customer Number, Name, Amount Paid, and Current Due fields in the query. Type 0 as the criterion for the Current Due field. You need not enter a dollar sign or decimal point in the criterion. Point to the Run button on the Query Design toolbar.

The fields are selected and the criterion is entered (Figure 2-28).

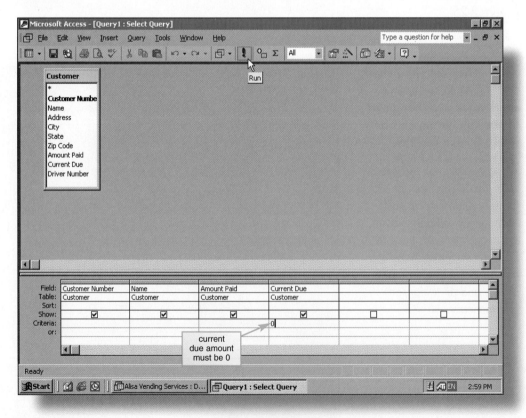

FIGURE 2-28

3 Click the Run button to run the query.

The results display (Figure 2-29). Only those customers that have a current due amount of $0.00 are included.

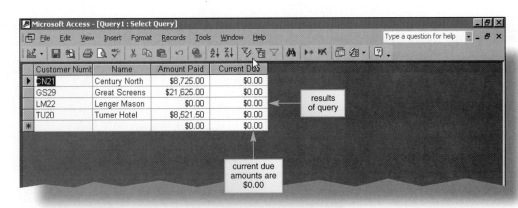

FIGURE 2-29

Using Comparison Operators

Unless you specify otherwise, Access assumes that the criteria you enter involve equality (exact matches). In the last query, for example, you were requesting those customers whose current due amount was equal to 0 (zero). If you want something other than an exact match, you must enter the appropriate **comparison operator**. The comparison operators are > (greater than), < (less than), >= (greater than or equal to), <= (less than or equal to), and NOT (not equal to).

Perform the following steps to use the > operator to find all customers whose amount paid is greater than $20,000.

Steps **To Use a Comparison Operator in a Criterion**

1 Click the View button on the Query Datasheet toolbar to return to the Query1 : Select Query window. On the Edit menu, click Clear Grid.

Access clears the design grid so you can enter the next query.

2 Include the Customer Number, Name, Amount Paid, and Current Due fields in the query. Type >20000 as the criterion for the Amount Paid field.

The fields are selected and the criterion is entered (Figure 2-30).

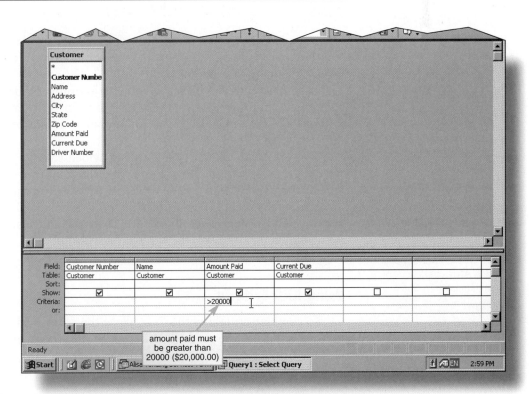

FIGURE 2-30

3 **Click the Run button on the Query Design toolbar to run the query.**

The results display (Figure 2-31). Only those customers who have an amount paid greater than $20,000 are included.

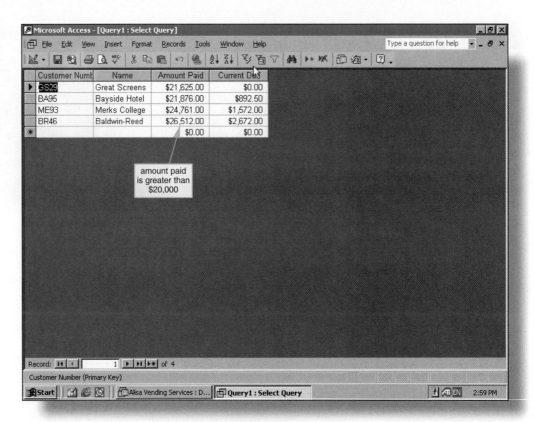

FIGURE 2-31

Using Compound Criteria

Often you will have more than one criterion that the data for which you are searching must satisfy. This type of criterion is called a **compound criterion**. Two types of compound criteria exist.

In an **AND criterion**, each individual criterion must be true in order for the compound criterion to be true. For example, an AND criterion would allow you to find those customers that have an amount paid greater than $20,000 and whose driver is driver 60.

Conversely, an **OR criterion** is true provided either individual criterion is true. An OR criterion would allow you to find those customers that have an amount paid greater than $20,000 or whose driver is driver 60. In this case, any customer whose amount paid is greater than $20,000 would be included in the answer whether or not the customer's driver is driver 60. Likewise, any customer whose driver is driver 60 would be included whether or not the customer had an amount paid greater than $20,000.

Using AND Criteria

To combine criteria with AND, place the criteria on the same line. Perform the following steps to use an AND criterion to find those customers whose amount paid is greater than $20,000 and whose driver is driver 60.

Compound Criteria

The BETWEEN operator allows you to search for a range of values in one field. For example, to find all customers whose amount paid amount is between $5,000 and $10,000, you would enter Between 5000 and 10000 in the Criteria row for the Amount Paid field. It also is possible to create compound criteria involving both OR and AND operators. For more information, visit the Access 2002 More About Web page (scsite.com/ac2002/more.htm) and then click Compound Criteria.

Steps **To Use a Compound Criterion Involving AND**

1 Click the View
button on the Query
Datasheet toolbar to return
to the Query1 : Select
Query window. Include the
Driver Number field in the
query. Be sure >20000 is
entered in the Criteria row
for the Amount Paid field.
Click the Criteria entry for
the Driver Number field
and then type 60 as the
criterion for the Driver
Number field.

*Criteria have been entered
for the Amount Paid and
Driver Number fields
(Figure 2-32).*

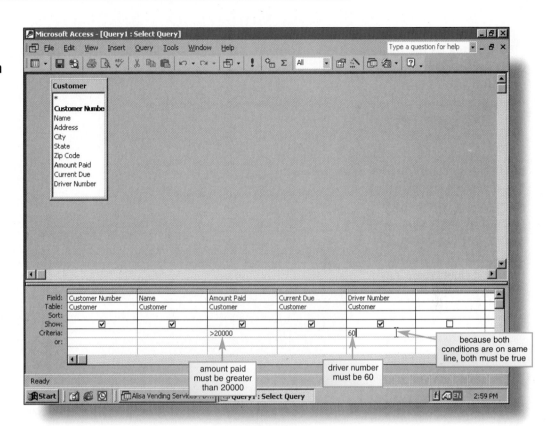

FIGURE 2-32

2 Click the Run button
on the Query Design
toolbar to run the query.

*The results display (Figure
2-33). Only the customers
whose amount paid is greater
than $20,000 and whose
driver number is 60 are
included.*

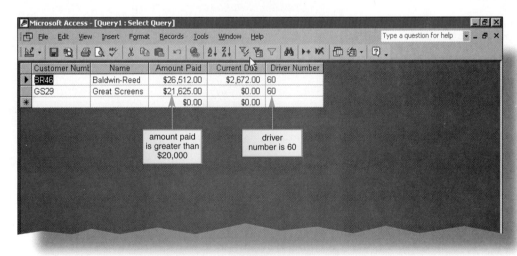

FIGURE 2-33

Using OR Criteria

To combine criteria with OR, the criteria must go on separate lines in the
Criteria area of the grid. The steps on the next page use an OR criterion to find
those customers whose amount paid is greater than $20,000 or whose driver is
driver 60 (or both).

Steps To Use a Compound Criterion Involving OR

1 **Click the View button on the Query Datasheet toolbar to return to the Query1 : Select Query window.**

2 **If necessary, click the Criteria entry for the Driver Number field. Use the BACKSPACE key or the DELETE key to delete the entry ("60"). Click the or: row (below the Criteria row) for the Driver Number field and then type 60 as the entry.**

The criteria are entered for the Amount Paid and Driver Number fields on different lines (Figure 2-34).

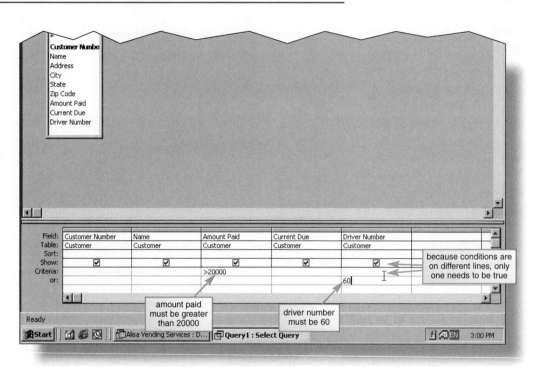

FIGURE 2-34

3 **Click the Run button on the Query Design toolbar to run the query.**

The results display (Figure 2-35). Only those customers whose amount paid is greater than $20,000 or whose driver number is 60 are included.

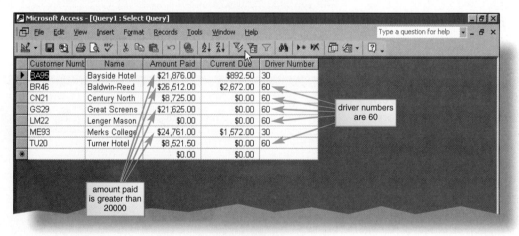

FIGURE 2-35

Sorting Data in a Query

In some queries, the order in which the records are displayed really does not matter. All you need be concerned about are the records that appear in the results. It does not matter which one is first or which one is last.

In other queries, however, the order can be very important. You may want to see the cities in which customers are located and would like them arranged alphabetically. Perhaps you want to see the customers listed by driver number. Further, within all the customers of any given driver, you would like them to be listed by amount paid.

To order the records in the answer to a query in a particular way, you **sort** the records. The field or fields on which the records are sorted is called the **sort key**. If you are sorting on more than one field (such as sorting by amount paid within driver number), the more important field (Driver Number) is called the **major key** (also called the **primary sort key**) and the less important field (Amount Paid) is called the **minor key** (also called the **secondary sort key**).

To sort in Microsoft Access, specify the sort order in the Sort row of the design grid below the field that is the sort key. If you specify more than one sort key, the sort key on the left will be the major sort key and the one on the right will be the minor sort key.

The following steps sort the cities in the Customer table.

More About

Sorting Data in a Query

When sorting data in a query, the records in the underlying tables (the tables on which the query is based) are not actually rearranged. Instead, the DBMS will determine the most efficient method of simply displaying the records in the requested order. The records in the underlying tables remain in their original order.

Steps: To Sort Data in a Query

1 **Click the View button on the Query Datasheet toolbar to return to the Query1 : Select Query window. On the Edit menu, click Clear Grid.**

2 **Include the City field in the design grid. Click the Sort row below the City field, and then click the Sort row arrow that displays.**

The City field is included (Figure 2-36). A list of available sort orders displays.

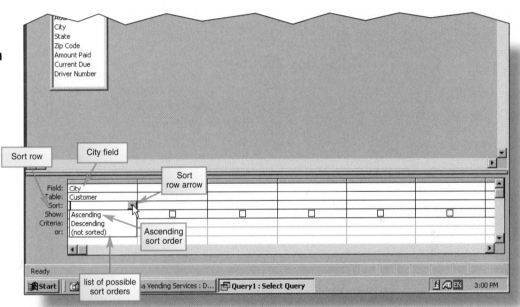

FIGURE 2-36

3 **Click Ascending.**

Ascending is selected as the order (Figure 2-37).

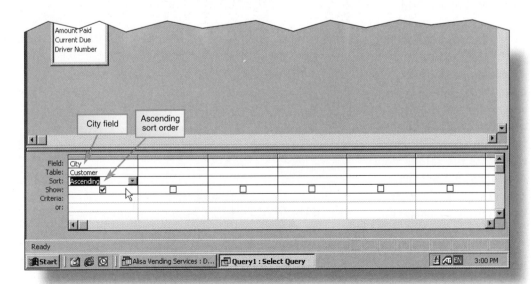

FIGURE 2-37

4 **Click the Run button on the Query Design toolbar to run the query.**

The results contain the cities from the Customer table (Figure 2-38). The cities display in alphabetical order. Duplicates, also called identical rows, are included.

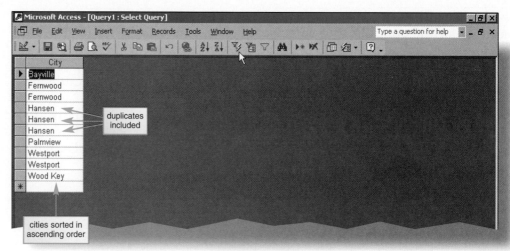

duplicates included

cities sorted in ascending order

FIGURE 2-38

Omitting Duplicates

When you sort data, duplicates normally are included. In Figure 2-38, for example, Fernwood appeared twice, Hansen appeared three times, and Westport appeared twice. If you do not want duplicates included, use the Properties command and specify Unique Values Only. Perform the following steps to produce a sorted list of the cities in the Customer table in which each city is listed only once.

Steps **To Omit Duplicates**

1 **Click the View button on the Query Datasheet toolbar to return to the Query1 : Select Query window. On the Edit menu, click Clear Grid.**

2 **Include the City field, click Ascending as the sort order, and right-click the second field in the design grid (the empty field following City). (You must right-click the second field or you will not get the correct results.) Point to the Properties command.**

The shortcut menu displays (Figure 2-39).

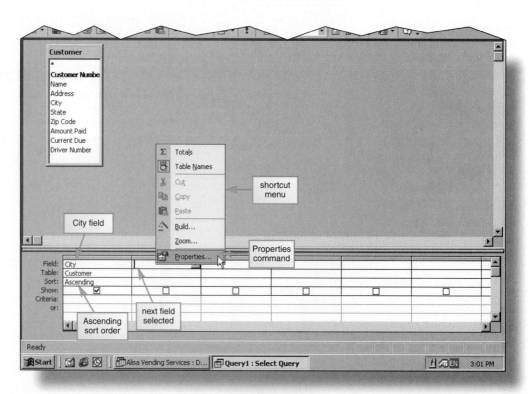

shortcut menu

City field

Properties command

Ascending sort order

next field selected

FIGURE 2-39

3 Click Properties on the shortcut menu and then point to the Unique Values property box.

The Query Properties sheet displays (Figure 2-40). (If your sheet looks different, you right-clicked the wrong place. Close the sheet that displays and right-click the second field in the grid.)

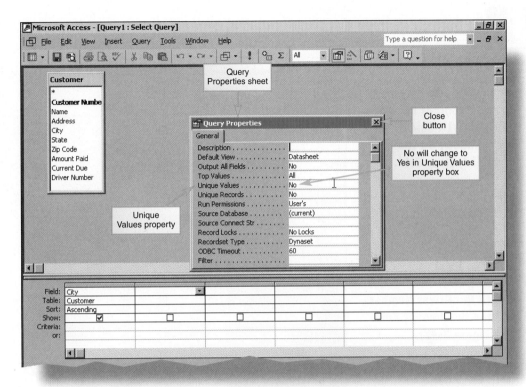

FIGURE 2-40

4 Click the Unique Values property box, and then click the arrow that displays to produce a list of available choices for Unique Values. Click Yes and then close the Query Properties sheet by clicking its Close button. Click the Run button on the Query Design toolbar to run the query.

The results display (Figure 2-41). The cities are sorted alphabetically. Each city is included only once.

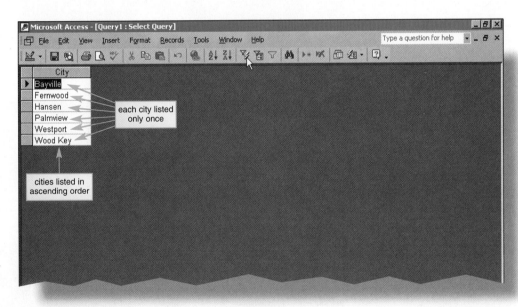

FIGURE 2-41

Sorting on Multiple Keys

The next example lists the number, name, driver number, and amount paid for all customers. The data is to be sorted by amount paid within driver number, which means that the Driver Number field is the major key and the Amount Paid field is the minor key.

The steps on the next page accomplish this sorting by specifying the Driver Number and Amount Paid fields as sort keys.

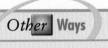

Other Ways

1. Click Properties button on toolbar
2. On View menu click Properties
3. In Voice Command mode, say "Properties"

Steps To Sort on Multiple Keys

1 Click the View button on the Query Datasheet toolbar to return to the Query1 : Select Query window. On the Edit menu, click Clear Grid.

2 Include the Customer Number, Name, Driver Number, and Amount Paid fields in the query in this order. Select Ascending as the sort order for both the Driver Number field and the Amount Paid field (Figure 2-42).

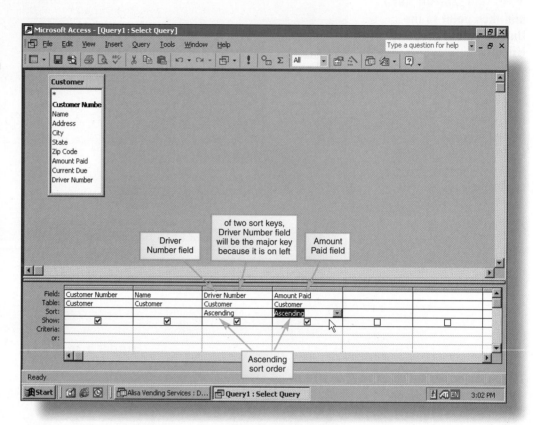

FIGURE 2-42

3 Click the Run button on the Query Design toolbar to run the query.

The results display (Figure 2-43). The customers are sorted by driver number. Within the collection of customers having the same driver, the customers are sorted by amount paid.

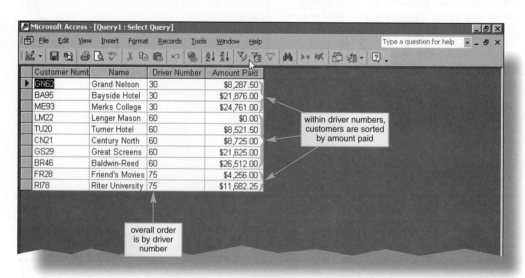

FIGURE 2-43

It is important to remember that the major sort key must appear to the left of the minor sort key in the design grid. If you attempted to sort by amount paid within driver number, but placed the Amount Paid field to the left of the Driver Number field, your results would be incorrect.

Joining Tables

Alisa Vending Services needs to list the number and name of each customer along with the number and name of the customer's driver. The customer's name is in the Customer table, whereas the driver's name is in the Driver table. Thus, this query cannot be satisfied using a single table. You need to **join** the tables; that is, to find records in the two tables that have identical values in matching fields (Figure 2-44). In this example, you need to find records in the Customer table and the Driver table that have the same value in the Driver Number fields.

Give me the number and name of each customer along with the number and name of the customer's driver.

Customer table

CUSTOMER NUMBER	NAME	. . .	DRIVER NUMBER
BA95	Bayside Hotel	...	30
BR46	Baldwin-Reed	...	60
CN21	Century North	...	60
FR28	Friend's Movies	...	75
GN62	Grand Nelson	...	30
GS29	Great Screens	...	60
LM22	Lenger Mason	...	60
ME93	Merks College	...	30
RI78	Riter University	...	75
TU20	Turner Hotel	...	60

Driver table

DRIVER NUMBER	LAST NAME	FIRST NAME	. . .
30	Tuttle	Larissa	...
60	Powers	Frank	...
75	Ortiz	Jose	...

CUSTOMER NUMBER	NAME	. . .	DRIVER NUMBER	LAST NAME	FIRST NAME	. . .
BA95	Bayside Hotel	...	30	Tuttle	Larissa	...
BR46	Baldwin-Reed	...	60	Powers	Frank	...
CN21	Century North	...	60	Powers	Frank	...
FR28	Friend's Movies	...	75	Ortiz	Jose	...
GN62	Grand Nelson	...	30	Tuttle	Larissa	...
GS29	Great Screens	...	60	Powers	Frank	...
LM22	Lenger Mason	...	60	Powers	Frank	...
ME93	Merks College	...	30	Tuttle	Larissa	...
RI78	Riter University	...	75	Ortiz	Jose	...
TU20	Turner Hotel	...	60	Powers	Frank	...

FIGURE 2-44

To join tables in Access, first you bring field lists for both tables to the upper pane of the Select Query window. Access will draw a line, called a **join line**, between matching fields in the two tables indicating that the tables are related. You then can select fields from either table. Access will join the tables automatically.

The first step is to add an additional table, the Driver table, to the query. A join line will display connecting the Driver Number fields in the two field lists. This join line indicates how the tables are related; that is, linked through these matching fields. (If you fail to give the matching fields the same name, Access will not insert the line. You can insert it manually, however, by clicking one of the two matching fields and dragging the mouse pointer to the other matching field.)

The following steps add the Driver table and then select the appropriate fields.

To Join Tables

1 **Click the View button on the Query Datasheet toolbar to return to the Query1 : Select Query window. On the Edit menu, click Clear Grid.**

2 **Right-click any open area in the upper pane of the Query1 : Select Query window and then point to Show Table on the shortcut menu.**

The shortcut menu displays (Figure 2-45).

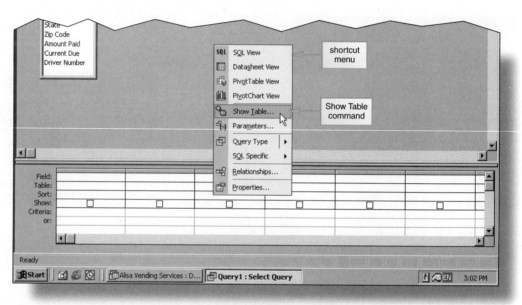

FIGURE 2-45

3 **Click Show Table on the shortcut menu and then point to Driver.**

The Show Table dialog box displays (Figure 2-46).

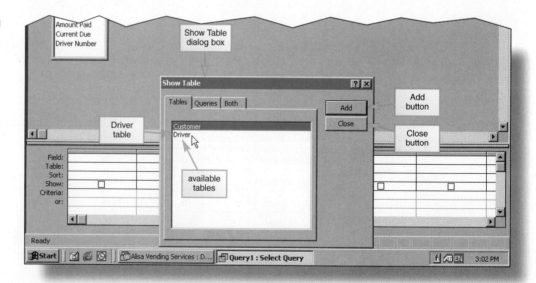

FIGURE 2-46

4 Click Driver to select the Driver table and then click the Add button. Close the Show Table dialog box by clicking the Close button. Expand the size of the field list so all the fields in the Driver table display.

The field lists for both tables display (Figure 2-47). A join line connects the two field lists.

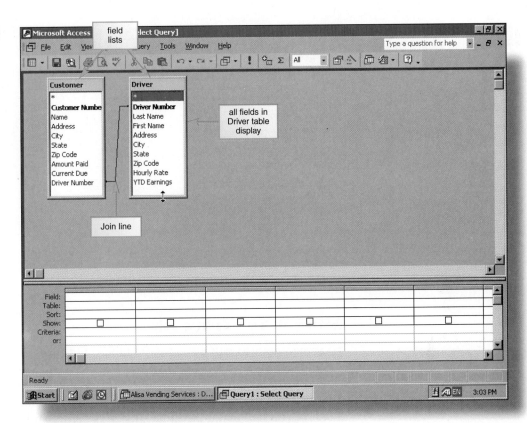

FIGURE 2-47

5 Include the Customer Number, Name, and Driver Number fields from the Customer table and the Last Name and First Name fields from the Driver table.

The fields from both tables are selected (Figure 2-48).

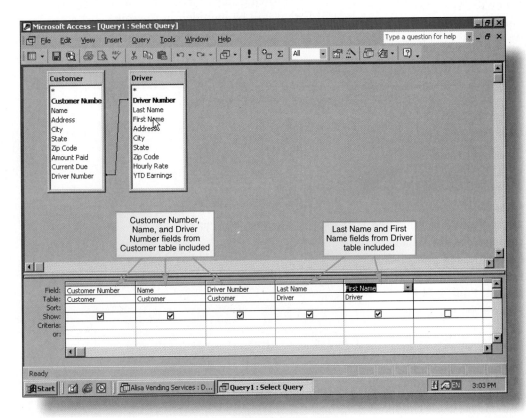

FIGURE 2-48

6 Click the Run button on the Query Design toolbar to run the query.

The results display (Figure 2-49). They contain data from both the Customer and the Driver tables.

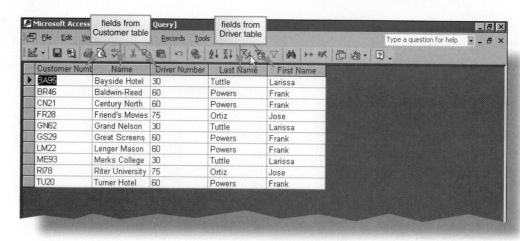

FIGURE 2-49

Restricting Records in a Join

Sometimes you will want to join tables, but you will not want to include all possible records. In such cases, you will relate the tables and include fields just as you did before. You also will include criteria. For example, to include the same fields as in the previous query, but only those customers whose amount paid is greater than $20,000, you will make the same entries as before and then also type >20000 as a criterion for the Amount Paid field.

The following steps modify the query from the previous example to restrict the records that will be included in the join.

Steps **To Restrict the Records in a Join**

1 Click the View button on the Query Datasheet toolbar to return to the Query1 : Select Query window. Add the Amount Paid field to the query. Type >20000 as the criterion for the Amount Paid field and then click the Show check box for the Amount Paid field to remove the check mark.

The Amount Paid field displays in the design grid (Figure 2-50). A criterion is entered for the Amount Paid field and the Show check box is empty, indicating that the field will not display in the results of the query.

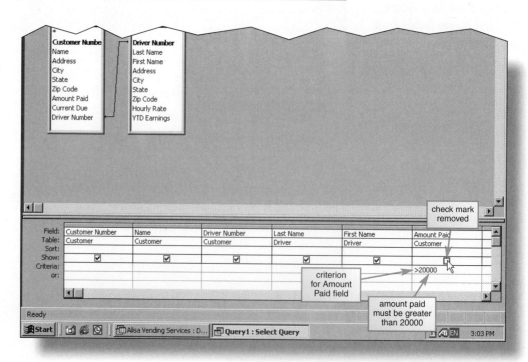

FIGURE 2-50

2 Click the Run button on the Query Design toolbar to run the query.

The results display (Figure 2-51). Only those customers with an amount paid greater than $20,000 display in the result. The Amount Paid field does not display.

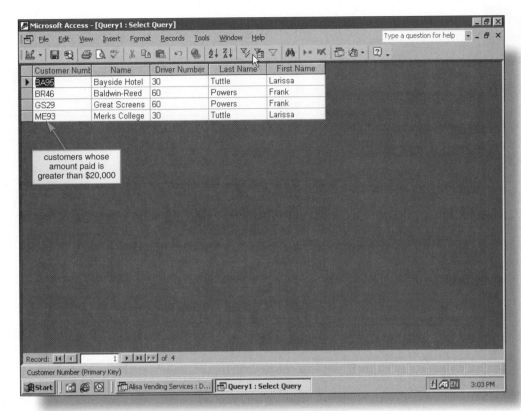

customers whose amount paid is greater than $20,000

FIGURE 2-51

Using Calculated Fields in a Query

It is important to Alisa Vending Services to know the total amount for each customer; that is, the amount paid plus the current due amount. This poses a problem because the Customer table does not include a field for total amount. You can calculate it, however, because the total amount is equal to the amount paid plus the current due amount. Such a field is called a **calculated field**.

To include calculated fields in queries, you enter a name for the calculated field, a colon, and then the expression in one of the columns in the Field row. Any fields included in the expression must be enclosed in square brackets ([ ]). For the total amount, for example, you will type `Total Amount:[Amount Paid]+[Current Due]` as the expression.

You can type the expression directly into the Field row. You will not be able to see the entire entry, however, because the Field row is not large enough. The preferred way is to select the column in the Field row, right-click to display the shortcut menu, and then click Zoom. The Zoom dialog box displays where you can type the expression.

You are not restricted to addition in calculations. You can use subtraction (-), multiplication (*), or division (/). You also can include parentheses in your calculations to indicate which calculations should be done first.

Perform the steps on the next page to remove the Driver table from the query (it is not needed), and then use a calculated field to display the number, name, and total amount of all customers.

More About

Calculated Fields

Because it is easy to compute values in a query, there is no need to store calculated fields, also called computed fields, in a database.

More About

Formatting Results in a Calculated Field

When you create a calculated field, you may want the results to display in a specific format, for example, currency. To format the results of a calculated field, right-click the calculated field in the design grid. When the property sheet for the field displays, click the Format property box, click the property box arrow, and then select the appropriate format.

Steps **To Use a Calculated Field in a Query**

1 Click the View button on the Query Datasheet toolbar to return to the Query1 : Select Query window. Right-click any field in the Driver table field list. Point to Remove Table on the shortcut menu.

The shortcut menu displays (Figure 2-52).

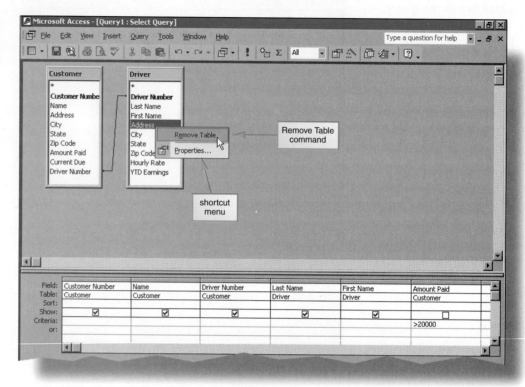

FIGURE 2-52

2 Click Remove Table to remove the Driver table from the Query1 : Select Query window. On the Edit menu, click Clear Grid.

3 Include the Customer Number and Name fields. Right-click the Field row in the first open column in the design grid and then point to Zoom on the shortcut menu.

The shortcut menu displays (Figure 2-53).

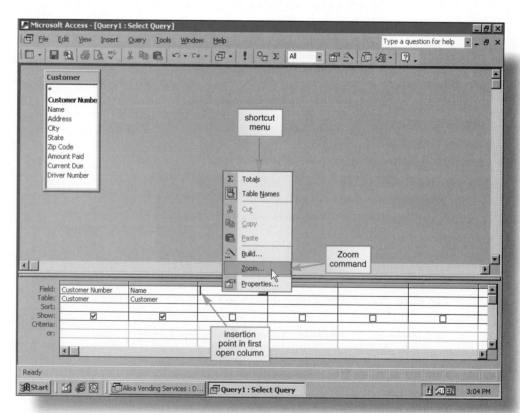

FIGURE 2-53

4 Click Zoom on the shortcut menu. Type `Total Amount:[Amount Paid]+[Current Due]` in the Zoom dialog box that displays. Point to the OK button.

The Zoom dialog box displays (Figure 2-54). The expression you typed displays within the dialog box.

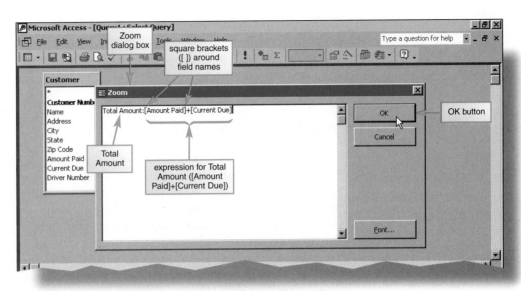

FIGURE 2-54

5 Click the OK button.

The Zoom dialog box no longer displays (Figure 2-55). A portion of the expression you entered displays in the third field in the design grid.

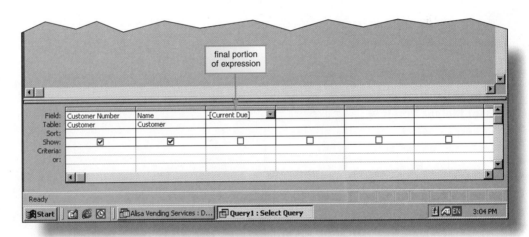

FIGURE 2-55

6 Click the Run button on the Query Design toolbar to run the query.

The results display (Figure 2-56). Microsoft Access has calculated and displayed the total amounts.

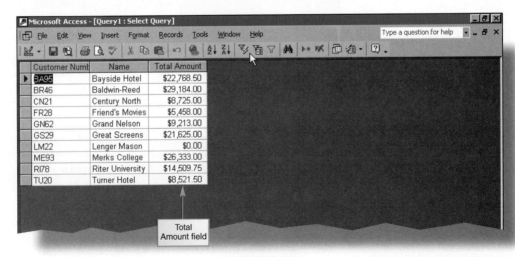

FIGURE 2-56

Other Ways

1. Press SHIFT+F2

Calculating Statistics

Virtually all database management systems support the basic set of statistical calculations: sum, average, count, maximum, and minimum as part of their query feature. Some systems, including Access, add several more, such as standard deviation, variance, first, and last.

Instead of clicking Zoom on the shortcut menu, you can click Build. The Build dialog box then will display. This dialog box provides assistance in creating the expression. If you know the expression you will need, however, it usually is easier to enter it using Zoom.

Calculating Statistics

Microsoft Access supports the built-in statistics: COUNT, SUM, AVG (average), MAX (largest value), MIN (smallest value), STDEV (standard deviation), VAR (variance), FIRST, and LAST. These statistics are called aggregate functions. An **aggregate function** is a function that performs some mathematical function against a group of records. To use any of these aggregate functions in a query, you include it in the Total row in the design grid. The Total row routinely does not appear in the grid. To include it, right-click the grid, and then click Totals on the shortcut menu.

The following example illustrates how you use these functions by calculating the average amount paid for all customers.

 To Calculate Statistics

1 **Click the View button on the Query Datasheet toolbar to return to the Query1 : Select Query window. On the Edit menu, click Clear Grid. Right-click the grid and point to Totals on the shortcut menu.**

The shortcut menu displays (Figure 2-57).

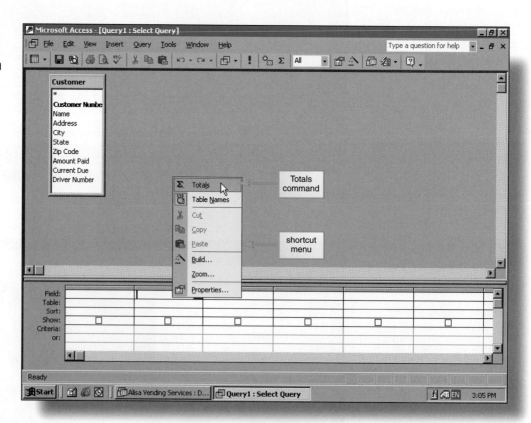

FIGURE 2-57

2 **Click Totals on the shortcut menu and then include the Amount Paid field. Point to the Total row in the Amount Paid column.**

The Total row now is included in the design grid (Figure 2-58). The Amount Paid field is included, and the entry in the Total row is Group By. The mouse pointer, which has changed shape to an I-beam, is positioned on the Total row under the Amount Paid field.

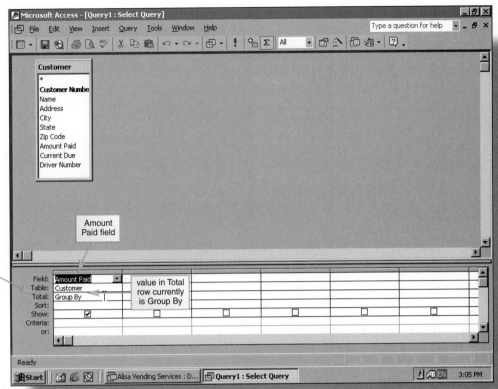

FIGURE 2-58

3 **Click the Total row in the Amount Paid column, and then click the row arrow that displays. Point to Avg in the list that displays.**

The list of available selections displays (Figure 2-59).

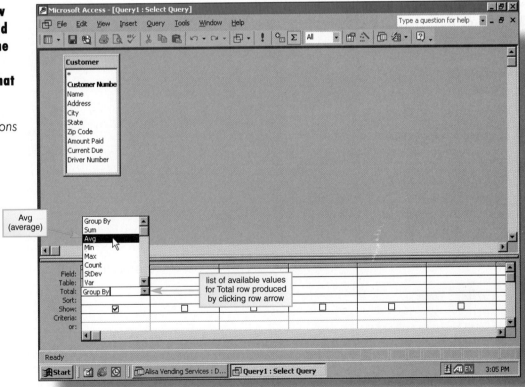

FIGURE 2-59

4 Click Avg.

Avg is selected (Figure 2-60).

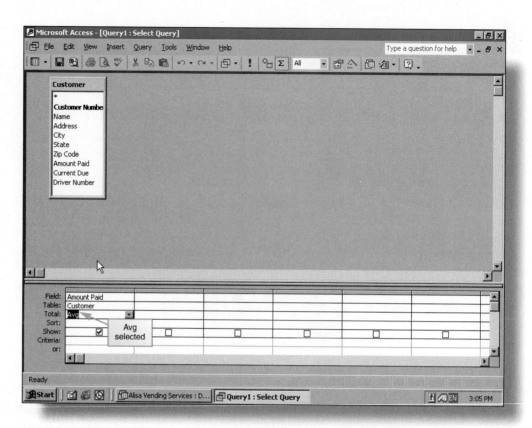

FIGURE 2-60

5 Click the Run button on the Query Design toolbar to run the query.

The result displays (Figure 2-61), showing the average amount paid for all customers.

FIGURE 2-61

Using Criteria in Calculating Statistics

Sometimes calculating statistics for all the records in the table is appropriate. In other cases, however, you will need to calculate the statistics for only those records that satisfy certain criteria. To enter a criterion in a field, first you select Where as the entry in the Total row for the field and then enter the criterion in the Criteria row. The following steps use this technique to calculate the average amount paid for customers of driver 60.

Steps: To Use Criteria in Calculating Statistics

1 Click the View button on the Query Datasheet toolbar to return to the Query1 : Select Query window.

2 Include the Driver Number field in the design grid. Produce the list of available options for the Total row entry just as you did when you selected Avg for the Amount Paid field. Use the vertical scroll bar to move through the options until the word, **Where**, displays. Point to the word, Where, in the list that displays.

The list of available selections displays (Figure 2-62). The Group By entry in the Driver Number field may not be highlighted on your screen depending on where you clicked in the Total row.

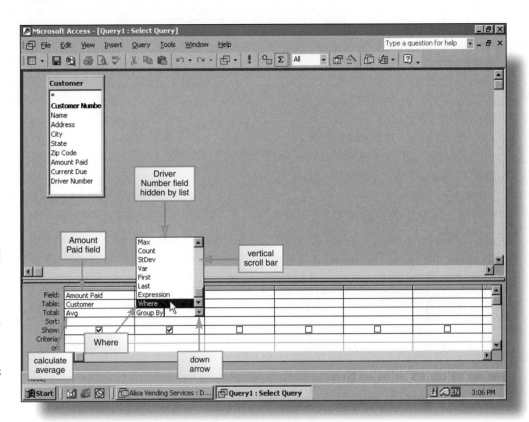

FIGURE 2-62

3 Click Where. Type 60 **as the criterion for the Driver Number field.**

Where is selected as the entry in the Total row for the Driver Number field (Figure 2-63) and 60 is entered as the Criterion.

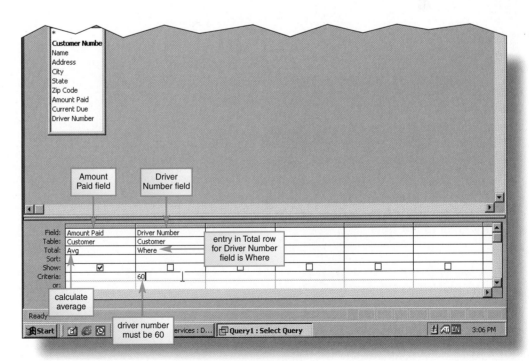

FIGURE 2-63

4 **Click the Run button to run the query.**

The result displays (Figure 2-64), giving the average amount paid for customers of driver 60.

average of amounts paid for customers of driver 60

FIGURE 2-64

More About

Quick Reference

For a table that lists how to complete tasks covered in this book using the mouse, menu, shortcut menu, and keyboard, see the Quick Reference Summary at the back of this book or visit the Shelly Cashman Series Office XP Web page (scsite.com/offxp/qr.htm) and then click Microsoft Access 2002.

Grouping

Another way statistics often are used is in combination with grouping; that is, statistics are calculated for groups of records. You may, for example, need to calculate the average amount paid for the customers of each driver. You will want the average for the customers of driver 30, the average for customers of driver 60, and so on.

Grouping means creating groups of records that share some common characteristic. In grouping by the Driver Number field, for example, the customers of driver 30 would form one group, the customers of driver 60 would be a second, and the customers of driver 75 form a third. The calculations then are made for each group. To indicate grouping in Access, select Group By as the entry in the Total row for the field to be used for grouping.

Perform the following steps to calculate the average amount paid for customers of each driver.

Steps **To Use Grouping**

1 **Click the View button on the Query Datasheet toolbar to return to the Query1 : Select Query window. On the Edit menu, click Clear Grid.**

2 **Include the Driver Number field.** **Include the Amount Paid field, and then click Avg as the calculation in the Total row.**

The Driver Number and Amount Paid fields are included (Figure 2-65). Group By currently is the entry in the Total row for the Driver Number field, which is correct; thus, it was not changed.

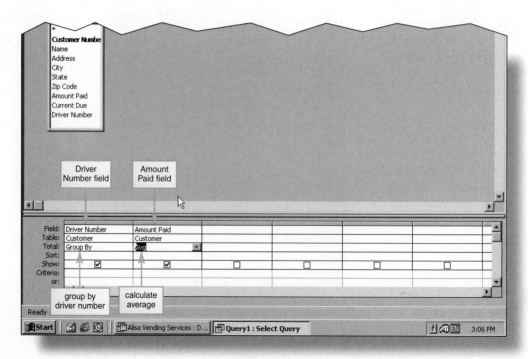

Driver Number field

Amount Paid field

group by driver number

calculate average

FIGURE 2-65

3 **Click the Run button to run the query.**

The result displays (Figure 2-66), showing each driver's number along with the average amount paid for the customers of that driver.

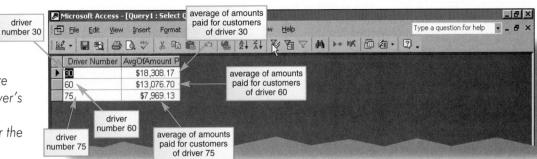

FIGURE 2-66

Saving a Query

In many cases, you will construct a query you will want to use again. By saving the query, you will eliminate the need to repeat all your entries. The following steps illustrate the process by saving the query you just have created and assigning it the name Average Amount Paid by Driver.

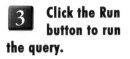 **To Save a Query**

1 **Click the View button on the Query Datasheet toolbar to return to the Query1 : Select Query window. Click the Close Window button to close the window containing the query. Click the Yes button in the Microsoft Access dialog box when asked if you want to save the changes to the design of the query. Type** Average Amount Paid by Driver **and then point to the OK button.**

The Save As dialog box displays with the query name you typed (Figure 2-67).

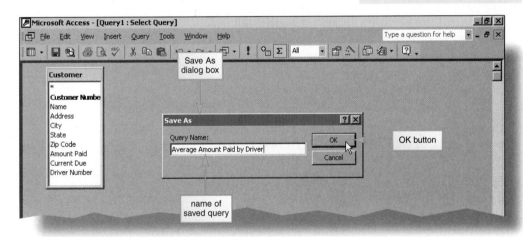

FIGURE 2-67

2 **Click the OK button to save the query.**

Access saves the query and closes the Query1 : Select Query window.

Once you have saved a query, you can use it at any time in the future by opening it. To open a saved query, click the Queries object in the Database window, right-click the query, and then click Open on the shortcut menu. You then could print the

More *About*

Microsoft Certification

The Microsoft Office User Specialist (MOUS) Certification program provides an opportunity for you to obtain a valuable industry credential — proof that you have the Access 2002 skills required by employers. For more information, see Appendix E or visit the Shelly Cashman Series MOUS Web page at scsite.com/offxp/cert.htm.

results by clicking the Print button. If you wish to change the design of the query, you would click Design View on the shortcut menu instead of Open. If you wanted to print it without first opening it, you would click Print on the shortcut menu.

The query is run against the current database. Thus, if changes have been made to the data since the last time you ran it, the results of the query may be different.

Closing a Database

The following step closes the database by closing its Database window.

TO CLOSE A DATABASE

1 Click the Close Window button for the Alisa Vending Services : Database window.

CASE PERSPECTIVE SUMMARY

In Project 2, you assisted the management of Alisa Vending Services by creating and running queries to obtain answers to important questions. You used various types of criteria in these queries. You joined tables in some of the queries. Some Alisa Vending Services queries used calculated fields and statistics. Finally, you saved one of the queries for future use.

Project Summary

In Project 2, you created and ran a variety of queries. You saw how to select fields in a query. You used text data and wildcards in criteria. You also used comparison operators in criteria involving numeric data. You combined criteria with both AND and OR. You saw how to sort the results of a query, how to join tables, and how to restrict the records in a join. You created computed fields and calculated statistics. You learned how to use grouping as well as how to save a query for future use.

What You Should Know

Having completed this project, you now should be able to perform the following tasks:

▶ Calculate Statistics *(A 2.36)*
▶ Clear a Query *(A 2.15)*
▶ Close a Database *(A 2.42)*
▶ Close the Query *(A 2.13)*
▶ Create a Query *(A 2.06)*
▶ Include All Fields in a Query *(A 2.14)*
▶ Include Fields in the Design Grid *(A 2.10)*
▶ Join Tables *(A 2.30)*
▶ Omit Duplicates *(A 2.26)*
▶ Open a Database *(A 2.06)*
▶ Print the Results of a Query *(A 2.11*
▶ Restrict the Records in a Join *(A 2.32)*
▶ Return to the Select Query Window *(A 2.12)*
▶ Run the Query *(A 2.11)*

▶ Save a Query *(A 2.41)*
▶ Sort Data in a Query *(A 2.25)*
▶ Sort on Multiple Keys *(A 2.28)*
▶ Use a Calculated Field in a Query *(A 2.34)*
▶ Use a Comparison Operator in a Criterion *(A 2.21)*
▶ Use a Compound Criterion Involving AND *(A 2.23)*
▶ Use a Compound Criterion Involving OR *(A 2.24)*
▶ Use a Number in a Criterion *(A 2.20)*
▶ Use a Wildcard *(A 2.18)*
▶ Use Criteria for a Field Not Included in the Results *(A 2.19)*
▶ Use Criteria in Calculating Statistics *(A 2.39)*
▶ Use Grouping *(A 2.40)*
▶ Use Text Data in a Criterion *(A 2.16)*

Learn It Online

Instructions: To complete the Learn It Online exercises, start your browser, click the Address bar, and then enter scsite.com/offxp/exs.htm. When the Office XP Learn It Online page displays, follow the instructions in the exercises below

1 Project Reinforcement TF, MC, and SA

Below Access Project 2, click the Project Reinforcement link. Print the quiz by clicking Print on the File menu. Answer each question. Write your first and last name at the top of each page, and then hand in the printout to your instructor.

2 Flash Cards

Below Access Project 2, click the Flash Cards link. When Flash Cards displays, read the instructions. Type 20 (or a number specified by your instructor) in the Number of Playing Cards text box, type your name in the Name text box, and then click the Flip Card button. When the flash card displays, read the question and then click the Answer box arrow to select an answer. Flip through Flash Cards. Click Print on the File menu to print the last flash card if your score is 15 (75%) correct or greater and then hand it in to your instructor. If your score is less than 15 (75%) correct, then redo this exercise by clicking the Replay button.

3 Practice Test

Below Access Project 2, click the Practice Test link. Answer each question, enter your first and last name at the bottom of the page, and then click the Grade Test button. When the graded practice test displays on your screen, click Print on the File menu to print a hard copy. Continue to take practice tests until you score 80% or better. Hand in a printout of the final practice test to your instructor.

4 Who Wants to Be a Computer Genius?

Below Access Project 2, click the Computer Genius link. Read the instructions, enter your first and last name at the bottom of the page, and then click the Play button. Hand in your score to your instructor.

5 Wheel of Terms

Below Access Project 2, click the Wheel of Terms link. Read the instructions, and then enter your first and last name and your school name. Click the Play button. Hand in your score to your instructor.

6 Crossword Puzzle Challenge

Below Access Project 2, click the Crossword Puzzle Challenge link. Read the instructions, and then enter your first and last name. Click the Play button. Work the crossword puzzle. When you are finished, click the Submit button. When the crossword puzzle redisplays, click the Print button. Hand in the printout.

7 Tips and Tricks

Below Access Project 2, click the Tips and Tricks link. Click a topic that pertains to Project 2. Right-click the information and then click Print on the shortcut menu. Construct a brief example of what the information relates to in Access to confirm you understand how to use the tip or trick. Hand in the example and printed information.

8 Newsgroups

Below Access Project 2, click the Newsgroups link. Click a topic that pertains to Project 2. Print three comments. Hand in the comments to your instructor.

9 Expanding Your Horizons

Below Access Project 2, click the Articles for Microsoft Access link. Click a topic that pertains to Project 2. Print the information. Construct a brief example of what the information relates to in Access to confirm you understand the contents of the article. Hand in the example and printed information to your instructor.

10 Search Sleuth

Below Access Project 2, click the Search Sleuth link. To search for a term that pertains to this project, select a term below the Project 2 title and then use the Google search engine at google.com (or any major search engine) to display and print two Web pages that present information on the term. Hand in the printouts to your instructor.

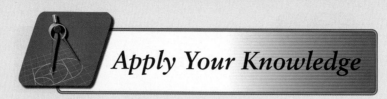

Apply Your Knowledge

1 Querying the Beyond Clean Database

Instructions: Start Access. Open the database Beyond Clean that you used in Project 1 or see your instructor for information on accessing the files required for this book. Perform the following tasks.

1. Create a new query for the Client table.
2. Add the Client Number, Name, and Address fields to the design grid.
3. Restrict retrieval to only those records where the customer has an address on Mallery.
4. Run the query and print the results. *Query 1*
5. Return to Design view and clear the grid.
6. Add the Client Number, Name, Address, Telephone Number, and Balance fields to the design grid.
7. Restrict retrieval to only those records where the balance is greater than $125.
8. Run the query and print the results. *QUERY 2*
9. Return to Design view and clear the grid.
10. Add the Client Number, Name, Address, and Custodian Id to the design grid.
11. Restrict retrieval to only those records where the Custodian Id is either 011 or 013.
12. Run the query and print the results. *QUERY 3*
13. Return to Design view and clear the grid.
14. Display and print the cities in ascending order. Each city should display only once.
15. Run the query and print the results. *QUERY 4*
16. Return to Design view and clear the grid.
17. Join the Client and Custodian tables. Add the Client Number, Name, and Custodian Id fields from the Client table and the First Name and Last Name fields from the Custodian table.
18. Sort the records in ascending order by Custodian Id.
19. Run the query and print the results. *QUERY 5*

In the Lab

1 Querying the Wooden Crafts Database

Problem: Jan Merchant has determined a number of questions she wants the database management system to answer. You must obtain the answers to the questions posed by Jan.

Instructions: Use the database created in the In the Lab 1 of Project 1 for this assignment or see your instructor for information on accessing the files required for this book. Perform the following tasks.

1. Open the Wooden Crafts database.
2. Use the Simple Query Wizard to create a new query to display and print the Product Id, Description, On Hand, and Selling Price for records in the table as shown in Figure 2-68. (*Hint:* See More About Queries: The Simple Query Wizard on page A 2.06 to solve this problem.)

In the Lab

3. Display all fields and print all the records in the table.

4. Display and print the Product Id, Description, Cost, and Supplier Code fields for all products where the Supplier Code is AP.

5. Display and print the Product Id and Description fields for all items where the description includes the letters, rail.

6. Display and print the Product Id, Description, and Supplier Code fields for all items with a cost less than $15.

7. Display and print the Product Id and Description fields for all products that have a selling price greater than $30.

8. Display and print all fields for those items with a selling price greater than $10 and where the number on hand is at least 10.

9. Display and print all fields for those items that have a supplier code of PL or a selling price greater than $30.

10. Join the Product table and the Supplier table. Display the Product Id, Description, Cost, First Name, Last Name, and Telephone Number fields. Run the query and print the results.

11. Restrict the records retrieved in task 10 above to only those products where number on hand is less than 5. Run the query and print the results.

12. Remove the Supplier table and clear the design grid.

13. Include the Product Id and Description fields in the design grid. Calculate the on-hand value (on hand * cost) for all records in the table. Run the query and print the results.

Product Id	Description	On Hand	Selling Price
BF01	Barnyard Friend	3	$60.00
BL23	Blocks in Box	5	$32.00
CC14	Coal Car	8	$18.00
FT05	Fire Truck	7	$12.00
LB34	Lacing Bear	4	$16.00
MR06	Midget Railroad	3	$34.00
PJ12	Pets Jigsaw	10	$12.00
RB02	Railway Bridge	1	$20.00
SK10	Skyscraper	6	$30.00
UM09	USA Map	12	$18.00
		0	$0.00

FIGURE 2-68

14. Display and print the average selling price of all products.

15. Display and print the average selling price of products grouped by supplier code.

16. Join the Product and Supplier tables. Include the Supplier Code, First Name, and Last Name fields from the Supplier table. Include the Product Id, Description, Cost, and On Hand fields from the Product table. Sort the query in ascending order by the Supplier Code field. Run the query and print the results. Save the query as Suppliers and Products.

2 Querying the Restaurant Supply Database

Problem: The restaurant supply company has determined a number of questions that they want the database management system to answer. You must obtain the answers to the questions posed by the company.

(continued)

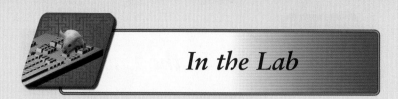

In the Lab

Querying the Restaurant Supply Database *(continued)*

Instructions: Use the database created in the In the Lab 2 of Project 1 for this assignment or see your instructor for information on accessing the files required for this book. Perform the following tasks.

1. Open the Restaurant Supply database and create a new query for the Customer table.
2. Display and print the Customer Number, Name, Balance, and Amount Paid fields for all the records in the table.
3. Display and print the Customer Number, Name, and Balance fields for all customers where the sales rep number is 51.
4. Display and print the Customer Number, Name, and Balance fields for all customers where the balance is greater than $100.
5. Display and print the Customer Number, Name, and Amount Paid fields for all customers where the sales rep number is 49 and the amount paid is greater than $1,000.
6. Display and print the Customer Number, Name, and Address fields for all customers with an address on Devon.
7. Display and print the Customer Number, Name, and Balance fields for all customers where the sales rep number is 49 or the balance is less than $50.
8. Include the Customer Number, Name, and Balance fields in the design grid. Sort the records in descending order by the Balance field. Display and print the results.
9. Display and print the Customer Number, Name, and Amount Paid fields for all customers where the sales rep number is 44 or 49 and the balance is greater than $100. (*Hint:* See More About Compound Criteria on page A 2.22 to solve this problem.)
10. Display and print the Customer Number, Name, Balance, and Amount Paid fields from the Customer table and the First Name, Last Name, and Comm Rate fields from the Sales Rep table.
11. Restrict the records retrieved in task 10 above to only those customers that have a balance of 0. Display and print the results.
12. Clear the design grid and add the First Name, Last Name, and Comm Rate fields from the Sales Rep table to the grid. Add the Name and Balance fields from the Customer table. Calculate the pending commission (balance * comm rate) for the Sales Rep table. Sort the records in ascending order by last name and format pending commission as currency. (*Hint:* See More About Formatting Results in a Calculated Field on page A 2.33 to solve this problem.) Run the query and print the results.
13. Display and print the following statistics: the total balance and total amount paid for all customers; the total balance for customers of sales rep 44; and the total amount paid for each sales rep.
14. Create a query that includes the Sales Rep Number, Last Name, First Name, Customer Number, Name, Balance, and Amount Paid fields. Sort the query in ascending order by the Sales Rep Number field. Run the query and then save the query as Sales Reps and Customers.

3 Querying the Condo Management Database

Problem: The condo management company has determined a number of questions that they want the database management system to answer. You must obtain the answers to the questions posed by the company.

1:40 - 2:10

In the Lab

Instructions: Use the database created in the In the Lab 3 of Project 1 for this assignment or see your instructor for information on accessing the files required for this book. Perform the following tasks.

1. Open the Condo Management database and create a new query for the Condo table.

2. Display and print the Unit Number, Weekly Rate, and Owner Id fields for all the records in the table as shown in Figure 2-69.

Microsoft Access - [Query1 : Select Query]

File Edit View Insert Format Records Tools Window Help   Type a question for help

Unit Number	Weekly Rate	Owner Id
101	$675.00	HJ05
108	$1,050.00	AB10
202	$1,400.00	BR18
204	$1,100.00	BR18
206	$925.00	GM50
308	$950.00	GM50
403	$700.00	HJ05
405	$750.00	AB10
500	$1,100.00	AB10
510	$825.00	BR18
*	$0.00	

FIGURE 2-69

3. Display and print the Unit Number and Weekly Rate fields for all units that rent for less than $1,000 per week.

4. Display and print the Unit Number, Sleeps, and Weekly Rate for all units that sleep more than four people and have a powder room.

5. Display and print the Unit Number, Bedrooms, and Weekly Rate fields for all units that have 2 bedrooms and a powder room or that have 3 bedrooms. (**Hint:** See More About Compound Criteria on page A 2.22 to solve this problem.)

6. Display and print the Unit Number and Weekly Rate fields for all units that are on the fifth floor. (**Hint:** The first digit of the Unit Number field indicates the floor.)

7. Display and print the Unit Number, Bedrooms, and Weekly Rate fields for all units that have more than one bedroom and more than one bathroom and provide linens.

8. Include the Unit Number, Bedrooms, Sleeps, and Weekly Rate fields in the design grid. Sort the records in descending order by bedrooms within sleeps. The Bedrooms field should display in the result to the left of the Sleeps field. (**Hint:** Use Microsoft Access Help to solve this problem.)

9. Display and print the weekly rates in descending order. Each rate should display only once.

10. Display and print the Unit Number and Weekly Rate fields from the Condo table and First Name, Last Name, and Telephone fields from the Owner table.

11. Restrict the records retrieved in task 10 above to only those units that rent for more than $1,000 per week. Display and print the results.

12. Clear the design grid and remove the Owner table from the query. Owner BR18 offers a 15 percent discount on the weekly rate if renters rent for more than one week at a time. What is the discounted weekly rental rate for her units? Display the unit number, bedrooms, bathrooms, sleeps, and discounted weekly rate in your result. Format the discounted weekly rate as currency. (**Hint:** See More About Formatting Results in a Calculated Field on page A 2.33 to solve this problem.) Run the query and print the results.

13. Display and print the average weekly rate for each owner.

14. Create a query that includes the Owner Id, First Name, Last Name, Unit Number, and Weekly Rate fields. Sort the query in ascending order by the Owner Id field. Save the query as Owners and Condo Units.

0:20

10:40

Cases and Places

The difficulty of these case studies varies:
▶ are the least difficult; ▶▶ are more difficult; and ▶▶▶ are the most difficult.

1 ▶ Use the Computer Expertise database you created in Case Study 1 of Project 1 for this assignment. You now want to use the database to find answers to questions that will help you manage your company better. Perform the following: (a) Display and print the customer number, name, and telephone number of all customers whose name begins with the letter L. (b) Display and print the customer number, name, telephone number, and balance for all customers who have a balance greater than $150. (c) Display and print the customer number, name, balance, helper first name, and helper last name for all customers. Sort the records in ascending order by helper last name. (d) Display and print the average balance of all customers. (e) Display and print the average balance of customers grouped by helper. (f) Display and print the total balance of all customers.

2 ▶ Use the Baseball database you created in Case Study 2 of Project 1 for this assignment. The marketing team has put together a list of the most common type of questions they would like to ask the database. They want to know if the database you created can answer these questions. Perform the following: (a) Display and print the description, cost, and units on hand of all items supplied by Beverage Holders. (b) Display and print the item id, description, and on-hand value (units on hand * cost) of all items. (c) Display and print the item id, description, units on hand, and current profit (selling price – cost) of all items that have a selling price greater than $15. (d) Display and print the item id, description, units on hand, supplier name, and supplier telephone number for all items where there are less than 10 items on hand. (e) Display and print the description and selling price sorted in ascending order by selling price. (f) Find the lowest priced item and the highest priced item.

3 ▶▶ Use the local attractions database you created in Case Study 3 of Project 1 for this assignment. The tourism director is pleased with the database you have created. You have asked her to put together a list of questions for which she regularly will need the answers. Perform the following: (a) List the name and telephone number of all attractions. (b) List all attractions by type of attraction. (c) List all attractions that have no cost associated with them. (d) List all attractions that do have a cost associated with them. (e) List all attractions that are open on Sunday. (f) List all attractions that are historic homes.

4 ▶▶ Use the high school Math club database you created in Case Study 4 of Project 1 for this assignment. Display and print the following: (a) A list of all high school students involved in the tutoring program. (b) A list of all elementary students being tutored. (c) A list of all high school students along with the students they are tutoring. Sort the list by high school student. (d) The elementary school student with the highest number of points. (e) The high school student with the highest number of hours tutored. (f) The total number of hours spent tutoring. (g) The total number of hours spent tutoring by high school student.

5 ▶▶▶ Use the hobby or collection database you created in Case Study 5 of Project 1 for this assignment. Develop a list of questions that you want the database to be able to answer. Query the database using the list you developed and print the results.

Microsoft Access 2002

3

Maintaining a Database Using the Design and Update Features of Access

You will have mastered the material in this project when you can:

O B J E C T I V E S

- Add records to a table
- Locate records
- Filter records
- Change the contents of records in a table
- Delete records from a table
- Restructure a table
- Change field characteristics
- Add a field
- Save the changes to the structure
- Update the contents of a single field
- Make changes to groups of records
- Delete groups of records
- Create validation rules
- Update a table with validation rules
- Specify referential integrity
- Use subdatasheets
- Order records
- Create single-field and multiple-field indexes

Database Maintenance
Promises Top Performance

The Chicago River flooded basements in Loop buildings because of a construction accident at the Kinzie Street Bridge over the North Branch. Abandoned railroad tunnels built in the 1800s fill with water from Lake Michigan that roars into office buildings, ruining computers, irreplaceable paper files, and sophisticated environmental equipment. This underground flood of Chicago, which took place early on the morning of April 13, 1992, devastated Chicago's downtown commerce district with the worst business disaster ever in that city; the kind of event for which disaster recovery planners prepare, but hope they never have to experience.

Due to a lack of maintenance, what started out as a minor crack grew into a torrent that city workers desperately tried to reinforce while city administrators sent requests for competitive bids. Regrettably, the river would not wait and continued to devastate the city as the condition worsened. If officials had acted immediately, an estimated $75,000 repair job could have saved the city the eventual

$1 billion loss.Individuals seldom are faced with problems that have such massive financial impact. Unlike the Maytag repairman, however, people must contend with maintenance issues on a regular basis: cars, homes, dental work, even personal computers. All are issues important to health, safety, and well-being. How a person handles these can make the difference between a happy life and a trying one. Likewise, for many business people, scientific researchers, and self-employed individuals, professional survival depends on maintaining their computer databases.

Information flows in today's world like the waters of all the rivers combined. From telephone lines, customer service terminals, satellite feeds, the mail, and so on, literally billions of pieces of data enter daily into the databases of entities such as insurance companies, banks, mail-order firms, astronomical observatories, medical research labs, doctors' offices, automobile dealerships, home-based businesses, and multitudes of others. Based on the content of this information, decisions are made and actions taken, often triggering a corresponding flow of information to other interested users. The process of handling this data — the lifeblood of today's information-based society — is known as database maintenance.

Microsoft Access 2002 is a powerful tool that facilitates designing the database and then maintaining it with ease. Effective design and update features in Access allow you to add, change, and delete records in a table, change the size of or add new fields to the database, and then quickly update the restructured database. In this project, you will learn the techniques to maintain any type of database with which you might work in your academic or professional life.

During college, you may use a personal database to organize and maintain information such as names, addresses, and telephone numbers of friends, family, and club members, or possessions such as a CD or tape collection, videos, or books. As a club member, you may be asked to design, update, and maintain a database of club members and information.

Your first use for a database may come when you start your search for the right graduate school or as you begin your mailing campaign for future employment opportunities. Once employed, you will be exposed to the use of databases in all facets of business. Learning the important skills associated with database maintenance will pave the way for opportunity in the workplace.

Although a mundane task at best, the effort you expend in database maintenance will assure you are prepared when restoring computer operations in the event of a disaster.

Microsoft Access 2002

Maintaining a Database Using the Design and Update Features of Access

CASE PERSPECTIVE

Alisa Vending Services has created and loaded its database. The management and staff have received many benefits from the database, including the ability to ask a variety of questions concerning the data in the database. They now face the task of keeping the database up to date. They must add new records as they take on new customers and drivers. They must make changes to existing records to reflect additional billings, payments, changes of address, and so on. Alisa Vending Services also found that it needed to change the structure of the database in two specific ways. The management decided they needed to categorize the customers by type, so they need to add a Customer Type field to the Customer table. They also discovered the Name field was too short to contain the name of one of the customers so they need to enlarge the field. In addition, they want to establish rules for the data entered in the database to ensure that users can enter only valid data. Finally, they determined they want to improve the efficiency of certain types of processing, specifically sorting and retrieving data. Your task is to help Alisa Vending Services in all these activities.

Introduction

Once a database has been created and loaded with data, it must be maintained. **Maintaining the database** means modifying the data to keep it up to date, such as adding new records, changing the data for existing records, and deleting records. **Updating** can include **mass updates** or **mass deletions**; that is, updates to, or deletions of, many records at the same time.

In addition to adding, changing, and deleting records, maintenance of a database periodically can involve the need to **restructure** the database; that is, to change the database structure. This can include adding new fields to a table, changing the characteristics of existing fields, and removing existing fields. It also can involve the creation of **indexes**, which are similar to indexes found in the back of books and are used to improve the efficiency of certain operations.

Figure 3-1 summarizes some of the various types of activities involved in maintaining a database.

Project Three — Maintaining the Alisa Vending Services Database

You are to make the changes to the data in the Alisa Vending Services database as requested by the management of Alisa Vending Services. You must restructure the database to meet the current needs of Alisa Vending Services. This includes adding an additional field as well as increasing the width of one of the existing fields. You must modify the structure of the database in a way that prevents users from entering invalid data. Finally, management is concerned that some operations, for example, those involving sorting the data, are taking longer than they would like. You are to create indexes to attempt to address this problem.

Add new records
Change records
Delete records
Change field width
Add new field
Use update and delete queries
Create validation rules
Specify default values
Specify relationships
Sort records
Create indexes to improve performance

FIGURE 3-1

Opening the Database

Before carrying out the steps in this project, first you must open the database. To do so, perform the following steps.

TO OPEN A DATABASE

1 Click the Start button, click Programs on the Start menu, and then click Microsoft Access on the Programs submenu.

2 Click Open on the Database toolbar and then click 3½ Floppy (A:) in the Look in box. If necessary, click the Alisa Vending Services database name.

3 Click the Open button.

The database opens and the Alisa Vending Services : Database window displays.

Maintaining a Database: Recovery

If a problem occurs that damages either the data in the database or the structure of the database, the database is recovered by copying the backup copy over it. To do so, use the copy features of Windows to copy the backup version (for example, Alisa Vending Backup) over the actual database (for example, Alisa Vending Services). This will return the database to the state it was in when the backup was made.

Adding, Changing, and Deleting

Keeping the data in a database up to date requires three tasks: adding new records, changing the data in existing records, and deleting existing records.

Adding Records

In Project 1, you added records to a database using Datasheet view; that is, as you were adding records, the records were displayed on the screen in the form of a datasheet, or table. When you need to add additional records, you can use the same techniques.

In Project 1, you used a form to view records. This is called **Form view**. You also can use Form view to update the data in a table. To add new records, change existing records, or delete records, you will use the same techniques you used in Datasheet view. To add a record to the Customer table with a form, for example, use the following steps. These steps use the Customer form you created in Project 1.

 To Use a Form to Add Records

1 With the Alisa Vending Services database open, point to Forms on the Objects bar (Figure 3-2).

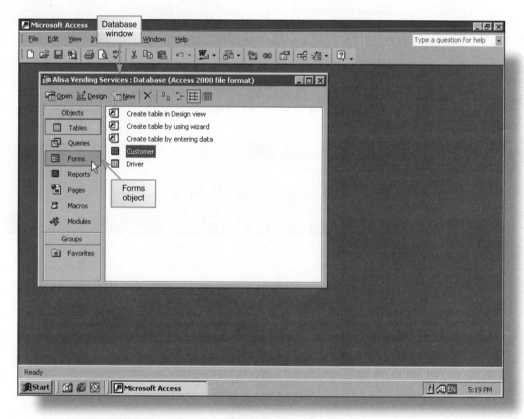

FIGURE 3-2

2 Click Forms. Right-click Customer and then point to Open on the shortcut menu.

The shortcut menu displays (Figure 3-3).

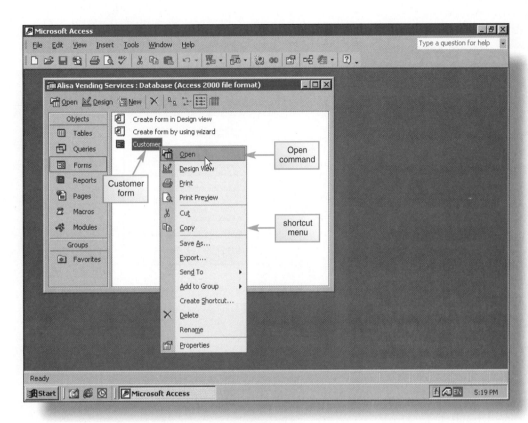

FIGURE 3-3

3 Click Open on the shortcut menu and then point to the New Record button.

The form for the Customer table displays (Figure 3-4).

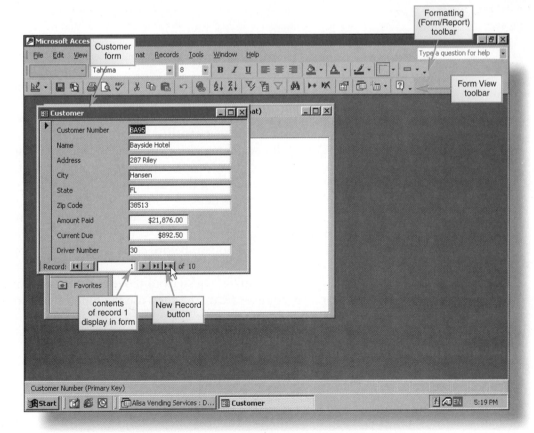

FIGURE 3-4

Microsoft **Access 2002**

 Click the New Record button and then type the data for the new record as shown in Figure 3-5. Press the TAB key after typing the data in each field, except after typing the final field (Driver Number).

The record displays.

5 **Press the TAB key.**

The record now is added to the Customer table and the contents of the form are erased.

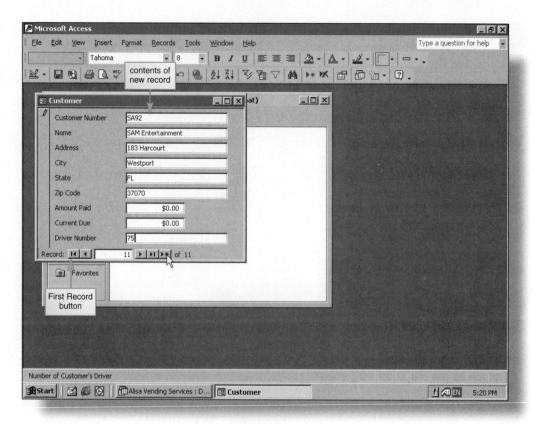

FIGURE 3-5

 *Other* **Ways**

1. Click New Record button on Form View toolbar
2. On Insert menu click New Record
3. In Voice Command mode, say "Insert, New Record"

Searching for a Record

In the database environment, **searching** means looking for records that satisfy some criteria. Looking for the customer whose number is LM22 is an example of searching. The queries in Project 2 also were examples of searching. Access had to locate those records that satisfied the criteria.

A need for searching also exists when using Form view or Datasheet view. To update customer LM22, for example, first you need to find the customer. In a small table, repeatedly pressing the Next Record button until customer LM22 is on the screen may not be particularly difficult. In a large table with many records, however, this would be extremely cumbersome. You need a way to be able to go directly to a record just by giving the value in some field. This is the function of the **Find button** on the Form View toolbar. Before clicking the Find button, select the field for the search.

Perform the following steps to move to the first record in the table, select the Customer Number field, and then use the Find button to search for the customer whose number is LM22.

Steps **To Search for a Record**

1 **Make sure the Customer table is open and the form for the Customer table is on the screen. Click the First Record button (see Figure 3-5) to display the first record. If the Customer Number field currently is not selected, select it by clicking the field name. Point to the Find button on the Form View toolbar.**

The first record displays on the form (Figure 3-6).

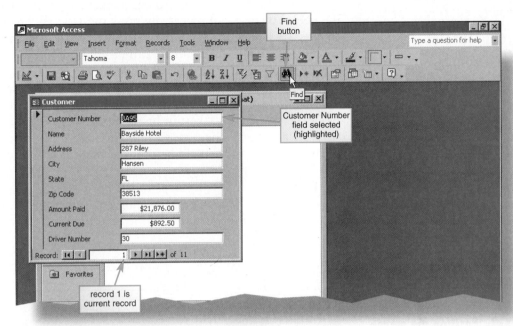

FIGURE 3-6

2 **Click the Find button. Type** LM22 **in the Find What text box in the Find and Replace dialog box and then click the Find Next button.**

Access locates the record for customer LM22. The Find and Replace dialog box displays and the Find What text box contains the entry, LM22 (Figure 3-7).

3 **Click the Close button in the Find and Replace dialog box.**

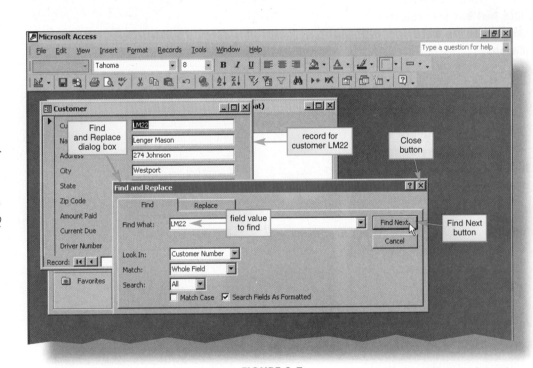

FIGURE 3-7

In some cases, after locating a record that satisfies a criterion, you might need to find the next record that satisfies the same criterion. For example, if you just found the first customer whose driver number is 30, you then may want to find the second such customer, then the third, and so on. To do so, repeat the same process. You will not need to retype the value, however.

Other Ways

1. On Edit menu click Find
2. Press CTRL+F
3. In Voice Command mode, say "Find"

More About

Changing the Contents of a Record

When you are changing the value in a field, clicking within the field will produce an insertion point. Clicking the name of the field will select the entire field. The new entry typed then will replace completely the previous entry.

Changing the Contents of a Record

After locating the record to be changed, select the field to be changed by clicking the field. You also can repeatedly press the TAB key. Then make the appropriate changes. (Clicking the field automatically produces an insertion point. If you use the TAB key, you will need to press F2 to produce an insertion point.)

Normally, Access is in **Insert mode**, so the characters typed will be inserted at the appropriate position. To change to **Overtype mode**, press the INSERT key. The letters, OVR, will display near the bottom right edge of the status bar. To return to Insert mode, press the INSERT key. In Insert mode, if the data in the field completely fills the field, no additional characters can be inserted. In this case, you would need to increase the size of the field before inserting the characters. You will see how to do this later in the project.

Perform the following steps to use Form view to change the name of customer LM22 to Lenger Mason's by inserting an apostrophe (') and the letter, s, after Mason. Sufficient room exists in the field to make this change.

Steps **To Update the Contents of a Field**

1 **Position the mouse pointer in the Name field text box for customer LM22 after the word, Mason.**

The mouse pointer shape is an I-beam (Figure 3-8).

2 **Click to produce an insertion point and then type 's to correct the name.**

The name now is Lenger Mason's.

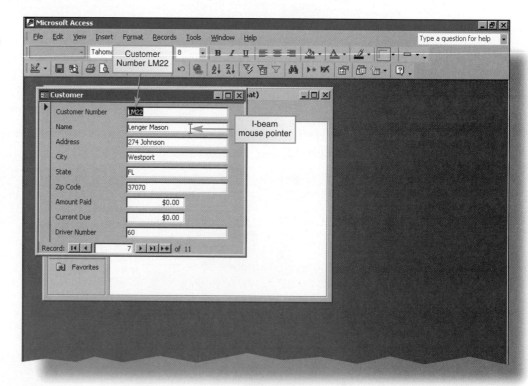

FIGURE 3-8

Switching Between Views

Sometimes, after working in Form view where you can see all fields, but only one record, it would be helpful to see several records at a time. To do so, switch to Datasheet view by clicking the View button arrow and then clicking Datasheet View. Perform the following steps to switch from Form view to Datasheet view.

Steps **To Switch from Form View to Datasheet View**

1 **Point to the View button arrow on the Form View toolbar (Figure 3-9).**

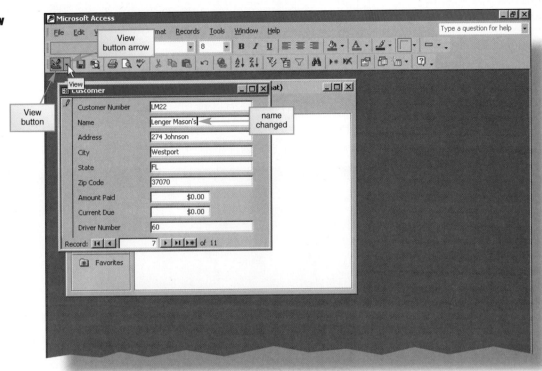

FIGURE 3-9

2 **Click the View button arrow and then point to Datasheet View.**

The View list displays (Figure 3-10).

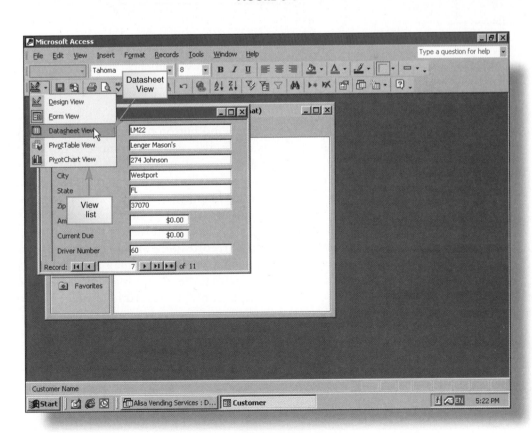

FIGURE 3-10

3 **Click Datasheet View and then maximize the window containing the datasheet.**

The datasheet displays (Figure 3-11). The position in the table is maintained. The current record selector points to customer LM22, the customer that displayed on the screen in Form view. The Name field, the field in which the insertion point is displayed, is selected. The new record for customer SA92 is currently the last record in the table. When you close the table and open it later, customer SA92 will be in its appropriate location.

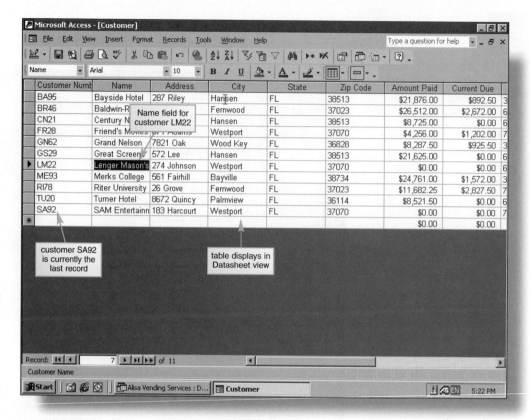

FIGURE 3-11

If you wanted to return to Form view, you would use the same process. The only difference is that you would click Form View rather than Datasheet View.

Filtering Records

You can use the Find button to locate a record quickly that satisfies some criterion (for example, the customer number is LM22). All records display, however, not just the record or records that satisfy the criterion. To have only the record or records that satisfy the criterion display, use a filter. The simplest type of filter is called **filter by selection**. To use filter by selection, give Access an example of the data you want by selecting the data within the table and then clicking the Filter By Selection button on the Datasheet View toolbar. For example, if only the record or records on which the customer name is Lenger Mason's are to be included, you would select the Name field on the record for customer LM22, because the name on that record is Lenger Mason's. The following steps use filter by selection to display only the record for Lenger Mason's.

Steps: To Filter Records

1 Make sure the name for customer LM22 (Lenger Mason's) is selected and then point to the Filter By Selection button on the Datasheet View toolbar (Figure 3-12).

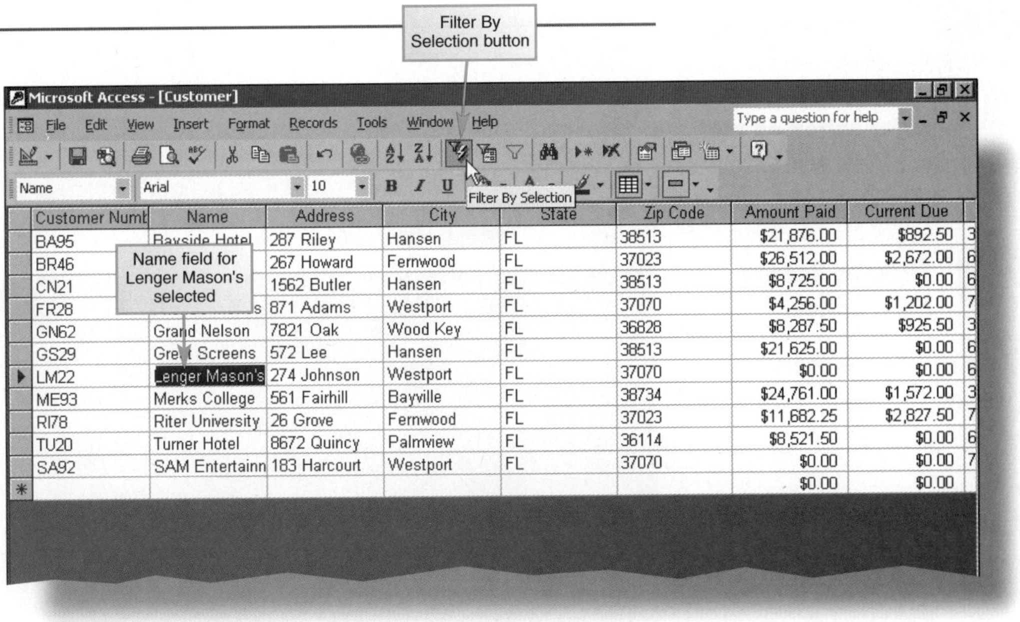

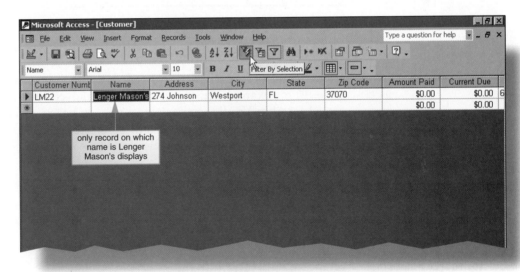

FIGURE 3-12

2 Click the Filter By Selection button.

Only the customer whose name is Lenger Mason's displays (Figure 3-13).

FIGURE 3-13

Because there is only one customer in the database with the name Lenger Mason's, only one customer displays. If you instead had selected the City field on the same record (Hansen) before clicking the Filter By Selection button, three customers would display, because there currently are three customers located in Hansen (customers BA95, CN21, and GS29).

In order to have all records once again display, remove the filter by clicking the Remove Filter button on the Datasheet View toolbar as in the steps on the next page.

More About

Filters: Filter by Form

If you want to filter records based on values in more than one field, click the Filter by Form button instead of the Filter by Selection button. You then will be able to fill in values in as many fields as you want. Once you are finished, click the Apply Filter button. Only those records containing all the values you entered will display.

Steps **To Remove a Filter**

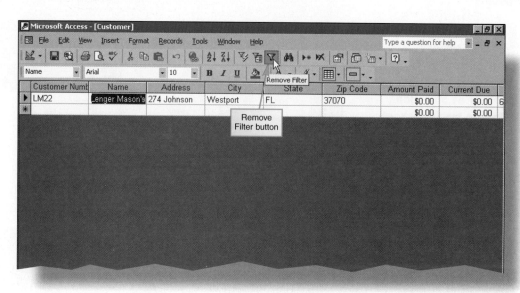

1 **Point to the Remove Filter button on the Datasheet View toolbar (Figure 3-14).**

2 **Click the Remove Filter button.**

All records once again display.

FIGURE 3-14

Other **Ways**

1. On Records menu click Filter, then click Filter By Selection
2. In Voice Command mode, say "Filter By Selection"

Deleting Records

When records are no longer needed, **delete the records** (remove them) from the table. If, for example, customer GN62 has moved its offices to a city that is not served by Alisa Vending Services and already has received its final payment, that customer's record should be deleted. To delete a record, first locate it and then press the DELETE key. Complete the following steps to delete customer GN62.

Steps **To Delete a Record**

1 **With the datasheet for the Customer table on the screen, position the mouse pointer on the record selector of the record in which the customer number is GN62 (Figure 3-15).**

Custom	Name	Address	City	State	Zip Code	Amount Paid	Current Due	
BA95	side Hotel	287 Riley	Hansen	FL	38513	$21,876.00	$892.50	3
BR46	Baldwin-Reed	267 Howard	Fernwood	FL	37023	$26,512.00	$2,672.00	6
CN21	Century North	1562 Butler	Hansen	FL	38513	$8,725.00	$0.00	6
FR28	Friend's Movies	871 Adams	Westport	FL	37070	$4,256.00	$1,202.00	7
GN62	Grand Nelson	7821 Oak	Wood Key	FL	36828	$8,287.50	$925.50	6
GS29	Great Screens	572 Lee	Hansen	FL	38513	$21,625.00	$0.00	6
LM22	Lenger Mason's	274 Johnson	Westport	FL	37070	$0.00	$0.00	6
ME93	Merks College	561 Fairhill	Bayville	FL	38734	$24,761.00	$1,572.00	3
RI78	Riter University	26 Grove	Fernwood	FL	37023	$11,682.25	$2,827.50	7
SA92	SAM Entertainn	183 Harcourt	Westport	FL	37070	$0.00	$0.00	7
TU20	Turner Hotel	8672 Quincy	Palmview	FL	36114	$8,521.50	$0.00	6
*						$0.00	$0.00	

FIGURE 3-15

2 **Click the record
selector to select the
record, press the DELETE key
to delete the record, and
then point to the Yes
button in the Microsoft
Access dialog box.**

*The Microsoft Access dialog
box displays (Figure 3-16).
The message indicates that
one record will be deleted.*

3 **Click the Yes button
to complete the
deletion. Close the window
containing the table by
clicking its Close Window
button.**

*The record is deleted and the
table no longer displays.*

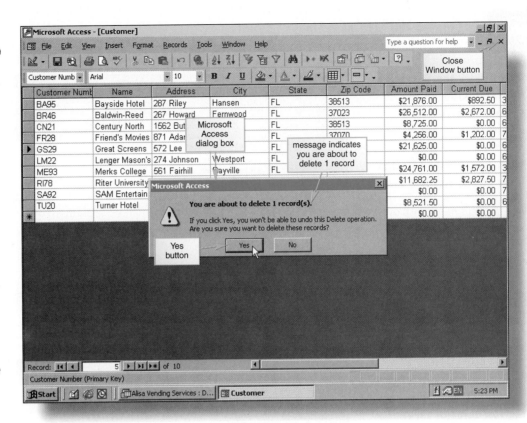

FIGURE 3-16

Changing the Structure

When you initially create a database, you define its **structure**; that is, you indicate the names, types, and sizes of all the fields. In many cases, the structure you first defined will not continue to be appropriate as you use the database. A variety of reasons exist why the structure of a table might need to change. Changes in the needs of users of the database may require additional fields to be added. In the Customer table, for example, if it is important to store a code indicating the customer type of a customer, you need to add such a field.

Characteristics of a given field may need to change. For example, the customer Century North's name is stored incorrectly in the database. It actually should be Century North Industries. The Name field is not large enough, however, to hold the correct name. To accommodate this change, you need to increase the width of the Name field.

It may be that a field currently in the table no longer is necessary. If no one ever uses a particular field, it is not needed in the table. Because it is occupying space and serving no useful purpose, it should be removed from the table. You also would need to delete the field from any forms, reports, or queries that include it.

To make any of these changes, click Design View on the shortcut menu.

Changing the Size of a Field

The steps on the next page change the size of the Name field from 20 to 25 to accommodate the change of name from Century North to Century North Industries.

> **More About**
>
> **Changing the Structure**
>
> A major advantage of using a full-featured database management system is the ease with which you can change the structure of the tables that make up the database. In a non-database environment, changes to the structure can be very cumbersome, requiring difficult and time-consuming changes to many programs.

Steps **To Change the Size of a Field**

1 **With the Database window on the screen, click Tables on the Objects bar and then right-click Customer. Point to Design View on the shortcut menu.**

The shortcut menu displays (Figure 3-17).

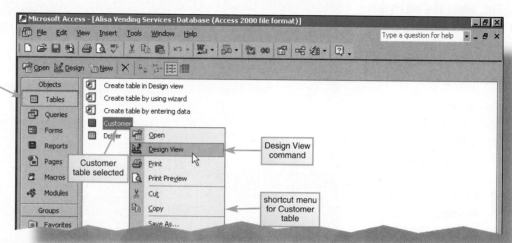

FIGURE 3-17

2 **Click Design View on the shortcut menu and then point to the row selector for the Name field.**

The Customer : Table window displays (Figure 3-18).

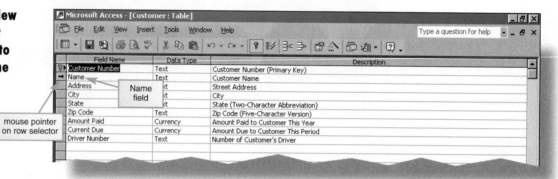

FIGURE 3-18

3 **Click the row selector for the Name field.**

The Name field is selected (Figure 3-19).

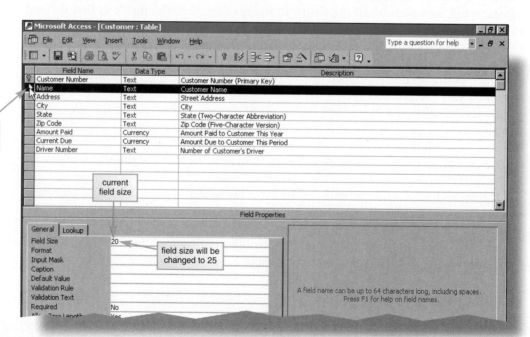

FIGURE 3-19

4 Press F6 to select the field size, type 25 as the new size, and press F6 again.

The size is changed (Figure 3-20).

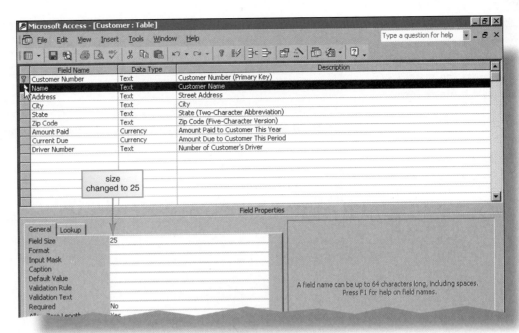

FIGURE 3-20

Adding a New Field

The management of Alisa Vending Services decided they needed to categorize the customers. To do so, they want to add an additional field, Customer Type. The possible values for Customer Type are EDU (which indicates the customer is an educational institution), MAN (which indicates the customer is a manufacturing organization), or SER (which indicates the customer is a service organization).

To be able to store the customer type, the following steps add a new field, called Customer Type, to the table. The possible entries in this field are EDU, MAN, and SER. The new field will follow the Zip Code field in the list of fields; that is, it will be the seventh field in the restructured table. The current seventh field (Amount Paid) will become the eighth field, Current Due will become the ninth field, and so on. Complete the following steps to add the field.

Adding a New Field

Tables frequently need to be expanded to include additional fields for a variety of reasons. Users' needs can change. The field may have been omitted by mistake when the table first was created. Government regulations may change in such a way that the organization needs to maintain additional information.

 To Add a Field to a Table

1 Point to the row selector for the Amount Paid field (Figure 3-21).

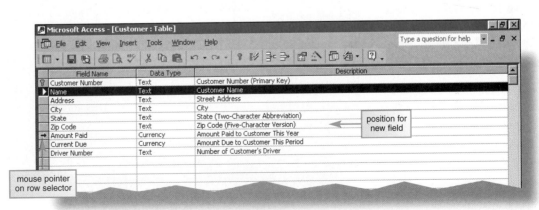

FIGURE 3-21

Microsoft **Access 2002**

2 Click the row selector for the Amount Paid field and then press the INSERT key to insert a blank row.

A blank row displays in the position for the new field (Figure 3-22).

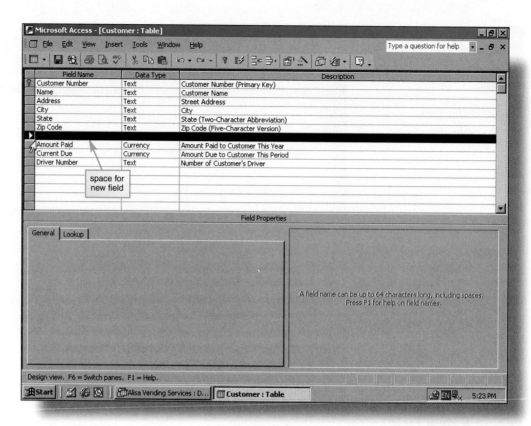

FIGURE 3-22

3 Click the Field Name column for the new field. Type Customer Type as the field name and then press the TAB key. Select the Text data type by pressing the TAB key. Type Customer Type (EDU - Education, MAN - Manufacturing, or SER - Service) as the description. Press F6 to move to the Field Size text box, type 3 (the size of the Customer Type field), and press F6 again.

The entries for the new field are complete (Figure 3-23).

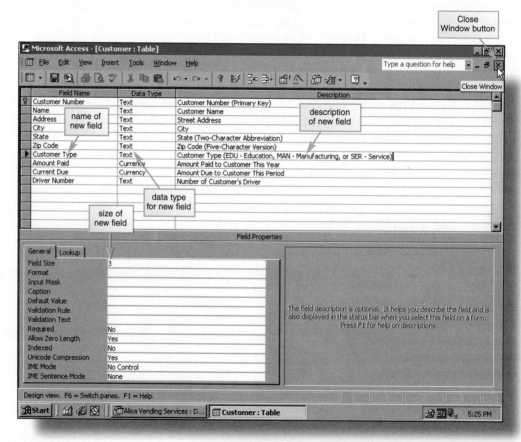

FIGURE 3-23

4 **Close the Customer : Table window by clicking its Close Window button. Point to the Yes button in the Microsoft Access dialog box.**

The Microsoft Access dialog box displays (Figure 3-24).

5 **Click the Yes button to save the changes.**

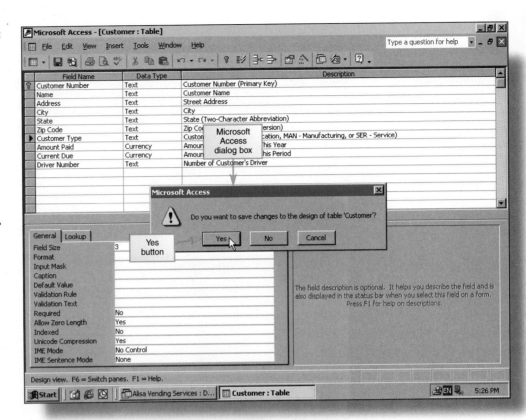

FIGURE 3-24

Deleting a Field

It is possible to find that a field in one of your tables is no longer needed. It may no longer serve a useful purpose or it may have been included by mistake. In such a case, you should delete the field. To do so, you first would open the table in Design view and then click the row selector for the field to select it. You then would press the DELETE key to delete the field. Access would request confirmation that you do indeed wish to delete the field. If you click the Yes button and then save your changes, the field will be removed from the table.

Updating the Restructured Database

Changes to the structure are available immediately. The Name field is longer, although it does not appear that way on the screen, and the new Customer Type field is included.

To make a change to a single field, such as changing the name from Century North to Century North Industries, click the field to be changed, and then make the necessary correction. If the record to be changed is not on the screen, use the Navigation buttons (Next Record, Previous Record) to move to it. If the field to be corrected simply is not visible on the screen, use the horizontal scroll bar along the bottom of the screen to shift all the fields until the correct one displays. Then make the change.

Perform the steps on the next page to change the name of Century North to Century North Industries.

More About

The Access Help System

Need Help? It is no further than the Ask a Question box in the upper-right corner of the window. Click the box that contains the text, Type a question for help (Figure 3-24), type help, and then press the ENTER key. Access will respond with a list of items you can click to learn about obtaining help on any Access-related topic. To find out what is new in Access 2002, type what's new in Access in the Ask a Question box.

Steps To Update the Contents of a Field

1 Right-click Customer. Click Open on the shortcut menu. Position the I-beam mouse pointer to the right of the letter h in Century North (customer CN21).

The datasheet displays (Figure 3-25).

2 Click immediately to the right of the letter h in Century North, press the SPACEBAR, and then type Industries to change the name.

The name is changed from Century North to Century North Industries.

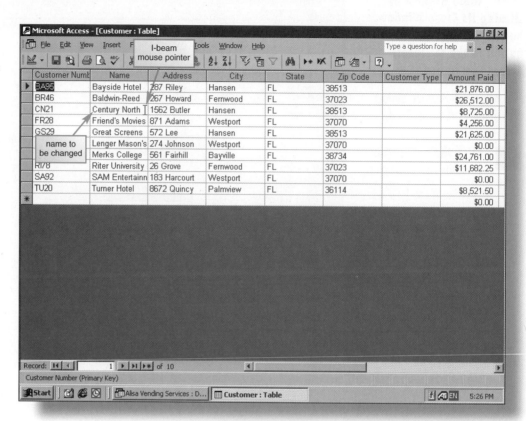

FIGURE 3-25

Resizing Columns

After you have changed the size of a field, the forms you have created will not reflect your changes. If you used the AutoForm command, you can change the field sizes by simply recreating the form. To do so, right-click the form, click Delete, and then create the form as you did in Project 1.

Resizing Columns

The default column sizes provided by Access do not always allow all the data in the field to display. You can correct this problem by **resizing the column** (changing its size) in the datasheet. In some instances, you actually may want to reduce the size of a column. The City field, for example, is short enough that it does not require all the space on the screen that is allotted to it.

Both types of changes are made the same way. Position the mouse pointer on the right boundary of the column's **field selector** (the line in the column heading immediately to the right of the name of the column to be resized). The mouse pointer will change to a two-headed arrow with a vertical bar. You then can drag the line to resize the column. In addition, you can double-click in the line, in which case Access will determine the best size for the column.

The following steps illustrate the process for resizing the Name column to the size that best fits the data.

Steps | **To Resize a Column**

1 Point to the right boundary of the field selector for the Name field (Figure 3-26).

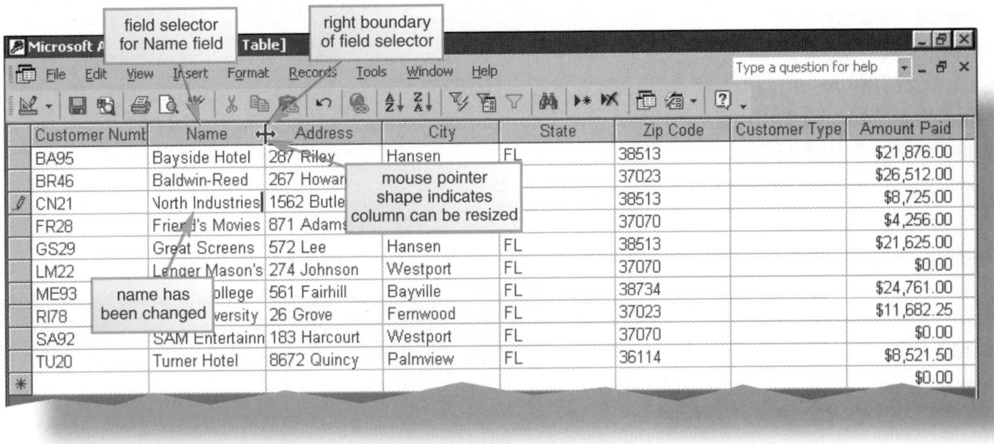

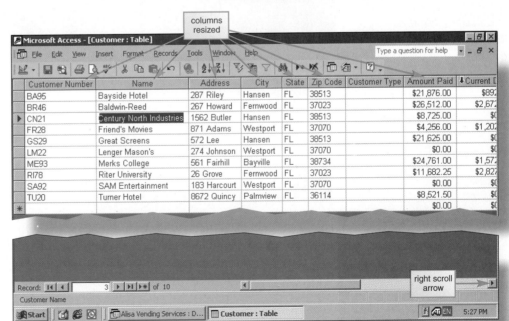

field selector for Name field

right boundary of field selector

mouse pointer shape indicates column can be resized

name has been changed

FIGURE 3-26

2 Double-click the right boundary of the field selector for the Name field.

The Name column has been resized (Figure 3-27).

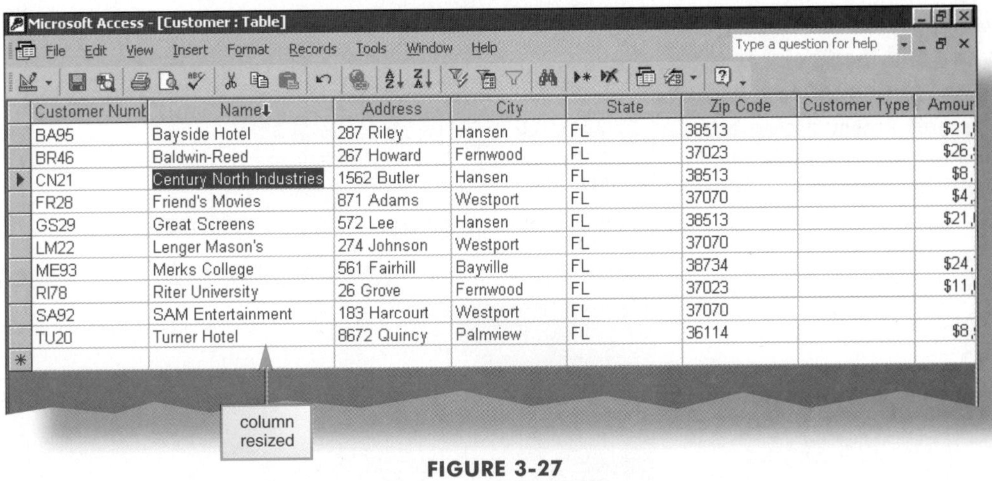

column resized

FIGURE 3-27

3 Use the same technique to resize the Customer Number, Address, City, State, Zip Code, and Amount Paid columns to best fit the data.

The columns have been resized (Figure 3-28).

columns resized

right scroll arrow

FIGURE 3-28

4 If necessary, click the right scroll arrow to display the Current Due and Driver Number columns, and then resize the columns to best fit the data. Point to the Close Window button for the Customer : Table window.

All the columns have been resized (Figure 3-29).

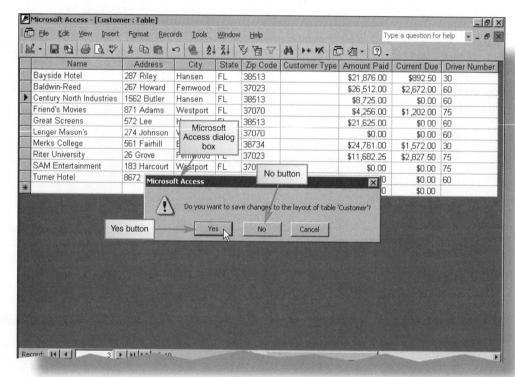

FIGURE 3-29

5 Close the Customer : Table window by clicking its Close Window button and then point to the Yes button in the Microsoft Access dialog box.

The Microsoft Access dialog box displays (Figure 3-30). Changing a column width changes the layout or design of a table.

6 Click the Yes button.

The change to the layout is saved. The next time the datasheet displays, the columns will have the new widths.

FIGURE 3-30

Other Ways

1. On Format menu click Column Width
2. In Voice Command mode, say "Format, Column Width"

Using an Update Query

The Customer Type field is blank on every record. One approach to entering the information for the field would be to step through the entire table, assigning each record its appropriate value. If most of the customers have the same type, a simpler approach is available.

At Alisa Vending Services, for example, most customers are type SER. Initially, you can set all the values to SER. To accomplish this quickly and easily, you use a special type of query called an **update query**. Later, you can change the type for educational institutions and manufacturing organizations.

The process for creating an update query begins the same as the process for creating the select queries in Project 2. After selecting the table for the query, right-click any open area of the upper pane, click Query Type on the shortcut menu, and then click Update Query on the menu of available query types. An extra row, Update To:, displays in the design grid. Use this additional row to indicate the way the data will be updated. If a criterion is entered, then only those records that satisfy the criterion will be updated.

Perform the following steps to change the value in the Customer Type field to SER for all the records. Because all records are to be updated, no criteria will be entered.

More About

Action Queries

An action query is a query that makes changes to many records in just one operation. There are four types of action queries: delete, update, append, and make-table. In this project you learn how to use update, delete, and append queries.

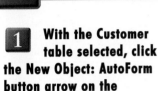 **To Use an Update Query to Update All Records**

1 **With the Customer table selected, click the New Object: AutoForm button arrow on the Database toolbar, and then point to Query on the list that displays.**

The New Object: AutoForm list displays (Figure 3-31).

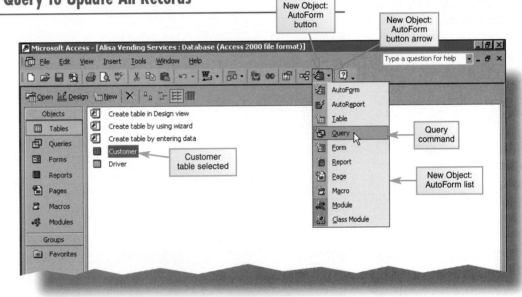

FIGURE 3-31

2 **Click Query and then point to the OK button in the New Query dialog box.**

The New Query dialog box displays (Figure 3-32). Design View is selected.

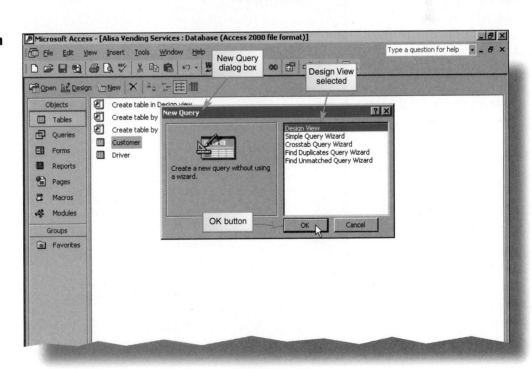

FIGURE 3-32

3 Click the OK button, and then be sure the Query1 : Select Query window is maximized. Resize the upper and lower panes of the window as well as the Customer table field list so all fields in the field list display (see page A 2.08 Project 2). Right-click the upper pane and point to Query Type on the shortcut menu. When the Query Type submenu displays, point to Update Query.

The shortcut menu displays (Figure 3-33). The Query Type submenu displays, showing available query types.

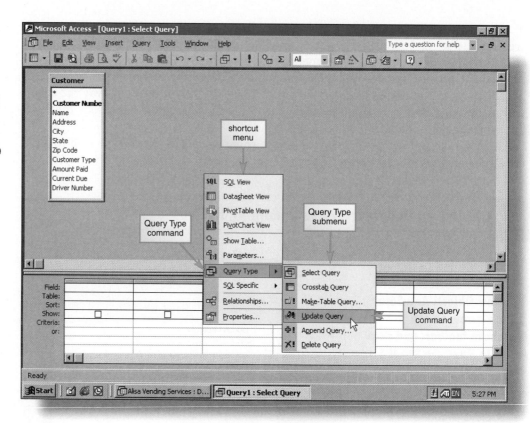

FIGURE 3-33

4 Click Update Query on the submenu, double-click the Customer Type field to select the field, click the Update To text box in the first column of the design grid, type SER as the new value, and then point to the Run button on the Query Design toolbar.

The Customer Type field is selected (Figure 3-34). In an Update Query, the Update To row displays in the design grid. The value to which the field is to be changed is entered as SER. Because no criteria are entered, the Customer Type value on every row will be changed to SER.

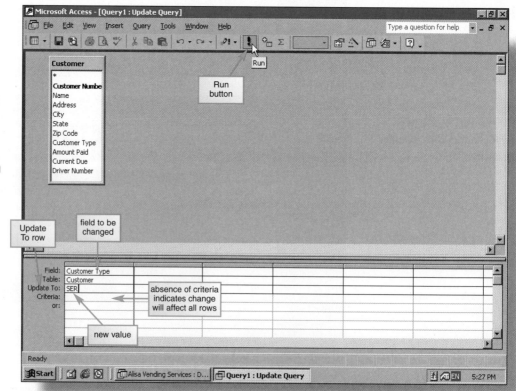

FIGURE 3-34

5 **Click the Run button and then point to the Yes button in the Microsoft Access dialog box.**

The Microsoft Access dialog box displays (Figure 3-35). The message indicates that 10 rows will be updated by the query.

6 **Click the Yes button.**

The changes are made.

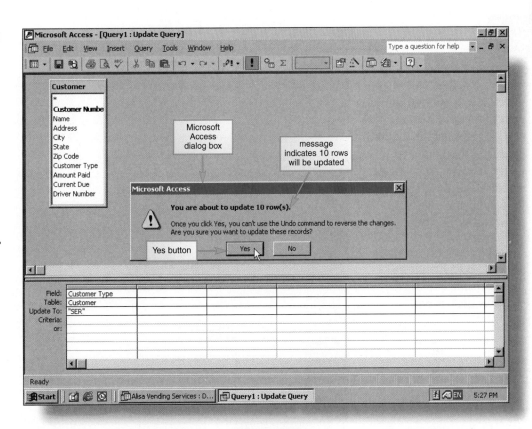

FIGURE 3-35

Using a Delete Query

In some cases, you may need to delete several records at a time. If, for example, all customers in a particular zip code are to be serviced by another firm, the customers with this zip code can be deleted from the Alisa Vending Services database. Instead of deleting these customers individually, which could be very cumbersome, you can delete them in one operation by using a **delete query**, which is a query that will delete all the records satisfying the criterion entered in the query.

Perform the steps on the next page to use a delete query to delete any customer whose zip code is 36114. (There happens to be only one such customer currently in the database.)

Other Ways

1. Click Query Type button arrow on Query Design toolbar, click Update Query
2. On Query menu click Update Query
3. In Voice Command mode, say "Query, Update Query"

More About

Action Queries: Append Queries

An append query adds a group of records from one table to the end of another table. For example, suppose that Alisa Vending Services acquires some new customers and a database containing a table on those customers. To avoid entering all this information manually, you can append it to the Customer table in the Alisa Vending Services database.

Steps To Use a Delete Query to Delete a Group of Records

1 **Click Edit on the menu bar and then click Clear Grid to clear the grid. Right-click the upper pane and then point to Query Type on the shortcut menu. When the Query Type submenu displays, point to Delete Query.**

The shortcut menu displays (Figure 3-36). The Query Type submenu displays the available query types.

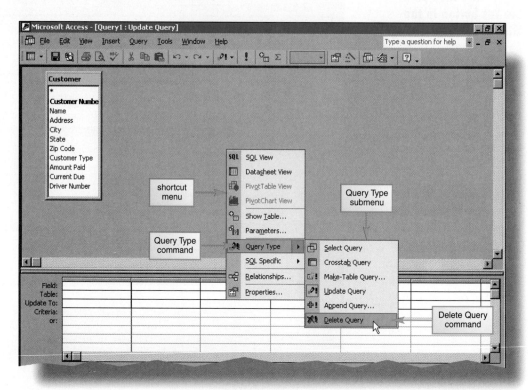

FIGURE 3-36

2 **Click Delete Query on the submenu, double-click the Zip Code field to select the field, and then click the Criteria row. Type** 36114 **as the criterion and then point to the Run button on the Query Design toolbar.**

The criterion is entered in the Zip Code column (Figure 3-37). In a delete query, the Delete row displays in the design grid.

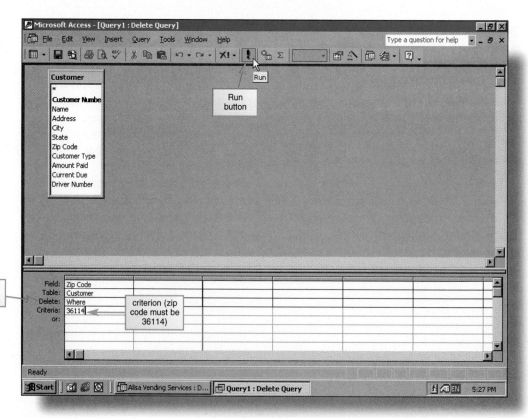

FIGURE 3-37

3 Click the Run button to run the query. Point to the Yes button in the Microsoft Access dialog box.

The Microsoft Access dialog box displays (Figure 3-38). The message indicates the query will delete 1 row (record).

4 Click the Yes button. Close the Query window. Do not save the query.

The customer with zip code 36114 has been removed from the table.

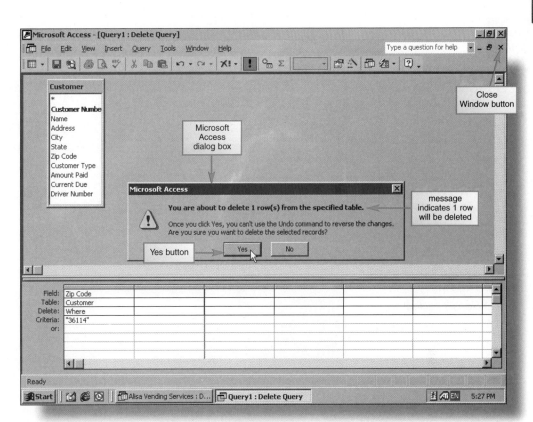

FIGURE 3-38

Other Ways

1. Click Query Type button arrow on Query Design toolbar, click Delete Query
2. On Query menu click Delete Query
3. In Voice Command mode, say "Query, Delete Query"

Creating Validation Rules

You now have created, loaded, queried, and updated a database. Nothing you have done so far, however, ensures that users enter only valid data. To do so, you create **validation rules**; that is, rules that the data entered by a user must follow. As you will see, Access will prevent users from entering data that does not follow the rules. The steps also specify **validation text**, which is the message that will be displayed if a user violates the validation rule.

Validation rules can indicate a **required field**, a field in which the user actually must enter data. For example, by making the Name field a required field, a user actually must enter a name (that is, the field cannot be blank). Validation rules can make sure a user's entry lies within a certain **range of values**; for example, that the values in the Amount Paid field are between $0.00 and $90,000.00. They can specify a **default value**; that is, a value that Access will display on the screen in a particular field before the user begins adding a record. To make data entry of customer numbers more convenient, you also can have lowercase letters displayed automatically as uppercase letters. Finally, validation rules can specify a collection of acceptable values; for example, that the only legitimate entries for the Customer Type field are EDU, MAN, and SER.

Specifying a Required Field

To specify that a field is to be required, change the value in the Required property box from No to Yes. The steps on the next page specify that the Name field is to be a required field.

More About

Creating Append Queries

To create an append query, create a select query for the table containing the records to append. In the design grid, indicate which fields to include. Then, right-click the upper pane, click Query Type, and then click Append Query on the Query Type submenu. When the Append Query dialog box displays, specify the name of the table to receive the new records, and its location.

To Specify a Required Field

1 **With the Database window on the screen and the Tables object selected, right-click Customer. Click Design View on the shortcut menu, and then select the Name field by clicking its row selector. Point to the Required property box.**

The Customer : Table window displays (Figure 3-39). The Name field is selected.

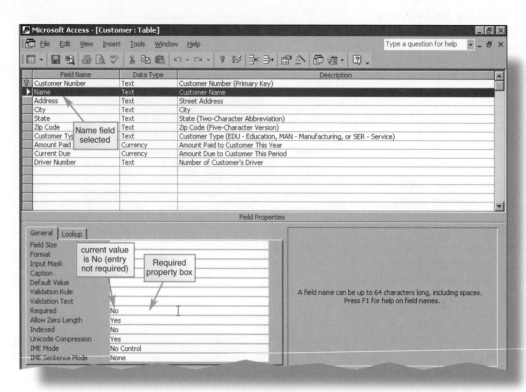

FIGURE 3-39

2 **Click the Required property box in the Field Properties pane, and then click the property box arrow that displays. Click Yes in the list.**

The value in the Required property box changes to Yes (Figure 3-40). It now is required that the user enter data into the Name field when adding a record.

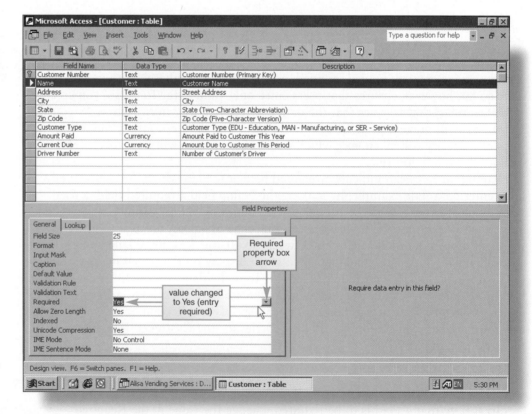

FIGURE 3-40

Specifying a Range

The following step specifies that entries in the Amount Paid field must be between $0.00 and $90,000.00. To indicate this range, you will enter a condition that specifies that the amount paid amount must be both >= 0 (greater than or equal to zero) and <= 90000 (less than or equal to 90000).

Steps | To Specify a Range

1 **Select the Amount Paid field by clicking its row selector. Click the Validation Rule property box to produce an insertion point, and then type** >=0 and <=90000 **as the rule. Click the Validation Text property box to produce an insertion point, and then type** Must be between $0.00 and $90,000.00 **as the text. In the Validation Text property box, you should type all the text, including the dollar signs and comma.**

The validation rule and text are entered (Figure 3-41). In the Validation Rule property box, Access automatically changed the lowercase letter, a, to uppercase in the word, and.

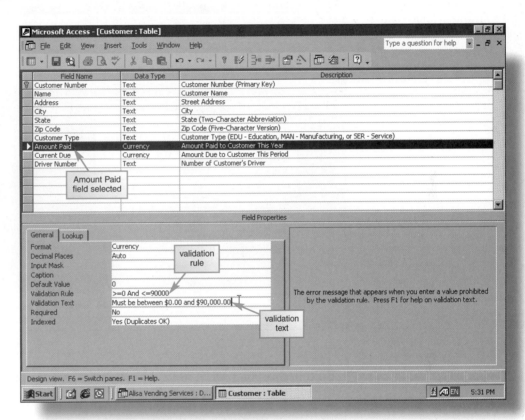

FIGURE 3-41

Users now will be prohibited from entering an amount paid amount that either is less than $0.00 or greater than $90,000.00 when they add records or change the value in the Amount Paid field.

Specifying a Default Value

To specify a default value, enter the value in the Default Value property box. The step on the next page specifies SER as the default value for the Customer Type field. This simply means that if users do not enter a customer type, the type will be SER.

Steps **To Specify a Default Value**

1 **Select the Customer Type field. Click the Default Value property box and then type** =SER **as the value.**

The Customer Type field is selected. The default value is entered in the Default Value property box (Figure 3-42).

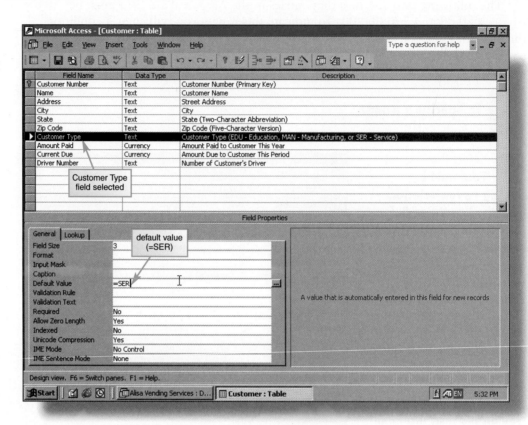

FIGURE 3-42

From this point on, if users do not make an entry in the Customer Type field when adding records, Access will set the value equal to SER.

Specifying a Collection of Legal Values

The only **legal values** for the Customer Type field are EDU, MAN, and SER. An appropriate validation rule for this field can direct Access to reject any entry other than these three possibilities. Perform the following step to specify the legal values for the Customer Type field.

Steps To Specify a Collection of Legal Values

1 Make sure the Customer Type field is selected. Click the Validation Rule property box and then type =EDU or =MAN or =SER as the validation rule. Click the Validation Text property box and then type Must be EDU, MAN, or SER as the validation text.

The Customer Type field is selected. The validation rule and text have been entered (Figure 3-43). In the Validation Rule property box, Access automatically inserted quotation marks around the EDU, MAN, and SER values and changed the lowercase letter, o, to uppercase in the word, or.

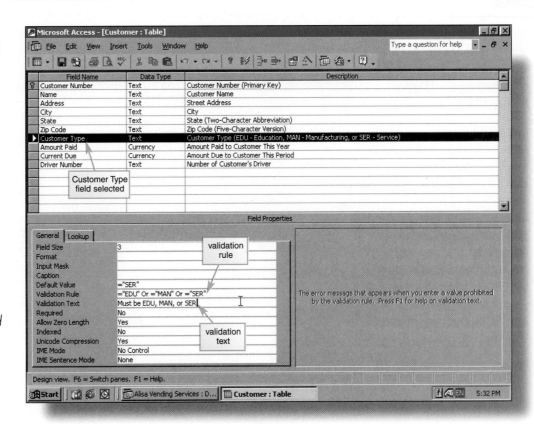

FIGURE 3-43

Users now will be allowed to enter only EDU, MAN, or SER in the Customer Type field when they add records or make changes to this field.

Using a Format

To affect the way data is displayed in a field, you can use a **format**. To use a format, you enter a special symbol, called a **format symbol**, in the field's Format property box. The step on the next page specifies a format for the Customer Number field in the Customer table. The format symbol used in the example is >, which causes Access to display lowercase letters automatically as uppercase. The format symbol < would cause Access to display uppercase letters automatically as lowercase.

Steps To Specify a Format

1 **Select the Customer Number field. Click the Format property box and then type > (Figure 3-44).**

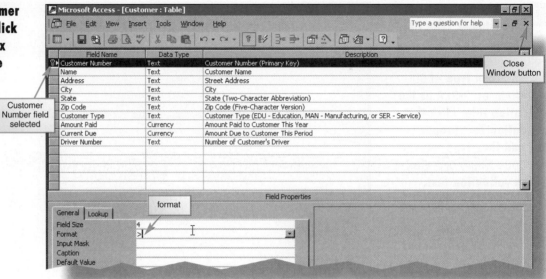

FIGURE 3-44

From this point on, any lowercase letters will be displayed automatically as uppercase when users add records or change the value in the Customer Number field.

Saving Rules, Values, and Formats

To save the validation rules, default values, and formats, perform the following steps.

Steps To Save the Validation Rules, Default Values, and Formats

1 **Click the Close Window button for the Customer : Table window to close the window and then point to the Yes button in the Microsoft Access dialog box.**

The Microsoft Access dialog box displays, asking if you want to save your changes (Figure 3-45).

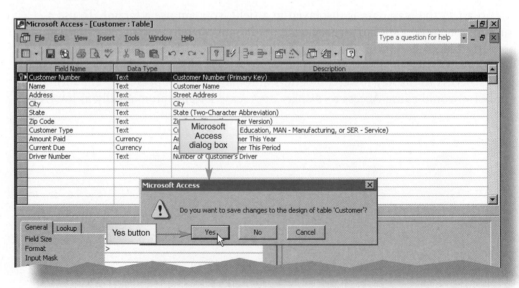

FIGURE 3-45

Click the Yes button to save the changes.

The Microsoft Access dialog box displays (Figure 3-46). This message asks if you want the new rules applied to current records. If this were a database used to run a business or to solve some other critical need, you would click Yes. You would want to be sure that the data already in the database does not violate the rules.

3 **Click the No button.**

The changes are saved.

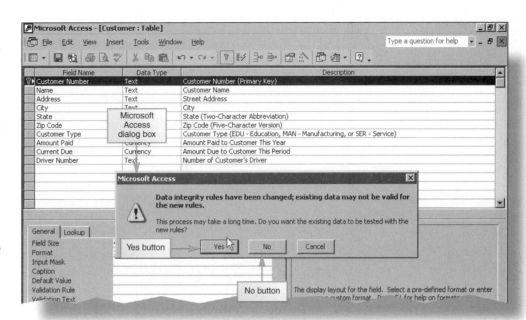

FIGURE 3-46

Updating a Table that Contains Validation Rules

When updating a table that contains validation rules, Access provides assistance in making sure the data entered is valid. It helps in making sure that data is formatted correctly. Access also will not accept invalid data. Entering a number that is out of the required range, for example, or entering a value that is not one of the possible choices, will produce an error message in the form of a dialog box. The database will not be updated until the error is corrected.

If the Customer number entered contains lowercase letters, such as dr22 (Figure 3-47), Access will display the data automatically as DR22 (Figure 3-48).

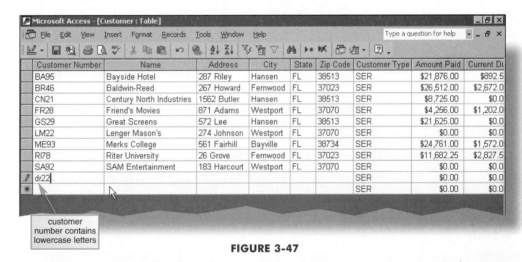

FIGURE 3-47

FIGURE 3-48

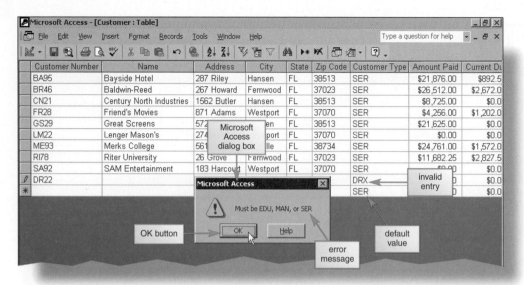

FIGURE 3-49

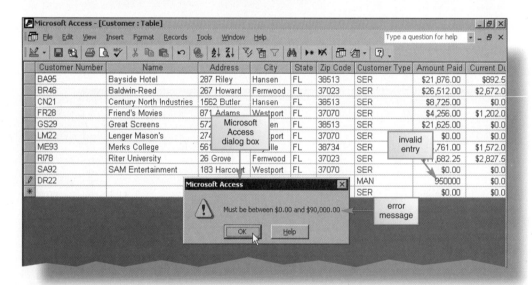

FIGURE 3-50

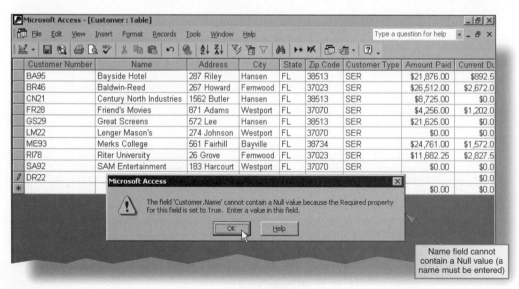

FIGURE 3-51

Instead of the Customer Type field initially being blank, it now contains the value SER, because SER is the default value. Thus, for any customer whose type is SER, it is not necessary to enter the value. By pressing the TAB key, the value SER is accepted.

If the customer type is not valid, such as DRX, Access will display the text message you specified (Figure 3-49) and not allow the data to enter the database.

If the amount paid value is not valid, such as 950000, which is too large, Access also displays the appropriate message (Figure 3-50) and refuses to accept the data.

If a required field contains no data, Access indicates this by displaying an error message as soon as you attempt to leave the record (Figure 3-51). The field must contain a valid entry before Access will move to a different record.

When entering data into a field with a validation rule, you may find that the system displays the error message and you find yourself unable to make the necessary correction. It may be that you cannot remember the validation rule you created or it was created incorrectly. In such a case, you will find that you neither can leave the field nor close the table because you have entered data into a field that violates the validation rule.

If this happens, first try again to type an acceptable entry. If this does not work, repeatedly press the BACKSPACE key to erase the contents of the field and then try to leave the field. If you are unsuccessful using this procedure, press the ESC key until the record is removed from the screen. The record will not be added to the database.

Should the need arise to take this drastic action, you probably have a faulty validation rule. Use the techniques of the previous sections to correct the existing validation rules for the field.

Making Individual Changes to a Field

Earlier, you changed all the entries in the Customer Type field to SER. You now have created a rule that will ensure that only legitimate values (EDU, MAN, or SER) can be entered in the field. To make a change, click the field to be changed to produce an insertion point, use the BACKSPACE or DELETE key to delete the current entry, and then type the new entry.

Complete the following steps to change the Customer Type value on the second and sixth records to MAN and on the seventh and eighth records to SER.

Steps To Make Individual Changes

1 Make sure the Customer table displays in Datasheet view. Click to the right of the SER entry in the Customer Type field on the second record.

An insertion point displays in the Customer Type field on the second record (Figure 3-52).

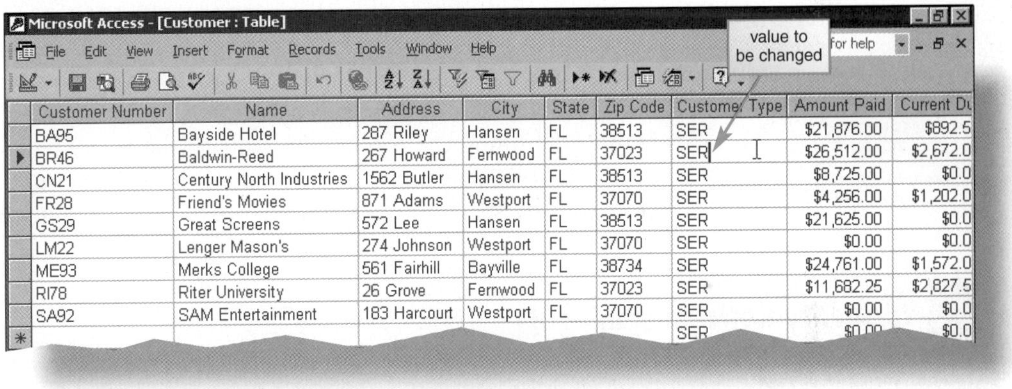

FIGURE 3-52

2 Press the BACKSPACE key three times to delete SER and then type MAN as the new value. In a similar fashion, change the SER on the sixth record to MAN, on the seventh record to EDU, and on the eighth record to EDU (Figure 3-53).

3 Close the Customer : Table window by clicking its Close Window button.

The Customer Type field changes now are complete.

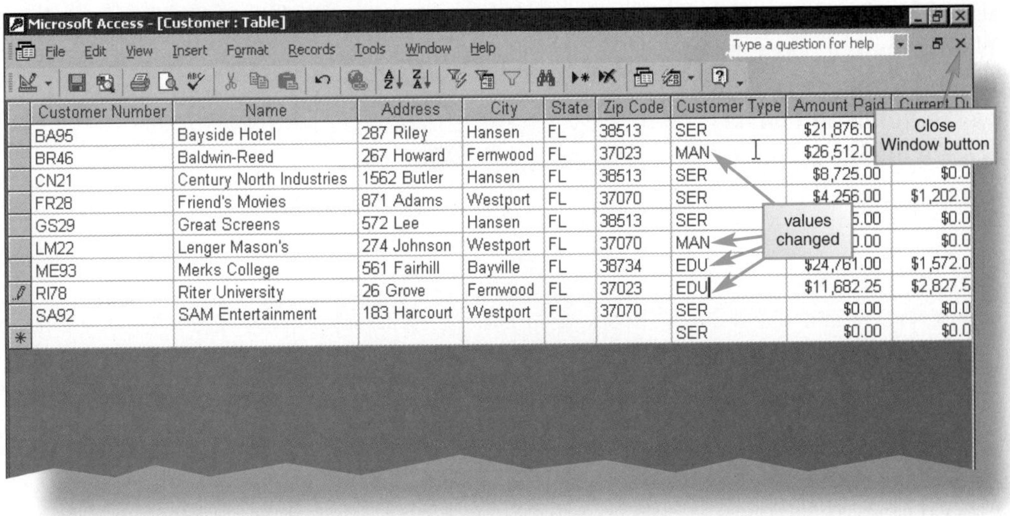

FIGURE 3-53

Specifying Referential Integrity

The property that ensures that the value in a foreign key must match that of another table's primary key is called **referential integrity**. A **foreign key** is a field in one table whose values are required to match the *primary key* of another table. In the Customer table, the Driver Number field is a foreign key that must match the primary key of the Driver table; that is, the driver number for any customer must be a driver currently in the Driver table. A customer whose driver number is 92, for example, should not be stored because there is no such driver.

In Access, to specify referential integrity, you must define a relationship between the tables by using the Relationships command. Access then prohibits any updates to the database that would violate the referential integrity. Access will not allow you to store a customer with a driver number that does not match a driver currently in the Driver table. Access also will prevent you from deleting a driver who currently has customers. Driver 60, for example, currently has customers in the Customer table. If you deleted driver 60, these customers' driver numbers would no longer match anyone in the Driver table.

The type of relationship between two tables specified by the Relationships command is referred to as a **one-to-many relationship**. This means that *one* record in the first table is related to (matches) *many* records in the second table, but each record in the second table is related to only *one* record in the first. In the Alisa Vending Services database, for example, a one-to-many relationship exists between the Driver table and the Customer table. *One* driver is associated with *many* customers, but each customer is associated with only a single driver. In general, the table containing the foreign key will be the *many* part of the relationship.

The following steps use the Relationships command to specify referential integrity by specifying a relationship between the Driver and Customer tables.

More *About*

Referential Integrity

Referential integrity is an essential property for databases, but providing support for it proved to be one of the most difficult tasks facing the developers of relational database management systems. For more information, visit the Access 2002 More About Web page (scsite.com/ac2002/more.htm) and then click Referential Integrity.

Steps **To Specify Referential Integrity**

1 **Close any open datasheet on the screen by clicking its Close Window button. Then, point to the Relationships button on the Database toolbar (Figure 3-54).**

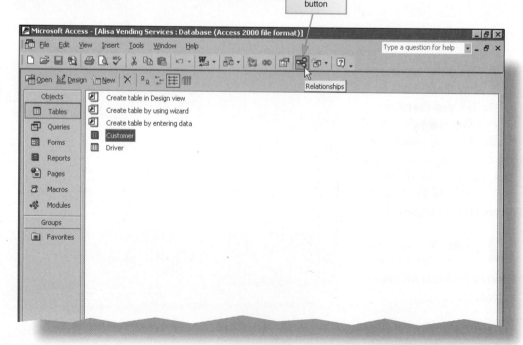

FIGURE 3-54

2 Click the Relationships button, select the Driver table and then point to the Add button in the Show Table dialog box.

The Show Table dialog box displays (Figure 3-55).

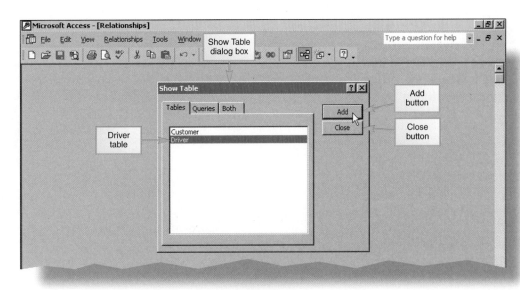

FIGURE 3-55

3 Click the Add button, click the Customer table, click the Add button again, and then click the Close button in the Show Table dialog box. Resize the field lists that display so all fields are visible. Point to the Driver Number field in the field list for the Driver table.

Field lists for the Driver and Customer tables display (Figure 3-56). The lists have been resized so all fields are visible.

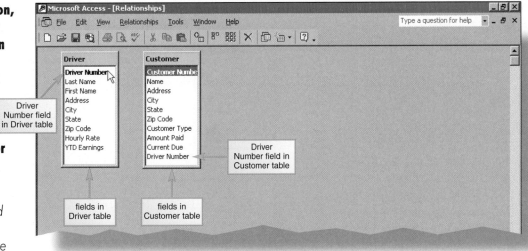

FIGURE 3-56

4 Drag the Driver Number field in the Driver table field list to the Driver Number field in the Customer table field list. Point to the Enforce Referential Integrity check box in the Edit Relationships dialog box.

The Edit Relationships dialog box displays (Figure 3-57). The correct fields (the Driver Number fields) have been identified as the matching fields.

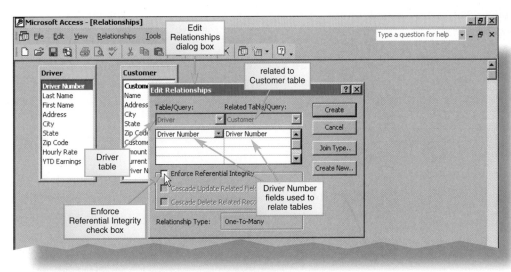

FIGURE 3-57

Microsoft **Access 2002**

5 **Click the Enforce Referential Integrity check box and point to the Create button in the Edit Relationships dialog box.**

Enforce Referential Integrity is selected (Figure 3-58). With Enforce Referential Integrity selected, Access will reject any update that would violate referential integrity.

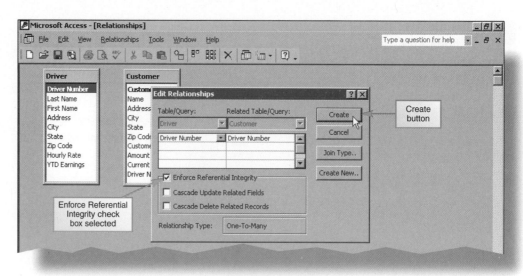

FIGURE 3-58

6 **Click the Create button. Point to the Close Window button for the Relationships window.**

*Access creates the relationship and displays it visually with the **relationship line** joining the two Driver Number fields (Figure 3-59). The number 1 at the top of the relationship line close to the Driver Number field in the Driver table indicates that the Driver table is the "one" part of the relationship. The infinity symbol at the other end of the relationship line indicates that the Customer table is the "many" part of the relationship.*

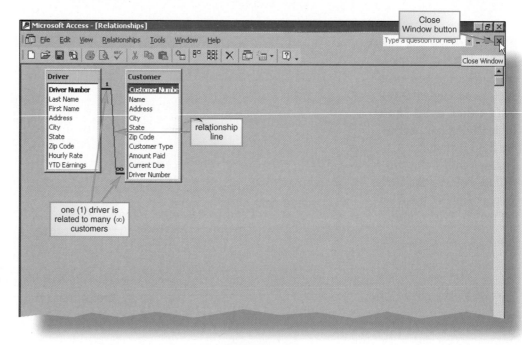

FIGURE 3-59

7 **Close the Relationships window by clicking its Close Window button. When the Microsoft Access dialog box displays, click the Yes button to save the relationship you created.**

Access now will reject any number in the Driver Number field in the Customer table that does not match a driver number in the Driver table. Attempting to add a customer whose Driver Number field does not match would result in the error message shown in Figure 3-60.

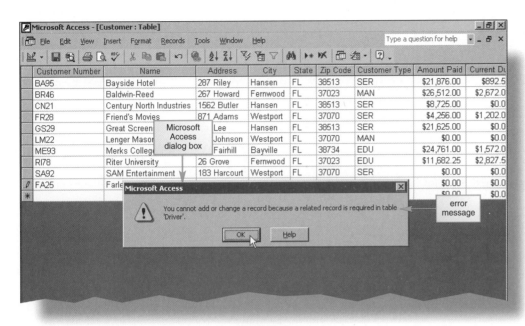

FIGURE 3-60

A deletion of a driver for whom related customers exist also would be rejected. Attempting to delete driver 60 from the Driver table, for example, would result in the message shown in Figure 3-61.

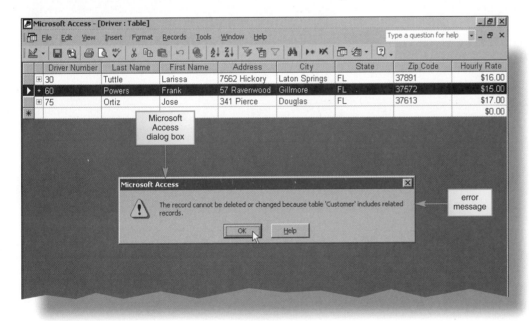

FIGURE 3-61

Using Subdatasheets

Now that the Driver table is related to the Customer table, it is possible to view the customers of a given driver when you are viewing the datasheet for the Driver table. The customers for the driver will display right under the driver in a **subdatasheet**. The fact that such a subdatasheet is available is indicated by a plus sign that displays in front of the rows in the Driver table. To display the subdatasheet, click the plus sign. The steps on the next page display the subdatasheet for driver 60.

More About

Relationships: The Find Unmatched Query Wizard

Occasionally, you may want to find records in one table that have no matching records in another table. For example, suppose the customers of Alisa Vending Services placed orders for vending machine maintenance. You may want to know which customers have no orders. The Find Unmatched Query Wizard allows you to find unmatched records. To use the Find Unmatched Query Wizard, click the New Object: Auto-Form button arrow, and then click Query. When the New Query dialog box displays, click the Find Unmatched Query Wizard. Follow the directions in the Find Unmatched Query Wizard dialog boxes.

More About

Relationships: Printing Relationships

You can obtain a printed copy of your relationships once you have created them. To do so, first click the Relationships button to display the relationships. Next, click File on the menu bar and then click Print Relationships.

Steps To Use a Subdatasheet

1 With the Database window on the screen and the Tables object selected, right-click Driver. Click Open on the shortcut menu. Point to the plus sign in front of the row for driver 60 (Figure 3-62).

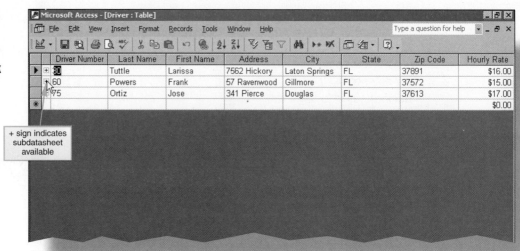

FIGURE 3-62

2 Click the plus sign in front of the row for driver 60.

The subdatasheet displays (Figure 3-63). It contains only those customers that are assigned to driver 60.

3 Click the minus sign to remove the subdatasheet and then close the datasheet for the Driver table by clicking its Close Window button.

The subdatasheet is removed and the datasheet no longer displays.

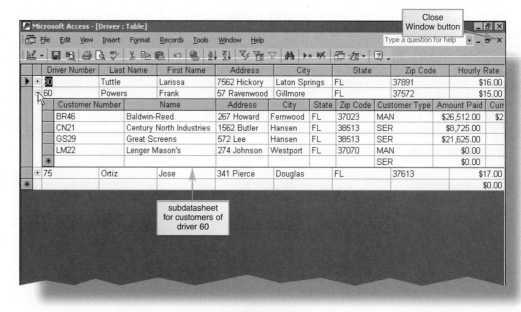

FIGURE 3-63

Ordering Records

Recall from previous discussions that Access sequences the records by customer number whenever listing them because the Customer Number field is the primary key. To change the order in which records display, use the Sort Ascending or Sort Descending buttons on the Table Datasheet toolbar. Either button reorders the records based on the field in which the insertion point is located.

Perform the following steps to order the records by city using the Sort Ascending button.

Steps: To Use the Sort Ascending Button to Order Records

1 **Open the Customer table in Datasheet view, and then click the City field on the first record (any other record would do as well). Point to the Sort Ascending button on the Table Datasheet toolbar (Figure 3-64).**

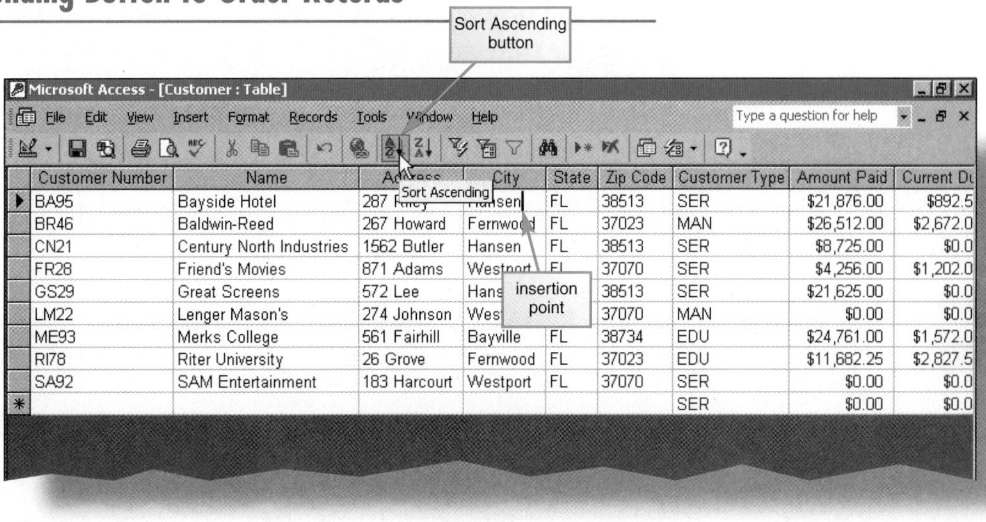

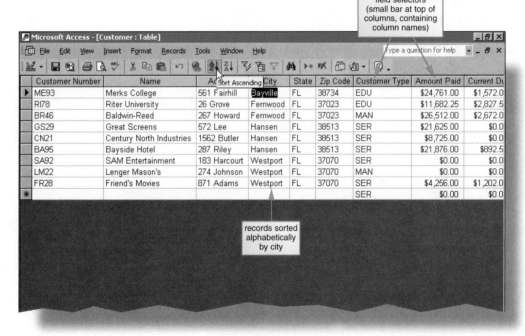

FIGURE 3-64

2 **Click the Sort Ascending button.**

The rows now are ordered by city (Figure 3-65).

FIGURE 3-65

If you wanted to sort the data in reverse order, you would click the Sort Descending button instead of the Sort Ascending button.

Ordering Records on Multiple Fields

Just as you are able to sort the answer to a query on multiple fields, you also can sort the data that displays in a datasheet on multiple fields. To do so, the major and minor keys must be next to each other in the datasheet with the major key on the left. (If this is not the case, you can drag the columns into the correct position. Instead of dragging, however, usually it will be easier to use a query that has the data sorted in the desired order.)

Other Ways

1. On Records menu click Sort, then click Sort Ascending
2. In Voice Command mode, say "Sort Ascending"

Given that the major and minor keys are in the correct position, select both fields and then click the Sort Ascending button on the Table Datasheet toolbar. To select the fields, use the **field selector**, the small bar at the top of the column that you click to select an entire field in a datasheet. Click the field selector for the first field (the major key). Next, hold down the SHIFT key and then click the field selector for the second field (the minor key).

Order records on the combination of the Customer Type and Amount Paid fields using the Sort Ascending button by completing the following steps.

Steps To Use the Sort Ascending Button to Order Records on Multiple Fields

1 Click the field selector (see Figure 3-65 on the previous page) at the top of the Customer Type column to select the entire column. Hold down the SHIFT key and then click the field selector for the Amount Paid column. Point to the Sort Ascending button on the Table Datasheet toolbar.

The Customer Type and Amount Paid columns both are selected (Figure 3-66).

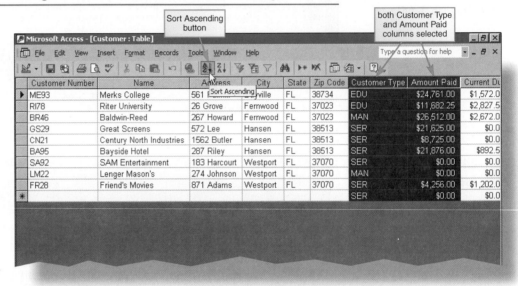

FIGURE 3-66

2 Click the Sort Ascending button.

The rows are ordered by customer type (Figure 3-67). Within each group of customers of the same type, the rows are ordered by the amount paid amount.

3 Close the Customer : Table window by clicking its Close Window button. Click the No button in the Microsoft Access dialog box to abandon the changes.

The next time the table is open, the records will display in their original order.

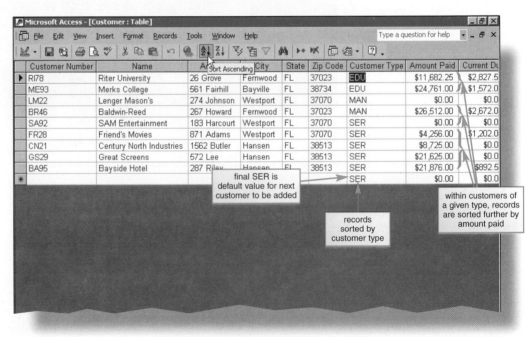

FIGURE 3-67

Creating and Using Indexes

You already are familiar with the concept of an index. The index in the back of a book contains important words or phrases together with a list of pages on which the given words or phrases can be found. An **index** for a table is similar. Figure 3-68, for example, shows the Customer table along with an index built on names. In this case, the items of interest are names instead of keywords or phrases as is the case in the back of this book. The field or fields on which the index is built is called the **index key**. Thus, in Figure 3-68, the Name field is the index key. (The structure of an index actually is a little more complicated than the one shown in the figure and is beyond the scope of this book. The concept is the same, however, and the structure shown in the figure illustrates the important concepts.)

Index on Name			Customer Table						
NAME	RECORD NUMBER		RECORD NUMBER	CUSTOMER NUMBER	NAME	ADDRESS	CITY	STATE	ZIP CODE
Baldwin-Reed	2		1	BA95	Bayside Hotel	287 Riley	Hansen	FL	38513 ...
Bayside Hotel	1		2	BR46	Baldwin-Reed	267 Howard	Fernwood	FL	37023 ...
Century North Industries	3		3	CN21	Century North Industries	1562 Butler	Hansen	FL	38513 ...
Friend's Movies	4		4	FR28	Friend's Movies	871 Adams	Westport	FL	37070 ...
Great Screens	5		5	GS29	Great Screens	572 Lee	Hansen	FL	38513 ...
Lenger Mason's	6		6	LM22	Lenger Mason's	274 Johnson	Westport	FL	37070 ...
Merks College	7		7	ME93	Merks College	561 Fairhill	Bayville	FL	38734
Riter University	8		8	RI78	Riter University	26 Grove	Fernwood	FL	37023
SAM Entertainment	9		9	SA92	SAM Entertainment	183 Harcourt	Westport	FL	37070

FIGURE 3-68

Each name occurs in the index along with the number of the record on which the corresponding customer is located. Further, the names appear in the index in alphabetical order. If Access were to use this index to find the record on which the name is Friend's Movies, for example, it could scan rapidly the names in the index to find Friend's Movies. Once it did, it would determine the corresponding record number (4) and then go immediately to record 4 in the Customer table, thus finding this customer more quickly than if it had to look through the entire Customer table one record at a time. Indexes make the process of retrieving records very fast and efficient. (With relatively small tables, the increased efficiency associated with indexes will not be apparent readily. In practice, it is common to encounter tables with thousands, tens of thousands, or even hundreds of thousands, of records. In such cases, the increase in efficiency is dramatic. In fact, without indexes, many operations in such databases would simply not be practical. They would take too long to complete.)

More About

Indexes

The most common structure for high-performance indexes is called a B-tree. It is a highly efficient structure that supports very rapid access to records in the database as well as a rapid alternative to sorting records. Virtually all systems use some version of the B-tree structure. For more information, visit the Access 2002 More About Web page (scsite.com/ac2002/more.htm) and then click B-tree.

Because no two customers happen to have the same name, the Record Number column contains only single values. This may not always be the case. Consider the index on the Zip Code field shown in Figure 3-69. In this index, the Record Number column contains several values, namely all the records on which the corresponding zip code displays. The first row, for example, indicates that zip code 37023 is found on records 2 and 8; the second row indicates that zip code 37070 is found on records 4, 6, and 9. If Access were to use this index to find all customers in zip code 37070, it could scan rapidly the zip codes in the index to find 37070. Once it did, it would determine the corresponding record numbers (4, 6, and 9) and then go immediately to these records. It would not have to examine any other records in the Customer table.

Index on Zip Code		Customer Table							
ZIP CODE	*RECORD NUMBER*	*RECORD NUMBER*	*CUSTOMER NUMBER*	*NAME*	*ADDRESS*	*CITY*	*STATE*	*ZIP CODE*	...
37023	2,8	1	BA95	Bayside Hotel	287 Riley	Hansen	FL	38513	...
37070	4,6,9	2	BR46	Baldwin-Reed	267 Howard	Fernwood	FL	37023	...
38513	1,3,5	3	CN21	Century North Industries	1562 Butler	Hansen	FL	38513	
38734	7	4	FR28	Friend's Movies	871 Adams	Westport	FL	37070	...
		5	GS29	Great Screens	572 Lee	Hansen	FL	38513	...
		6	LM22	Lenger Mason's	274 Johnson	Westport	FL	37070	...
		7	ME93	Merks College	561 Fairhill	Bayville	FL	38734	
		8	RI78	Riter University	26 Grove	Fernwood	FL	37023	
		9	SA92	SAM Entertainment	183 Harcourt	Westport	FL	37070	...

FIGURE 3-69

Another benefit of indexes is that they provide an efficient way to order records. That is, if the records are to display in a certain order, Access can use an index instead of physically having to rearrange the records in the database. Physically rearranging the records in a different order, which is called **sorting**, can be a very time-consuming process.

To see how indexes can be used for alphabetizing records, look at the record numbers in the index (Figure 3-68 on the previous page). Suppose you used these to list all customers; that is, simply follow down the Record Number column, listing the corresponding customers. In this example, first you would list the customer on record 2 (Baldwin-Reed), then the customer on record 1 (Bayside Hotel), then the customer on record 3 (Century North Industries), and so on. The customers would be listed alphabetically by name without actually sorting the table.

To gain the benefits from an index, you first must create one. Access automatically creates an index on the primary key as well as some other special fields. If, as is the case with both the Customer and Driver tables, a table contains a field called Zip Code, for example, Access will create an index for it automatically. You must create any other indexes you feel you need, indicating the field or fields on which the index is to be built.

Although the index key usually will be a single field, it can be a combination of fields. For example, you might want to sort records by amount paid within customer type. In other words, the records are ordered by a combination of fields: Customer Type and Amount Paid. An index can be used for this purpose by using a combination of fields for the index key. In this case, you must assign a name to the index. It is a good idea to assign a name that represents the combination of fields. For example, an index whose key is the combination of the Customer Type and Amount Paid fields, might be called TypePaid.

How Does Access Use an Index?

Access creates an index whenever you request that it do so. It takes care of all the work in setting up and maintaining the index. In addition, Access will use the index automatically.

If you request that data be sorted in a particular order and Access determines that an index is available that it can use to make the process efficient, it will do so. If no index is available, it still will sort the data in the order you requested; it will just take longer.

Similarly, if you request that Access locate a particular record that has a certain value in a particular field, Access will use an index if an appropriate one exists. If not, it will have to examine each record until it finds the one you want.

In both cases, the added efficiency provided by an index will not be apparent readily in tables that have only a few records. As you add more records to your tables, however, the difference can be dramatic. Even with only 50 to 100 records, you will notice a difference. You can imagine how dramatic the difference would be in a table with 50,000 records.

When Should You Create an Index?

An index improves efficiency for sorting and finding records. On the other hand, indexes occupy space on your disk. They also require Access to do extra work. Access must maintain all the indexes that have been created up to date. Thus, both advantages and disadvantages exist to using indexes. Consequently, the decision as to which indexes to create is an important one. The following guidelines should help you in this process.

Create an index on a field (or combination of fields) if one or more of the following conditions are present:

1. The field is the primary key of the table (Access will create this index automatically).
2. The field is the foreign key in a relationship you have created.
3. You frequently will need your data to be sorted on the field.
4. You frequently will need to locate a record based on a value in this field.

Because Access handles 1 automatically, you need only to concern yourself about 2, 3, and 4. If you think you will need to see customer data arranged in order of amount paid amounts, for example, you should create an index on the Amount Paid field. If you think you will need to see the data arranged by amount paid within driver number, you should create an index on the combination of the Driver Number field and the Amount Paid field. Similarly, if you think you will need to find a customer given the customer's name, you should create an index on the Name field.

More About

More About Quick Reference

For a table that lists how to complete tasks covered in this book using the mouse, menu, shortcut menu, and keyboard, see the Quick Reference Summary at the back of this book, or visit the Shelly Cashman Series Office XP Web page (scsite.com/offxp/qr.htm) and then click Microsoft Access 2002.

More About

Primary Keys: The Find Duplicates Query Wizard

One reason to include a primary key for a table is to eliminate duplicate records. There still is a possibility, however, that duplicate records can get into your database. (Perhaps, a customer's name was misspelled and the data entry person assumed it was a new customer.) The Find Duplicates Query Wizard allows you to find duplicate records. To use the Find Duplicates Query Wizard, click the table that you want to query, click the New Object: AutoForm button arrow, and then click Query. When the New Query dialog box displays, click the Find Duplicates Query Wizard. Follow the directions in the Find Duplicates Query Wizard dialog boxes.

Creating Single-Field Indexes

A **single-field index** is an index whose key is a single field. In this case, the index key is to be the Name field. In creating an index, you need to indicate whether to allow duplicates in the index key; that is, two records that have the same value. For example, in the index for the Name field, if duplicates are not allowed, Access would not allow the addition of a customer whose name is the same as the name of a customer already in the database. In the index for the Name field, duplicates will be allowed. Perform the following steps to create a single-field index.

 To Create a Single-Field Index

1 **Right-click Customer. Click Design View on the shortcut menu, and then, if necessary, maximize the Customer : Table window. Click the row selector to select the Name field. Click the Indexed property box in the Field Properties pane. Click the property box arrow that displays.**

The Indexed list displays (Figure 3-70). The items in the list are No (no index), Yes (Duplicates OK) (create an index and allow duplicates), and Yes (No Duplicates) (create an index but reject (do not allow) duplicates).

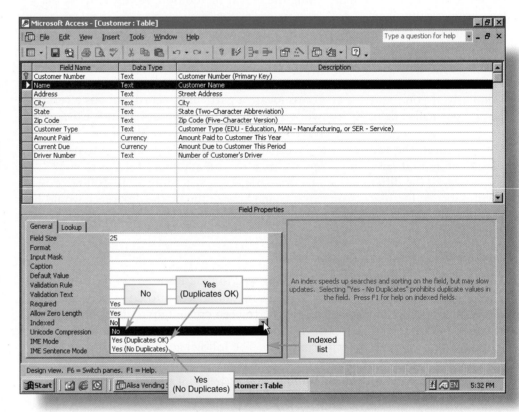

2 **Click the Yes (Duplicates OK) item in the list.**

FIGURE 3-70

The index on the Name field now will be created and is ready for use as soon as you save your work.

Creating Multiple-Field Indexes

Creating **multiple-field indexes**, that is, indexes whose key is a combination of fields, involves a different process from creating single-field indexes. To create multiple-field indexes, you will use the **Indexes button** on the Table Design toolbar, enter a name for the index, and then enter the combination of fields that make up the index key. The following steps create a multiple-field index with the name TypePaid. The key will be the combination of the Customer Type field and the Amount Paid fields.

Steps **To Create a Multiple-Field Index**

1 **Point to the Indexes button on the Table Design toolbar (Figure 3-71).**

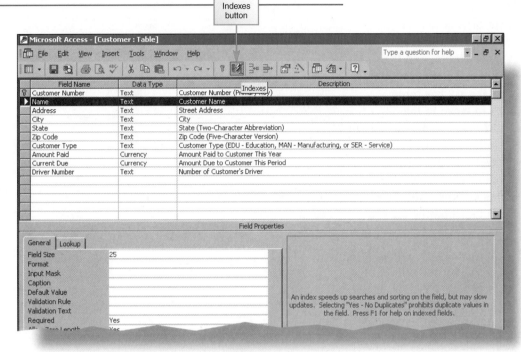

FIGURE 3-71

2 **Click the Indexes button. Click the blank row (the row following Name) in the Index Name column in the Indexes: Customer dialog box. Type** TypePaid **as the index name, and then press the TAB key. Point to the down arrow.**

The Indexes: Customer dialog box displays. It shows the indexes that already have been created and allows you to create additional indexes (Figure 3-72). The index name has been entered as TypePaid. An insertion point displays in the Field Name column. The index on the Customer Number field is the primary index and was created automatically by Access. The index on the Name field is the one just created.

Access created other indexes (for example, the Zip Code and Amount Paid fields) automatically. In this dialog box, you can create additional indexes.

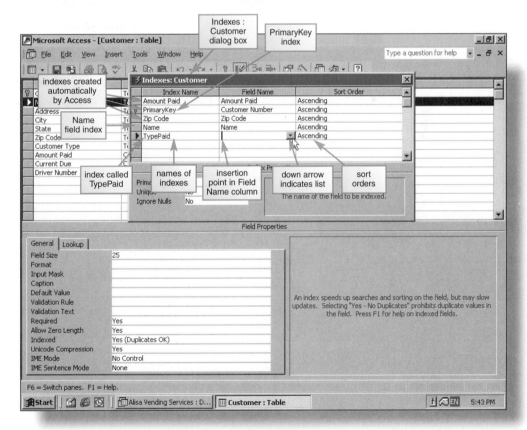

FIGURE 3-72

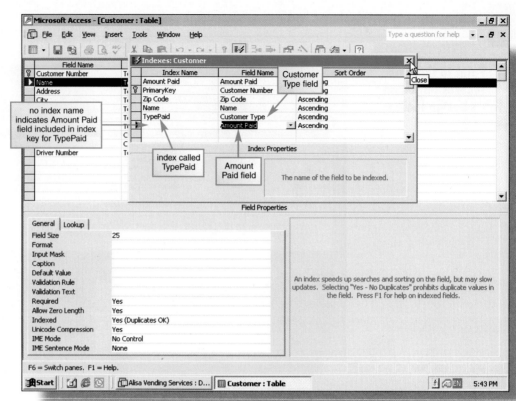

3 Click the down arrow in the Field Name column to produce a list of fields in the Customer table, and then select Customer Type. Press the TAB key three times to move to the Field Name column on the following row. Select the Amount Paid field in the same manner as the Customer Type field. Point to the Close button for the Indexes: Customer dialog box.

Customer Type and Amount Paid are selected as the two fields for the TypePaid index (Figure 3-73). The absence of an index name on the row containing the Amount Paid field indicates that it is part of the previous index, TypePaid.

FIGURE 3-73

4 Close the Indexes: Customer dialog box by clicking its Close button, and then close the Customer : Table window by clicking its Close Window button. When the Microsoft Access dialog box displays, click the Yes button to save your changes.

The indexes are created and the Database window displays.

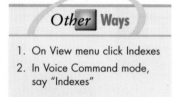

Other Ways

1. On View menu click Indexes
2. In Voice Command mode, say "Indexes"

More About

Microsoft Certification

The Microsoft Office User Specialist (MOUS) Certification program provides an opportunity for you to obtain a valuable industry credential — proof that you have the Access 2002 skills required by employers. For more information, see Appendix E or visit the Shelly Cashman Series MOUS Web page at scsite.com/offxp/cert.htm.

The indexes now have been created. Access will use them automatically whenever possible to improve efficiency of ordering or finding records. Access also will maintain them automatically. That is, whenever the data in the Customer table is changed, Access will make appropriate changes in the indexes automatically.

Closing the Database

The following step closes the database by closing its Database window.

TO CLOSE A DATABASE

1 Click the Close button for the Alisa Vending Services : Database window.

The database closes.

CASE PERSPECTIVE SUMMARY

In Project 3, you assisted Alisa Vending Services in the maintenance of the database. You used Form view to add a record to the database and searched for a record satisfying a criterion. You used a filter so you could view only the record you needed. You changed and deleted records. You changed the structure of the Customer table in the Alisa Vending Services database, created validation rules, and specified referential integrity. You used a subdatasheet to view the customers assigned to a driver while viewing driver data. You made mass changes and created indexes to improve performance.

Project Summary

In Project 3, you learned how to maintain a database. You saw how to use Form view to add records to a table. You learned how to locate and filter records. You saw how to change the contents of records in a table and how to delete records from a table. You restructured a table, both by changing field characteristics and by adding a new field. You saw how to make changes to groups of records and how to delete groups of records. You learned how to create a variety of validation rules to specify a required field, specify a range, specify a default value, specify legal values, and specify a format. You examined the issues involved in updating a table with validation rules. You also saw how to specify referential integrity. You learned how to view related data by using subdatasheets. You learned how to order records. Finally, you saw how to improve performance by creating single-field and multiple-field indexes.

What You Should Know

Having completed this project, you now should be able to perform the following tasks:

- Add a Field to a Table (A 3.17)
- Change the Size of a Field (A 3.16)
- Close a Database (A 3.48)
- Create a Multiple-Field Index (A 3.47)
- Create a Single-Field Index (A 3.46)
- Delete a Record (A 3.14)
- Filter Records (A 3.13)
- Make Individual Changes (A 3.35)
- Open a Database (A 3.05)
- Remove a Filter (A 3.14)
- Resize a Column (A 3.21)
- Save the Validation Rules, Default Values, and Formats (A 3.32)
- Search for a Record (A 3.09)
- Specify a Collection of Legal Values (A 3.31)
- Specify a Default Value (A 3.30)
- Specify a Format (A 3.32)
- Specify a Range (A 3.29)
- Specify a Required Field (A 3.29)
- Specify Referential Integrity (A 3.36)
- Switch from Form View to Datasheet View (A 3.11)
- Update the Contents of a Field (A 3.10, A 3.20)
- Use a Delete Query to Delete a Group of Records (A 3.26)
- Use a Form to Add Records (A 3.06)
- Use a Subdatasheet (A 3.40)
- Use an Update Query to Update All Records (A 3.23)
- Use the Sort Ascending Button to Order Records (A 3.41)
- Use the Sort Ascending Button to Order Records on Multiple Fields (A 3.42)

Learn It Online

Instructions: To complete the Learn It Online exercises, start your browser, click the Address bar, and then enter scsite.com/offxp/exs.htm. When the Office XP Learn It Online page displays, follow the instructions in the exercises below.

1 Project Reinforcement TF, MC, and SA

Below Access Project 3, click the Project Reinforcement link. Print the quiz by clicking Print on the File menu. Answer each question. Write your first and last name at the top of each page, and then hand in the printout to your instructor.

2 Flash Cards

Below Access Project 3, click the Flash Cards link. When Flash Cards displays, read the instructions. Type 20 (or a number specified by your instructor) in the Number of Playing Cards text box, type your name in the Name text box, and then click the Flip Card button. When the flash card displays, read the question and then click the Answer box arrow to select an answer. Flip through Flash Cards. Click Print on the File menu to print the last flash card if your score is 15 (75%) correct or greater and then hand it in to your instructor. If your score is less than 15 (75%) correct, then redo this exercise by clicking the Replay button.

3 Practice Test

Below Access Project 3, click the Practice Test link. Answer each question, enter your first and last name at the bottom of the page, and then click the Grade Test button. When the graded practice test displays on your screen, click Print on the File menu to print a hard copy. Continue to take practice tests until you score 80% or better. Hand in a printout of the final practice test to your instructor.

4 Who Wants to Be a Computer Genius?

Below Access Project 3, click the Computer Genius link. Read the instructions, enter your first and last name at the bottom of the page, and then click the Play button. Hand in your score to your instructor.

5 Wheel of Terms

Below Access Project 3, click the Wheel of Terms link. Read the instructions, and then enter your first and last name and your school name. Click the Play button. Hand in your score.

6 Crossword Puzzle Challenge

Below Access Project 3, click the Crossword Puzzle Challenge link. Read the instructions, and then enter your first and last name. Click the Play button. Work the crossword puzzle. When you are finished, click the Submit button. When the crossword puzzle redisplays, click the Print button. Hand in the printout.

7 Tips and Tricks

Below Access Project 3, click the Tips and Tricks link. Click a topic that pertains to Project 3. Right-click the information and then click Print on the shortcut menu. Construct a brief example of what the information relates to in Access to confirm you understand how to use the tip or trick. Hand in the example and printed information.

8 Newsgroups

Below Access Project 3, click the Newsgroups link. Click a topic that pertains to Project 3. Print three comments. Hand in the comments.

9 Expanding Your Horizons

Below Access Project 3, click the Articles for Microsoft Access link. Click a topic that pertains to Project 3. Print the information. Construct a brief example of what the information relates to in Access to confirm you understand the contents of the article. Hand in the example and printed information.

10 Search Sleuth

Below Access Project 3, click the Search Sleuth link. To search for a term that pertains to this project, select a term below the Project 3 title and then use the Google search engine at google.com (or any major search engine) to display and print two Web pages that present information on the term. Hand in the printout.

online

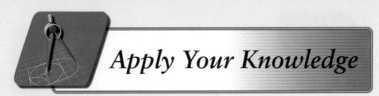

Apply Your Knowledge

1 Maintaining the Beyond Clean Database

Instructions: Start Access. Open the database Beyond Clean that you used in Project 2 or see your instructor for information on accessing the files required for this book. Perform the following tasks.

1. Open the Client table in Design view as shown in Figure 3-74.

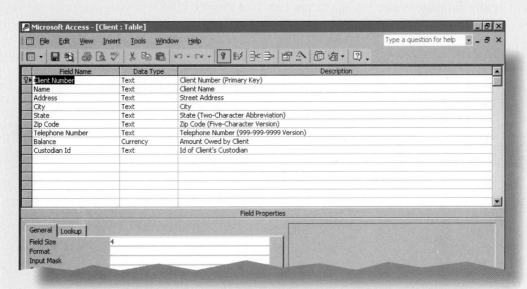

FIGURE 3-74

2. Increase the size of the Name field to 25.
3. Format the Client Number and State fields so any lowercase letters display in uppercase.
4. Make the Name field a required field.
5. Specify that balance amounts must be less than or equal to $200.00. Include validation text.
6. Create an index that allows duplicates for the Name field.
7. Save the changes to the structure.
8. Open the Client table in Datasheet view.
9. Change the name of client HA09 to Halyards Manufacturing.
10. Resize the Name column so the complete name for client HA09 displays. Resize the State, Zip Code, Balance, and Custodian Id columns to the best size.
11. Close the table and click Yes to save the changes to the layout of the table.
12. Print the table. If necessary, change the margins so the table prints on one page in landscape orientation.
13. Open the Client table and use Filter By Selection to find the record for client BE29. Delete the record.
14. Remove the filter and then print the table.
15. Sort the data in ascending order by balance.
16. Print the table. Close the table. If you are asked to save changes to the design of the table, click the No button.
17. Establish referential integrity between the Custodian table (the one table) and the Client table (the many table). Print the Relationships window by making sure the Relationships window is open, clicking File on the menu bar, and then clicking Print Relationships.

In the Lab

1 Maintaining the Wooden Crafts Database

Problem: Jan Merchant would like to make some changes to the Wooden Crafts database structure. She needs to increase the size of the Description field and add an additional index. She also would like to add some validation rules to the database. Finally, some new products must be added to the database.

Instructions: Use the database created in the In the Lab 1 of Project 1 for this assignment or see your instructor for information on accessing the files required for this book. Perform the following tasks.

1. Open the Wooden Crafts database and open the Product table in Design view as shown in Figure 3-75.

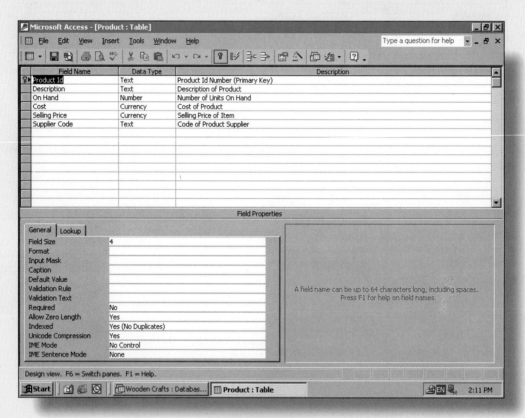

FIGURE 3-75

2. Create an index for the Description field. Be sure to allow duplicates.
3. Create and save the following validation rules for the Product table. List the steps involved on your own paper.
   a. Make the Description field a required field.
   b. Ensure that any lowercase letters entered in the Product Id field are displayed as uppercase.
   c. Specify that the on hand units must be between 0 and 20. Include validation text.
4. Save the changes.

In the Lab

5. Open the Product form you created in Project 1, and then add the following record to the Product table:

PRODUCT ID	DESCRIPTION	ON HAND	COST	SELLING PRICE	SUPPLIER CODE
AD01	Animal Dominoes	5	$18.00	$21.00	BH

6. Switch to Datasheet view and sort the records in descending order on the combination of the On Hand and Cost fields.

7. Print the table. Close the table. If you are asked to save changes to the design of the table, click the No button.

8. Create a new query for the Product table.

9. Using a query, delete all records in the Product table where the description starts with the letter R. (*Hint:* Use online Help to solve this problem.) Close the query without saving it.

10. Print the Product table.

11. Open the Supplier table in Design view and add a new field to the end of the table. Name the field, Fax Number. This new field has the same data type and length as Telephone Number. Enter the same comment as Telephone Number but replace Telephone with Fax. Save the change to the table design.

12. Open the Supplier table in Datasheet view, and then add the following data to the Fax Number field.

SUPPLIER CODE	FAX NUMBER
AP	505-555-6574
BH	707-555-8967
PL	602-555-9991

13. Resize all columns in the Supplier table to the best size.

14. Print the table. If necessary, change the margins so the table prints on one page in landscape orientation. Save the change to the layout of the table.

15. Specify referential integrity between the Supplier table (the one table) and the Product table (the many table). Print the Relationships window by making sure the Relationships window is open, clicking File on the menu bar, and then clicking Print Relationships.

2 Maintaining the Restaurant Supply Database

Problem: The restaurant supply company has purchased the business of an independent contractor who also serviced restaurants. You now need to merge the customers of the two businesses. Because the business has expanded, you also need to change the database structure and add some validation rules to the database.

Instructions: Use both the Restaurant Supply database created in the In the Lab 2 of Project 1 and the Independent Supply database for this assignment. Be sure both databases are on the same disk before starting In the Lab 2. If you do not know how to do this, see your instructor for assistance. Perform the following tasks.

1. Open the Independent Supply database from the Data Disk. See the preface at the front of this book for instructions for downloading the Data Disk or see your instructor for information on accessing the files required in this book.

(continued)

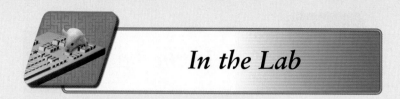

In the Lab

Maintaining the Restaurant Supply Database *(continued)*

2. Create a new query for the Customer table and double-click the asterisk in the field list to add all fields to the query.
3. Change the query type to an Append Query.
4. When the Append dialog box displays, make the entries shown in Figure 3-76 and then click the OK button. If your Restaurant Supply database is not located on the disk in drive A, you will need to enter the appropriate information in the File Name text box.

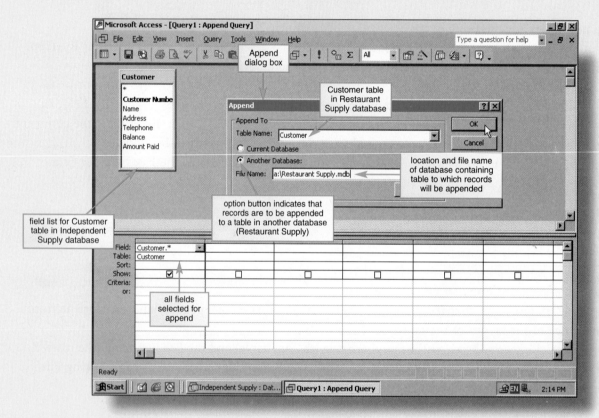

FIGURE 3-76

5. Click the Run button to run the Append query. When the Microsoft Access dialog box displays with the message that you are about to append 3 rows, click Yes.
6. Close the append query without saving it, and then close the Independent Supply database. Open the Restaurant Supply database, and then open the Customer table in Datasheet view. There should be 13 records in the table.
7. The customers added from the Independent Supply database do not have a sales rep assigned to them. Assign customer PP43 to sales rep 44, customer RR15 to sales rep 49, and customer TD01 to sales rep 51. Print the Customer table. If necessary, change the margins so the table prints on one page in landscape orientation. Close the table.
8. Open the Customer table in Design view.

In the Lab

9. Add the field, Dining Type, to the Customer table. Define the field as text with a width of 3. Insert the field after the Telephone field. This field will contain data on the type of restaurant. Restaurants are classified as fine dining (FIN), family (FAM), and fast food/takeout (FFT). Save these changes.

10. Using a query, change all the entries in the Dining Type column to FAM. This will be the type of most restaurants. Do not save the query.

11. Open the Customer table and resize all columns to best fit the data. Print the table. Save the changes to the layout of the table.

12. Create the following validation rules for the Customer table and save the changes to the table. List the steps involved on your own paper.

    a. Make the Name field a required field.

    b. Specify the legal values FIN, FAM, and FFT for the Dining Type field.

    c. Ensure that any letters entered in the Customer Number field are displayed as uppercase.

    d. Specify that balance must be less than or equal to $500.000. Include validation text.

13. You can use either Form view or Datasheet view to change records in a table. To use Form view, you must replace the form you created in Project 1 with a form that includes the new field, Dining Type. With the Customer table selected, click the New Object: AutoForm button arrow on the Database Window toolbar. Click AutoForm. Use this form that contains the new field to change the dining type for the following records:

CUSTOMER NUMBER	DINING TYPE
AM23	FFT
BI15	FIN
EG07	FIN
RD03	FFT
VG21	FFT

14. Close the form. Click the Yes button when asked if you want to save the form. Save the form as Customer. Click the Yes button when asked if you want to replace the Customer form you created in Project 1.

15. Open the table in Datasheet view and print the table.

16. Use Filter By Form to find all records where the customer has a balance of $350.00 and has the Dining Type of FAM. Delete these records. (*Hint*: Read the More About: Filter By Form on page A 3.13 to solve this problem.)

17. Remove the filter and print the Customer table. If you are asked to save changes to the design of the table, click the No button.

18. Specify referential integrity between the Sales Rep table (the one table) and the Customer table (the many table). Print the Relationships window by making sure the Relationships window is open, clicking File on the menu bar, and then clicking Print Relationships.

In the Lab

3 Maintaining the Condo Management Database

Problem: The condo management company has determined that some changes must be made to the database structure. Another field must be added. Because several different individuals update the data, the company also would like to add some validation rules to the database. Finally, some additions and deletions are required to the database.

Instructions: Use the database created in the In the Lab 3 of Project 1 for this assignment or see your instructor for information on accessing the files required for this book. Perform the following tasks.

1. Open the Condo Management database and open the Condo table in Design view as shown in Figure 3-77.

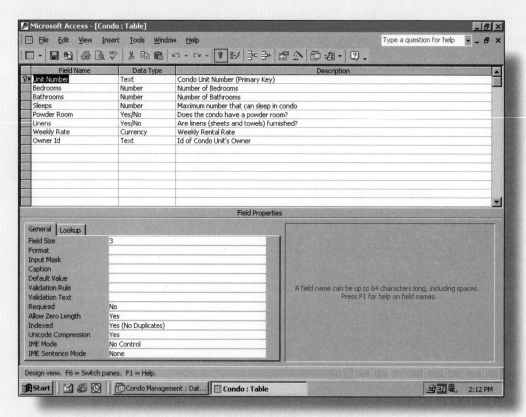

FIGURE 3-77

2. Create an index on the combination of the Bedrooms and Bathrooms fields. Name the index Bedbath. Create an index on the combination of the Sleeps and Bedrooms field. Name the index SleepBed. Save these changes.
3. Display the Condo table in Datasheet view and use the Sort Ascending button to order the records by bathrooms within bedrooms.
4. Print the table and then close the table. If you are asked to save changes to the design of the table, click the No button.

In the Lab

5. Add the field, For Sale, to the Condo table. Define the field as a Yes/No field. Insert the field after the Weekly Rate field. This field will indicate whether or not the condo unit is for sale.

6. Save these changes and display the Condo table in Datasheet view.

7. Units 101, 108, and 403 are for sale. Update the records for these condo units. Decrease the width of the For Sale column.

8. Print the table. If necessary, change the page orientation and margins so the table prints on one page. Close the table. Save the layout changes to the table.

9. Create the following validation rules for the Condo table and save the changes to the table. List the steps involved on your own paper.
    a. Make the Bedrooms, Bathrooms, and Sleeps field required fields.
    b. Assign a default value of 1 to the Bedrooms and Bathrooms fields. Assign a default value of 2 to the Sleeps field.
    c. Specify that the Bedrooms and Bathrooms fields must be at least one and the Sleeps field must be at least two. Include validation text.
    d. Specify that weekly rate must be between $600 and $1,800. Include validation text.

10. The management office has just received a new listing from Mark Graty. It is unit 300. The unit sleeps 10, has 3 bedrooms, 2 bathrooms, a powder room, and linens are provided. The weekly rate is $1,300 and the owner is interested in selling the unit. Add this record to your database. You can use either Form view or Datasheet view to add records to a table. To use Form view, you must replace the form you created in Project 1 with a form that includes the new field, For Sale. With the Condo table selected, click the New Object: AutoForm button arrow on the Database window toolbar. Click , and then use the form to add the record.

11. If necessary, close the form. Click Yes when asked if you want to save the form. Save the form as Condo. Click the Yes button when asked if you want to replace the Condo form you created in Project 1.

12. Change to Datasheet view and print the table.

13. Using a query, delete all records in the table where the condo has 2 bedrooms, 1 bathroom, and no powder room.

14. Print the Condo table.

15. Specify referential integrity between the Owner table (the one table) and the Condo table (the many table). Print the Relationships window by making sure the Relationships window is open, clicking File on the menu bar, and then clicking Print Relationships.

Cases and Places

The difficulty of these case studies varies:
❱ are the least difficult; ❱❱ are more difficult; and ❱❱❱ are the most difficult.

1 ❱ Use the Computer Expertise database you created in Case Study 1 of Project 1 for this assignment. Perform each of the following tasks and then print the results:

(a) The name for customer LK23 should really be Learn n Kids Day Care.
(b) To help manage the business better, it is important to know the type of customer being served. Customer types are RET (retail), SER (service), MFG (manufacturing), and DIN (dining.) No other customer type should be entered in the database. Customers AL35, BK18, and LB42 are retail organizations. Customers CL45, LK23, and SR34 are service organizations. Customers AR43 and ME30 are manufacturing organizations and customers CJ78 and RE20 are dining establishments.
(c) Ready Eats now has a balance of $175.00.
(d) Specify referential integrity between the two tables in the database.

2 ❱ Use the Baseball database you created in Case Study 2 of Project 1 for this assignment. Perform each of these tasks and then print the results:

(a) The description for item 7930 is really Coffee Travel Mug.
(b) Logo Goods has increased the cost of their items by 10 percent. The marketing team has decided to raise the selling price by 5 percent for these items. (*Hint:* Use an update query to solve this problem.)
(c) The team has sold seven tee shirts and five baseball caps.
(d) Only numbers should be entered as item ids and the supplier codes always should display in uppercase.
(e) Specify referential integrity between the two tables in the database.

3 ❱❱ Use the local attractions database you created in Case Study 3 of Project 1 for this assignment:

(a) Determine and create the appropriate validity check for the type of attraction.
(b) Ensure that data always is entered in the Name, Address, and Telephone Number fields.
(c) Create an index on the combination of attraction type and attraction name.
(d) Add two records to the database.

4 ❱❱ Use the high school Math club database you created in Case Study 4 of Project 1 for this assignment:

(a) Add a field to the database to store the date an elementary student started in the tutoring program. Enter some sample data for this field.
(b) Determine and create appropriate validity checks for the fields in your database.
(c) Add two records to the database.
(d) Determine and create appropriate indexes for your database. Use the indexes to sort the data.
(e) Analyze the database and determine if you have a one-to-many relationship between any tables. If so, specify referential integrity between the one table and the many table.

Cases and Places

5 ▶▶▶ Use the hobby or collection database you created in Case Study 5 of Project 1 for this assignment:

(a) Analyze the database and determine if you need any additional fields. Do you have a field for the date you acquired the item in your collection? Do you have a price or cost associated with each item? Add any fields that you now think would be useful to the database. Determine if there are any duplicate records in your database. (*Hint*: See More About Primary Keys: The Find Duplicate Query Wizard on page A 3.45 to solve this problem.)

(b) Determine and create appropriate validity checks for the fields in your database.

(c) Add two records to the database.

(d) Determine and create appropriate indexes for your database. Use the indexes to sort the data.

(e) Analyze the database and determine if you have a one-to-many relationship between any tables. If so, specify referential integrity between the one table and the many table. Determine if there are any records in one table that do not have related records in another table. (*Hint:* See More About Relationships: The Find Unmatched Query Wizard on page A 3.36 to solve this problem.)

Microsoft Access 2002

Publishing to the Internet Using Data Access Pages

CASE PERSPECTIVE

Alisa Vending Services is pleased with all the work you have done for them thus far. They appreciate the database you have designed and created. They also like the ease with which they can query the database. They find the default values, validation rules, validation text, and the relationships you created to be useful in ensuring the database contains only valid data. They also find the report you created in Project 1 to be useful. They are pleased with the form you created for them in Project 1, which they have used to view and update customer data. They would like to use a Web page that would be similar to this form in order to view and/or update customer data over the Internet. They would like you to develop a sample of such a Web page, which they then would review. If they determine that it satisfies their needs, they will instruct the network administrator to make both the database and your Web page accessible on the Internet.

Introduction

Microsoft Access 2002 supports data access pages. A **data access page** is an HTML document that can be bound directly to data in the database. The fact that it is an HTML document implies that it can be run in the Internet Explorer browser. The fact that it is bound directly to the database means that it can access data in the database directly.

Figure 1 on the next page shows a sample data access page run in the Internet Explorer browser. Notice that it is similar to the form created in Project 1 (see Figure 1-56 on page A 1.38). Although running in the browser, the data access page is displaying data in the Alisa Vending Services database. Furthermore, the page can be used to change this data. You can use it to change the contents of existing records, to delete records, and to add new records.

In this project, you will create the data access page shown in Figure 1 on the next page. (This data access page is located on a disk in drive A. The database it is accessing also is located on the disk. In order to use this page on the Internet, both the page and the database would need to be located on some server that would be available to the Internet. The address entered in the browser would be changed to reflect the true location of the page.)

Opening the Database

Before carrying out the steps in this project, you first must open the database. To do so, perform the steps on the next page.

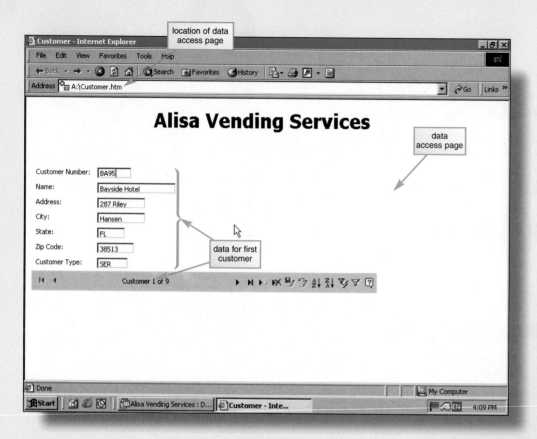

FIGURE 1

1 Click the Start button, click Programs on the Start menu, and then click Microsoft Access.

2 Click the Open button on the Database toolbar and then click 3½ Floppy (A:) in the Look in box. If necessary, click the Alisa Vending Services database name.

3 Click the Open button.

The database opens and the Alisa Vending Services : Database window displays.

Creating a Data Access Page

To create a data access page, use the Page Wizard as shown in the following steps.

Steps **To Create a Data Access Page**

1 **With the Customer table selected, click the New Object: AutoForm button arrow on the Database toolbar. Point to Page on the New Object: AutoForm button list.**

The list of available objects displays (Figure 2).

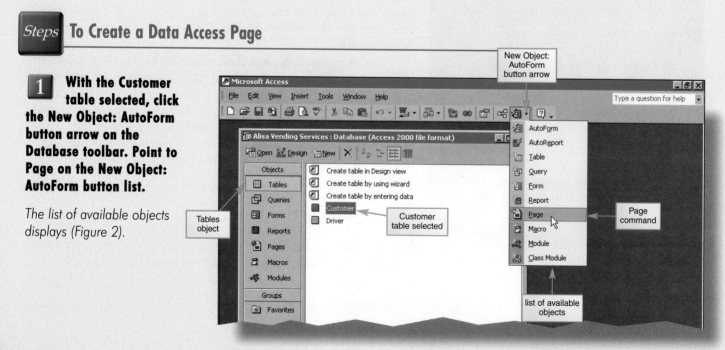

FIGURE 2

2 **Click Page, select Page Wizard in the New Data Access Page dialog box, and then point to the OK button.**

The New Data Access Page dialog box displays (Figure 3).

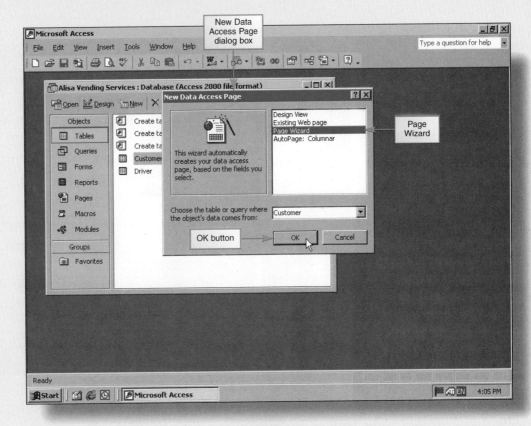

FIGURE 3

3 **Click the OK button and then point to the Add Field button.**

The Page Wizard dialog box displays (Figure 4). The fields in the Customer table display in the list of available fields. The Customer Number field currently is selected.

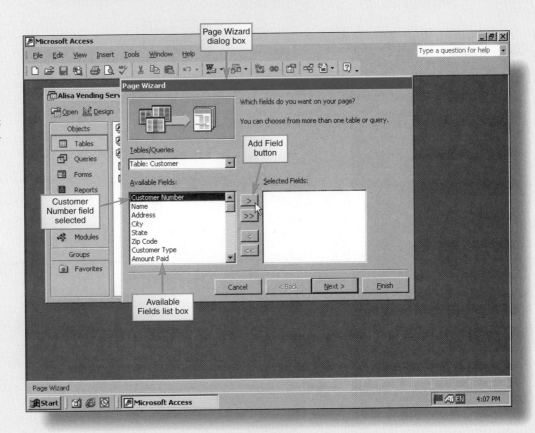

FIGURE 4

4 **Click the Add Field button to add the Customer Number field to the list of selected fields. Click the Add Field button six more times to add the Name, Address, City, State, Zip Code, and Customer Type fields. Point to the Next button.**

The Customer Number, Name, Address, City, State, Zip Code, and Customer Type fields are selected (Figure 5).

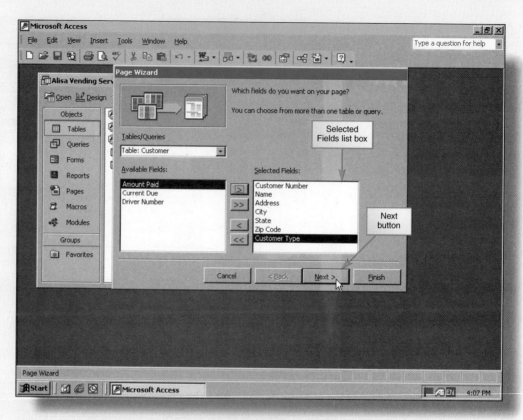

FIGURE 5

5 **Click the Next button.**

The Page Wizard dialog box displays, asking if you want to add any grouping levels (Figure 6).

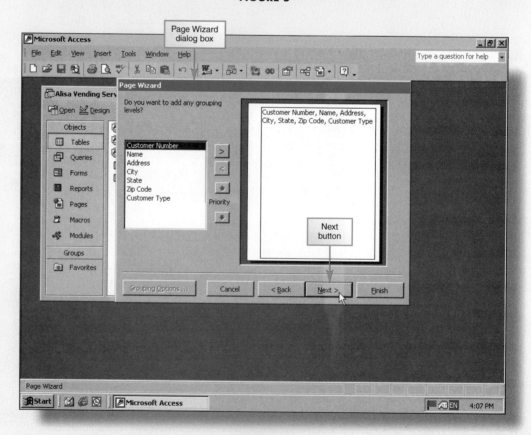

FIGURE 6

6   **Click the Next button because you do not need any grouping levels. Click the Next button a second time because you do not need to make any changes on the following screen, which enables you to specify a special sort order. Point to the Finish button.**

The Page Wizard dialog box displays (Figure 7).

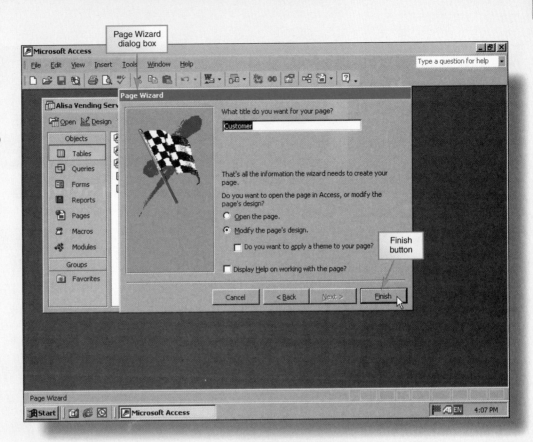

FIGURE 7

7   **Click the Finish button. The Field List pane may display. (The contents of your Field List pane may be different.) If the Field List pane does display, point to the Close button for the Field List pane.**

The Customer data access page displays (Figure 8).

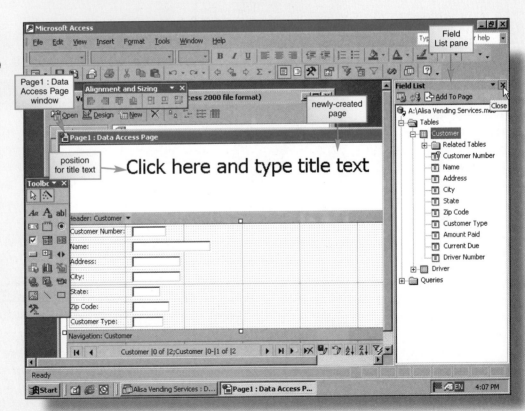

FIGURE 8

8 If the Field List pane displays, click the Close button for the Field List pane. Click anywhere in the portion of the screen labeled "Click here and type title text" and then type Alisa Vending Services as the title text. Point to the Close button for the Page1 : Data Access Page window.

The data access page displays (Figure 9). The title is changed to Alisa Vending Services.

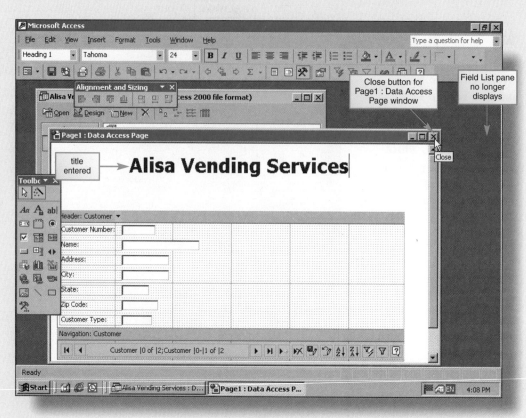

FIGURE 9

9 Click the Close button for the Page1 : Data Access Page window to close the window and then click the Yes button in the Microsoft Access dialog box to indicate you want to save your changes. When the Save As Data Access Page dialog box displays, be sure 3½ Floppy (A:) is selected and that the file name is Customer. Point to the Save button.

The Save As Data Access Page dialog box displays (Figure 10).

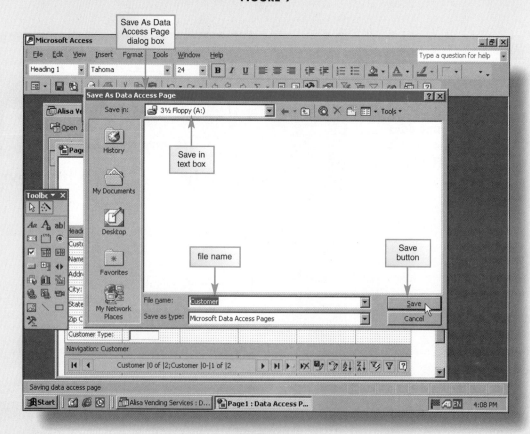

FIGURE 10

10 **Click the Save button. If you see a message similar to the one in Figure 11, click the OK button because the file location you specified is acceptable. (This message indicates that you will need to specify a Universal Naming Convention (UNC) address, instead of the file location you have specified if you want the page to be accessible over a network.)**

The data access page is created.

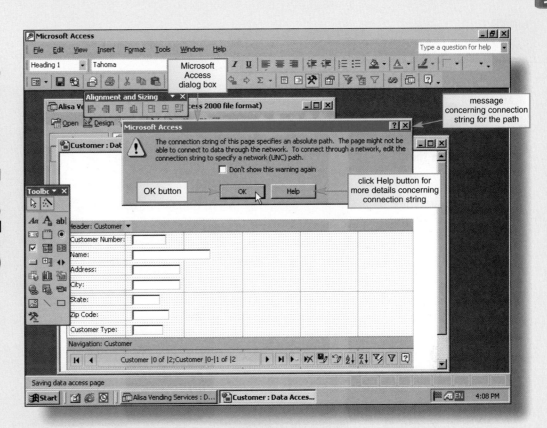

FIGURE 11

Viewing the Data Access Page

If you are connected to the Internet, you can view the data access page in the browser (see Figure 1 on page AW 1.02). To do this you use the Web Page Preview command on the shortcut menu. When not connected to the Internet, you can view the data access page using the Open command on the shortcut menu. The following steps use the Open command to view the data access page that was just created.

More *About*

Quick Reference

For a table that lists how to complete tasks covered in this book using the mouse, menu, shortcut menu, and keyboard, see the Quick Reference Summary at the back of this book or visit the Shelly Cashman Series Office XP Web page (scsite.com/offxp/qr.htm) and then click Microsoft Access 2002.

Steps View the Data Access Page

1 **With the Database window open, click the Pages object. Right-click Customer and then point to Open on the shortcut menu.**

The shortcut menu for the Customer data access page displays (Figure 12).

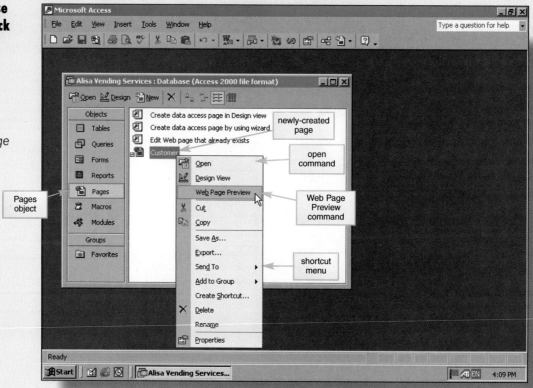

FIGURE 12

2 **Click Open on the shortcut menu and then maximize the window.**

The page displays (Figure 13).

3 **Click the Close Window button to close the data access page. Close the database.**

The page no longer displays. The database is closed.

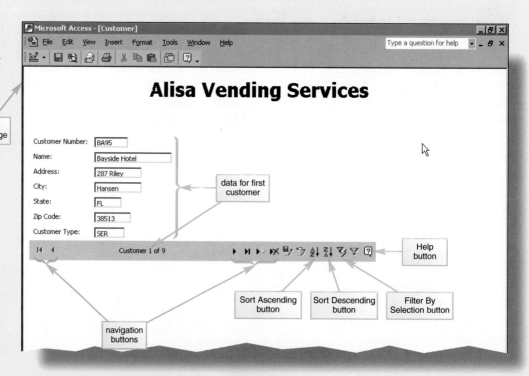

FIGURE 13

Using the Data Access Page

To use the data access page, start Internet Explorer, type the location of the data access page (for example, a:\customer.htm if you created the page on your disk), and then press the ENTER key. The page then will display and look similar to the one in Figure 1 on page AW 1.02.

You can use the navigation buttons, the Sort Ascending and Sort Descending buttons, and the Filter By Selection button just as you do when viewing a datasheet or a form in Access. You can get help on the way you use the page by clicking the Help button (see Figure 13). A book icon indicates subtopics are available. Double-clicking the icon displays the subtopics. A question mark icon indicates that information on the topic will display when you click the question mark. In Figure 14, for example, the subtopics for both Getting Started and Getting Help display. The question mark in front of "Get Help using a data access page" has been clicked so the information on that topic displays. In addition, the window has been maximized, which makes it easier to read the help information.

More About

Microsoft Certification

The Microsoft User Specialist (MOUS) Certification program provides an opportunity for you to obtain a valuable industry credential — proof that you have the Access 2002 skills required by employers. For more information, see Appendix E or visit the Shelly Cashman Series MOUS Web page at (scsite.com/offxp/cert.htm).

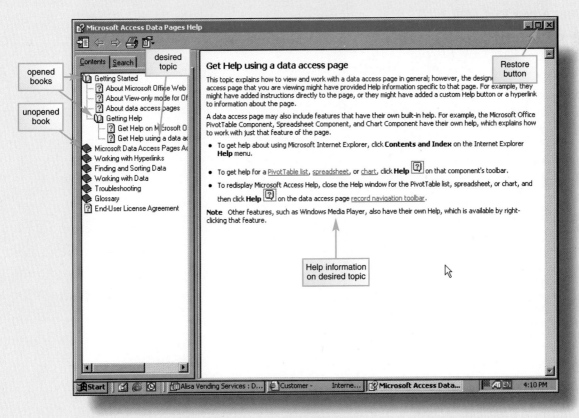

FIGURE 14

C A S E   P E R S P E C T I V E   S U M M A R Y

In this Web Feature, you created a data access page for the Customer table in the Alisa Vending Services database. This page will enable Alisa to access their database using the Internet.

Web Feature Summary

In this Web Feature, you created a data access page for the Customer table in the Alisa Vending Services database. To do so, you used the Page Wizard. You then saw how to view the data access page from within Access. Finally, you saw how to use the data access page.

What You Should Know

Having completed this Web Feature, you now should be able to perform the following tasks:

▶ Create a Data Access Page (*AW 1.02*)
▶ Open a Database (*AW 1.02*)
▶ View a Data Access Page (*AW 1.07*)

More *About*

Publishing to the Internet: Saving Other Objects

You also can publish other objects such as reports and datasheets to the Internet. To publish a datasheet or a report to the Internet, save the object as a Web page in HTML format. To do so, select the name of the object in the Database window, click File on the menu bar, and then click Export. In the Save As Type box, click HTML Documents.

In the Lab

1 Creating a Data Access Page for the Beyond Clean Database

Instructions: Start Access. Open the Beyond Clean database that you used in Project 3 or see your instructor for information on accessing the files required for this book. Perform the following tasks.

1. Use the Page Wizard to create a data access page for the Custodian table (Figure 15). When the Page Wizard dialog box displays that asks what sort order you want for your records, select Custodian Id.

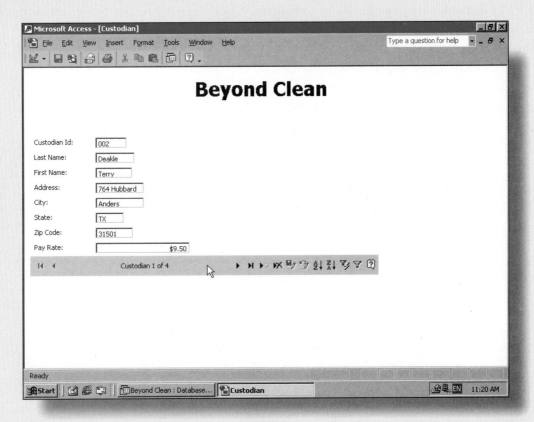

FIGURE 15

2. Print the data access page. To print the page, open the page, click File on the menu bar, and then click Print.

In the Lab

2 Using a Data Access Page

Instructions: Make sure the disk containing the Beyond Clean database and the data access page you created in the In the Lab 1 is in drive A. Perform the following tasks.

1. Start Access and then open the Custodian data access page.
2. Use the data access page to add yourself as a new record to the Custodian table. Use 099 as the custodian id, and $9.25 as the hourly pay rate. Refer to Figure 1-81 on page A 1.55 for the maximum field sizes for the remaining fields. Close the data access page.
3. Open the Custodian table in Datasheet view. You now should have five records. Print the table.
4. Open the Custodian data access page.
5. Use the data access page to delete the record you just added and then close the page.
6. Open the Custodian table in Datasheet view. Print the table and then quit Access.

Microsoft Access 2002

PROJECT

4

Reports, Forms, and Combo Boxes

You will have mastered the material in this project when you can:

OBJECTIVES

- Create a query for a report
- Use the Report Wizard to create a report
- Use the Report window to modify a report design
- Move between Design view and Print Preview
- Recognize sections in a report
- Save and close a report
- Print a report
- Create a report with grouping and subtotals
- Use the Form Wizard to create an initial form
- Use the Form window to modify a form design
- Place a calculated field on a form
- Place a combo box on a form
- Place a title on a form
- View data using a form

The Art of Navigation

"There will come an age in the far-off years When ocean shall unloose the bonds of things, When the whole broad earth shall be revealed."

—Lucius Annaeus Seneca

Whether traveling by car, boat, or airplane, your goal is to arrive safely at your destination. As you make the journey, you may interact with some of the latest technology. Many vehicles manufactured today include some type of onboard navigation system to help point drivers in the right direction. The pocket-sized computers used in these systems include databases similar to the database you have developed in the Access projects in this book; only these databases cover the Earth's surface.

These computers collect radio signals emitted from government

you are here X

satellites and calculate the user's position and altitude. Then, they interface with commercial databases and display such useful information as where the closest automated teller machine is located or how long it will take to get to the campground.

The technology is the offspring of once-secret military Cold War technology. The Department of Defense spent an estimated $10 billion developing the global positioning system (GPS) during the 1970s and launched its first satellite in 1978. Now, 24 GPS satellites orbit high above the Earth.

Expanding on the military's technological successes using the GPS during Operation Desert Storm, enterprising engineers developed civilian satellite-navigation systems that use mapped data from databases to guide users in a variety of applications.

Advanced mobile GPS technology allows these systems to map out a route to any known destination on a small color screen positioned near the dashboard and track the precise location of a vehicle as it moves along that route. The systems recalibrate if a motorist makes a wrong turn, and some supply audio directions in addition to the in-dash visual display. The OnStar® system, available with many makes and models, has an emergency function that can be used at the touch of a single button on the OnStar handset. The GPS automatically calculates the vehicle's location and displays it on the Advisor's screen so the information can be relayed to an emergency provider with the request for assistance.

In another system, GPS technology in airplanes helps pilots save time and fuel. Databases contain information on airport locations and radio frequencies, and they interact with the satellite signals to compute the aircraft's precise location, direct route to an airport, time enroute, airspeed, and ground speed.

Hikers and boaters benefit from handheld GPS navigating technology. Databases for hikers contain details on popular campgrounds, fishing holes, and hiking trails, and the computer can calculate current position, walking speed, direction to these sites, and estimated time of arrival. GPSs for boaters display the course traveled, distance to go, miles off course, latitude and longitude, and speed.

Entrepreneurial developers have engineered systems for trucking companies to track the location of their vehicles on the roads, for farmers to analyze their crops, police to track drug dealers, and scientists to check movements of the San Andreas fault.

Ancient travelers looked to the heavens to chart their courses — the sun by day and the stars by night, mariners mapped their voyages using drawings and charts, and over the centuries, sailors developed increasingly sophisticated instruments to navigate the seas. Today, the most important advances in the age-old art of navigation are the mobile computers and extensive databases that comprise the global positioning system satellites that watch from above.

Microsoft Access 2002

Reports, Forms, and Combo Boxes

PROJECT

4

C A S E   P E R S P E C T I V E

Alisa Vending Services has realized several benefits from its database of customers and drivers. For example, the management and staff greatly appreciate the ease with which they can query the database. They hope to realize additional benefits using two custom reports. The first report includes the number, name, address, city, state, Zip code, and total amount (amount paid plus current due amount) of each customer. The second report groups the records by driver number. Subtotals of the amount paid and current due amounts display after each group, and grand totals display at the end of the report. The management also wants to improve the data-entry process by using a custom form. In addition to a title, the form will contain the fields arranged in two columns and include the total amount, to be calculated automatically by adding the amount paid and current due amounts. To assist users in entering the correct customer type, users should be able to select from a list of possible customer types. To help users in entering the correct driver number, users should be able to select from a list of existing drivers. Your task is to help Alisa Vending Services with these requirements.

Introduction

This project creates two reports and a form. The first report is shown in Figure 4-1. This report includes the customer number, name, address, city, state, Zip code, and total amount (amount paid plus current due amount) of each customer. It is similar to the one produced by clicking the Print button on the toolbar. It has two significant differences, however.

First, not all fields are included. The Customer table includes a Customer Type field (added in Project 3), an Amount Paid field, a Current Due field, and a Driver Number field, none of which appears on this report. Second, this report contains a Total Amount field, which is not included in the Customer table.

The second report is shown in Figure 4-2 on page 4.06. It is similar to the report shown in Figure 4-1 but contains an additional feature, grouping. **Grouping** means creating separate collections of records sharing some common characteristic. In the report shown in Figure 4-2, for example, the records are grouped by driver number. The report includes three separate groups: one for driver 30, one for driver 60, and one for driver 75. The appropriate driver number appears before each group, and the total of the amount paid and current due amounts for the customers in the group (called a **subtotal**) displays after the group. At the end of the report is a grand total of the amount paid and current due amounts for all groups.

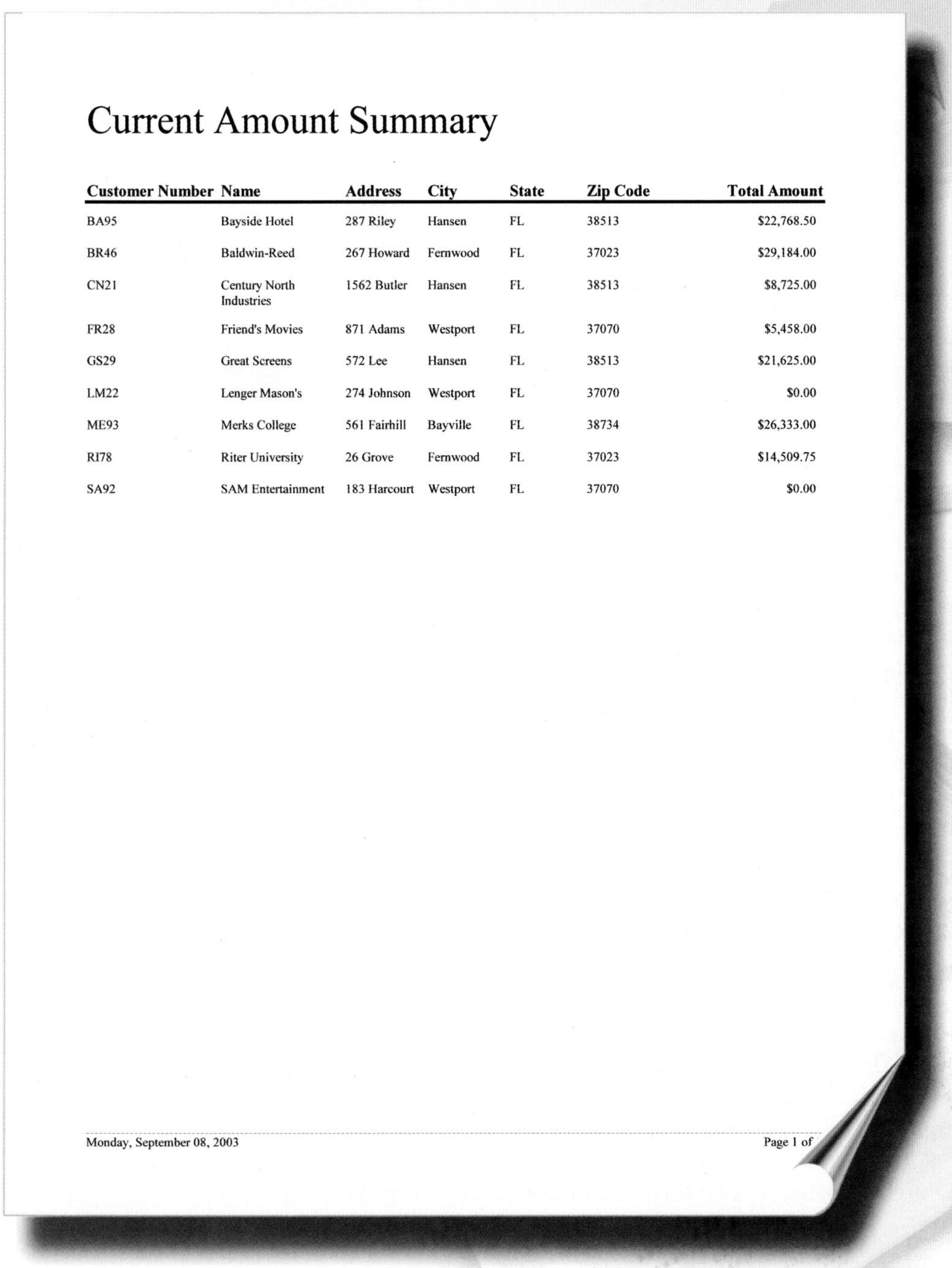

Current Amount Summary

Customer Number	Name	Address	City	State	Zip Code	Total Amount
BA95	Bayside Hotel	287 Riley	Hansen	FL	38513	$22,768.50
BR46	Baldwin-Reed	267 Howard	Fernwood	FL	37023	$29,184.00
CN21	Century North Industries	1562 Butler	Hansen	FL	38513	$8,725.00
FR28	Friend's Movies	871 Adams	Westport	FL	37070	$5,458.00
GS29	Great Screens	572 Lee	Hansen	FL	38513	$21,625.00
LM22	Lenger Mason's	274 Johnson	Westport	FL	37070	$0.00
ME93	Merks College	561 Fairhill	Bayville	FL	38734	$26,333.00
RI78	Riter University	26 Grove	Fernwood	FL	37023	$14,509.75
SA92	SAM Entertainment	183 Harcourt	Westport	FL	37070	$0.00

Monday, September 08, 2003   Page 1 of

FIGURE 4-1

Driver/Customer Report

Driver Number	First Name	Last Name	Customer Number	Name	Amount Paid	Current Due
30	Larissa	Tuttle				
			BA95	Bayside Hotel	$21,876.00	$892.50
			ME93	Merks College	$24,761.00	$1,572.00
					$46,637.00	$2,464.50
60	Frank	Powers				
			BR46	Baldwin-Reed	$26,512.00	$2,672.00
			CN21	Century North Industries	$8,725.00	$0.00
			GS29	Great Screens	$21,625.00	$0.00
			LM22	Lenger Mason's	$0.00	$0.00
					$56,862.00	$2,672.00
75	Jose	Ortiz				
			FR28	Friend's Movies	$4,256.00	$1,202.00
			RI78	Riter University	$11,682.25	$2,827.50
			SA92	SAM Entertainment	$0.00	$0.00
					$15,938.25	$4,029.50
Grand Total					$119,437.25	$9,166.00

Monday, September 08, 2003 Page 1 c

FIGURE 4-2

The **custom form** to be created is shown in Figure 4-3. Although similar to the form created in Project 1, it offers some distinct advantages. Some of the differences are merely aesthetic. The form has a title and the fields are rearranged in two columns. In addition, two other major differences are present. This form displays the total amount and will calculate it automatically by adding the amount paid and current due amounts. Second, to assist users in entering the correct customer type and driver number, the form contains **combo boxes**, which are boxes that allow you to select entries from a list. An arrow displays in the Driver Number field, for example. Clicking the arrow causes a list of the drivers in the Driver table to display as shown in the figure. You then either can type the desired driver number or click the desired driver.

> **More About**
>
> **The Access Help System**
>
> Need Help? It is no further than the Ask a Question box in the upper-right corner of the window. Click the box that contains the text, Type a question for help (Figure 4-3), type `help`, and then press the ENTER key. Access will respond with a list of items you can click to learn about obtaining help on any Access-related topic. To find out what is new in Access 2002, type `what's new in Access` in the Ask a Question box.

Project Four — Creating Reports and Forms for Alisa Vending Services

You are to create the reports requested by the management of Alisa Vending Services. In the first report you will use a query that includes a calculated field as the basis for the report. In the second report you will group records by driver number and display subtotal and grand total amounts.

You also must create the form the management deems to be important to the data-entry process. The form includes two combo boxes.

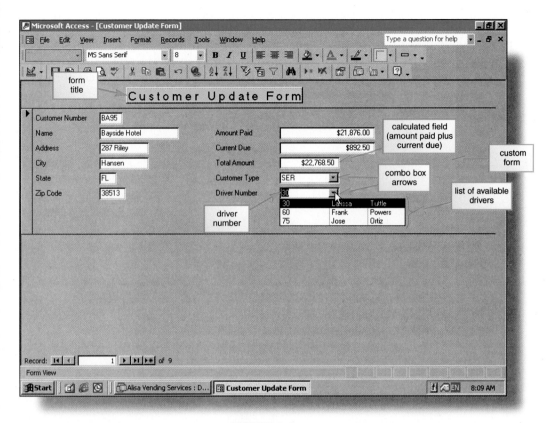

FIGURE 4-3

Opening the Database

Before you create the reports or forms, you must open the database. Perform the following steps to complete this task.

TO OPEN A DATABASE

1 Click the Start button, click Programs on the Start menu, and then click Microsoft Access on the Programs submenu.

2 Click Open on the Database toolbar and then click 3½ Floppy (A:) in the Look in box. Make sure the database called Alisa Vending Services is selected.

3 Click the Open button.

The database is open and the Alisa Vending Services : Database window displays.

Report Creation

The simplest way to create a report design is to use the **Report Wizard**. For some reports, the Report Wizard can produce exactly the desired report. For others, however, you first must use the Report Wizard to produce a report that is as close as possible to the desired report. Then use the **Report window** to modify the report and transform it into the correct report. In either case, once the report is created and saved, you can print it at any time. Access will use the current data in the database for the report, formatting and arranging it in exactly the way you specified when the report was created.

Creating a Report

There are two alternatives to using the Report Wizard to create reports. You can use AutoReport to create a very simple report that includes all fields and records in the table or query. Design view also allows you to create a report from scratch.

Using Queries for Reports

The records in the report will display in the specified order if you have sorted the data in the query. You also can enter criteria in the query, in which case only records that satisfy the criteria will be included in the report. Reports based on queries open faster than those based on tables.

If a report uses only the fields in a single table, use the table as a basis for the report. If the report uses extra fields (such as Total Amount), however, the simplest way to create the report is to create a query using the steps you learned in Project 2. The query should contain only the fields required for the report. This query forms the basis for the report.

Creating a Query

The process of creating a query for a report is identical to the process of creating queries for any other purpose. Perform the following steps to create the query for the first report.

 To Create a Query

1 If necessary, in the Database window click Tables on the Objects bar, and then click Customer. Click the New Object: AutoForm button arrow on the Database toolbar. Click Query. Be sure Design View is selected, and then click the OK button. Maximize the Query1 : Select Query window. Resize the upper and lower panes and the Customer field list so all the fields in the Customer table display.

2 Double-click Customer Number. Select Ascending as the sort order for the field. Double-click the names of the fields to include the Name, Address, City, State, and Zip Code fields in the design grid. If necessary, click the right scroll arrow to scroll the fields so a blank column displays after the column containing the Zip Code field. Right-click in the Field row of the column for the additional field (the field after the Zip Code field). Point to Zoom on the shortcut menu.

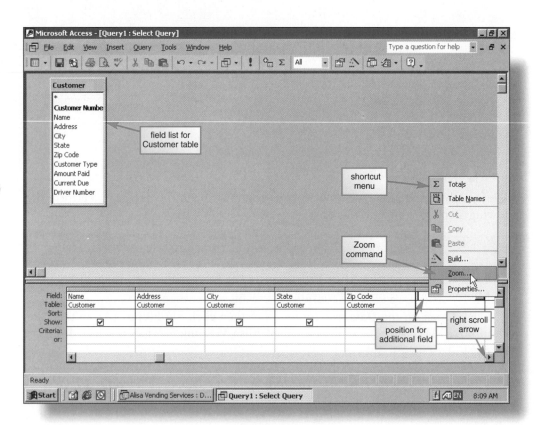

FIGURE 4-4

The shortcut menu for the extra field displays (Figure 4-4). The Customer Number field has been shifted to the left and does not display.

3 Click Zoom on the shortcut menu. Type Total Amount:[Amount Paid]+[Current Due] in the Zoom dialog box and then point to the OK button (Figure 4-5).

4 Click the OK button. Click the Close Window button for the Select Query window and then click the Yes button.

5 Type Customer Amount Query as the name of the query and then click the OK button.

The query is saved, and the Select Query window closes.

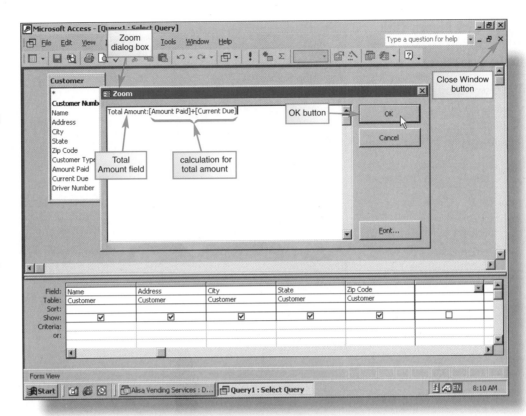

FIGURE 4-5

Creating a Report

Next, you will create a report using the Report Wizard. Access leads you through a series of choices and questions and then creates the report automatically. Perform the following steps to create the report shown in Figure 4-1 on page A 4.05.

Steps **To Create a Report**

1 If necessary, in the Database window click Queries on the Objects bar, and then click Customer Amount Query. Click the New Object: Query button arrow on the Database toolbar and then point to Report (Figure 4-6).

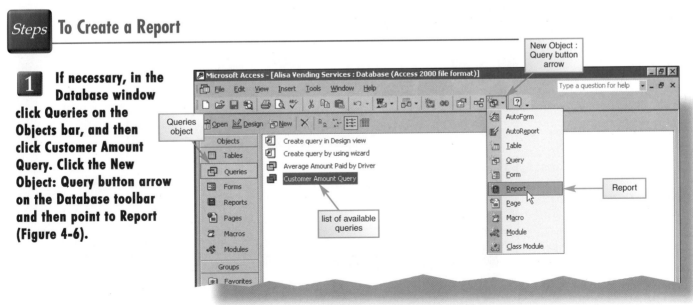

FIGURE 4-6

2 **Click Report. Click Report Wizard. Point to the OK button.**

The New Report dialog box displays and the Customer Amount Query is selected (Figure 4-7).

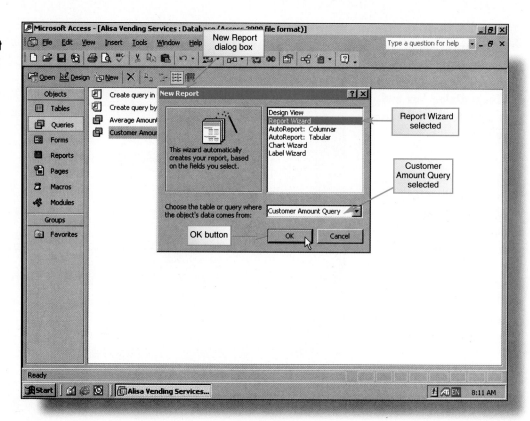

FIGURE 4-7

3 **Click the OK button and then point to the Add All Fields button.**

The Report Wizard dialog box displays, requesting the fields for the report (Figure 4-8). To add the selected field to the list of fields on the report, use the Add Field button. To add all fields, use the Add All Fields button.

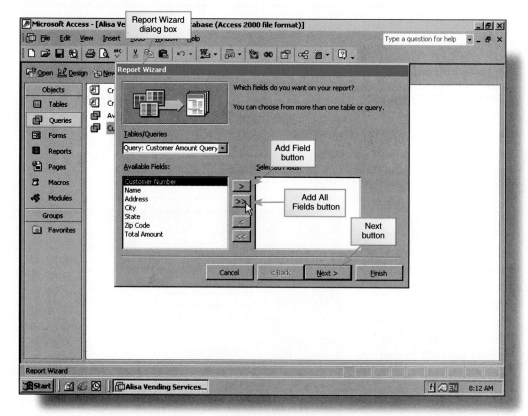

FIGURE 4-8

4 **Click the Add All Fields button to add all the fields, and then click the Next button.**

The next Report Wizard dialog box displays, requesting the field or fields for grouping levels (Figure 4-9). This report will not include grouping levels.

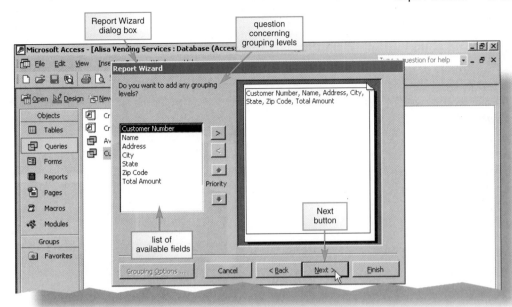

FIGURE 4-9

5 **Click the Next button.**

The next Report Wizard dialog box displays, requesting the sort order for the report (Figure 4-10). The query already is sorted in the appropriate order, so you will not need to specify a sort order.

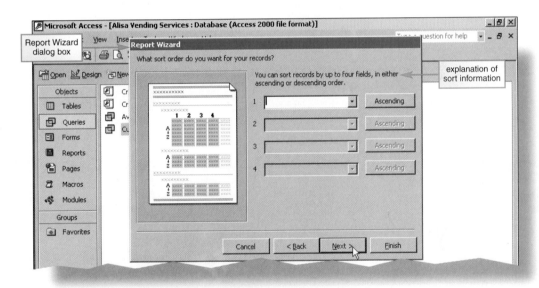

FIGURE 4-10

6 **Click the Next button.**

The next Report Wizard dialog box displays, requesting your report layout preference (Figure 4-11).

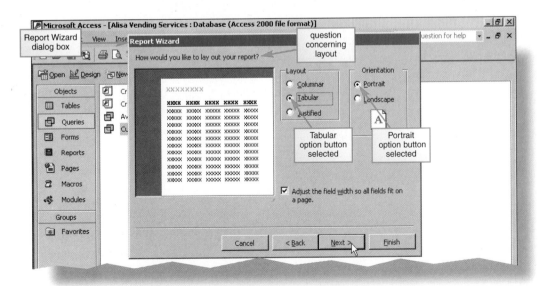

FIGURE 4-11

Microsoft **Access 2002**

| 7 | **Be sure the options selected in the Report Wizard dialog box on your screen match those shown in Figure 4-11 on the previous page, and then click the Next button. If Formal is not already selected, click Formal to select it. Point to the Next button.** |

The next Report Wizard dialog box displays, requesting a style for the report (Figure 4-12). The Formal style is selected.

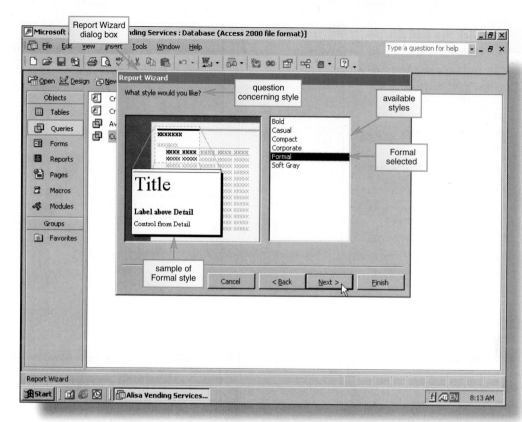

FIGURE 4-12

| 8 | **Click the Next button and then type** Current Amount Summary **as the report title. Point to the Finish button.** |

The next Report Wizard dialog box displays, requesting a title for the report (Figure 4-13). Current Amount Summary is entered as the title.

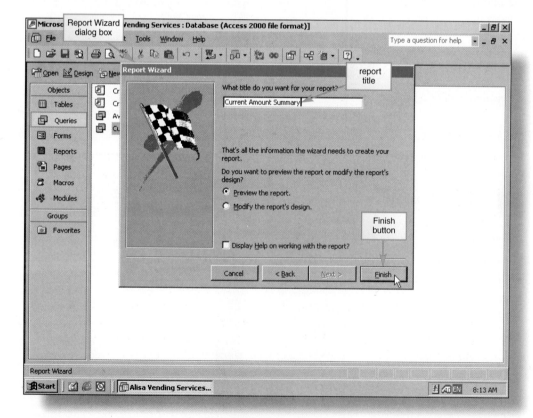

FIGURE 4-13

9 **Click the Finish button.**

The report design is complete and displays in Print Preview (Figure 4-14). (If your computer displays an entire page of the report, click the portion of the report displaying the mouse pointer.)

10 **Click the Close Window button in the window containing the report to close the report.**

The report no longer displays.

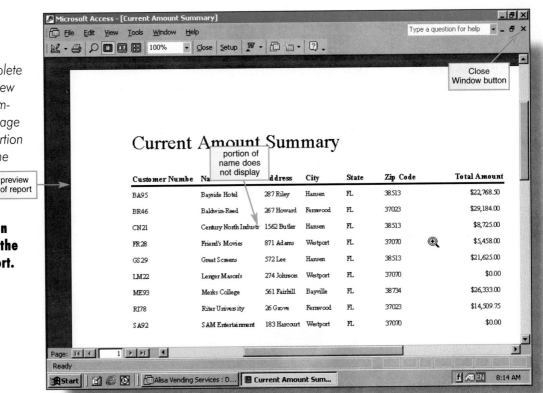

FIGURE 4-14

Because of the insufficient amount of space allowed in the report shown in Figure 4-14, some of the data does not display completely. The final portion of the name of Century North Industries does not display, for example. You will need to correct this problem.

Using Design View

Within the Report window, the different possible views are Design view and Print Preview. Use **Design view** to modify the design (layout) of the report. Use **Print Preview** to see the report with sample data. To move from Design view to Print Preview, click the Print Preview button on the Report Design toolbar. To move from Print Preview to Design view, click the button labeled Close on the Print Preview toolbar.

Within Print Preview, you can switch between viewing an entire page and viewing a portion of a page. To do so, click somewhere within the report. When pointing within the report, the mouse pointer will change shape to a magnifying glass.

In Design view, you can modify the design of the report. A **toolbox** is available in Design view that allows you to create special objects for the report. The toolbox also can obscure a portion of the report. You can use the Toolbox button on the Report Design toolbar to remove it and then return it to the screen when needed. Because you use the toolbox frequently when modifying report and form designs, it is desirable to leave it on the screen, however. You can move the toolbar to different positions on the screen using a process referred to as **docking**. To dock the toolbox in a different position, simply drag the title bar of the toolbox to one of the edges of the window. The bottom of the screen usually is a good position for it.

Perform the steps on the next page to move to Design view. You also will remove the **field list** that displays, because you will not need it.

Other Ways

1. Click Reports on Objects bar, click New button, click Report Wizard to create report
2. Click Reports on Objects bar, click Create report by using wizard
3. On Insert menu click Report, click Report Wizard to create report
4. In Voice Command mode, say "Insert, Report"

More About

Previewing a Report

You can view two pages at the same time when previewing a report by clicking the Two Pages button on the toolbar. You can view multiple pages by clicking Multiple Pages on the toolbar, and then clicking the number of pages to view.

Steps **To Move to Design View and Dock the Toolbox**

1 **Click the Reports object in the Database window, right-click Current Amount Summary, and then click Design View on the shortcut menu. If a field list displays, point to its Close button.**

The report displays in Design view (Figure 4-15).

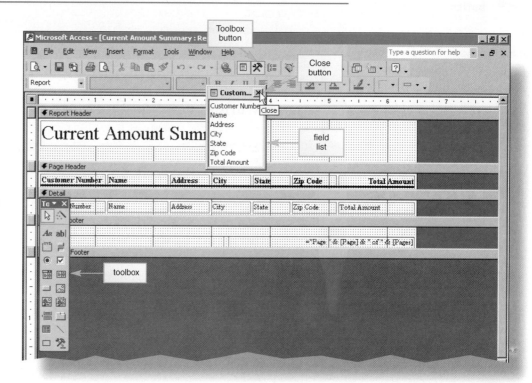

FIGURE 4-15

2 **If a field list displays, click its Close button to remove the field list from the screen. If necessary, click the Toolbox button on the Report Design toolbar to display the toolbox. If the toolbox is not docked at the bottom of the screen, dock it there by dragging its title bar to the bottom of the screen.**

The field list no longer displays, and the toolbox is docked at the bottom of the screen (Figure 4-16).

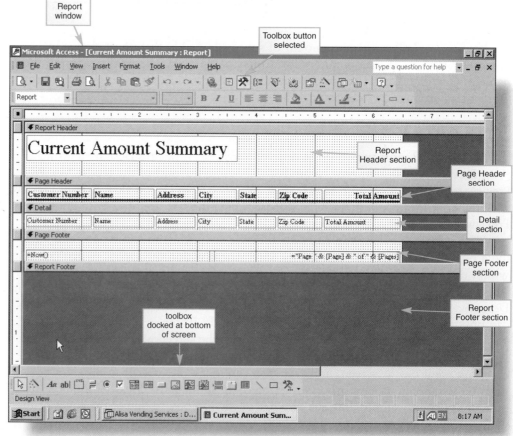

FIGURE 4-16

Other Ways

1. With report selected, click Design button
2. In Voice Command mode with report selected, say "Design"

Report Sections

Each portion of the report is described in what is termed a **section**. The sections are labeled on the screen (see Figure 4-16). Notice the following sections: Report Header section, Page Header section, Detail section, Page Footer section, and Report Footer section.

The contents of the **Report Header section** print once at the beginning of the report. The contents of the **Report Footer section** print once at the end of the report. The contents of the **Page Header section** print once at the top of each page, and the contents of the **Page Footer section** print once at the bottom of each page. The contents of the **Detail section** print once for each record in the table.

The various rectangles displaying in Figure 4-16 (Current Amount Summary, Customer Number, Name, and so on) are called **controls**. All the information on a report or form is contained in the controls. The control containing Current Amount Summary displays the report title; that is, it displays the words, Current Amount Summary. The control in the Page Header section containing Name displays the word, Name.

The controls in the Detail section display the contents of the corresponding fields. The control containing Name, for example, will display the customer's name. The controls in the Page Header section serve as **captions** for the data. The Customer Number control in this section, for example, will display the words, Customer Number, immediately above the column of customer numbers, thus making it clear to anyone reading the report that the items in the column are, in fact, customer numbers.

To move, resize, delete, or modify a control, click it. Small squares called **sizing handles** display around the border of the control. Drag the control to move it, drag one of the sizing handles to resize it, or press the DELETE key to delete it. Clicking a second time produces an insertion point in the control in order to modify its contents.

Changing Properties

Some of the changes you may make will involve using the property sheet for the control to be changed. The **property sheet** for each control is a list of properties that can be modified. By using the property sheet, you can change one or more of the control's properties. To produce the property sheet, right-click the desired control and then click Properties on the shortcut menu.

The problem of the missing data in the report shown in Figure 4-14 on page A 4.13 can be corrected in several ways.

1. Move the controls to allow more space in between them. Then, drag the appropriate handles on the controls that need to be expanded to enlarge them.
2. Use the Font Size property to select a smaller font size. This will allow more data to print in the same space.
3. Use the Can Grow property. By changing the value of this property from No to Yes, the data can be spread over two lines, thus allowing all the data to print. The name of customer CN21, for example, will have Century North on one line and Industries on the next line. Access will split data at natural break points, such as commas, spaces, and hyphens.

The first approach will work and you will use this in the second report. It can be cumbersome, however. The second approach also works but makes the report more difficult to read. The third approach, changing the Can Grow property, is the simplest method to use and generally produces a very readable report. Perform the steps on the next page to change the Can Grow property for the Detail section.

More About

Report Sections

Another common term for the sections in a report is band. The term, band-oriented applied to a report tool means that the tool is very similar to the report design feature in Access; that is, you design a report by simply modifying the contents of the various sections (bands).

More About

Changing Properties

There are a large number of properties that can be changed using the property sheet. The properties determine the structure and appearance of a control, and the characteristics of the data the control contains. For details on a particular property, click Help on the menu bar, click What's This?, and then click the property.

Steps | To Change the Can Grow Property

1 **Point below the section selector for the Detail section (Figure 4-17).**

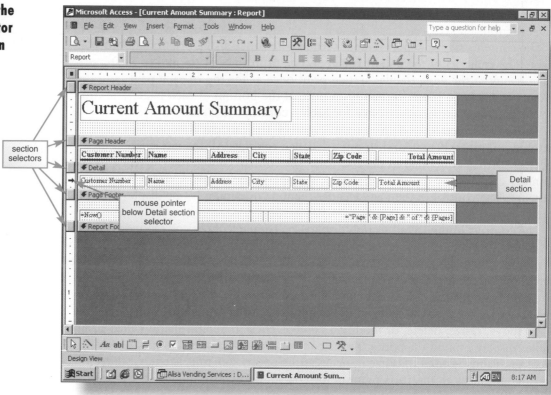

FIGURE 4-17

2 **Right-click and then point to Properties on the shortcut menu.**

The shortcut menu displays (Figure 4-18). All the controls in the Detail section are selected.

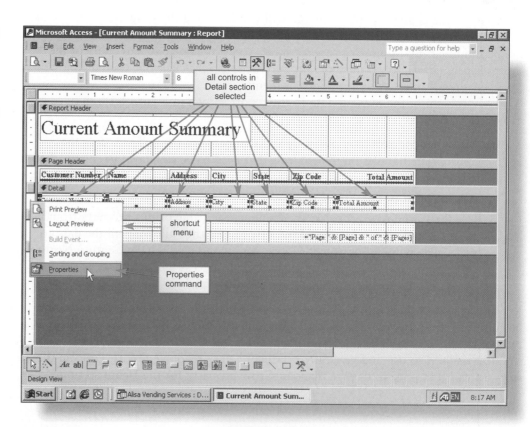

FIGURE 4-18

3 Click Properties and, if necessary, then click the All tab to ensure that all available properties display. Click the Can Grow property, click the Can Grow property box arrow, and then click Yes in the list that displays. Point to the Close button for the property sheet.

The Multiple selection property sheet displays (Figure 4-19). All the properties display in the All sheet. The value for the Can Grow property has been changed to Yes.

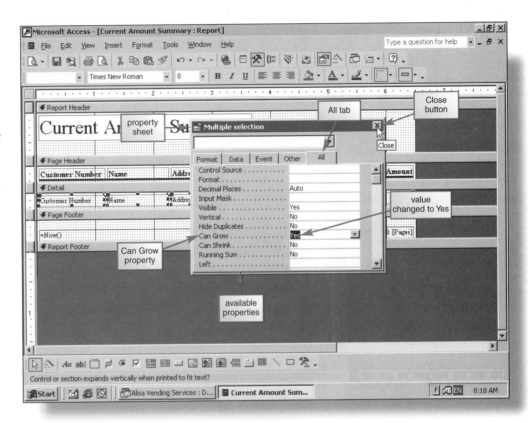

FIGURE 4-19

4 Close the property sheet by clicking its Close button, and then point to the Print Preview button on the Report Design toolbar (Figure 4-20).

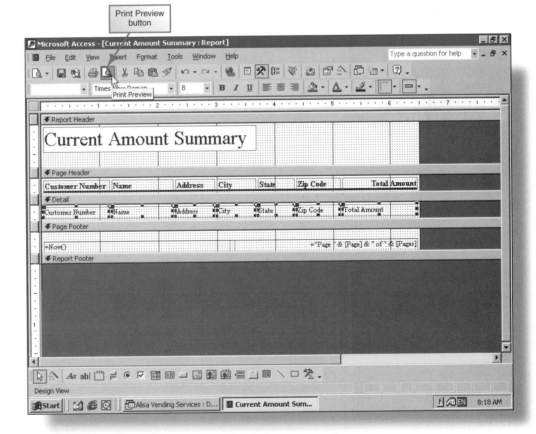

FIGURE 4-20

5 Click the Print Preview button.

A portion of the report displays (Figure 4-21). The names now display completely by extending to a second line. (If your computer displays an entire page, click the portion of the report displaying the mouse pointer in the figure.)

preview of report

Microsoft Access - [Current Amount Summary]

File   Edit   View   Tools   Window   Help

Type a question for help

100%   Close   Setup

Close button

Current Amount Summary

entire name displays (split over two lines)

Customer Numbe	Name			State	Zip Code	Total Amount
BA95	Bayside Hotel			FL	38513	$22,768.50
BR46	Baldwin-Reed	267 Howard	Fernwood	FL	37023	$29,184.00
CN21	Century North Industries	1562 Butler	Hansen	FL	38513	$8,725.00
FR28	Friend's Movies	871 Adams	Westport	FL	37070	$5,458.00
GS29	Great Screens	572 Lee	Hansen	FL	38513	$21,625.00
LM22	Lenger Mason's	274 Johnson	Westport	FL	37070	$0.00
ME93	Merks College	561 Fairhill	Bayville	FL	38734	$26,333.00
RI78	Riter University	26 Grove	Fernwood	FL	37023	$14,509.75
SA92	SAM Entertainment	183 Harcourt	Westport	FL	37070	$0.00

Page: 1

Ready

Start   Alisa Vending Services : D...   Current Amount Sum...   EN   8:19 AM

FIGURE 4-21

Enlarging Controls

If you want to make a slight adjustment to a control, it often is easier to hold down the SHIFT key and use the appropriate arrow key.

Enlarging Controls

In some cases, the contents of a control may appear to display completely in Design View, but yet not completely display in the report. In such a case, it typically is the last letter that does not display. For example, the control in the Page Header section might show Customer Number completely, but the report might read Customer Numbe. (The final r is missing.)

To fix this problem, it usually is sufficient to expand slightly the size of the control. To do so, click the control to select it and then drag the right sizing handle slightly to the right. If your report displays correctly, skip the following steps. Otherwise, perform the following steps to enlarge slightly the Customer Number control in the Page Header section, if necessary.

To Enlarge Controls

1 **Click the Close button on the Print Preview toolbar (Figure 4-21) to return to the Report window in Design view. Point to the Customer Number control in the Page Header section (Figure 4-22).**

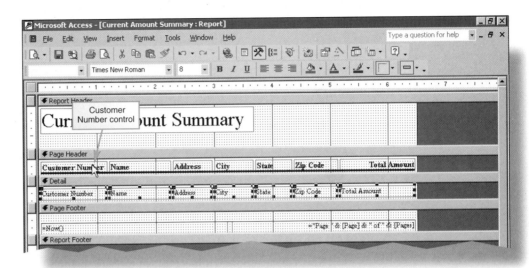

FIGURE 4-22

2 **Click the Customer Number control and then point to the right sizing handle.**

The Customer Number control is selected and the mouse pointer shape has changed to a two-headed horizontal arrow (Figure 4-23).

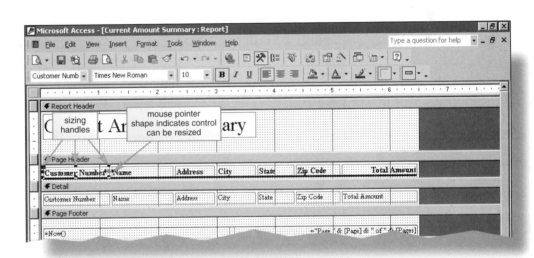

FIGURE 4-23

3 **Drag the right sizing handle slightly to the right to the approximate position shown in Figure 4-24. You can check to see if you have enlarged the control sufficiently by previewing the report. If the contents still do not display completely, return to the report design and expand the control further.**

FIGURE 4-24

In some cases, you may not have enough room to expand a control in the Page Header section. If so, you will need to take another approach, such as breaking the heading over two lines, as illustrated in the next report you will create.

Saving and Closing a Report

To close a report, close the window using the window's Close Window button in the upper-right corner of the window. Then indicate whether or not you want to save your changes. Perform the following step to close the report.

TO SAVE AND CLOSE A REPORT

1 Close the Report window and then click the Yes button to save the report.

The report no longer displays. The changes are saved.

Printing a Report

To print a report, right-click the report in the Database window, and then click Print on the shortcut menu. Perform the following steps to print the Current Amount Summary report.

TO PRINT A REPORT

1 If necessary, click the Reports object in the Database window and then right-click Current Amount Summary.

2 Click Print on the shortcut menu.

The report prints. It should look like the report shown in Figure 4-1 on page A 4.05.

More *About*

Grouping in a Report

To force each group to begin on a new page of the report, change the value of the ForceNewPage property for the Group Header section from None to Before Section. The ForceNewPage property does not apply to Page Header or Page Footer sections.

Grouping in a Report

Grouping arranges the records in your report. When records are grouped in a report, separate collections of records are created from those that share a common characteristic. In the report shown in Figure 4-2 on page A 4.06, for example, the records are grouped by driver number. Three separate groups were formed, one for each driver.

In grouping, reports typically include two additional types of sections: a group header and a group footer. A **group header** is printed before the records in a particular group are printed, and a **group footer** is printed after the group. In Figure 4-2, the group header indicates the driver number and name. The group footer includes the total of the amount paid and current due amounts for the customers assigned to that driver. Such a total is called a **subtotal**, because it is a subset of the overall total.

Creating a Second Report

As you did when you created the first report, you will use the Report Wizard to create the second report. This time, however, you will select fields from two tables. To do so, you will select the first table (for example, Driver) and then select the fields from this table you would like to include. Next, you will select the second table (for example, Customer) and then select the fields from the second table. Perform the following steps to create the report shown in Figure 4-2.

Steps **To Create a Second Report**

1 In the Database window, click the Reports object and then right-click Create report by using wizard. Click Design View on the shortcut menu. When the Report Wizard dialog box displays, click the Tables/Queries box arrow and then click Table: Driver. Point to the Add Field button.

The Report Wizard dialog box displays, requesting the fields for the report (Figure 4-25). Fields from the Driver table display. The Driver Number field is selected.

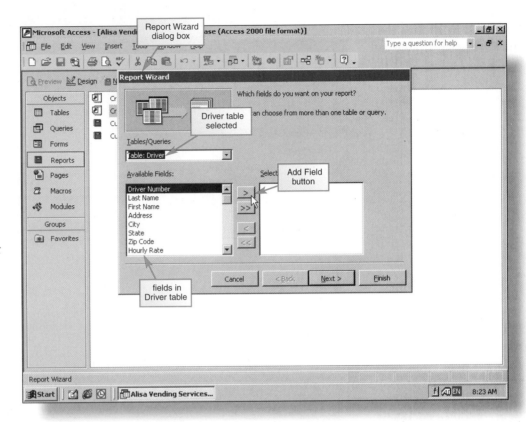

FIGURE 4-25

2 Click the Add Field button to add the Driver Number field. Add the First Name field by clicking it and then clicking the Add Field button. Add the Last Name field in the same manner. Select Table: Customer in the Tables/Queries list box and then point to the Add Field button.

The Driver Number, First Name, and Last Name fields are selected (Figure 4-26). The fields from the Customer table display in the Available Fields box.

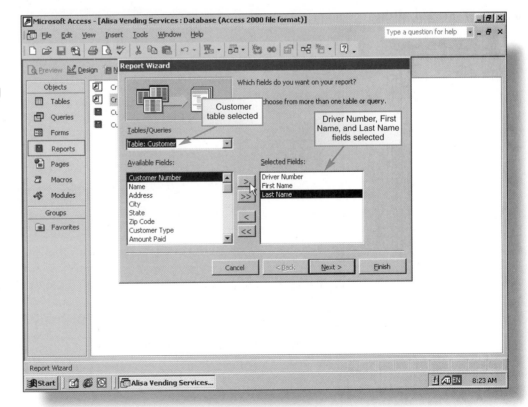

FIGURE 4-26

3 Add the Customer Number, Name, Amount Paid, and Current Due fields by clicking the field and then clicking the Add Field button. Click the Next button.

The next Report Wizard dialog box displays (Figure 4-27). Because the Driver and Customer tables are related, the wizard is asking you to indicate how the data is to be viewed; that is, the way the report is to be organized. The report may be organized by Driver or by Customer.

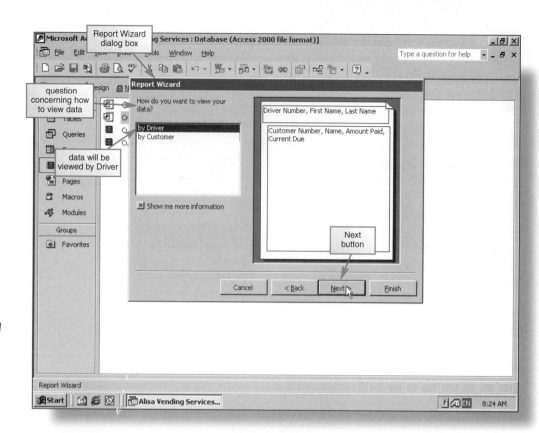

FIGURE 4-27

4 Because the report is to be viewed by driver and by Driver already is selected, click the Next button.

Access groups the report automatically by Driver Number, which is the primary key of the Driver table (Figure 4-28). The next Report Wizard dialog box displays, asking for additional grouping levels other than the Driver Number.

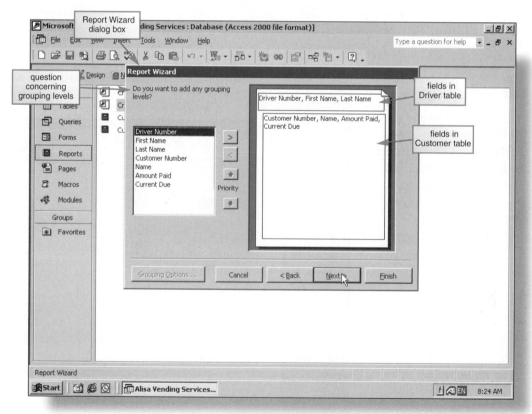

FIGURE 4-28

5 Because no additional grouping levels are required, click the Next button. Click the box 1 box arrow and then click the Customer Number field in the list. Point to the Summary Options button.

The next Report Wizard dialog box displays, requesting the sort order for detail records in the report; that is, the way in which records will be sorted within each of the groups (Figure 4-29). The Customer Number field is selected for the sort order, indicating that within the group of customers of any driver, the customers will be sorted by customer number.

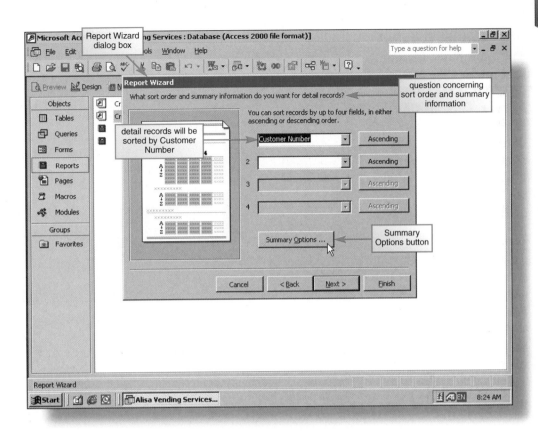

FIGURE 4-29

6 Click the Summary Options button. Point to the Sum check box in the row labeled Amount Paid.

The Summary Options dialog box displays (Figure 4-30). This dialog box allows you to indicate any statistics you want calculated in the report by clicking the appropriate check box.

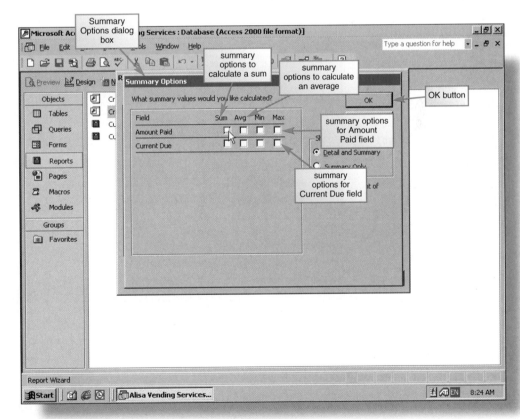

FIGURE 4-30

7 Click the Sum check box in the Amount Paid row and the Sum check box in the Current Due row. Click the OK button in the Summary Options dialog box, and then click the Next button in the Report Wizard dialog box. Click the Landscape option button.

The next Report Wizard dialog box displays, requesting your report layout preference (Figure 4-31). The Stepped layout, which is the correct one, already is selected. To see the effect of any of the others, click the appropriate option button. Landscape orientation is selected.

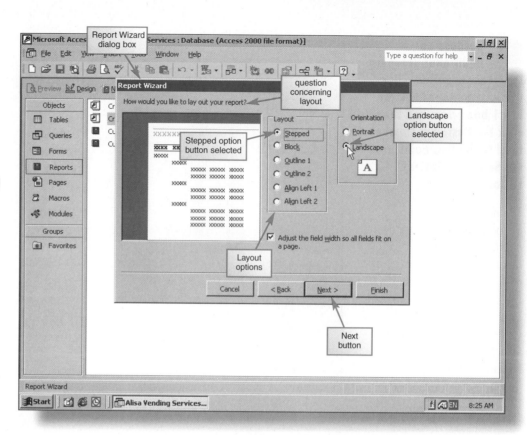

FIGURE 4-31

8 Be sure the options selected in the Report Wizard dialog box on your screen match those shown in Figure 4-31, and then click the Next button. If necessary, click Formal to select it.

The next Report Wizard dialog box displays, requesting a style for the report. The Formal style is selected (Figure 4-32).

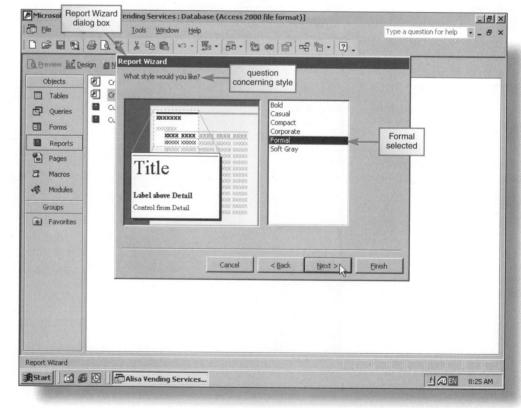

FIGURE 4-32

9 **Click the Next button and then type** Driver/Customer Report **as the report title. Point to the Finish button.**

The next Report Wizard dialog box displays, requesting a title for the report (Figure 4-33). Driver/Customer Report is typed as the title.

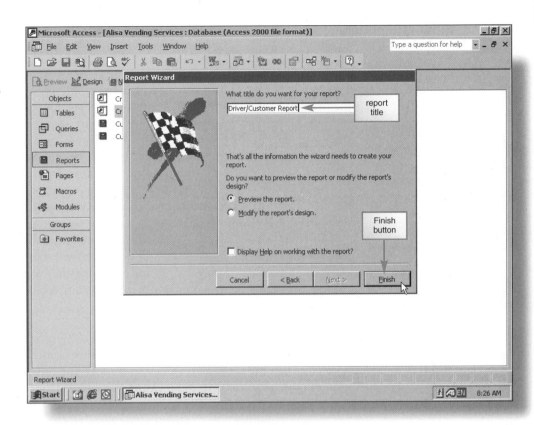

FIGURE 4-33

10 **Click the Finish button.**

The report design is complete and displays in the Print Preview window (Figure 4-34).

11 **Close the report by clicking the Close Window button for the window containing the report.**

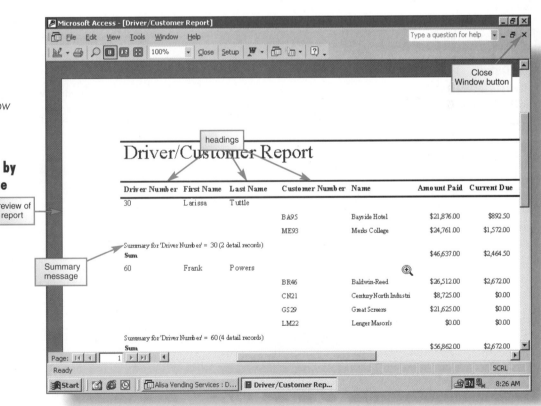

FIGURE 4-34

Reviewing the Report Design

You will find three major differences between the report shown in Figure 4-34 on the previous page and the one illustrated in Figure 4-2 on page A 4.06. The first is that all the column headings in Figure 4-34 are on a single line, whereas they extend over two lines in the report in Figure 4-2. The second difference is that the report in Figure 4-2 does not contain the message that begins, Summary for Driver Number. There are other messages found on the report in Figure 4-34 that are not on the report in Figure 4-2, but they are included in a portion of the report that does not display. The third difference is that the customer name for Century North Industries does not display completely.

To complete the report design, you must change the column headings and remove these extra messages. In addition, you will move the Amount Paid and Current Due fields to make room for enlarging the Name field. You then will enlarge the Name field so the values display completely.

Removing Unwanted Controls

To remove the extra messages, or any other control, first click the control to select it. Then press the DELETE key to remove the unwanted control. Perform the following steps to remove the unwanted controls from the report.

Steps: To Remove Unwanted Controls

1 Be sure the Reports object is selected in the Database window, right-click Driver/Customer Report, and then click Design View on the shortcut menu. If a field list displays, remove it from the screen by clicking its Close button. Point to the control that begins, ="Summary for " (Figure 4-35).

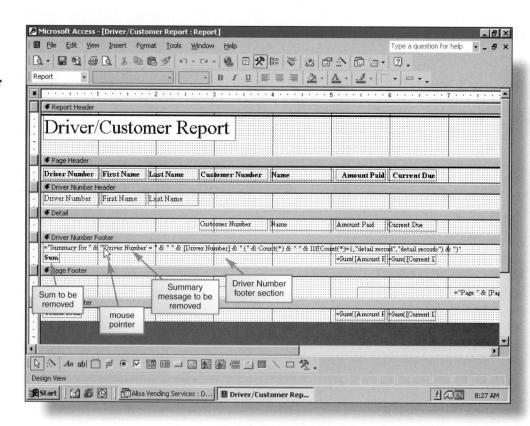

FIGURE 4-35

2 **Click the control to select it, and then press the DELETE key to delete it. In a similar fashion, delete the control below that contains Sum.**

The controls have been removed (Figure 4-36).

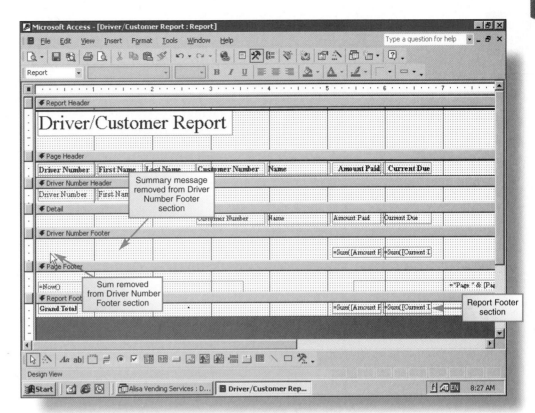

FIGURE 4-36

Enlarging the Page Header Section

The current Page Header section is not large enough to encompass the desired column headings because several of them extend over two lines. Thus, before changing the column headings, you must **enlarge** the Page Header. To do so, drag the bottom border of the Page Header section down. A bold line in the Page Header section immediately below the column headings also must be dragged down.

Perform the steps on the next page to enlarge the Page Header section and move the bold line.

Steps **To Enlarge the Page Header Section**

1 Point to the bottom border of the Page Header section (Figure 4-37). The mouse pointer shape changes to a two-headed vertical arrow with a crossbar.

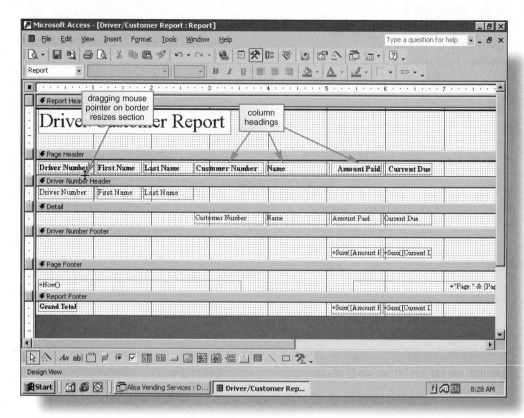

FIGURE 4-37

2 Drag the mouse pointer down to enlarge the size of the Page Header section to that shown in Figure 4-38, click the bold line in the Page Header section, and then drag the bold line down to the position shown in the figure. The mouse pointer will display as a hand as you drag the line.

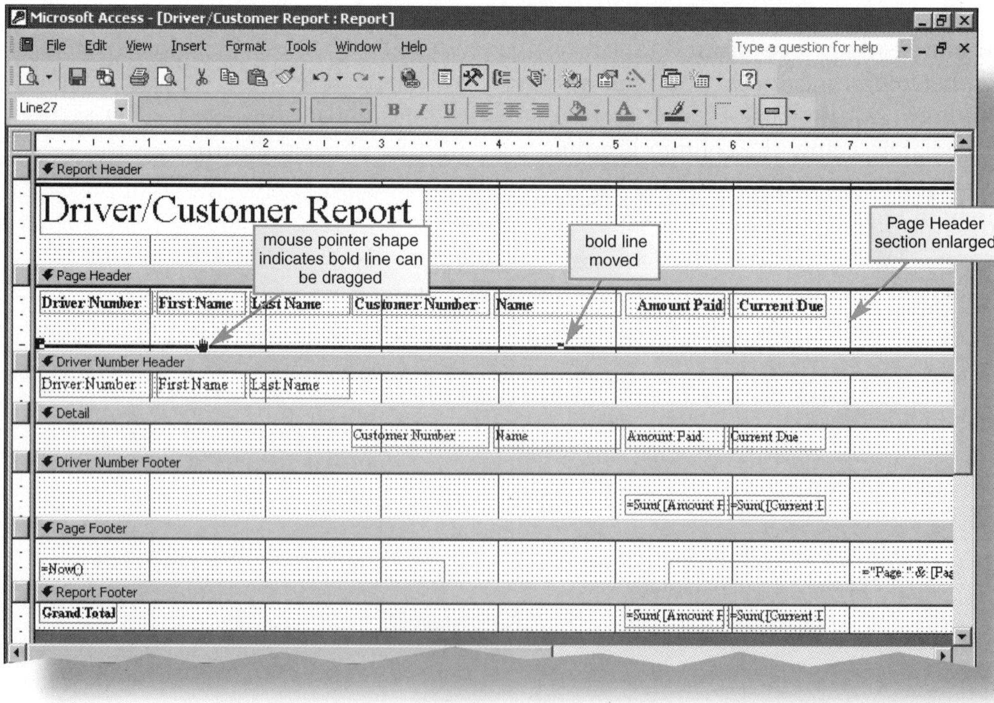

FIGURE 4-38

Changing Column Headings

To change a column heading, point to the position where you would like to display an insertion point. Click once to select the heading. Handles will display around the border of the heading after clicking. Then, click a second time to display the insertion point. Then you can make the desired changes. To delete a character, press the DELETE key to delete the character following the insertion point, or press the BACKSPACE key to delete the character preceding the insertion point. To insert a new character, simply type the character. To move the portion following the insertion point to a second line, press SHIFT+ENTER.

If you click the second time too rapidly, Access will assume that you have double-clicked the heading. Double-clicking a control is another way to produce the control's property sheet. If this happens, simply close the property sheet and begin the process again.

Perform the following steps to change the column headings.

To Change the Column Headings

1 **Point immediately in front of the N in Number in the heading for the first field. Click the column heading for the first field to select it. Click it a second time to produce an insertion point in front of the N, and then press SHIFT+ENTER.**

The heading is split over two lines (Figure 4-39).

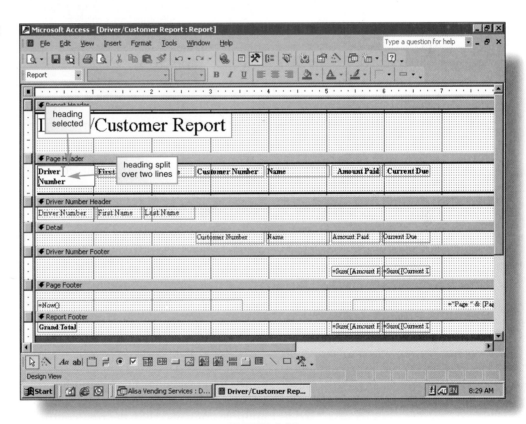

FIGURE 4-39

2 Use the same technique to split the headings for the First Name, Last Name, Customer Number, Amount Paid, and Current Due fields over two lines.

The headings are changed (Figure 4-40).

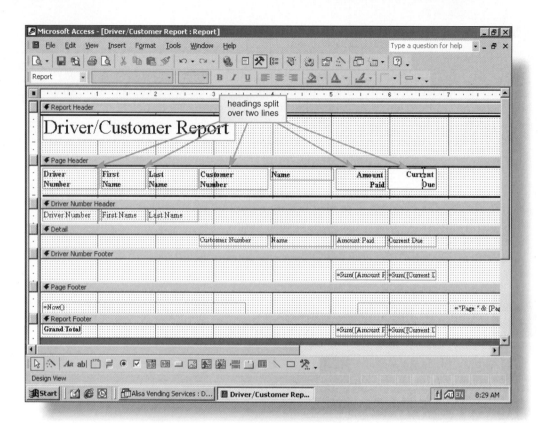

FIGURE 4-40

The changes to the header now are complete.

Moving and Resizing Controls

To move, resize, delete, or modify a single control, click it. Sizing handles display around the border of the control. To move the control, point to the boundary of the control, but away from any sizing handle. The mouse pointer changes shape to a hand. You then can drag the control to move it. To resize the control, drag one of the sizing handles.

You can move or resize several controls at the same time by selecting all of them before dragging. This is especially useful when controls must line up in a column. For example, the Amount Paid control in the Page Header should line up above the Amount Paid control in the Detail section. These controls also should line up with the controls in the Driver Number Footer and Report Footer sections that will display the sum of the Amount Paid amounts.

To select multiple controls, click the first control you wish to select. Then hold down the SHIFT key while you click each of the others. The following steps first will select the controls in the Page Header, Detail, Driver Number Footer, and Report Footer sections that relate to the Current Due field. You then will move all these controls at once. Next, you will use the same technique to move the controls that relate to the Amount Paid field. Finally, to ensure enough room for complete names, you will enlarge the Name controls in the Page Header and Detail sections.

Steps **To Move and Resize Controls**

1 **Click the Current Due control in the Page Header section to select it. While holding down the SHIFT key, click the Current Due control in the Detail section, the control for the sum of the Current Due amounts in the Driver Number Footer section, and the control for the sum of the Current Due amounts in the Report Footer section, and then release the SHIFT key. Point to the border of the Current Due control in the Page Header section but away from any handle. The mouse pointer shape should change to a hand.**

Multiple controls are selected, and the mouse pointer changes to a hand (Figure 4-41).

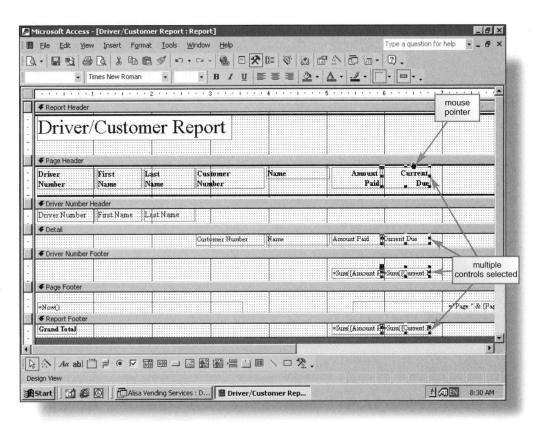

FIGURE 4-41

2 **Drag the Current Due control in the Page Header section to the position shown in Figure 4-42.**

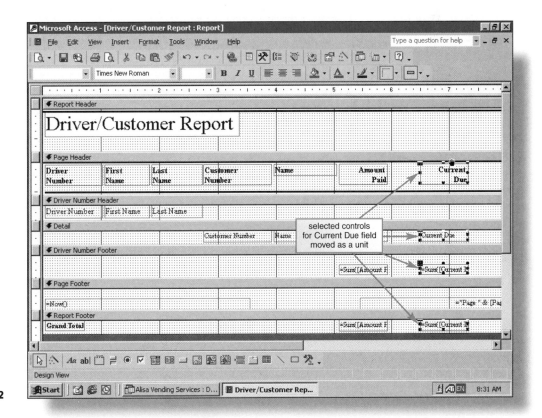

FIGURE 4-42

3 Use the same technique to move the controls for the Amount Paid field to the position shown in Figure 4-43.

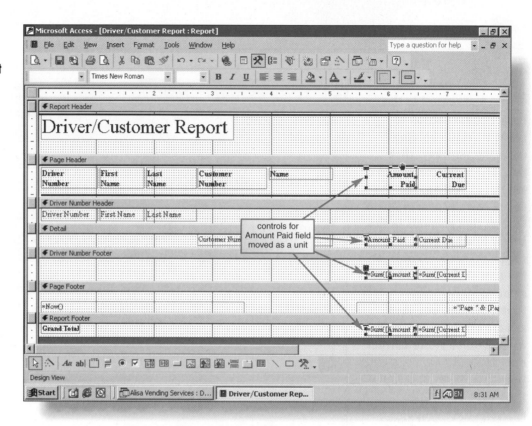

FIGURE 4-43

4 Select the Name control in the Page Header section and the Name control in the Detail section. Drag the right sizing handle for the Name control in the Page Header section to the approximate position shown in Figure 4-44.

The Name controls are resized.

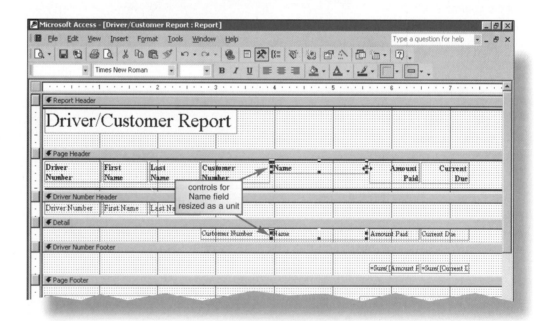

FIGURE 4-44

Previewing a Report

To see what the report looks like with sample data, preview the report by clicking the Print Preview button on the Report Design toolbar as illustrated in the following step.

TO PREVIEW A REPORT

 Click the Print Preview button on the Report Design toolbar. If the entire width of the report does not display, click anywhere within the report.

A preview of the report displays. The extra messages have been removed. The column headings have been changed and now extend over two lines.

Saving and Closing a Report

To close a report, close the window containing the report. Then, indicate whether you want to save your changes. Perform the following step to close and save the report.

TO SAVE AND CLOSE A REPORT

 Click the Close Window button for the window containing the report to close the window. Click the Yes button to save the design of the report.

The report no longer displays. The changes are saved.

Printing a Report

To print the report, right-click the report name in the Database window, and then click Print on the shortcut menu as shown in the following step.

TO PRINT A REPORT

1 Be sure the Reports object is selected in the Database window. Right-click Driver/Customer Report and then click Print on the shortcut menu.

The report prints. It should look like the report shown in Figure 4-2 on page A 4.06.

Report Design Considerations

When designing and creating reports, keep in mind the following guidelines.

1. The purpose of any report is to provide specific information. Ask yourself if the report conveys this information effectively. Are the meanings of the rows and columns in the report clear? Are the column captions easily understood? Are all abbreviations used in the report clear to those looking at the report?

2. Be sure to allow sufficient white space between groups. If you feel the amount is insufficient, add more space by enlarging the group footer.

3. You can use different fonts and sizes by changing the appropriate properties. It is important not to overuse them, however. Consistently using several different fonts and sizes often gives a cluttered and amateurish look to the report.

4. Be consistent when creating reports. Once you have decided on a general style, stick with it.

More About

Calculated Controls in a Report

You can add a calculated control to a report. To add a calculated control, use the Text Box tool in the toolbox, and place the calculated control in the appropriate section on the report. Then, enter the expression for the calculated control. For example, to create a calculated control Total Amount for the Detail section of the Driver/Customer Report, place the text box control in the Detail section to the right of the Current Due control. Enter =[Amount Paid]+[Current Due] as an expression in the text box. Then, you can format the control, delete the label in the Detail section, and add a label to the Page Header section. You also could add a calculated control to the Driver Number Footer section, and to the Page Footer section to sum the total amounts.

More About

Report Design

Proper report design is critical because users judge the value of information based on the way it is presented. Many organizations have formal rules governing the design of printed documents. For more information on report design, visit the Access 2002 More About Web page (scsite.com/ac2002/more.htm) and then click Report Design.

Creating and Using Custom Forms

More About

Creating Forms

Two alternatives to using the Form Wizard to create forms are available. You can use AutoForm to create a very simple form that includes all fields in the table or query. You also can use Design view to create a form totally from scratch.

Thus far, you have used a form to add new records to a table and change existing records. When you did, you created a basic form using the AutoForm command. Although the form did provide some assistance in the task, the form was not particularly pleasing. The standard form stacked fields on top of each other at the left side of the screen. This section covers custom forms that you can use in place of the basic form created by the Form Wizard. To create such a form, first use the Form Wizard to create a basic form. Then modify the design of this form, transforming it into the one you want.

Beginning the Form Creation

To create a form, click the Tables object and then select the table. Click the New Object : Report button arrow and then Form. Next, use the Form Wizard to create the form. The Form Wizard will lead you through a series of choices and questions. Access then will create the form automatically.

Perform the following steps to create an initial form. This form later will be modified to produce the form shown in Figure 4-3 on page A 4.07.

Steps | To Begin Creating a Form

1 **Make sure the Tables object is selected and, if necessary, then click Customer. Click the New Object : Report button arrow, click Form, and then click Form Wizard. Click the OK button and then point to the Add Field button.**

The Form Wizard dialog box displays (Figure 4-45). The Customer Number field is selected.

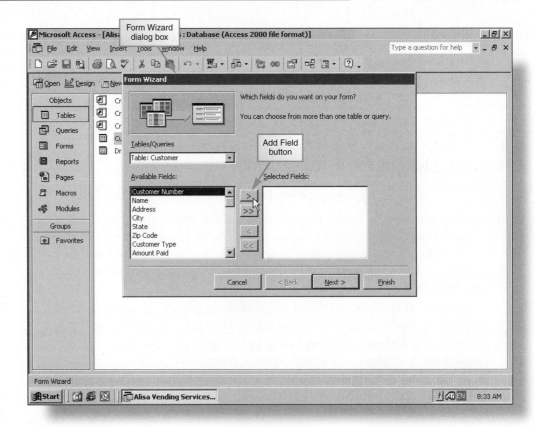

FIGURE 4-45

2 Use the Add Field button to add all the fields except the Customer Type and Driver Number fields. Then click the Next button. When asked for a layout, be sure Columnar is selected, and then click the Next button again.

The Form Wizard dialog box displays, requesting a form style (Figure 4-46).

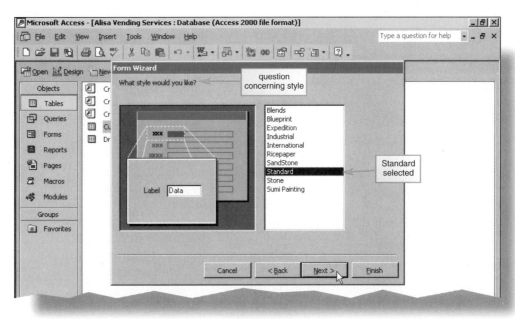

FIGURE 4-46

3 Be sure Standard is selected, click the Next button, and then type Customer Update Form as the title for the form. Click the Finish button to complete and display the form.

The form displays (Figure 4-47).

4 Click the Close Window button for the Customer Update Form window to close the form.

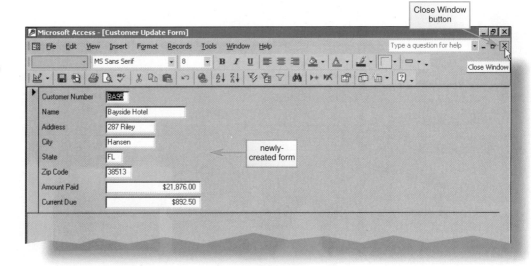

FIGURE 4-47

Modifying the Form Design

To modify the design of an existing form, right-click the form in the Database window, and then click Design View on the shortcut menu. Then, you can modify the design. The modifications can include moving fields, adding new fields, and changing field characteristics. In addition, you can add special features, such as combo boxes and titles and change the colors.

Just as with reports, the various items on a form are called **controls**. The three types are bound controls, unbound controls, and calculated controls. **Bound controls** are used to display data that comes from the database, such as the customer number and name. Bound controls have attached labels that typically display the name of the field that furnishes the data for the control. The **attached label** for the Customer Number field, for example, is the portion of the screen immediately to the left of the field. It contains the words, Customer Number.

Other Ways

1. Click Forms on Objects bar, click New button, click Form Wizard
2. Click Forms on Objects bar, click Create form by using wizard
3. On Insert menu click Form, click Form Wizard
4. In Voice Command mode, say "Forms, New"

Unbound controls are not associated with data from the database and are used to display such things as the form's title. Finally, **calculated controls** are used to display data that is calculated from other data in the database, such as the Total Amount, which is calculated by adding the amount paid and current due amounts.

To move, resize, delete, or modify a control, click it. Clicking a second time produces an insertion point in the control to let you modify its contents. When a control is selected, handles display around the border of the control and, if appropriate, around the attached label. If you point to the border of the control, but away from any handle, the pointer shape will change to a hand. You then can drag the control to move it. If an attached label displays, it will move along with the control. If you wish to move the control or the attached label separately, drag the large handle in the upper-left corner of the control or label. To resize the control, drag one of the sizing handles; and to delete it, press the DELETE key.

Just as with reports, some of the changes you wish to make to a control will involve using the property sheet for the control. You will use the property sheet of the Total Amount control, for example, to change the format that Access uses to display the contents of the control.

Perform the following steps to modify the design of the Customer Update Form and dock the toolbox at the bottom of the screen, if necessary.

Steps **To Modify the Form Design**

1 **In the Alisa Vending Services: Database window, click the Forms object. Right-click Customer Update Form and then click Design View on the shortcut menu. If necessary, maximize the window. If a field list displays, click its Close button. Be sure the toolbox displays and is docked at the bottom of the screen. Click the control for the Amount Paid field, and then move the mouse pointer until the shape changes to a hand. (You will need to point to the border of the control but away from any handle.)**

Move handles display, indicating the field is selected (Figure 4-48). The shape of the mouse pointer changes to a hand.

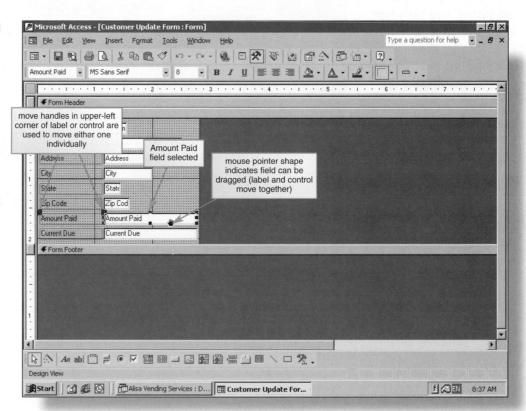

FIGURE 4-48

2 Drag the Amount Paid field to the approximate position shown in Figure 4-49. The form will expand automatically in size to accommodate the new position for the field.

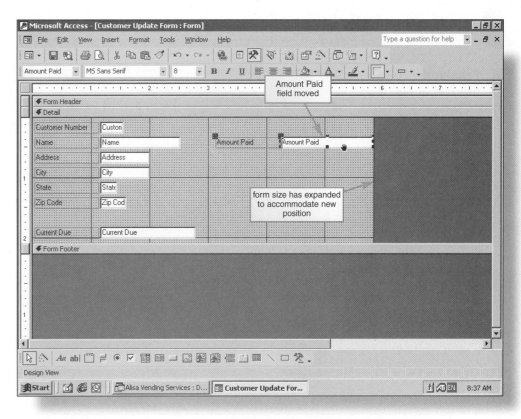

FIGURE 4-49

3 Use the same steps to move the Current Due field to the position shown in Figure 4-50.

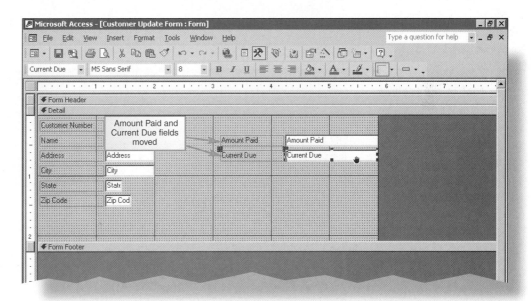

FIGURE 4-50

Adding a New Field

To add a new field, use the Text Box tool in the toolbox to add a field. After clicking the Text Box tool, click the position for the field on the form, and then indicate the contents of the field. Perform the steps on the next page to add the Total Amount field to the form.

Attached Labels

You can remove an attached label by clicking the label and then pressing the DELETE key. The label will be removed, but the control will remain.

Steps To Add a New Field

1 Point to the Text Box tool in the toolbox (Figure 4-51).

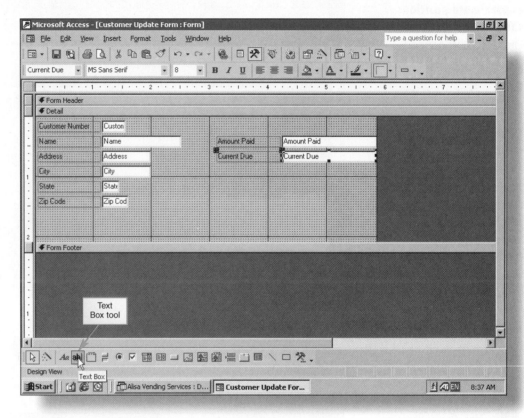

FIGURE 4-51

2 Click the Text Box tool in the toolbox, and then move the mouse pointer, which has changed shape to a small plus symbol accompanied by a text box, to the position shown in Figure 4-52.

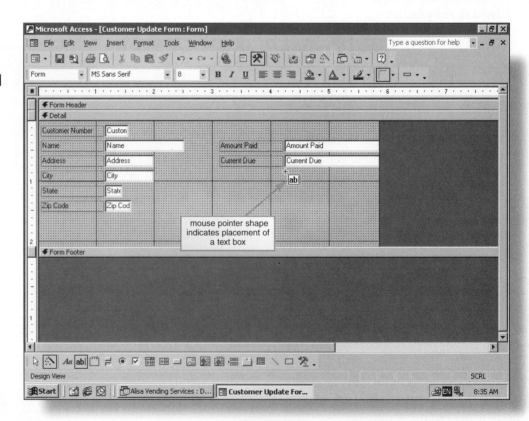

FIGURE 4-52

3 Click the position shown in Figure 4-52 to place a text box. Click inside the text box and type =[Amount Paid]+[Current Due] as the expression in the text box. Click the field label (the box that contains the word Text) twice, once to select it and a second time to display an insertion point. Use the DELETE key or the BACKSPACE key to delete the current entry. Type Total Amount as the new entry.

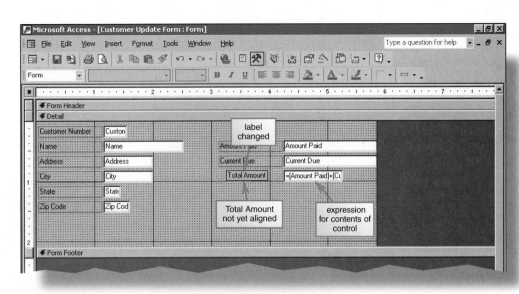

FIGURE 4-53

The expression for the field has been entered and the label has been changed to Total Amount (Figure 4-53).

4 Click outside the Total Amount control to deselect it. Then, click the control to select it once more. Handles will display around the control. Move the label portion so its left edge lines up with the labels for the Amount Paid and Current Due fields by dragging the move handle in its upper-left corner.

The label is moved (Figure 4-54). The mouse pointer has assumed the pointing finger shape.

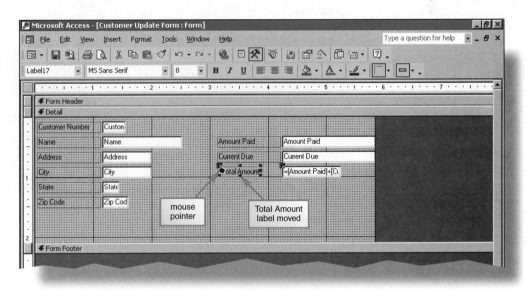

FIGURE 4-54

5 Click somewhere outside the control to deselect it.

The control is no longer selected.

Changing the Format of a Field

Access automatically formats fields from the database appropriately because it knows their data types. Usually, you will find the formats assigned by Access to be acceptable. For calculated fields, such as Total Amount, however, Access just assigns a general format. The value will not display automatically with two decimal places and a dollar sign.

More About

Changing a Format

Access assigns formats to database fields, but changing the Format property can change these formats. The specific formats that are available depend on the data type of the field. The Format list also contains samples of the way the data would display with the various formats.

To change to a special format, such as Currency, which displays the number with a dollar sign and two decimal places, requires using the field's property sheet to change the Format property. Perform the following steps to change the format for the Total Amount field to Currency.

Steps ## To Change the Format of a Field

1 **Right-click the control for the Total Amount field (the box containing the expression) to produce its shortcut menu and then click Properties on the shortcut menu. If necessary, click the All tab so all the properties display, and then click the Format property. Point to the Format property box arrow.**

The property sheet for the field displays (Figure 4-55).

2 **Click the Format property box arrow to produce a list of available formats. Scroll down so Currency displays and then click Currency. Close the property sheet by clicking its Close button.**

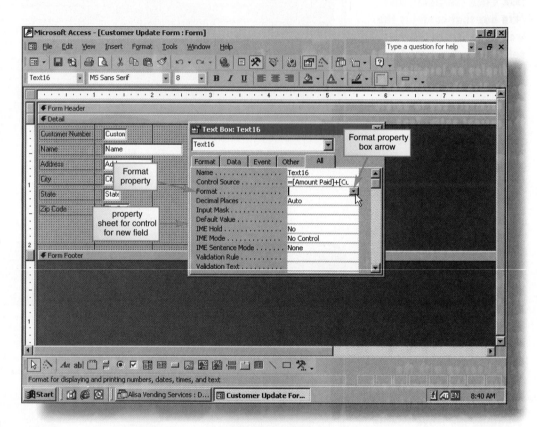

FIGURE 4-55

The property sheet no longer displays. The values in the Total Amount field will display in Currency format, which includes a dollar sign and two decimal places.

Combo Boxes

When entering a value for the customer type, there are only three legitimate values: EDU, MAN, and SER. When entering a driver number, the value must match the number of a driver currently in the Driver table. To assist the users in entering this data, the form will contain combo boxes. With a **combo box**, the user can type the data, if that is convenient. Alternatively, the user can click the combo box arrow to display a list of possible values and then select an item from the list.

To place a combo box in the form, use the Combo Box tool in the toolbox. If the **Control Wizards tool** in the toolbox is selected, you can use a wizard to guide you through the process of creating the combo box. Perform the following steps to place a combo box for the Customer Type field on the form.

To Place a Combo Box that Selects Values from a List

1 If necessary, click the Control Wizards tool in the toolbox to select it. Point to the Combo Box tool in the toolbox (Figure 4-56).

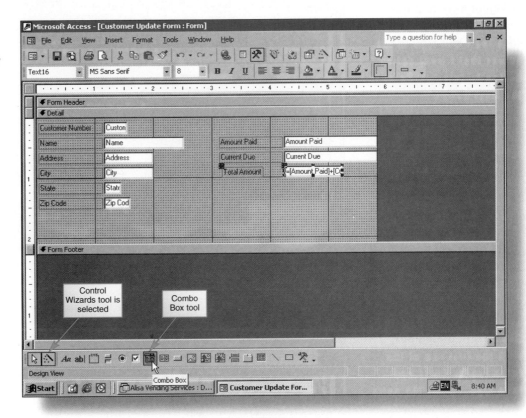

FIGURE 4-56

2 Click the Combo Box tool in the toolbox, and then move the mouse pointer, whose shape has changed to a small plus symbol accompanied by a combo box, to the position shown in Figure 4-57.

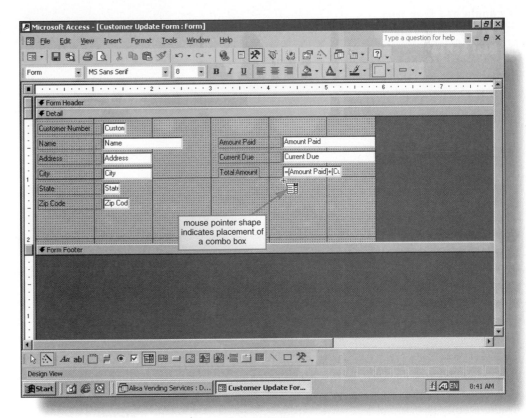

FIGURE 4-57

3 **Click the position shown in Figure 4-57 to place a combo box. If necessary, click the I will type in the values that I want option button to select it. Point to the Next button.**

The Combo Box Wizard dialog box displays, requesting that you indicate how the combo box is to receive values for the list (Figure 4-58). The I will type in the values that I want option button is selected.

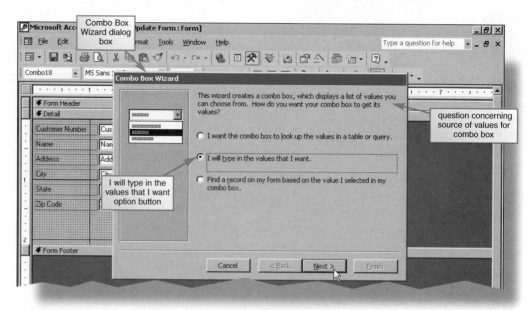

FIGURE 4-58

4 **Click the Next button in the Combo Box Wizard dialog box, click the first row of the table (under Col1) and then type EDU as the entry. Press the DOWN ARROW key and then type MAN as the entry. Press the DOWN ARROW key again and then type SER as the entry. Point to the Next button.**

The list of values for the combo box is entered (Figure 4-59).

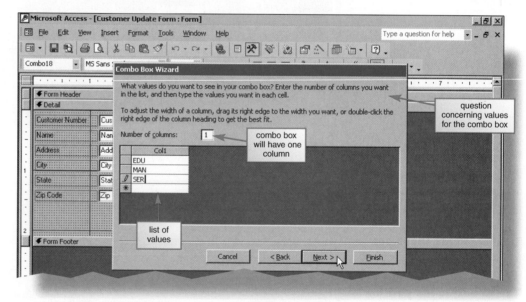

FIGURE 4-59

5 **Click the Next button. Click the Store that value in this field option button. Click the Store that value in this field box arrow, and then click Customer Type. Point to the Next button.**

The Store that value in this field option button is selected, and the Customer Type field is selected (Figure 4-60).

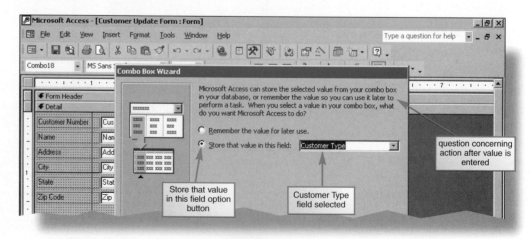

FIGURE 4-60

6 Click the Next button. Type Customer Type as the label for the combo box and point to the Finish button.

The label is entered (Figure 4-61).

7 Click the Finish button. Click the label for the combo box, and then drag its move handle to move the label so its left edge aligns with the left edge of the labels for the Amount Paid, Current Due, and Total Amount fields.

The combo box is placed on the form.

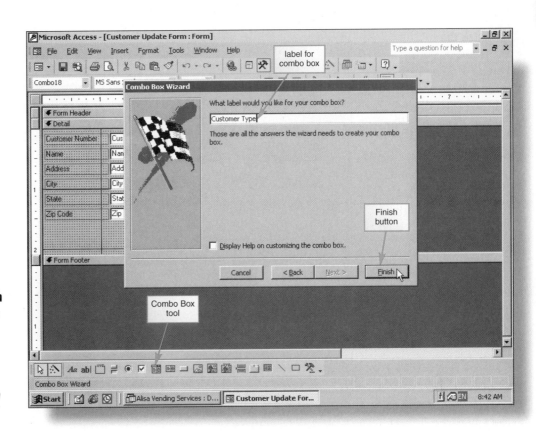

FIGURE 4-61

The steps for placing a combo box to select values from a table are similar to those for placing a combo box to select values from a list. The only difference is the source of the data. Perform the following steps to place a combo box for the Driver Number field on the form.

 To Place a Combo Box that Selects Values from a Related Table

1 With the Control Wizards tool in the toolbox selected, click the Combo Box tool in the toolbox, and then move the mouse pointer, whose shape has changed to a small plus symbol accompanied by a combo box, to the position shown in Figure 4-62.

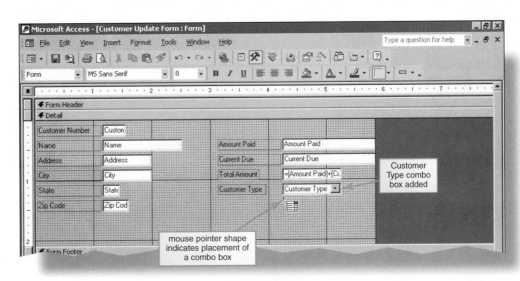

FIGURE 4-62

2 **Click the position shown in Figure 4-62 to place a combo box. In the Combo Box wizard, click the I want the combo box to look up the values in a table or query option button if it is not already selected. Click the Next button, click Table: Driver, and then point to the Next button.**

The Driver table is selected as the table to provide values for the combo box (Figure 4-63).

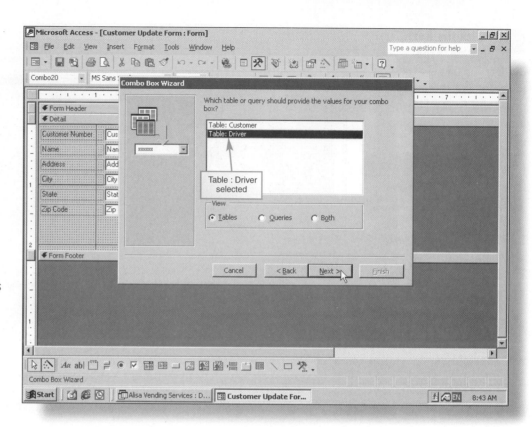

FIGURE 4-63

3 **Click the Next button. Click the Add Field button to add the Driver Number as a field in the combo box. Click the First Name field and then click the Add Field button. Click the Last Name field and then click the Add Field button. Point to the Next button.**

The Driver Number, First Name, and Last Name fields are selected for the combo box (Figure 4-64).

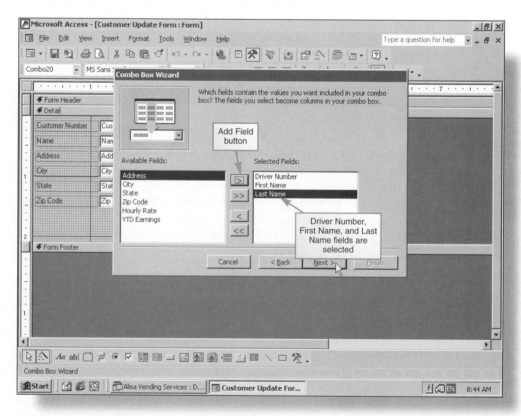

FIGURE 4-64

4 Click the Next button. Point to the Hide key column (recommended) check box.

The next Combo Box Wizard dialog box displays (Figure 4-65). You can use this dialog box to change the sizes of the fields. You also can use it to indicate whether the key field, in this case the Driver Number field, should be hidden.

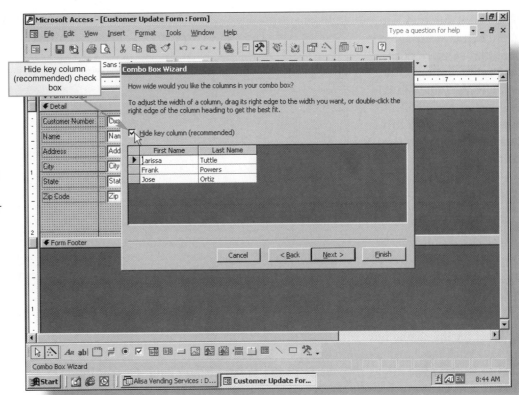

FIGURE 4-65

5 Click the Hide key column (recommended) check box to remove the check mark to ensure the Driver Number field displays along with the First Name and Last Name fields. Resize each column to best fit the data by double-clicking the right-hand border of the column heading. Click the Next button.

The Combo Box Wizard dialog box displays, asking you to choose a field that uniquely identifies a row in the combo box (Figure 4-66). The Driver Number field, which is the correct field, already is selected.

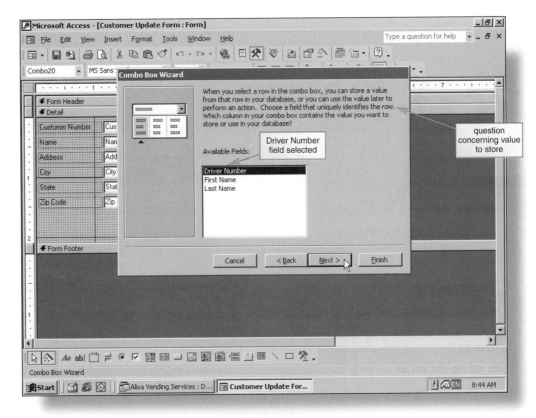

FIGURE 4-66

6 Click the Next button. Click the Store that value in this field option button. Click the Store that value in this field box arrow, scroll down, and then click Driver Number. Point to the Next button.

The Driver Number field is selected as the field in which to store the value (Figure 4-67).

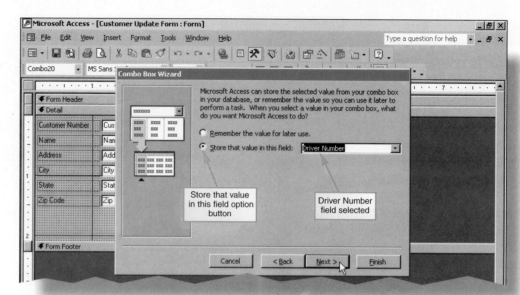

FIGURE 4-67

7 Click the Next button. If necessary, type `Driver Number` as the label for the combo box and then click the Finish button. Click the label for the combo box, and then move the label so its left edge aligns with the left edge of the Amount Paid, Current Due, Total Amount, and Customer Type fields.

The combo box is placed on the form.

Adding a Title

The form in Figure 4-3 on page A 4.07 contains a title, Customer Update Form, that displays in a large, light blue label at the top of the form. To add a title, first expand the Form Header section to allow room for the title. Next, use the Label tool in the toolbox to place the label in the Form Header section. Finally, type the title in the label. Perform the following steps to add a title to the form.

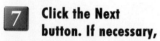 **To Add a Title**

1 Point to the bottom border of the Form Header section. The mouse pointer changes shape to a two-headed vertical arrow with a crossbar as shown in Figure 4-68.

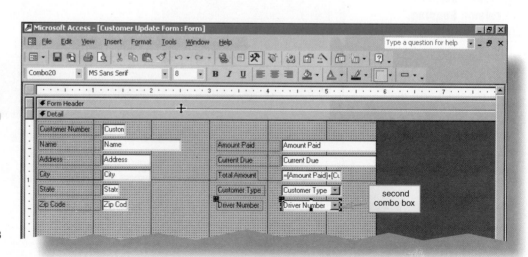

FIGURE 4-68

2 Drag the bottom border of the Form Header section to the approximate position shown in Figure 4-69, and then point to the Label tool in the toolbox.

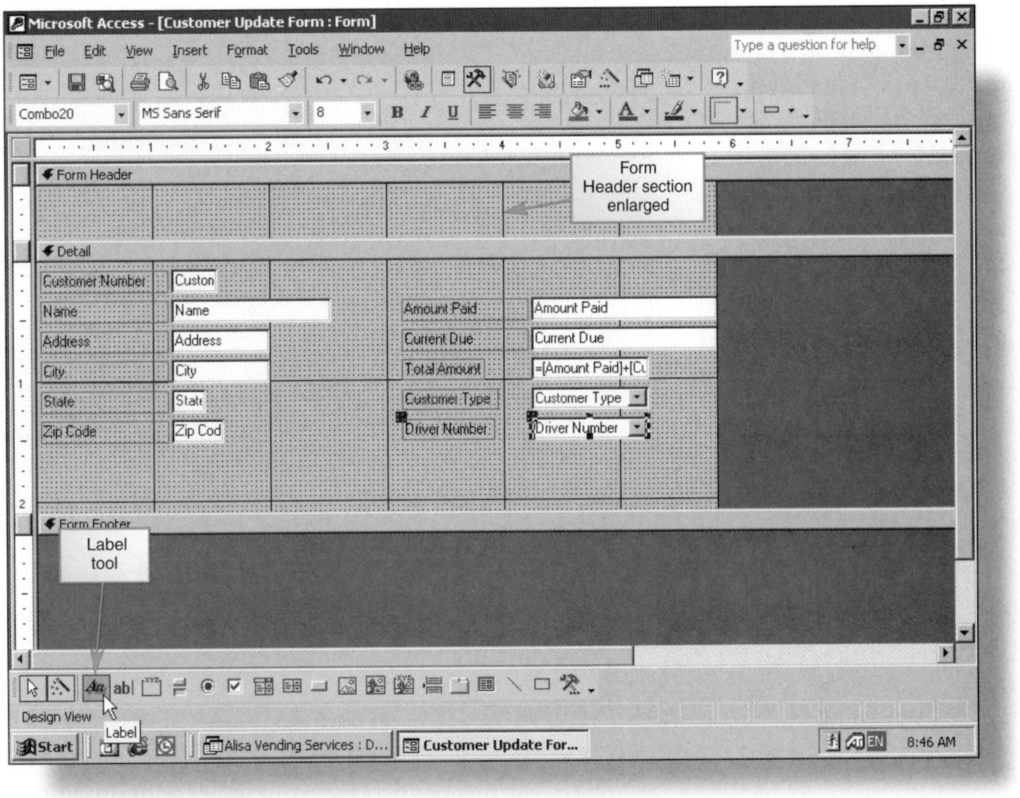

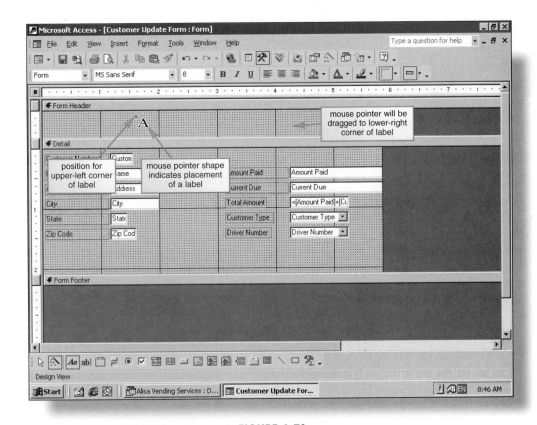

FIGURE 4-69

3 Click the Label tool in the toolbox and then move the mouse pointer, whose shape has changed to a small plus symbol accompanied by a label, into the position shown in Figure 4-70.

FIGURE 4-70

4 Drag the pointer to the opposite corner of the Form Header section to form the label shown in Figure 4-71 and then release the left mouse button.

5 Type Customer Update Form as the form title.

The title is entered.

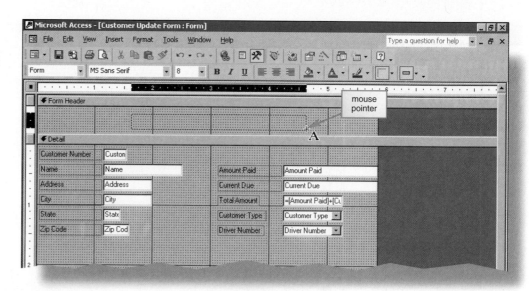

FIGURE 4-71

Enhancing a Title

The form now contains a title. You can enhance the appearance of the title by changing various properties of the label containing the title. The following steps change the color of the label, make the label appear to be raised from the screen, change the font size of the title, and change the alignment of the title within the label.

 To Enhance a Title

1 Click somewhere outside the label containing the title to deselect the label. Deselecting is required or right-clicking the label will have no effect. Next, right-click the label containing the title. Point to Properties on the shortcut menu.

The shortcut menu for the label displays (Figure 4-72).

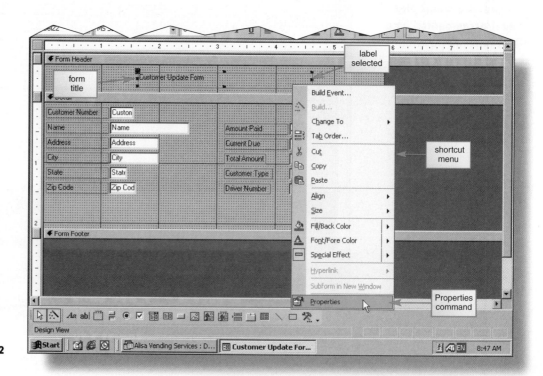

FIGURE 4-72

2 Click Properties. If necessary, click the All tab in the property sheet. Click the down scroll arrow to display the Back Color property, click Back Color, and then point to the Build button (the button with the three dots).

The property sheet for the label displays (Figure 4-73). The insertion point displays in the Back Color property and the Build button displays.

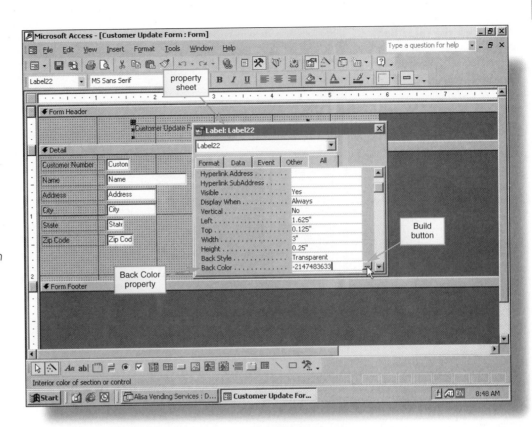

FIGURE 4-73

3 Click the Build button to display the Color dialog box and then point to the color light blue in row 2 column 5 in row 2, column 5 as shown in Figure 4-74.

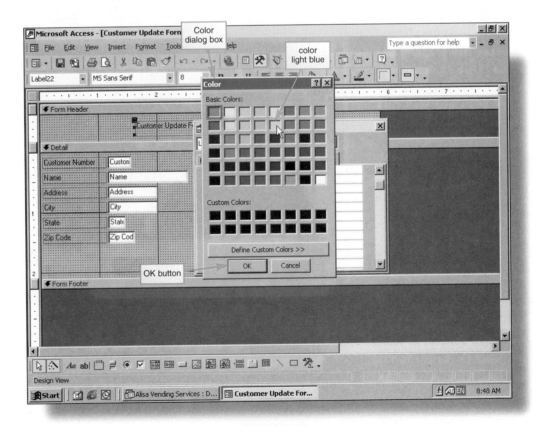

FIGURE 4-74

4 **Click the color light blue, and then click the OK button. Scroll down the property sheet, click the Special Effect property, and then click the Special Effect property box arrow. Point to Raised.**

The list of available values for the Special Effect property displays (Figure 4-75).

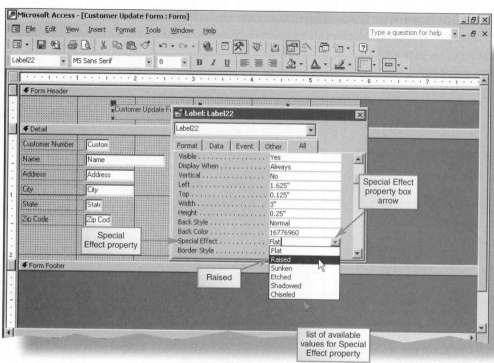

FIGURE 4-75

5 **Click Raised. Scroll down the property sheet and then click the Font Size property. Click the Font Size property box arrow. Click 14 in the list of font sizes that displays. Scroll down and then click the Text Align property. Click the Text Align property box arrow. Point to Distribute.**

The list of available values for the Text Align property displays (Figure 4-76).

6 **Click Distribute. Close the property sheet by clicking its Close button. If necessary, use the sizing handles to resize the label so the entire title displays. Click outside the label to deselect it.**

The enhancements to the title now are complete.

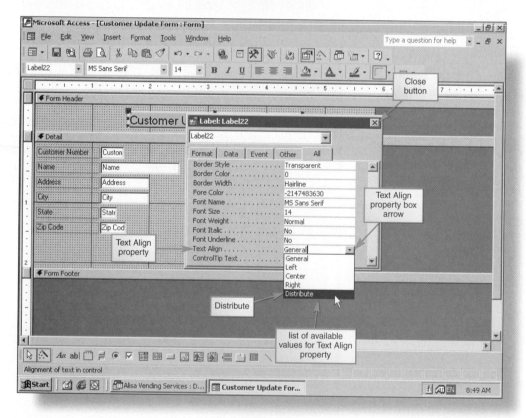

FIGURE 4-76

Changing Tab Stops

Users cannot change the value for the total amount. Instead, it will be recalculated automatically whenever the amount paid or current due amounts change. Consequently, if users repeatedly press the TAB key to move through the controls on the form, the Total Amount control should be bypassed. In order to force this to happen, change the Tab Stop property for the control from Yes to No as illustrated in the following steps.

Steps To Change a Tab Stop

1 **Right-click the Total Amount control, and then click Properties on the shortcut menu. Click the down scroll arrow until the Tab Stop property displays, click the Tab Stop property, click the Tab Stop property box arrow, and then point to No (Figure 4-77).**

2 **Click No, and then close the property sheet.**

The modifications to the control are complete. With this change, tabbing through the controls on the form will bypass the total amount.

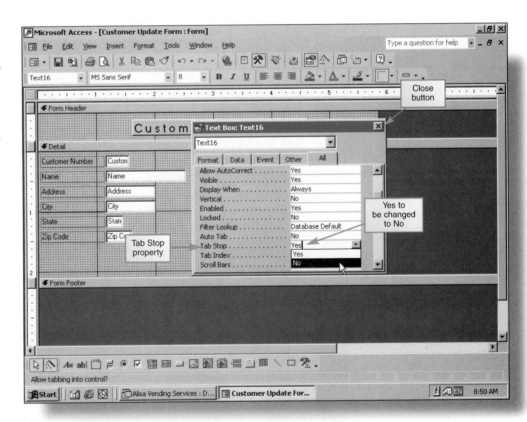

FIGURE 4-77

Saving and Closing a Form

To close a form, close the window using the window's Close button. Then indicate whether you want to save your changes. Perform the following step to save and close the form.

TO SAVE AND CLOSE A FORM

1 Click the window's Close Window button to close the window, and then click the Yes button to save the design of the form.

The form no longer displays. The changes are saved.

Opening a Form

To open a form, right-click a form in the Database window, and then click Open on the shortcut menu. The form will display and can be used to examine and update data. Perform the following step to open the Customer Update Form.

TO OPEN A FORM

1 With the Forms object selected, right-click the Customer Update Form to display the shortcut menu. Click Open on the shortcut menu.

The form displays. It should look like the form shown in Figure 4-3 on page A 4.07.

Using a Form

You use this form as you used the form in Project 3, with two differences. Access will not allow changes to the total amount, because Access calculates this amount automatically by adding the amount paid and current due amounts. The other difference is that this form contains combo boxes.

To use a combo box, click the arrow. Clicking the arrow in the Customer Type combo box produces a list of customer types (Figure 4-78). Clicking the arrow in the Driver Number combo box produces a list of numbers and the names of available drivers display as shown in Figure 4-3. In either case, you can type the appropriate value from the list you see on the screen or you can simply click the value in the list. With either method, the combo box helps you enter the correct value.

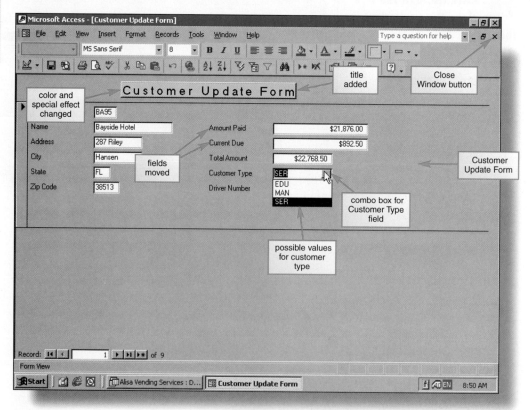

FIGURE 4-78

Closing a Form

To close a form, simply close the window containing the form. Perform the following step to close the form.

TO CLOSE A FORM

1 Click the Close Window button for the Form window.

Form Design Considerations

As you design and create custom forms, keep in mind the following guidelines.

1. Remember that someone using your form may be looking at the form for several hours at a time. Forms that are cluttered or contain too many different effects (colors, fonts, frame styles, and so on) can become very hard on the eyes.
2. Place the fields in logical groupings. Fields that relate to each other should be close to one another on the form.
3. If the data that a user will enter comes from a paper form, make the screen form resemble the paper form as closely as possible.

More About

Form Design

Forms should be appealing visually and present data logically and clearly. Properly designed forms improve both the speed and accuracy of data entry. For more information on form design, visit the Access 2002 More About Web page (scsite.com/ ac2002/more.htm) and then click Form Design.

Closing the Database

The following step closes the database by closing its Database window.

TO CLOSE A DATABASE

1 Click the Close Window button for the Alisa Vending Services : Database window.

CASE PERSPECTIVE SUMMARY

In Project 4, you assisted the management of Alisa Vending Services by creating two custom reports and a data entry form. You created the first report from a query that used a calculated field. In the second report, you grouped records by driver number and displayed subtotal and grand total amounts. You created a custom form that used a calculated control and combo boxes.

Project Summary

In Project 4, you created two reports and a form. To create the reports, you learned the purpose of the various sections and how to modify their contents. You used grouping in a report. Then, you created and used a custom form. Steps and techniques were presented showing you how to move controls, create new controls, add combo boxes, and add a title. You changed the characteristics of various objects in the form. You also learned general principles to help you design effective reports and forms.

What You Should Know

Having completed this project, you now should be able to perform the following tasks:

▶ Add a New Field *(A 4.38)*

▶ Add a Title *(A 4.46)*

▶ Begin Creating a Form *(A 4.34)*

▶ Change the Can Grow Property *(A 4.16)*

▶ Change the Column Headings *(A 4.29)*

▶ Change the Format of a Field *(A 4.40)*

▶ Change a Tab Stop *(A 4.51)*

▶ Close a Database *(A 4.53)*

▶ Close a Form *(A 4.53)*

▶ Create a Report *(A 4.09)*

▶ Create a Query *(A 4.08)*

▶ Create a Second Report *(A 4.21)*

▶ Enhance a Title *(A 4.48)*

▶ Enlarge Controls *(A 4.19)*

▶ Enlarge the Page Header Section *(A 4.28)*

▶ Modify the Form Design *(A 4.36)*

▶ Move and Resize Controls *(A 4.31)*

▶ Move to Design View and Dock the Toolbox *(A 4.14)*

▶ Open a Database *(A 4.07)*

▶ Open a Form *(A 4.52)*

▶ Place a Combo Box that Selects Values from a List *(A 4.41)*

▶ Place a Combo Box that Select Values from a Related Table *(A 4.43)*

▶ Preview a Report *(A 4.33)*

▶ Print a Report *(A 4.20, A 4.33)*

▶ Remove Unwanted Controls *(A 4.26)*

▶ Save and Close a Form *(A 4.51)*

▶ Save and Close a Report *(A 4.20, A 4.33)*

Learn It Online

Instructions: To complete the Learn It Online exercises, start your browser, click the Address bar, and then enter scsite.com/offxp/exs.htm. When the Office XP Learn It Online page displays, follow the instructions in the exercises below.

1 Project Reinforcement TF, MC, and SA

Below Access Project 4, click the Project Reinforcement link. Print the quiz by clicking Print on the File menu. Answer each question. Write your first and last name at the top of each page, and then hand in the printout to your instructor.

2 Flash Cards

Below Access Project 4, click the Flash Cards link. When Flash Cards displays, read the instructions. Type 20 (or a number specified by your instructor) in the Number of Playing Cards text box, type your name in the Name text box, and then click the Flip Card button. When the flash card displays, read the question and then click the Answer box arrow to select an answer. Flip through Flash Cards. Click Print on the File menu to print the last flash card if your score is 15 (75%) correct or greater and then hand it in to your instructor. If your score is less than 15 (75%) correct, then redo this exercise by clicking the Replay button.

3 Practice Test

Below Access Project 4, click the Practice Test link. Answer each question, enter your first and last name at the bottom of the page, and then click the Grade Test button. When the graded practice test displays on your screen, click Print on the File menu to print a hard copy. Continue to take practice tests until you score 80% or better. Hand in a printout of the final practice test to your instructor.

4 Who Wants to Be a Computer Genius?

Below Access Project 4, click the Computer Genius link. Read the instructions, enter your first and last name at the bottom of the page, and then click the Play button. Hand in your score to your instructor.

5 Wheel of Terms

Below Access Project 4, click the Wheel of Terms link. Read the instructions, and then enter your first and last name and your school name. Click the Play button. Hand in your score to your instructor.

6 Crossword Puzzle Challenge

Below Access Project 4, click the Crossword Puzzle Challenge link. Read the instructions, and then enter your first and last name. Click the Play button. Work the crossword puzzle. When you are finished, click the Submit button. When the crossword puzzle redisplays, click the Print button. Hand in the printout.

7 Tips and Tricks

Below Access Project 4, click the Tips and Tricks link. Click a topic that pertains to Project 4. Right-click the information and then click Print on the shortcut menu. Construct a brief example of what the information relates to in Access to confirm you understand how to use the tip or trick. Hand in the example and printed information.

8 Newsgroups

Below Access Project 4, click the Newsgroups link. Click a topic that pertains to Project 4. Print three comments. Hand in the comments to your instructor.

9 Expanding Your Horizons

Below Access Project 4, click the Articles for Microsoft Access link. Click a topic that pertains to Project 4. Print the information. Construct a brief example of what the information relates to in Access to confirm you understand the contents of the article. Hand in the example and printed information to your instructor.

10 Search Sleuth

Below Access Project 4, click the Search Sleuth link. To search for a term that pertains to this project, select a term below the Project 4 title and then use the Google search engine at google.com (or any major search engine) to display and print two Web pages that present information on the term. Hand in the printouts to your instructor.

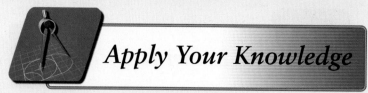

Apply Your Knowledge

1 Presenting Data in the Beyond Clean Database

Instructions: Start Access. If you are using the Microsoft Access 2002 Complete or the Microsoft Access 2002 Comprehensive text, open the Beyond Clean database that you used in Project 3. Otherwise, see the inside back cover for instructions for downloading the Data Disk or see your instructor for information on accessing the files required for this book. Perform the following tasks.

1. Create the report shown in Figure 4-79. Sort the report by Client Number within each group.
2. Print the report.
3. Using the Form Wizard, create a form for the Client table. Include all fields except Custodian Id on the form. Use Client Update Form as the title for the form.

4. Modify the form in the Design window to create the form shown in Figure 4-80. The form includes a combo box for the Custodian Id field.
5. Print the form. To print the form, open the form, click File on the menu bar, and then click Print. Click Selected Record(s) as the Print Range. Click the OK button.

Custodian/Client Report

Custodian Id	First Name	Last Name	Client Number	Name	Balance
002	Terry	Deakle			
			AD23	Adder Cleaners	$105.00
			CR67	Cricket Store	$0.00
			RO45	Royal Palms	$0.00
					$105.00
009	Michelle	Lee			
			AR76	The Artshop	$80.00
			HA09	Halyards Manufacturing	$145.00
			ST21	Steed's	$123.00
					$348.00
013	Juan	Torres			
			DL61	Del Sol	$135.00
			GR36	Great Foods	$104.00
			ME17	Merry Café	$168.00
					$407.00
Grand Total					$860.00

FIGURE 4-79

Microsoft Access - [Client Update Form]

File   Edit   View   Insert   Format   Records   Tools   Window   Help   Type a question for help

MS Sans Serif   8   B I U

Client Update Form

Client Number	AD23		
Name	Adder Cleaners	Zip Code	31501
Address	407 Mallery	Telephone Number	512-555-4070
City	Anders	Balance	$105.00
State	TX	Custodian Id	002

FIGURE 4-80

In the Lab

1 Presenting Data in the Wooden Crafts Database

Problem: Jan Merchant already has realized the benefits from the database of products and suppliers that you created. She now would like to prepare reports from the database. Jan greatly appreciates the validation rules that were added to ensure that data is entered correctly. She now feels she can improve the data entry process even further by creating custom forms.

Instructions: If you are using the Microsoft Access 2002 Complete or the Microsoft Access 2002 Comprehensive text, open the Wooden Crafts database that you used in Project 3. Otherwise, see the inside back cover for instructions for downloading the Data Disk or see your instructor for information on accessing the files required for this book. Perform the following tasks.

1. Create the On Hand Value Report shown in Figure 4-81 for the Product table. On Hand Value is the result of multiplying On Hand by Cost.

2. Print the report.

3. Create the Supplier/Products report shown in Figure 4-82. Profit is the difference between Selling Price and Cost.

4. Print the report.

5. Create the form shown in Figure 4-83. On Hand Value is a calculated control and is the result of multiplying On Hand by Cost. Include a combo box for Supplier Code.

6. Print the form. To print the form, open the form, click File on the menu bar, and then click Print. Click Selected Record(s) as the Print Range. Click the OK button.

FIGURE 4-81

On Hand Value Report

Product Id	Description	On Hand	Cost	On Hand Value
AD01	Animal Dominoes	5	$18.00	$90.00
BF01	Barnyard Friends	3	$54.00	$162.00
BL23	Blocks in Box	5	$29.00	$145.00
CC14	Coal Car	8	$14.00	$112.00
FT05	Fire Truck	7	$9.00	$63.00
LB34	Lacing Bear	4	$12.00	$48.00
MR06	Midget Railroad	3	$31.00	$93.00
PJ12	Pets Jigsaw	10	$8.00	$80.00
SK10	Skyscraper	6	$25.00	$150.00
UM09	USA Map	12	$14.00	$168.00

Supplier/Products Report

Supplier Code	First Name	Last Name	Product Id	Description	Selling Price	Cost	Profit
AP	Antonio	Patino					
			BL23	Blocks in Box	$32.00	$29.00	$3.00
			FT05	Fire Truck	$12.00	$9.00	$3.00
			LB34	Lacing Bear	$16.00	$12.00	$4.00
			UM09	USA Map	$18.00	$14.00	$4.00
BH	Bert	Huntington					
			AD01	Animal Dominoes	$21.00	$18.00	$3.00
			CC14	Coal Car	$18.00	$14.00	$4.00
			MR06	Midget Railroad	$34.00	$31.00	$3.00
PL	Ping	Luang					
			BF01	Barnyard Friends	$60.00	$54.00	$6.00
			PJ12	Pets Jigsaw	$12.00	$8.00	$4.00
			SK10	Skyscraper	$30.00	$25.00	$5.00

FIGURE 4-82

FIGURE 4-83

Microsoft Access - [Product Update Form]

File Edit View Insert Format Records Tools Window Help

Type a question for help

MS Sans Serif   8   B I U

Product Update Form

Product Id	AD01	On Hand	5
Description	Animal Dominoes	Cost	$18.00
Supplier Code	BH	Selling Price	$21.00
		On Hand Value	$90.00

In the Lab

2 Presenting Data in the Restaurant Supply Database

Problem: The restaurant supply company already has realized several benefits from the database you created. The company now would like to prepare reports from the database. The company greatly appreciates the validation rules that were added to ensure that data is entered correctly. They now feel the data entry process can be improved even further by creating custom forms.

Instructions: If you are using the Microsoft Access 2002 Complete or the Microsoft Access 2002 Comprehensive text, open the Restaurant Supply database that you used in Project 3. Otherwise, see the inside back cover for instructions for downloading the Data Disk or see your instructor for information on accessing the files required for this book. Perform the following tasks.

1. Create the Customer Income Report shown in Figure 4-84 for the Customer table. Customer Income is the sum of Balance and Amount Paid. Sort the report by Customer Number.
2. Print the report.
3. Create the Sales Rep/Customers report shown in Figure 4-85.
4. Print the report.
5. Create the form shown in Figure 4-86. Customer Income is a calculated control and is the sum of Balance and Amount Paid. Dining Type and Sales Rep Number are combo boxes.
6. Print the form. To print the form, open the form, click File on the menu bar, and then click Print. Click Selected Record(s) as the Print Range. Click the OK button.

Customer Income Report

Customer Number	Name	Address	Balance	Amount Paid	Customer Income
AM23	American Pie	223 Johnson	$95.00	$1,595.00	$1,690.00
BI15	Bavarian Inn	3294 Devon	$445.00	$1,250.00	$1,695.00
CB12	China Buffet	1632 Clark	$45.00	$610.00	$655.00
CM09	Curry and More	3140 Halsted	$195.00	$980.00	$1,175.00
EG07	El Gallo	185 Broad	$0.00	$1,600.00	$1,600.00
JS34	Joe's Seafood	2200 Lawrence	$260.00	$600.00	$860.00
LV20	Little Venice	13 Devon	$100.00	$1,150.00	$1,250.00
NC25	New Crete	1027 Wells	$140.00	$450.00	$590.00
PP43	Pan Pacific	3140 Halstead	$165.00	$0.00	$165.00
RD03	Reuben's Deli	787 Monroe	$0.00	$875.00	$875.00
TD01	Texas Diner	220 Lawrence	$280.00	$0.00	$280.00
VG21	Veggie Gourmet	1939 Congress	$60.00	$625.00	$685.00

FIGURE 4-84

Sales Rep/Customers Report

Sales Rep Number	First Name	Last Name	Customer Number	Name	Dining Type	Amount Paid	Balance
44	Pat	Charles					
			AM23	American Pie	FFT	$1,595.00	$95.00
			EG07	El Gallo	FIN	$1,600.00	$0.00
			NC25	New Crete	FAM	$450.00	$140.00
			PP43	Pan Pacific	FAM	$0.00	$165.00
			VG21	Veggie Gourmet	FFT	$625.00	$60.00
						$4,270.00	$460.00
49	Pinn	Gupta					
			BI15	Bavarian Inn	FIN	$1,250.00	$445.00
			CB12	China Buffet	FAM	$610.00	$45.00
			JS34	Joe's Seafood	FAM	$600.00	$260.00
			LV20	Little Venice	FAM	$1,150.00	$100.00
						$3,610.00	$850.00
51	Jose	Ortiz					
			CM09	Curry and More	FAM	$980.00	$195.00
			RD03	Reuben's Deli	FFT	$875.00	$0.00
			TD01	Texas Diner	FAM	$0.00	$280.00
						$1,855.00	$475.00
Grand Total						$9,735.00	$1,785.00

FIGURE 4-85

In the Lab

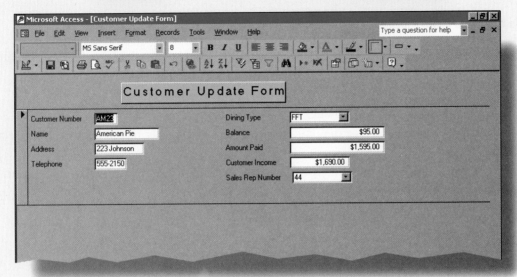

FIGURE 4-86

3 Presenting Data in the Condo Management Database

Problem: The condo management company already has realized several benefits from the database you created. The company now would like to prepare reports from the database. The company greatly appreciates the validation rules that were added to ensure that data is entered correctly. They now feel the data entry process can be improved even further by creating custom forms.

Instructions: If you are using the Microsoft Access 2002 Complete or the Microsoft Access 2002 Comprehensive text, open the Condo Management database that you used in Project 3. Otherwise, see the inside back cover for instructions for downloading the Data Disk or see your instructor for information on accessing the files required for this book. Perform the following tasks.

1. Create the Unit Rental Report shown in Figure 4-87. Sort the report in ascending order by unit number.
2. Print the report.

Unit Rental Report

Unit Number	Bedrooms	Bathrooms	Sleeps	Weekly Rate
101	1	1	2	$675.00
202	3	2	8	$1,400.00
204	2	2	6	$1,100.00
206	2	2	5	$925.00
300	3	2	10	$1,300.00
308	2	2	6	$950.00
403	1	1	2	$700.00
405	1	1	3	$750.00
500	3	3	8	$1,100.00
510	2	1	4	$825.00

FIGURE 4-87

(continued)

In the Lab

Presenting Data in the Condo Management Database *(continued)*

3. Create the Owner/Rental Units report shown in Figure 4-88. Sort the data by Unit Number within each group.
4. Print the report.
5. Create the form shown in Figure 4-89. Owner Id is a combo box.
6. Add the current date to the form. Place the date in the upper-right corner of the Form Header section. (*Hint:* Use Help to solve this problem.)
7. Print the form. To print the form, open the form, click File on the menu bar, and then click Print. Click Selected Record(s) as the Print Range. Click the OK button.

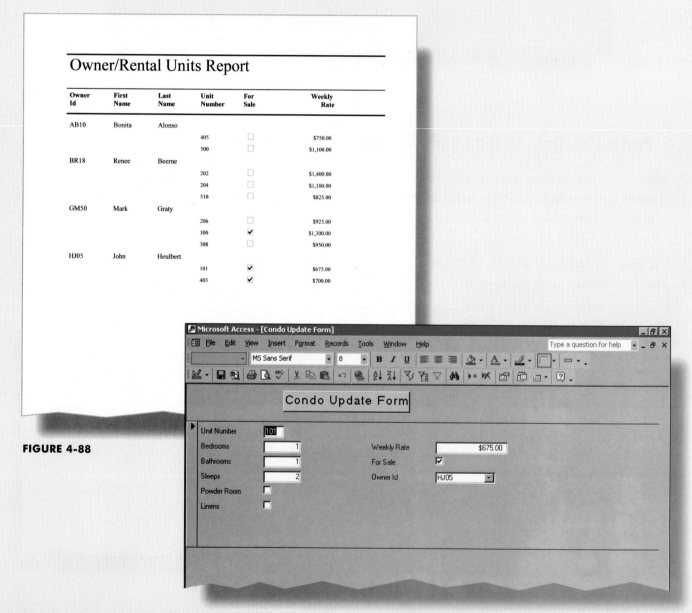

FIGURE 4-88

FIGURE 4-89

Cases and Places

The difficulty of these case studies varies:
▸ are the least difficult; ▸▸ are more difficult; and ▸▸▸ are the most difficult.

1 ▸ CompuWhiz is a small business formed by three college students to help organizations in need of computer expertise. CompuWhiz performs tasks such as, installation and maintenance of computer systems, computer training and back-up, and security tasks. The business uses a database to keep track of their customers. The CompuWhiz database is on the Access Data Disk. See the inside back cover for instructions for downloading the Data Disk or see your instructor for information on accessing the files required for this book. Use this database and create the report shown in Figure 4-90.

Technician/Clients Report

Technician Id	First Name	Last Name	Client Number	Name	Telephone Number	Balance
78	Yaowen	Chang				
			CJ78	Cindy Jo's	555-4242	$190.00
			LK23	Learn n Kids Day Care	555-4004	$75.00
			RE20	Real Food	555-9123	$185.00
82	Rick	Ortega				
			AR43	Artisan Co.	555-3434	$200.00
			BK18	Birdie's Kites	555-5678	$50.00
			LB42	Le Boutique	555-9012	$160.00
89	Irene	Smith				
			AL35	Aloha Gifts	555-1222	$165.00
			CL45	Class Act	555-9876	$150.00
			ME30	Mead Manufacturing.	555-0987	$195.00
			SR34	Shoe Repair	555-4378	$170.00

FIGURE 4-90

2 ▸ Using the database from Cases and Places 1 above, create the data entry form shown in Figure 4-91. Client Type and Technician Id are combo boxes. Print the form.

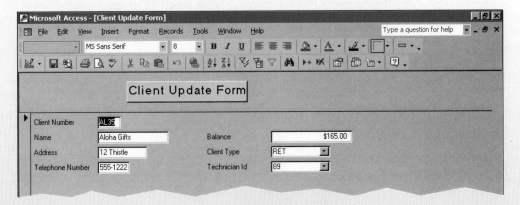

FIGURE 4-91

Cases and Places

3 ▶▶ A minor league ice hockey team recently moved to your town. The team has a small shop in the ice arena that sells items with the team logo. The shop manager uses a database to keep track of inventory and suppliers. The Hockey Shop database is on the Access Data Disk. See the inside back cover for instructions for downloading the Data Disk or see your instructor for information on accessing the files required for this book. Use this database to create a report similar to the one shown in Figure 4-81 on page A 4.57. Use a calculated control called Inventory Value that is the result of multiplying units on hand by cost. (*Hint:* See More About Calculated Controls in a Report on page A 4.33 to solve this problem). Sort the report in ascending order by item description. Print the report. Create the report shown in Figure 4-92. The report groups items by vendor and displays the average cost for each vendor.

Vendor/Items Report

Vendor Code	Name	Item Id	Description	On Hand	Cost
AC	Arnie Cheer				
		4593	Hockey Stick	8	$18.20
		5953	Knit Cap	10	$4.95
		6343	Sweatpants	9	$21.45
		7810	Sweatshirt	25	$27.50
					$18.03
BH	Beverage Holders				
		3683	Coffee Mug	20	$1.85
		4563	Glasses (4)	8	$8.20
					$5.03
LG	Logo Greats				
		3663	Baseball Cap	25	$9.25
		5923	Jacket	12	$49.23
		6189	Sports Towel	24	$3.58
		7930	Tee Shirt	11	$8.90
					$17.74

FIGURE 4-92

4 ▶▶ Using the database from Cases and Places 3 above, create an Item Update Form similar to the one shown in Figure 4-83 on page A 4.57. Use a calculated control called Inventory Value that is the result of multiplying units on hand by cost. Include a combo box for Vendor Code.

5 ▶▶▶ You are the president of the intramural swim club. Create a database to store information about the club's members. For each member, include member number, first name, last name, address (street address, city, state or province, zip or postal code), telephone number, birthdate, and a code to indicate swim specialty. Use swim specialties such as freestyle, backstroke, breaststroke, and butterfly. Create and print a report that lists members by swim specialty. In addition, create and print a form to help you update the database easily. Experiment with different styles.

Microsoft Access 2002

5

Enhancing Forms with OLE Fields, Hyperlinks, and Subforms

You will have mastered the material in this project when you can:

OBJECTIVES

- Add, update, and use date, memo, OLE, and hyperlink fields
- Change the row and column spacing in tables
- Save table properties
- Create a form with a subform
- Modify the subform design
- Move and resize fields on a form
- Change properties on a form
- Add a title to a form
- Use a form that contains a subform
- Use date and memo fields in a query
- Compact and repair a database

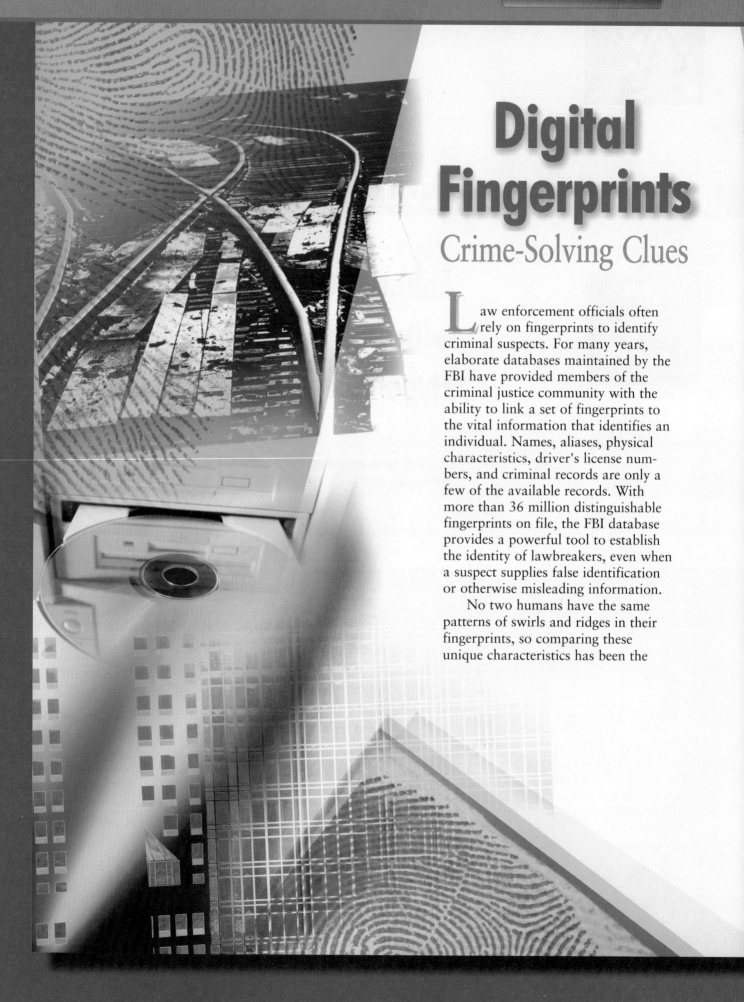

Digital Fingerprints
Crime-Solving Clues

Law enforcement officials often rely on fingerprints to identify criminal suspects. For many years, elaborate databases maintained by the FBI have provided members of the criminal justice community with the ability to link a set of fingerprints to the vital information that identifies an individual. Names, aliases, physical characteristics, driver's license numbers, and criminal records are only a few of the available records. With more than 36 million distinguishable fingerprints on file, the FBI database provides a powerful tool to establish the identity of lawbreakers, even when a suspect supplies false identification or otherwise misleading information.

No two humans have the same patterns of swirls and ridges in their fingerprints, so comparing these unique characteristics has been the

most powerful method of identifying people since Babylonians pioneered fingerprinting in 1700 b.c. Fingerprint identification technology is part of the growing field of biometrics, which identifies people based on physical characteristics. Manual comparisons of prints by looking through state and FBI files can take as long as three weeks, but computer database comparisons using search algorithms can make positive identifications in only two hours if a suspect is in custody.

The Federal Bureau of Investigation's Integrated Automated Fingerprint Identification System (IAFIS) is one of the largest of its kind, and the biggest single technology investment in FBI history. The system consists of a suite of powerful supercomputers, sophisticated image processing algorithms, and data management tools such as those available with Access 2002.

The FBI system is capable of rapidly and accurately searching a national criminal database with more than 400 million records. IAFIS is designed to be a rapid-response, paperless system that receives and processes electronic fingerprint images, criminal histories, and related data.

Law enforcement officials get the prints in two ways: when they arrest and book a suspect or when they obtain latent prints left accidentally at the crime scene. If the subject has been apprehended, the officer rolls the suspect's fingers on a small glass plate connected to a computer. If the suspect has not been identified or apprehended, an evidence technician goes to the crime scene

and uses special powders, chemicals, and lasers to lift and photograph the print. In both cases, the fingerprints are displayed on the computer monitor, traced with a stylus to enhance the lines, scanned, and digitized. These images then are transmitted electronically to the FBI and added to the database.

Using Remote Fingerprint Editing Software (RFES) freely distributed by the FBI, law enforcement agencies can transmit fingerprint images and query the IAFIS database from any personal computer. The FBI receives more than 50,000 such queries daily in an attempt to match prints with images stored in the database. To extend the capabilities of RFES, the FBI is working to develop Universal Latent Workstation (ULW) software. Using ULW, law enforcement officials can use a single digital image of a fingerprint to query not only the IAFIS, but fingerprint databases maintained by local or state authorities as well.

The IAFIS has marked the beginning of the end of the time-honored but laborious process of searching and checking fingerprints manually. Already, IAFIS has helped the FBI and other law enforcement officials nab nearly 3,000 fugitives a month. San Francisco investigators cleared nearly 14 times more latent cases during their first year using this system as compared with the previous year. Although electronic access to the IAFIS is not yet a reality for all state and local agencies, software such as RFES is helping to ensure that it will be.

Microsoft Access 2002

Enhancing Forms with OLE Fields, Hyperlinks, and Subforms

CASE PERSPECTIVE

After using the database, the management of Alisa Vending Services has found that it needs to maintain additional data on its drivers. Managers need to store the start date of each driver in the database. They want the database to contain a comment about each driver as well as the driver's picture. In addition, each driver now has a page on the Web, and the managers require easy access to this page from the database.

They would like to have a form created that incorporates some of the new fields with some of the existing fields. They want the form to include the customer number, name, amount paid, and current due amount for the customers of each driver. In addition, they need to display multiple customers on the screen at the same time. They want the capability of scrolling through all the customers of a driver and of accessing the driver's Web page directly from the form. They require queries that use the Start Date and Comment fields as criteria. Finally, they are concerned the database is getting larger than necessary and would like to compact the database to remove any wasted space. Your task is to help Alisa Vending Services make all these changes.

Introduction

This project creates the form shown in Figure 5-1. The form incorporates the following new features:

- New fields display on the form. The Comment field allows the organization to store notes concerning the driver. The Comment entry can be only as long as the organization desires. The Picture field holds a photograph of the driver.
- The Web Page field enables the user to access the driver's Web page directly from the database.
- The form not only shows data concerning the driver, but also the driver's customers. The customers are displayed as a table on the form.

Project Five — Enhancing the Alisa Vending Services Form

Before creating the required form for Alisa Vending Services, you must change the structure of the Driver table to incorporate the four new fields: Start Date, Comment, Picture, and Web Page. Each of these new fields uses a field type you have not encountered previously. Then, you must fill in these new fields with the appropriate data. The manner in which this is achieved depends on the field type. After entering data in the fields, you are to create the form including the table of customer data. You will create queries to obtain the answer to two important questions that reference the new fields. Finally, you will compact the database, thus ensuring the database does not occupy more space than is required.

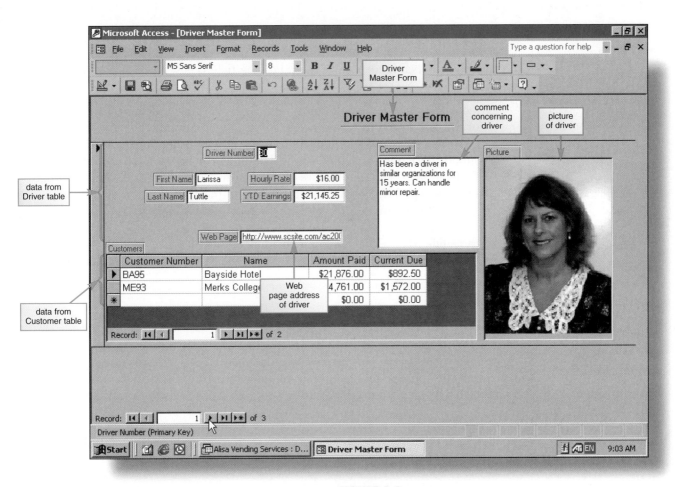

FIGURE 5-1

Note: A database containing pictures can get very large. Because this project illustrates adding pictures to a table, the Alisa Vending Services database is located in a folder called data on drive C and the pictures (bmp files) are located in a folder called pictures on drive C. You are encouraged to copy the Alisa Vending Services database to drive C or to a network drive, if possible. If you cannot do so, you will be instructed which steps to skip in this project.

Opening the Database

Before you can modify the Driver table and create the form, you must open the database. Perform the following steps to complete this task.

TO OPEN A DATABASE

1 Click the Start button, click Programs on the Start menu, and then click Microsoft Access on the Programs submenu.

2 Click Open on the Database toolbar, and then click Local Drive (C:) in the Look in box. Click the data folder (assuming that your database is stored in a folder called data), and then make sure the database called Alisa Vending Services is selected.

3 Click the Open button.

The database is open and the Alisa Vending Services : Database window displays.

More *About*

The Access Help System

Need Help? It is no further than the Ask a Question box in the upper-right corner of the window. Click the box that contains the text, Type a question for help (Figure 5-1) type help and then press the ENTER key. Access will respond with a list of items you can click to learn about obtaining help on any Access-related topic. To find out what is new is Access 2002, type what's new in Access in the Ask a Question box.

More About

OLE Data Type

A field with a data type of OLE can store data such as Microsoft Word or Excel documents, pictures, sound, and other types of binary data created in other programs. For more information, visit the Access 2002 More About page (scsite.com/ac2002/more.htm) and then click OLE Data Type.

Date, Memo, OLE, and Hyperlink Fields

The data to be added incorporates the following field types:

1. **Date** (**D**) — The field contains only valid dates.
2. **Memo** (**M**) — The field contains text that is variable in length. The length of the text stored in memo fields is virtually unlimited.
3. **OLE** (**O**) — The field contains objects created by other applications that support **OLE** (**Object Linking and Embedding**) as a server. Object Linking and Embedding is a special feature of Microsoft Windows that creates a special relationship between Microsoft Access and the application that created the object. When you edit the object, Microsoft Access returns automatically to the application that created the object.
4. **Hyperlink** (**H**) — This field contains links to other office documents or to Web pages. If the link is to a Web page, the field will contain the address of the Web page.

Adding Fields to a Table

You add new fields to the Driver table by modifying the design of the table and inserting the fields at the appropriate position in the table structure. Perform the following steps to add the Start Date, Comment, Picture, and Web Page fields to the Driver table.

Steps **To Add Fields to a Table**

1 **If necessary, click Tables on the Objects bar. Right-click Driver and then point to Design View on the shortcut menu.**

The shortcut menu for the Driver table displays, and the Design View command is highlighted (Figure 5-2).

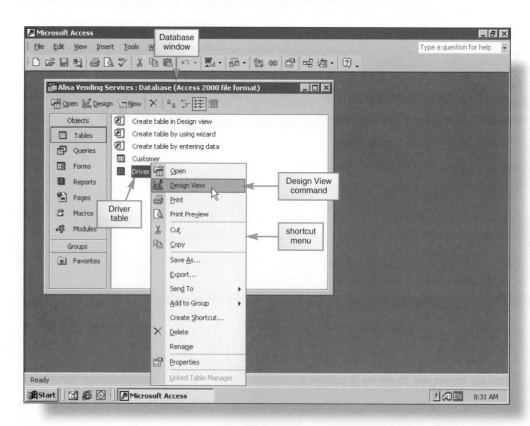

FIGURE 5-2

2 Click Design View on the shortcut menu and then maximize the Microsoft Access – [Driver : Table] window. Point to the position for the new field (the Field Name column in the row following the YTD Earnings field).

The Microsoft Access – [Driver : Table] window displays (Figure 5-3).

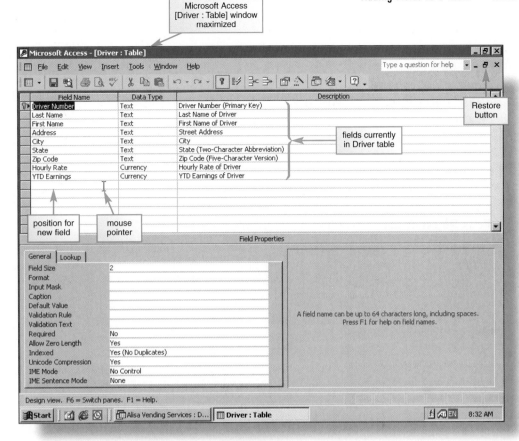

FIGURE 5-3

3 Click the position for the new field. **Type** Start Date **as the field name, press the TAB key, select Date/Time as the data type, press the TAB key, type** Start Date **as the description, and then press the TAB key.**

The Start Date field is entered (Figure 5-4).

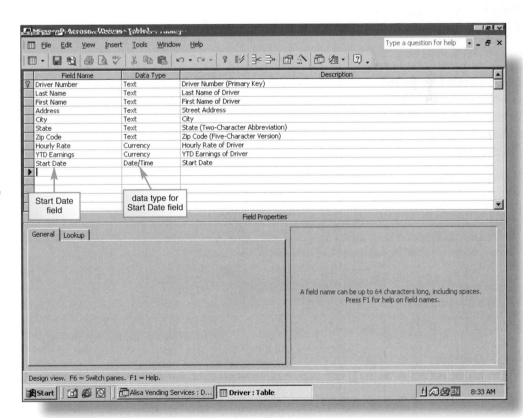

FIGURE 5-4

4 Type Comment **as the field name, press the TAB key, select Memo as the data type, press the TAB key, type** Comment Concerning Driver **as the description, and then press the TAB key. Type** Picture **as the field name, press the TAB key, select OLE Object as the data type, press the TAB key, type** Picture of Driver **as the description, and then press the TAB key. Type** Web Page **as the field name, press the TAB key, select Hyperlink as the data type, press the TAB key, and then type** Address of Driver's Web Page **as the description. Point to the Close Window button.**

The new fields are entered (Figure 5-5).

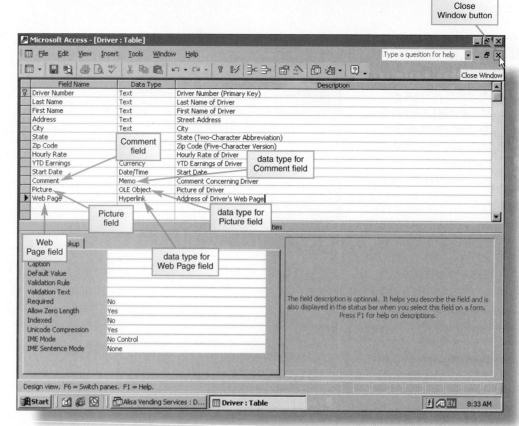

FIGURE 5-5

5 **Close the window by clicking its Close Window button. Click the Yes button in the Microsoft Access dialog box to save the changes.**

The new fields have been added to the structure of the Driver table.

Updating the New Fields

After adding the new fields to the table, the next task is to enter data into the fields. The manner in which this is accomplished depends on the field type. The following sections cover the methods for updating date fields, memo fields, OLE fields, and Hyperlink fields.

Entering Data in Date Fields

To enter data in **date fields,** simply type the dates and include slashes (/). Perform the following steps to add the start dates for all three drivers using Datasheet view.

 To Enter Data in Date Fields

1 **With the Database window on the screen, right-click the Driver table. Point to Open on the shortcut menu.**

The shortcut menu displays, and the Open command is highlighted (Figure 5-6).

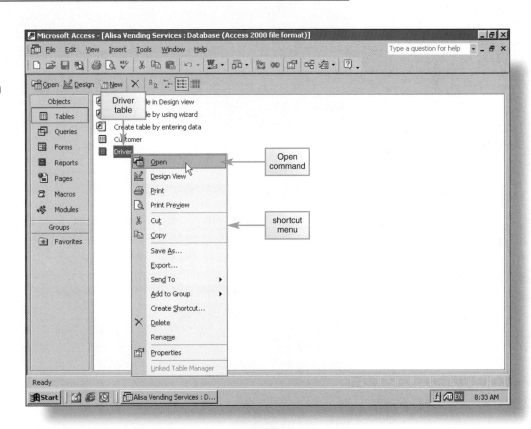

FIGURE 5-6

2 **Click Open on the shortcut menu and then, if necessary, maximize the window. Point to the right scroll arrow.**

The Driver table displays in Datasheet view in the maximized window (Figure 5-7).

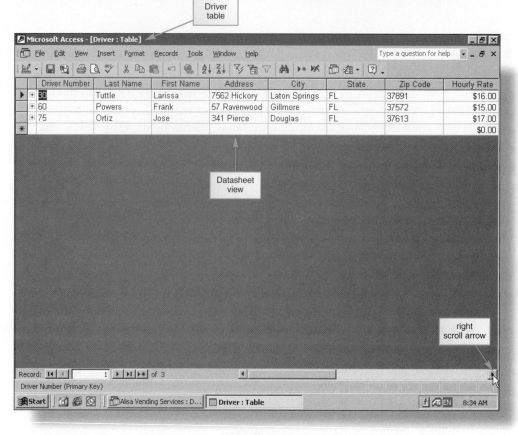

FIGURE 5-7

3 **Repeatedly click the right scroll arrow until the new fields display and then click the Start Date field on the first record (Figure 5-8).**

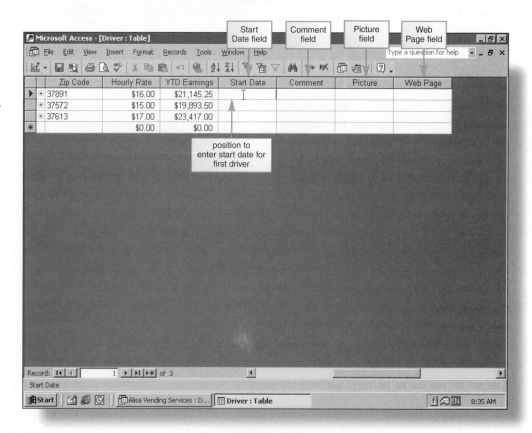

FIGURE 5-8

4 **Type** 9/15/2001 as the date. Press the DOWN ARROW key. **Type** 2/17/2001 as the start date on the second record and then press the DOWN ARROW key. **Type** 6/14/2001 as the start date on the third record.

The dates are entered (Figure 5-9). If the dates do not display with four-digit years, click the Start button, click Settings, and then click Control Panel. Double-click Regional Settings, click the Date tab, and then change the Short date style to MM/dd/yyyy. Click the OK button. Click the Close button on the Control Panel window title bar.

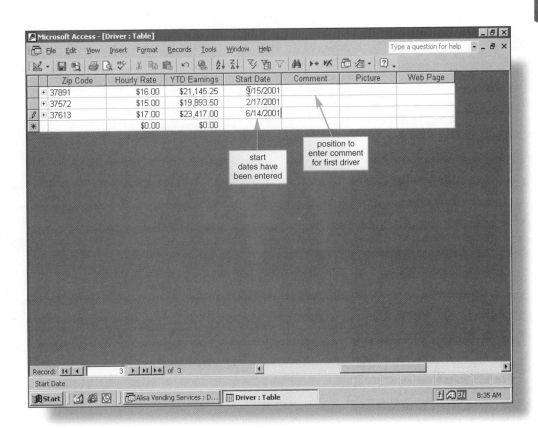

FIGURE 5-9

Entering Data in Memo Fields

To update a **memo field**, simply type the data in the field. With the current spacing on the screen, only a small portion of the memo will display. To correct this problem, you will change the spacing later to allow more room for the memo. Perform the following steps to enter each driver's comment.

Steps **To Enter Data in Memo Fields**

1 **If necessary, click the right scroll arrow so the Comment field displays. Click the Comment field on the first record. Type** Has been a driver in similar organizations for 15 years. Can handle minor repair. **as the entry.**

The last portion of the comment displays (Figure 5-10).

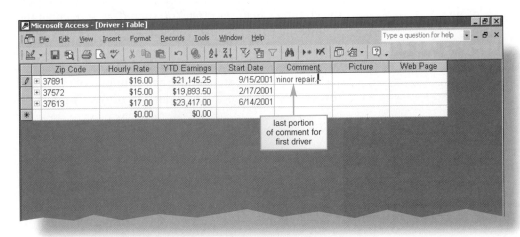

FIGURE 5-10

2 **Click the Comment field on the second record. Type** Previously worked for company that produced vending machines. Can handle significant repairs when problems occur. **as the entry.**

3 **Click the Comment field on the third record. Type** New to vending machines, but has been a driver in service-related industries for several years. **as the entry.**

All the comments are entered (Figure 5-11). The first portion of the comments for the first two drivers displays. Because the insertion point still is in the field for the third driver, only the last portion of the comment displays.

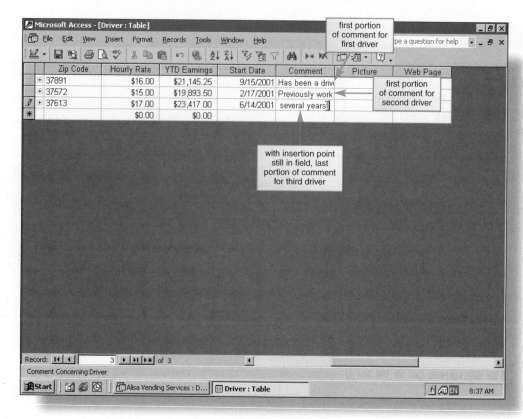

FIGURE 5-11

Changing the Row and Column Size

To undo changes to the row height, right-click the row selector, click Row Height on the shortcut menu, and then click the Standard Height check box in the Row Height dialog box. To undo changes to the column width, right-click the field selector, click Column Width on the shortcut menu, and then click the Standard Width check box in the Column Width dialog box.

Changing the Row and Column Size

Only a small portion of the comments displays in the datasheet. To allow more of the information to display, you can expand the size of the rows and the columns. You can change the size of a column by using the field selector. The **field selector** is the bar containing the field name. You position the mouse pointer on the right boundary of the column's field selector. You then drag to change the size of the column. To change the size of a row, you use a record's **record selector,** which is the small box at the beginning of each record. You position the mouse pointer on the lower boundary of the record's record selector and then drag to resize the row.

The following steps resize the column containing the Comment field and the rows of the table so a larger portion of the Comment field text will display.

To Change the Row and Column Size

1 **Point to the line between the column headings for the Comment and Picture columns.**

The mouse pointer changes to a two-headed horizontal arrow with a vertical crossbar, indicating you can drag the line to resize the column (Figure 5-12).

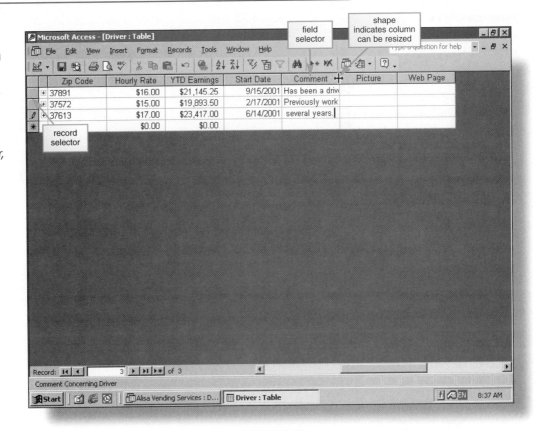

FIGURE 5-12

2 **Drag to the right to resize the Comment column to the approximate size shown in Figure 5-13 and then point to the line between the first and second record selectors as shown in the figure.**

The mouse pointer changes to a two-headed vertical arrow with a horizontal crossbar, indicating you can drag the line to resize the row.

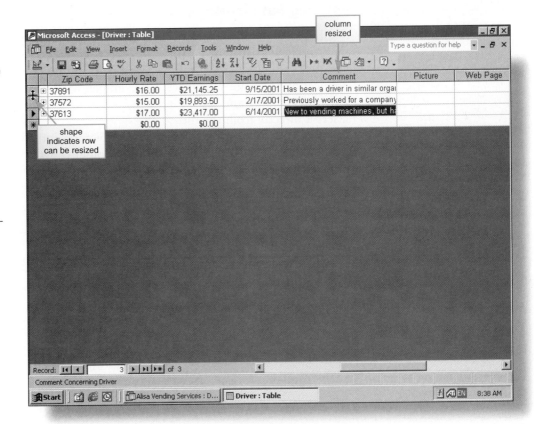

FIGURE 5-13

3 **Drag the edge of the row to approximately the position shown in Figure 5-14.**

All the rows are resized at the same time (Figure 5-14). The comments now display in their entirety. The last row has a different appearance from the other two because it still is selected.

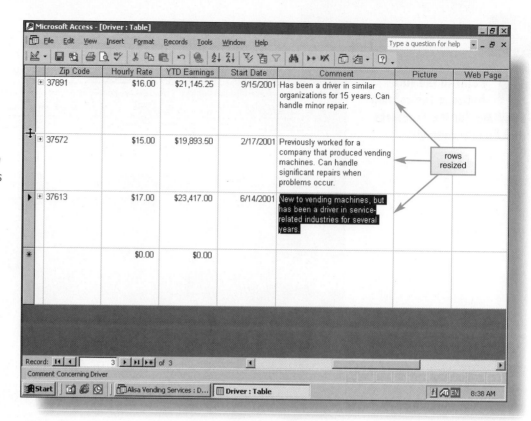

FIGURE 5-14

Entering Data in OLE Fields

To insert data into an OLE field, you will use the **Insert Object command** on the OLE field's shortcut menu. The Insert Object command presents a list of the various types of objects that can be inserted. Access then opens the corresponding application to create the object, for example, Microsoft Drawing. If the object already is created and stored in a file, as is the case in this project, you simply insert it directly from the file.

Perform the following steps to insert pictures into the Picture field. The steps assume that the pictures are located in a folder called pictures on drive C. If your pictures are located elsewhere, you will need to make the appropriate changes. The picture files to be inserted have the file extension, bmp.

Note: If your database is on a floppy disk (drive A), skip the steps in this section so your database will not become too large for your disk.

To Enter Data in OLE Fields and Convert the Data to Pictures

1 **Ensure the Picture field displays. Right-click the Picture field on the first record. Point to Insert Object on the shortcut menu.**

The shortcut menu for the Picture field displays (Figure 5-15). On your shortcut menu, the Paste command may be dimmed.

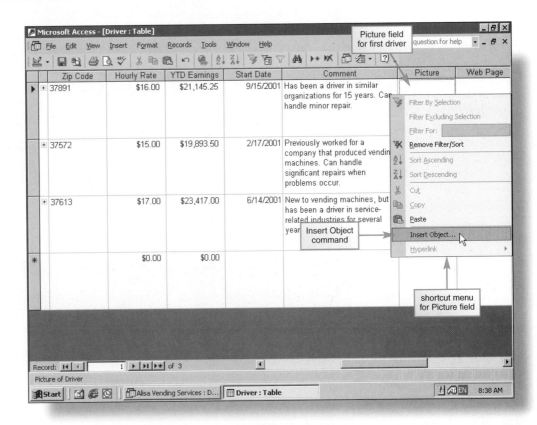

FIGURE 5-15

2 **Click Insert Object. Point to the Create from File option button in the Microsoft Access dialog box.**

The Microsoft Access dialog box, and the Object Type list display (Figure 5-16).

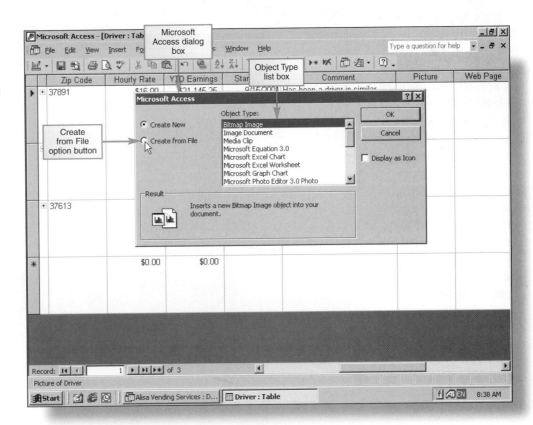

FIGURE 5-16

3 **Click Create from File.**

The Create from File option button is selected, and the location of the Alisa Vending Services database displays in the File text box (Figure 5-17).

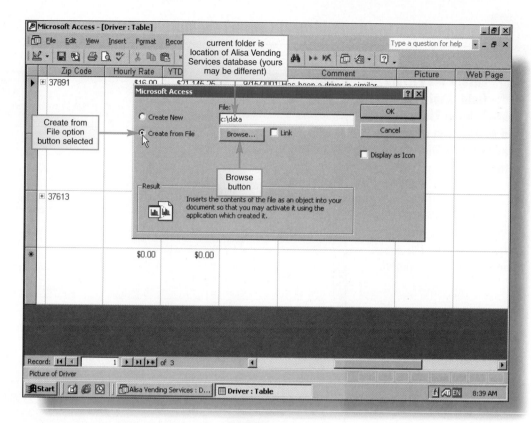

FIGURE 5-17

4 If necessary, use the BACKSPACE key or the DELETE key to delete the current entry in the File text box. Then, type c:\pictures in the File text box. (If your pictures are located elsewhere, type the name and location of the folder where they are located instead of c:\pictures.) Click the Browse button, click pict1, and then point to the OK button. If there is more than one pict1 file in your list, be sure the icon is the same as that shown in Figure 5-18.

The Browse dialog box displays (Figure 5-18). If you do not have the pictures, you will need to locate the folder in which yours are stored.

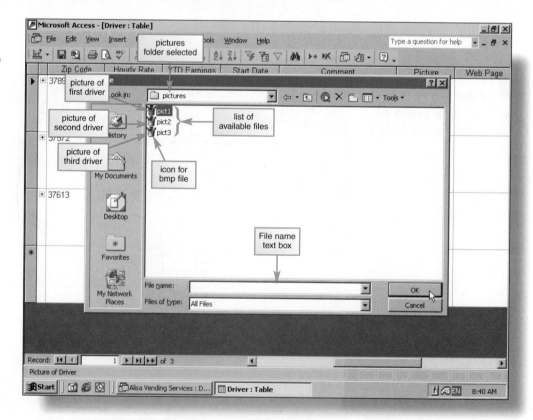

FIGURE 5-18

5 Click the OK button and then point to the OK button in the Microsoft Access dialog box.

The Browse dialog box closes and the Microsoft Access dialog box displays (Figure 5-19). The name of the selected picture displays in the File text box.

6 Click the OK button.

7 Insert the pictures into the second and third records using the techniques illustrated in Steps 1 through 6. For the second record, select the picture named pict2. For the third record, select the picture named pict3.

The pictures are inserted.

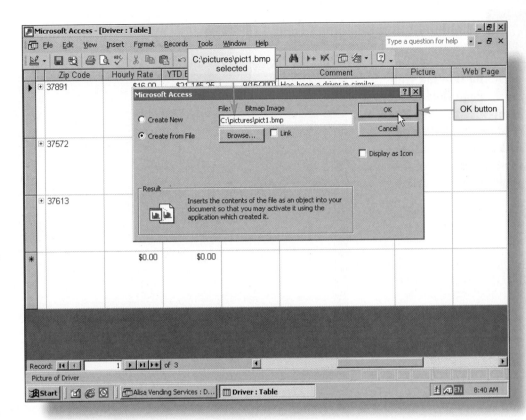

FIGURE 5-19

Entering Data in Hyperlink Fields

To insert data into a Hyperlink field, you will use the **Hyperlink command** on the Hyperlink field's shortcut menu. You then edit the hyperlink. You can enter the Web page address for the appropriate Web page or specify a file that contains the document to which you wish to link.

Perform the steps on the next page to insert data into the Web Page field.

Other **Ways**

1. On Insert menu click Object
2. In Voice Command mode, say "Insert, Object"

More **About**

Updating OLE Fields

OLE fields can occupy a great deal of space. To save space in your database, you can convert a picture from Bitmap Image to Picture (Device Independent Bitmap). To make the conversion, right-click the field, click Bitmap Image Object, click Convert, and then double-click Picture.

Steps **To Enter Data in Hyperlink Fields**

1 **Be sure the Web Page field displays.** **Right-click the Web Page field on the first record, click Hyperlink on the shortcut menu, and then point to Edit Hyperlink.**

The shortcut menu for the Web Page field displays (Figure 5-20). The submenu for the Hyperlink command also displays.

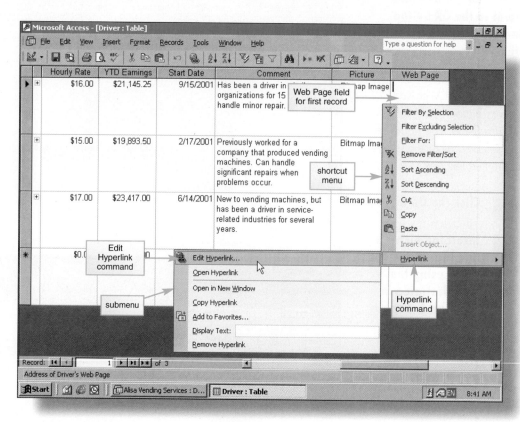

FIGURE 5-20

2 **Click Edit Hyperlink. Type** www.scsite.com/ac2002/driver1.htm **in the Address text box. Point to the OK button. (If you do not have access to the Internet, type** a:\driver1.htm **in the Address text box instead of www.scsite.com/ac2002/driver1.htm as the Web page address.)**

The Insert Hyperlink dialog box displays, and a list of browsed pages displays in the list box. Your list of browsed pages may be different or the contents of the current folder may display instead of browsed pages (Figure 5-21).

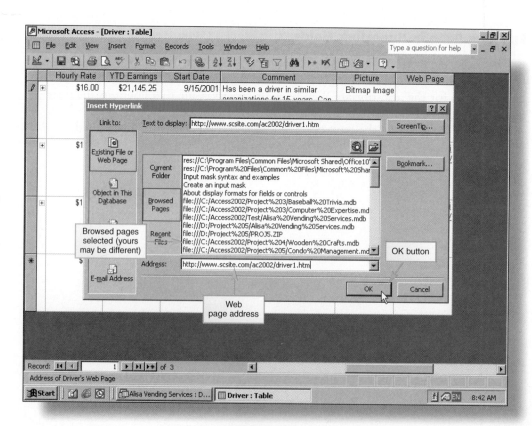

FIGURE 5-21

3 Click the OK button. Use the techniques described in Steps 1 and 2 to enter Web page data for the second and third drivers. For the second driver, type `www.scsite.com/ac2002/driver2.htm` **as the Web page address; and for the third, type** `www.scsite.com/ac2002/driver3.htm` **as the Web page address. (If you do not have access to the Internet, type** `a:\driver2.htm` **for the second driver and** `a:\driver3.htm` **for the third driver.) Point to the Close Window button.**

The Web page data is entered (Figure 5-22).

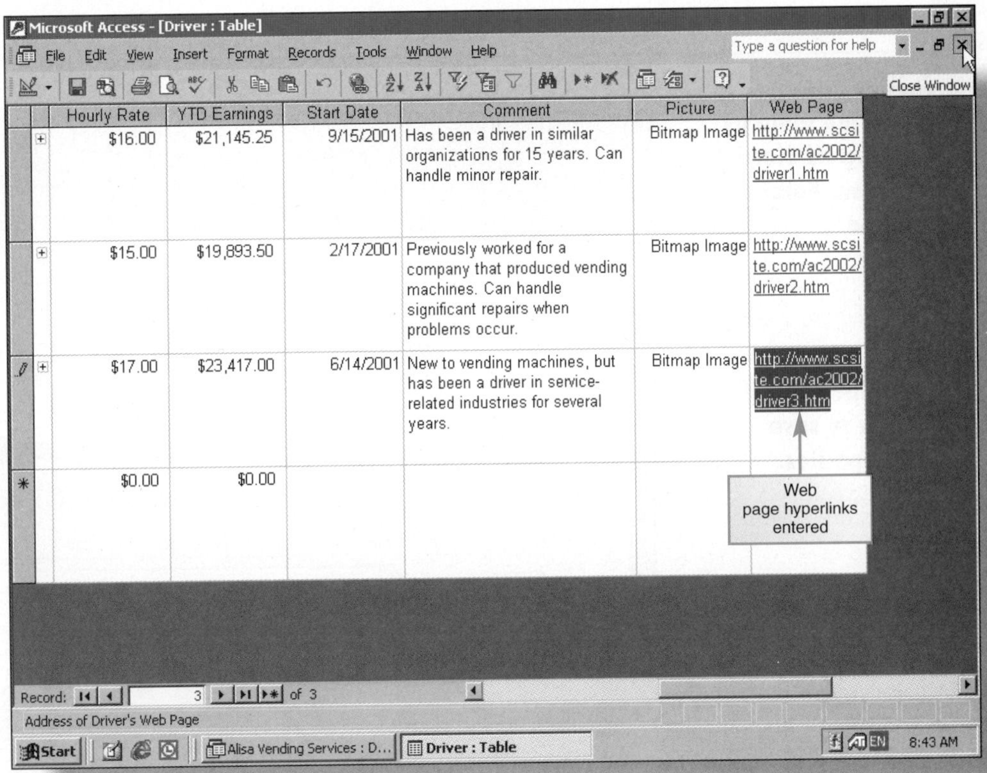

FIGURE 5-22

Other Ways

1. On Insert menu click Hyperlink
2. In Voice Command mode, say "Insert, Hyperlink"

Saving the Table Properties

The row and column spacing are **table properties**. When changing any table properties, the changes apply only as long as the table is active *unless they are saved*. If they are saved, they will apply every time the table is opened. To save them, simply close the table. If any properties have changed, a Microsoft Access dialog box will ask if you want to save the changes. By answering Yes, you can save the changes.

Perform the steps on the next page to close the table and save the properties that have been changed.

Steps **To Close the Table and Save the Properties**

1 Close the table by clicking its Close Window button. Point to the Yes button.

The Microsoft Access dialog box displays (Figure 5-23).

2 Click the Yes button to save the table properties.

The properties are saved.

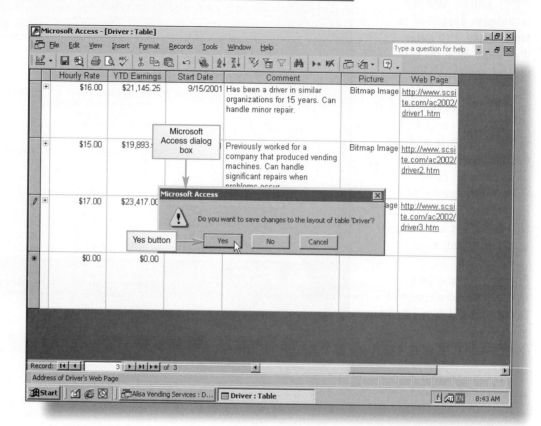

FIGURE 5-23

Although the pictures do not display on the screen, you can view them at any time. To view the picture of a particular driver, point to the Picture field for the driver, and then right-click to display the shortcut menu. Click Bitmap Image Object on the shortcut menu and then click Open. The picture will display. Once you have finished viewing the picture, close the window containing the picture by clicking its Close button. You also can view the Web page for a driver, by clicking the driver's Web Page field.

More About

Subforms

When you create forms with subforms, the tables for the main form and the subform must be related. The relationship must have been set previously in the Relationships window. To see if your tables are related, click the Relationships button. Relationships between tables display as lines connecting the tables.

Advanced Form Techniques

The form in this project includes data from both the Driver and Customer tables. The form will display data concerning one driver. It also will display data concerning the many customers to which the driver is assigned. Formally, the relationship between drivers and customers is called a **one-to-many relationship** (*one* driver services *many* customers).

To include the data for the many customers of a driver on the form, the customer data must display in a **subform,** which is a form that is contained within another form. The form in which the subform is contained is called the main form. Thus, the **main form** will contain driver data, and the subform will contain customer data.

Creating a Form with a Subform

No special action is required to create a form with a subform if you use the Form Wizard. You must, however, have created previously a one-to-many relationship between the two tables. The **Form Wizard** will create both the form and subform automatically once you have selected the tables and indicated the general organization of your data. Perform the following steps to create the form and subform.

Steps | **To Create a Form with a Subform Using the Form Wizard**

1 **Click Forms on the Objects bar, right-click Create form by using wizard and then point to Open on the shortcut menu.**

The shortcut menu displays (Figure 5-24).

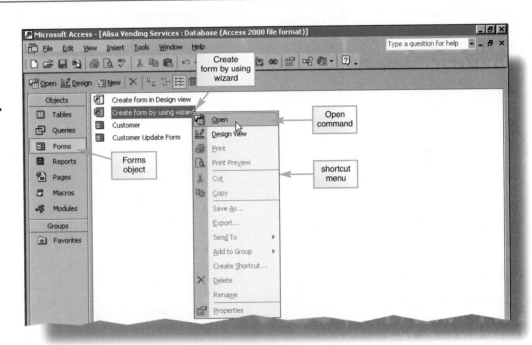

FIGURE 5-24

2 **Click Open on the shortcut menu, click the Tables/Queries box arrow, and then point to Table: Driver.**

The list of available tables and queries displays (Figure 5-25).

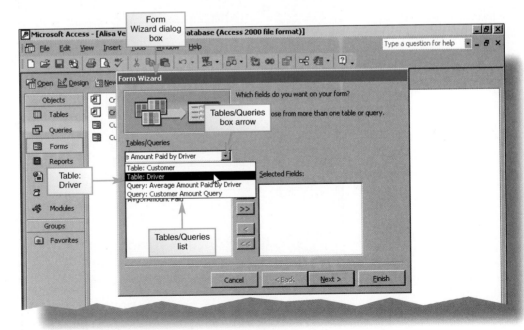

FIGURE 5-25

3 **Click Table: Driver. With the Driver Number field selected in the Available Fields box, click the Add Field button. Select the First Name, Last Name, Hourly Rate, YTD Earnings, Web Page, Comment, and Picture fields by clicking the field and then clicking the Add Field button. Click the Table/Queries box arrow and then point to Table: Customer.**

The fields from the Driver table are selected for the form (Figure 5-26).

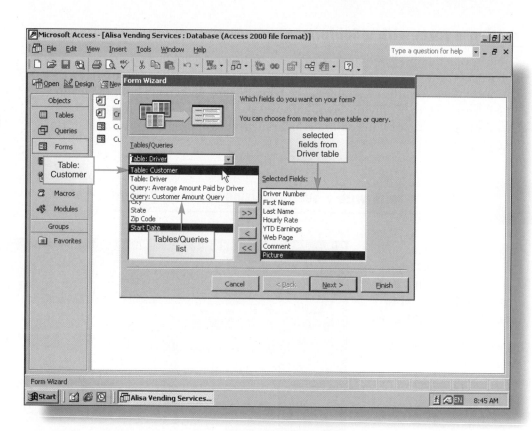

FIGURE 5-26

4 **Click Table: Customer. Select the Customer Number, Name, Amount Paid, and Current Due fields. Point to the Next button.**

The fields are selected (Figure 5-27).

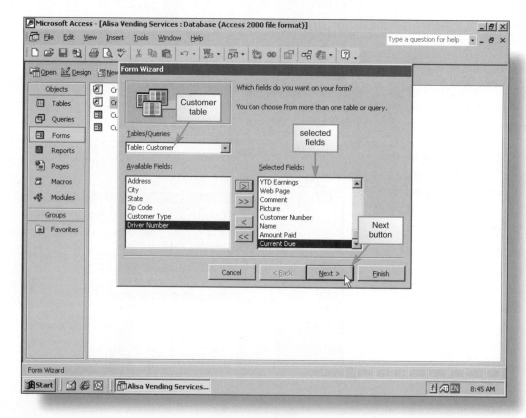

FIGURE 5-27

5 Click the Next button.

The Form Wizard dialog box displays, requesting how you want to view the data: by Driver or by Customer (Figure 5-28). The highlighted selection, by Driver, is correct. The box on the right indicates visually that the main organization is by Driver, with the Driver fields listed at the top. Contained within the form is a subform that contains customer data.

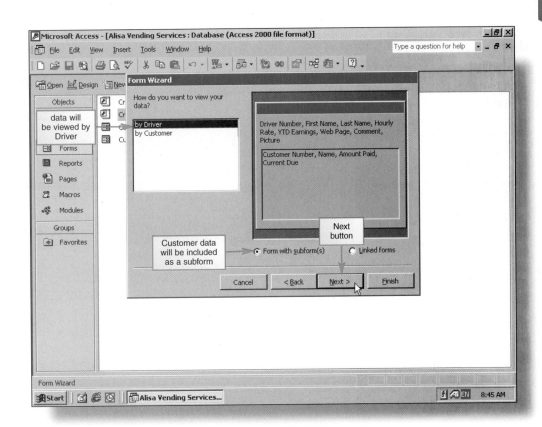

FIGURE 5-28

6 Click the Next button.

The Form Wizard dialog box displays, requesting the layout for the subform (Figure 5-29). This subform is to display in Datasheet view.

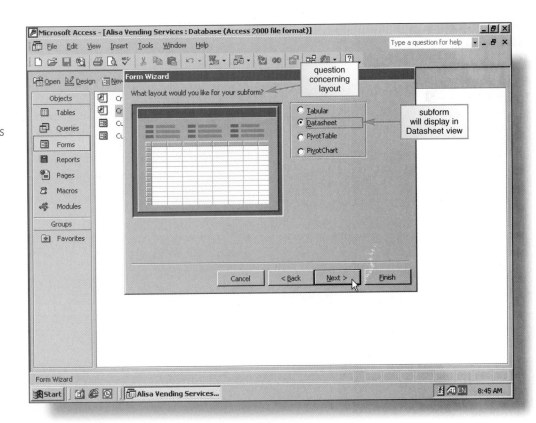

FIGURE 5-29

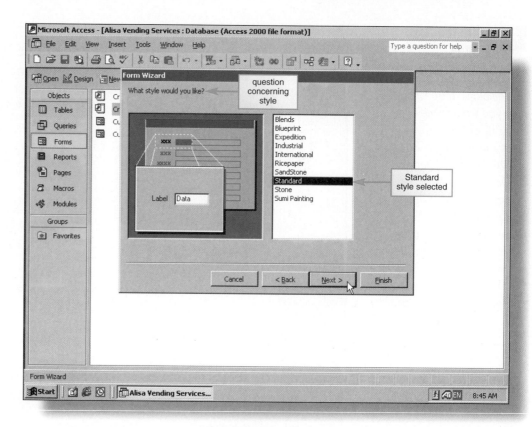

7 Be sure Datasheet is selected and then click the Next button. Ensure Standard style is selected.

The Form Wizard dialog box displays, requesting a style for the report, and Standard is selected (Figure 5-30).

FIGURE 5-30

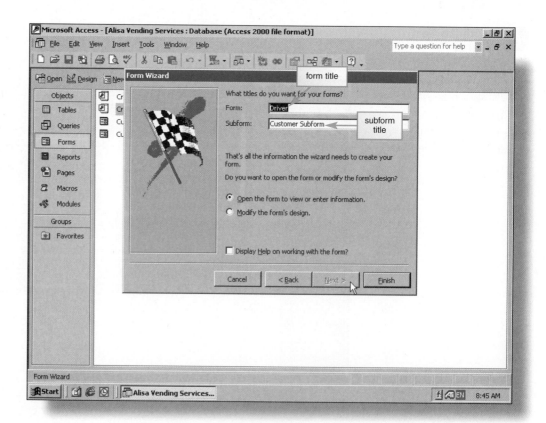

8 Click the Next button.

The Form Wizard dialog box displays (Figure 5-31). You use this dialog box to change the titles of the form and subform.

FIGURE 5-31

9 Type Driver Master Form **as the title of the form. Click the Subform text box, use the DELETE or BACKSPACE key to erase the current entry, and then type** Customers **as the name of the subform. Point to the Finish button.**

The titles are changed (Figure 5-32).

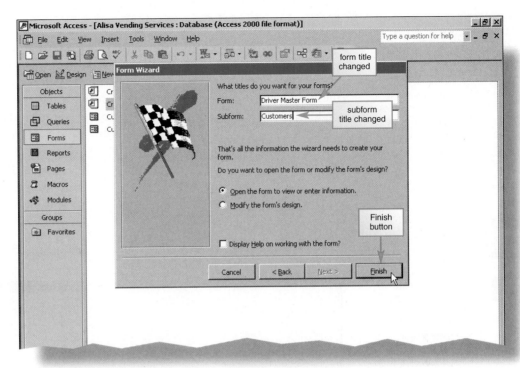

FIGURE 5-32

10 **Click the Finish button.**

The form displays (Figure 5-33). Your form layout may differ slightly. You will modify the layout in the following sections.

11 **Close the form by clicking its Close Window button.**

The form and subform now have been saved as part of the database and are available for future use.

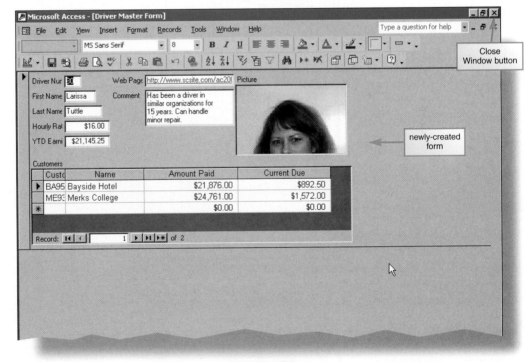

FIGURE 5-33

Other Ways

1. In Voice Command mode, say "Insert, Form, Form Wizard"

Subform Design

To change the appearance of the subform, make sure the subform control is not selected, right-click the form selector for the subform, click Properties, and then change the Default View property.

Modifying the Subform Design

The next task is to modify the spacing of the columns in the subform. The Customer Number column is so narrow that only the letters, Custo, display. Conversely, the Amount Paid column is much wider than needed. You can correct these problems by right-clicking the subform in the Database window and then clicking Design View. When the design of the subform displays, you then can convert it to Datasheet view. At this point, you resize each column by double-clicking the border to the right of the column name.

Perform the following steps to modify the subform design to improve the column spacing.

Steps **To Modify the Subform Design**

---

1 With the Forms object selected, right-click Customers. Point to Design View on the shortcut menu.

The shortcut menu for the subform displays (Figure 5-34).

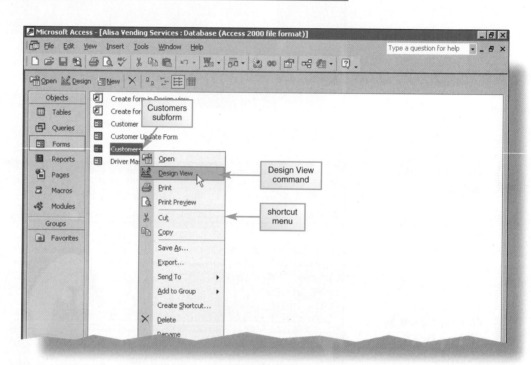

FIGURE 5-34

2 Click Design View on the shortcut menu. If the field list displays, point to its Close button (Figure 5-35).

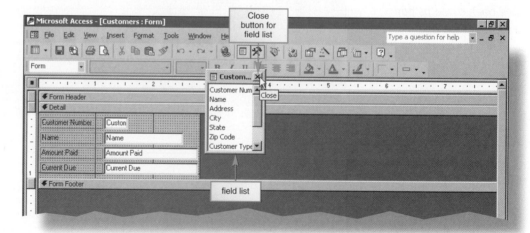

FIGURE 5-35

3 If the field list displays, click its Close button. Click the View button arrow on the Form Design toolbar and then point to Datasheet View.

The View list displays (Figure 5-36).

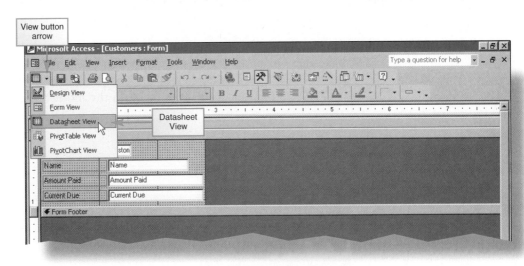

FIGURE 5-36

4 Click Datasheet View to display the subform in Datasheet view. Resize each of the columns by pointing to the right edge of the field selector (to the right of the column name) and double-clicking. Point to the Close Window button.

The subform displays in Datasheet view (Figure 5-37). The columns have been resized. You also can resize each column by dragging the right edge of the field selector.

5 Close the subform by clicking its Close Window button.

The changes are made and saved.

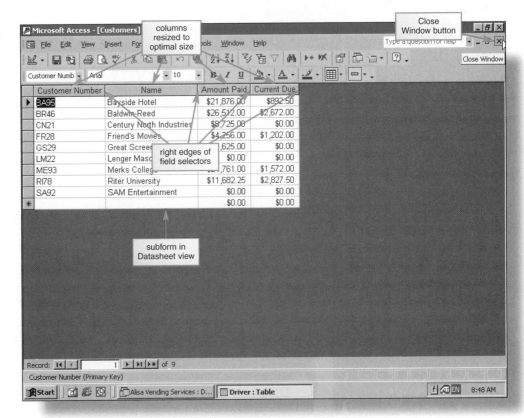

FIGURE 5-37

Modifying the Form Design

The next step is to make several changes to the form. Various objects need to be moved or resized. The properties of the picture need to be adjusted so the entire picture displays. The appearance of the labels needs to be changed, and a title needs to be added to the form.

Right-click the form in the Database window and then click Design View to make these or other changes to the design of the form. If the toolbox is on the screen, make sure it is docked at the bottom of the screen.

Perform the following steps to begin the modification of the form design.

Steps **To Modify the Form Design**

1 **Right-click Driver Master Form. Point to Design View on the shortcut menu.**

The shortcut menu for the form displays (Figure 5-38).

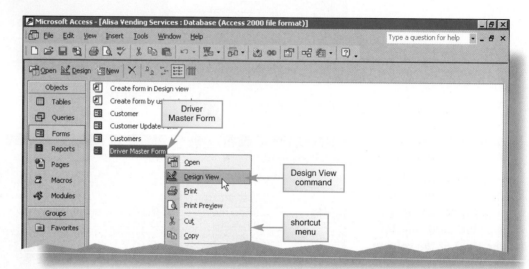

FIGURE 5-38

2 **Click Design View on the shortcut menu. If necessary, maximize the window. If the toolbox does not display, click the Toolbox button on the toolbar. Make sure it is docked at the bottom of the screen as shown in Figure 5-39. If it is not, drag its title bar to the bottom of the screen to dock it there. Your form layout may differ slightly. In the following sections, you will modify the form to match that shown in Figure 5-1 on page A 5.05.**

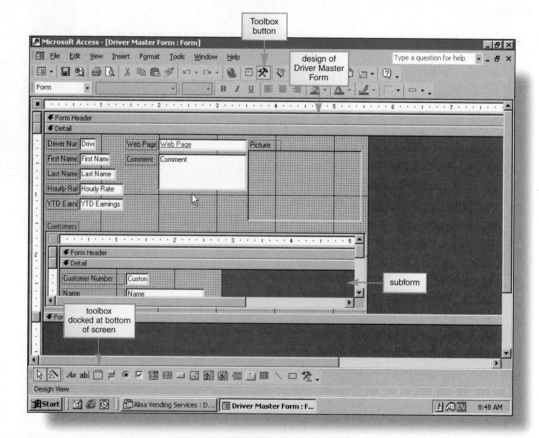

FIGURE 5-39

Moving and Resizing Fields

Fields on this form can be moved or resized just as they were in the form created in the previous project. First, click the field. To move it, move the mouse pointer to the boundary of the field so it becomes a hand and then drag the field. To resize a field, drag the appropriate sizing handle. The following steps move certain fields on the form. They also resize the fields appropriately.

 Steps **To Move and Resize Fields**

1 Click the Picture control, and then move the mouse pointer until the shape changes to a hand.

The Picture control is selected, and sizing handles display (Figure 5-40).

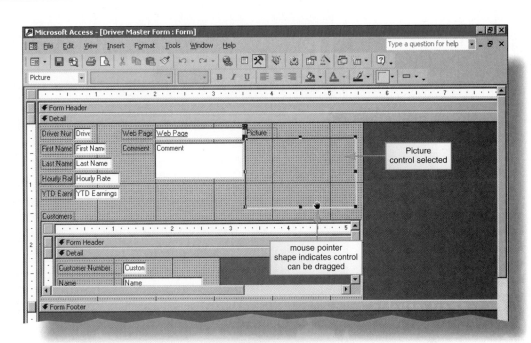

FIGURE 5-40

2 Drag the Picture control to approximately the position shown in Figure 5-41 and then point to the sizing handle on the lower edge of the control.

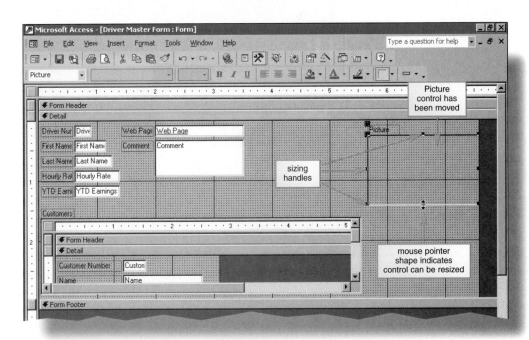

FIGURE 5-41

3 Drag the lower sizing handle to approximately the position shown in Figure 5-42.

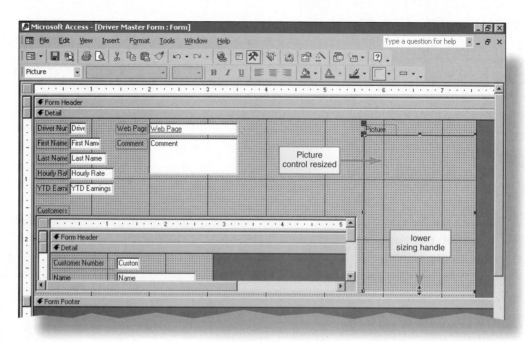

FIGURE 5-42

4 Move and resize the Comment control to the approximate position and size shown in Figure 5-43. Point to the Move handle for the label for the Comment control in preparation for the next task.

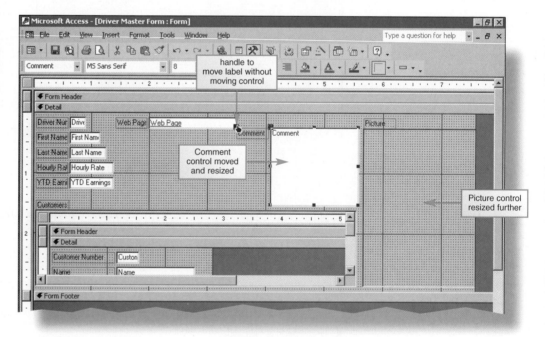

FIGURE 5-43

Moving Labels

To move a label independently from the field with which the label is associated, point to the large, **move handle** in the upper-left corner of the label. The shape of the mouse pointer changes to a hand with a pointing finger. By dragging this move handle, you will move the label without moving the associated field. Perform the following step to move the label of the Comment field without moving the field itself.

Steps To Move a Label

1 Be sure the Comment field is selected and then drag the Move handle for its label to the position shown in Figure 5-44.

The label is moved. The shape of the mouse pointer is a hand with a pointing finger.

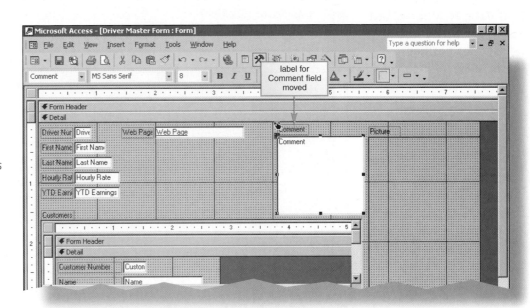

FIGURE 5-44

Moving Remaining Fields

The remaining fields on this form also need to be moved into appropriate positions. The following steps move these fields on the form.

Steps To Move Fields

1 Click the Web Page field, move the mouse pointer until the shape changes to a hand, and then drag the field to the position shown in Figure 5-45.

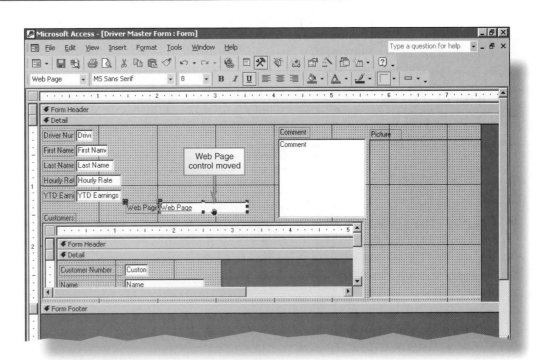

FIGURE 5-45

2 Drag the Hourly Rate, YTD Earnings, Start Date, First Name, Last Name, and Driver Number fields to the positions shown in Figure 5-46.

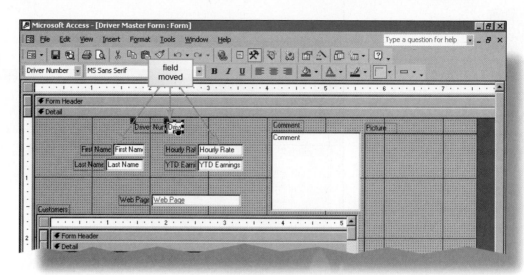

FIGURE 5-46

Changing Label Alignment

The labels for the Driver Number, First Name, Last Name, Hourly Rate, YTD Earnings, Start Date, and Web Page fields illustrated in Figure 5-1 on page A 5.05 are **right-aligned**, that is, aligned with the right margin. Because the labels currently are left-aligned, the alignment needs to be changed. To change the alignment, right-click the label to display the shortcut menu, click Properties, and then scroll to display the Text Align property. Click Text Align. In the property sheet, you can select the appropriate alignment.

In some cases, you will want to make the same change to several objects, perhaps to several labels at one time. Instead of making the changes individually, you can select all the objects at once and then make a single change. Perform the following steps to change the alignment of the labels.

Steps **To Change Label Alignment**

1 If the label for the Driver Number field is not already selected, click it.

The label for the Driver Number field is selected (Figure 5-47).

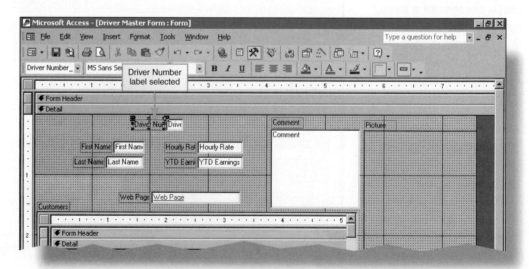

FIGURE 5-47

2 Select the labels for the First Name, Last Name, Hourly Rate, YTD Earnings, and Web Page fields by clicking them while holding down the SHIFT key. Right-click any of the selected labels and then point to Properties on the shortcut menu.

The shortcut menu displays (Figure 5-48).

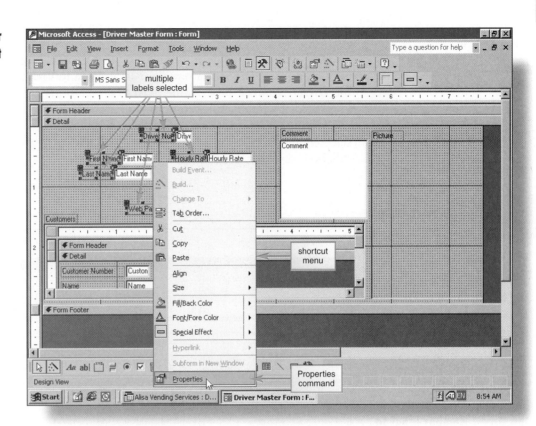

FIGURE 5-48

3 Click Properties and then click the down scroll arrow until the Text Align property displays. Click Text Align, click the Text Align property box arrow, and then point to Right.

The Multiple selection property sheet displays (Figure 5-49). The Text Align property is selected and the list of available options for the Text Align property displays. Depending on where you clicked in the property box, the General property may be highlighted.

4 Click Right to select right alignment for the labels. Close the Multiple selection property sheet by clicking its Close button.

The alignment is changed.

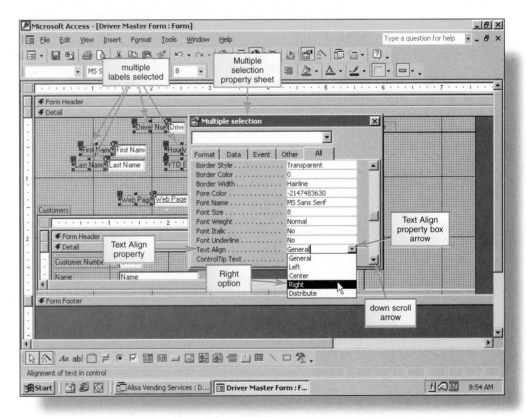

FIGURE 5-49

Resizing the Labels

To resize a label to optimum size, select the label by clicking it, and then double-click an appropriate sizing handle. Perform the following steps to resize the label for the Driver Number, First Name, Last Name, Hourly Rate, YTD Earnings, and Web Page fields by double-clicking the sizing handles at the left edge of the labels. You can resize them individually, but it is easier, however, to make sure they are all selected and then resize one of the labels. Access will automatically resize all the others as demonstrated in the following steps.

Steps **To Resize a Label**

1 With all the labels selected, point to the handle on the left edge of the Driver Number label (Figure 5-50).

2 Double-click the middle sizing handle on the left edge of the Driver Number label to resize all the labels to the optimal size.

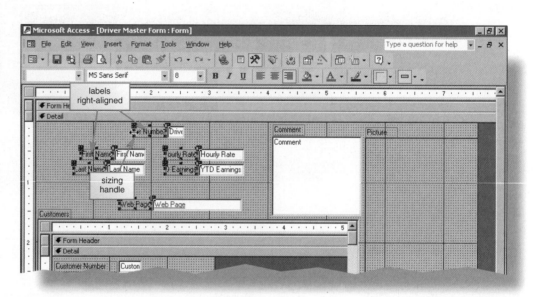

FIGURE 5-50

Changing the Size Mode of a Picture

The portion of a picture that displays as well as the way it displays is determined by the **size mode.** The possible size modes are as follows:

1. **Clip** — Displays only the portion of the picture that will fit in the space allocated to it.

2. **Stretch** — Expands or shrinks the picture to fit the precise space allocated on the screen. For photographs, usually this is not a good choice because fitting a photograph to the allocated space can distort the image, giving it a stretched appearance.

3. **Zoom** — Does the best job of fitting the picture to the allocated space without changing the look of the picture. The entire picture will display and be proportioned correctly. Some white space may be visible either above or to the right of the picture, however.

Currently, the size mode is Clip, and that is the reason only a portion of the picture may display. To see the whole picture, use the shortcut menu for the picture to change the size mode to Zoom as shown in the following steps.

Size Mode

The Clip setting for Size Mode is the most rapid to display, but may show only a portion of a picture. If your pictures have been created with a size such that the entire picture will display on the form with Clip as the setting for Size Mode, Clip is the best choice.

Steps **To Change the Size Mode of a Picture**

1 **Right-click the Picture control to produce its shortcut menu, click the All tab, if necessary, and then click Properties on the shortcut menu. Click the Size Mode property and then click the Size Mode property box arrow. Point to Zoom.**

The Bound Object Frame: Picture property sheet displays (Figure 5-51). The list of Size Mode property options displays.

2 **Click Zoom and then close the property sheet by clicking its Close button.**

The Size Mode property is changed. The entire picture now will display.

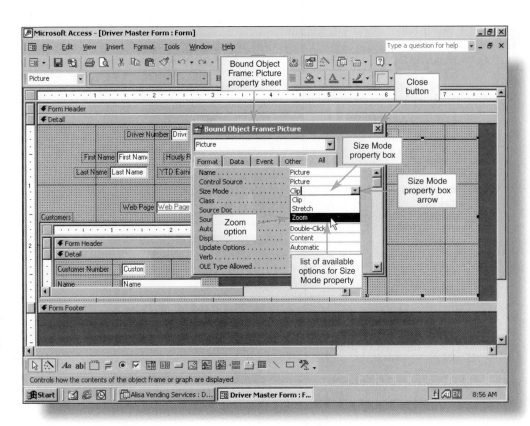

FIGURE 5-51

Changing the Special Effects and Colors of Labels

Access allows you to change a variety of the characteristics of the labels in the form. You can change the border style and color, the background color, and the font style and size. You also can give the label **special effects**, such as raised or sunken. To change the special effects and colors (characteristics) of a label, perform the steps on the next page.

More About

Colors of Labels

There are two different colors you can change for many objects, including labels. Changing Fore Color (foreground) changes the color of the letters that appear in the label. Changing Back Color (background) changes the color of the label itself.

Steps To Change Special Effects and Colors of Labels

1 **Click the Driver Number label to select it. Then select each of the remaining labels by holding the SHIFT key down while clicking the label. Be sure to include the Customers label for the subform. Right-click one of the selected labels and then point to Properties.**

All labels are selected (Figure 5-52). The shortcut menu displays.

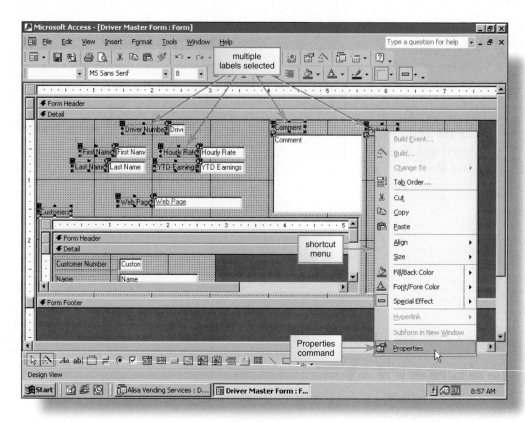

FIGURE 5-52

2 **Click Properties on the shortcut menu. Click the Special Effect property and then click the Special Effect property box arrow. Point to Etched.**

The Multiple selection property sheet displays (Figure 5-53). The list of options for the Special Effect property displays, and the Etched Special Effect property is highlighted.

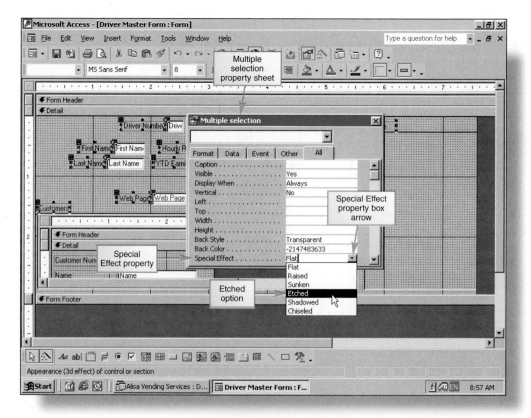

FIGURE 5-53

3 Click Etched. If necessary, click the down scroll arrow until the Fore Color property displays, and then click the Fore Color property. Point to the Build button (the button containing the three dots).

The Fore Color property is selected (Figure 5-54).

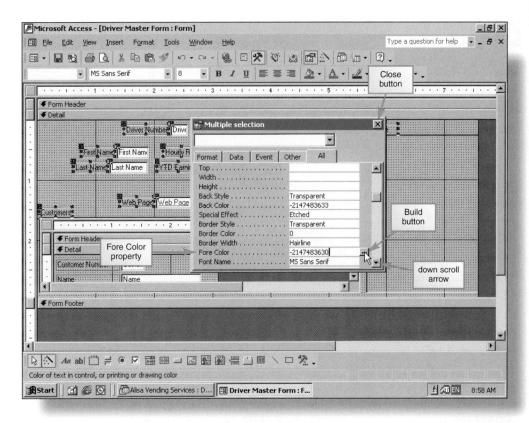

FIGURE 5-54

4 Click the Build button to display the Color dialog box and then point to the color blue in row 4, column 5, as shown in Figure 5-55.

5 Click the color blue and then click the OK button. Close the Multiple selection property sheet by clicking its Close button.

The changes to the labels are complete.

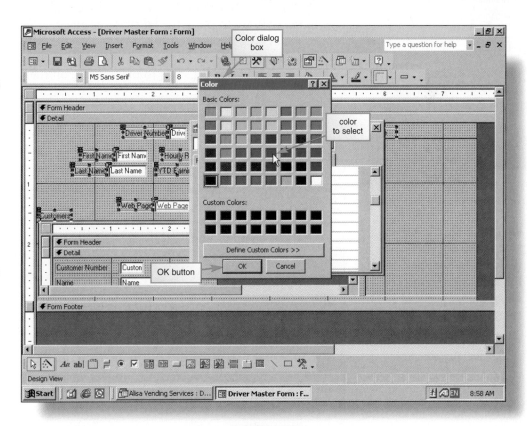

FIGURE 5-55

6 Click the View button to view the form.

The form displays (Figure 5-56). The fields have been moved and the appearance of the labels has been changed.

7 Click the View button a second time to return to Design view.

The form design displays.

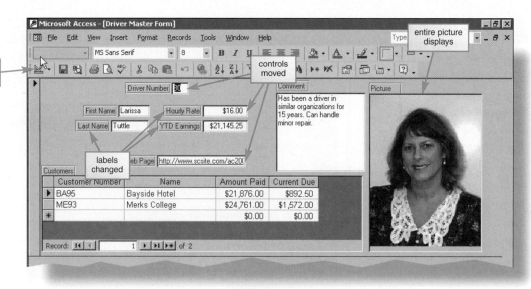

FIGURE 5-56

Selecting Multiple Controls

To select all the controls in a given column or row, you can use the rulers. To select all the controls in a column, click the horizontal ruler above the column. To select all the controls in a row, click the vertical ruler to the left of the row.

Adding a Form Title

Notice in Figure 5-1 on page A 5.05 that the form includes a title. To add a title to a form, add the title as a label in the Form Header section. To accomplish this task, first you will need to expand the size of the form header to accommodate the title by dragging the bottom border of the form header. Then, you can use the Label tool in the toolbox to place the label. After placing the label, you can type the title in the label. Using the Properties command on the label's shortcut menu, you can change various properties to improve the title's appearance, as well.

Perform the following steps to place a title on the form.

Steps To Add a Form Title

1 Resize the Form Header section by dragging down the line separating the Form Header section from the Detail section to the approximate position shown in Figure 5-57.

The shape of the mouse pointer changes to a two-headed vertical arrow with a horizontal crossbar, indicating you can drag the line to resize the Form Header section.

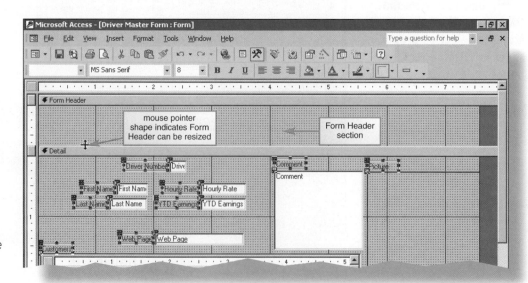

FIGURE 5-57

2 Point to the Label tool in the toolbox (Figure 5-58).

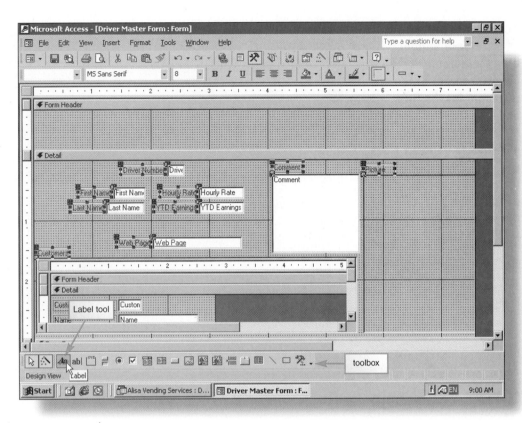

FIGURE 5-58

3 Click the Label tool and then position the mouse pointer as shown in Figure 5-59. The shape of the mouse pointer has changed, indicating you are placing a label.

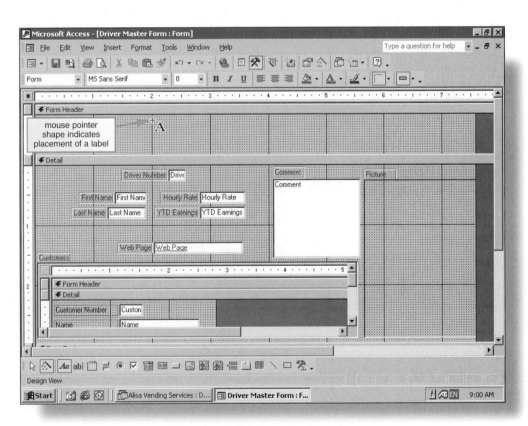

FIGURE 5-59

4 Press the left mouse button, drag the pointer to the opposite corner of the rectangle for the title, and type `Driver Master Form` as the title. You do not need to be exact when you drag the pointer to the opposite corner because you will resize the rectangle appropriately in a later step.

The label is placed on the form, and the title is entered (Figure 5-60).

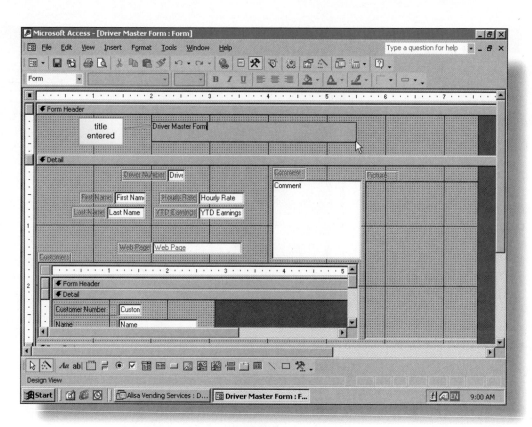

FIGURE 5-60

5 Click somewhere outside the rectangle containing the title to deselect the rectangle, and then right-click the rectangle containing the title. Click Properties on the shortcut menu that displays, click the Special Effect property, and then click the Special Effect property box arrow. Point to Chiseled.

The property sheet displays (Figure 5-61).

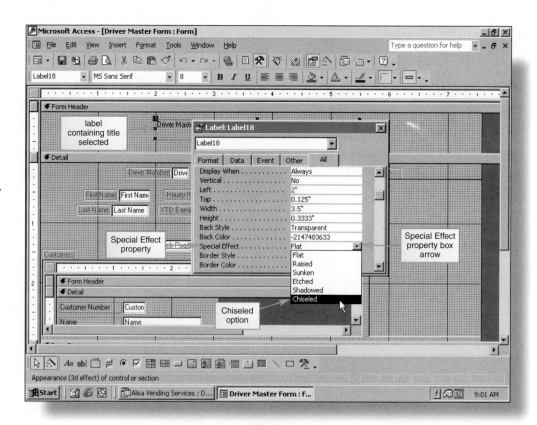

FIGURE 5-61

6 Click Chiseled. Click the down scroll arrow so the Font Size property displays. Click the Font Size property, click the Font Size property box arrow, and then click 12. If necessary, click the down scroll arrow to display the Font Weight property. Click the Font Weight property, click the Font Weight property box arrow, and then click Bold. Close the property sheet by clicking its Close button. Resize the label to fit the title and then move the label so it is centered over the form.

The form header is complete (Figure 5-62).

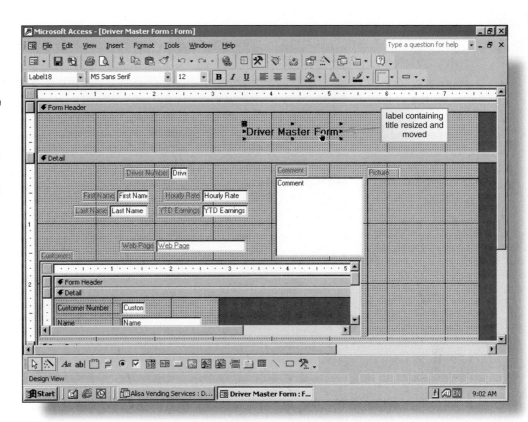

FIGURE 5-62

7 Close the window containing the form. When asked if you want to save the changes to the design of the form, click Yes.

The form is complete.

Viewing Data and Web Pages Using the Form

To use a form to view data, right-click the form in the Database window and then click Open on the shortcut menu that displays. You then can use the navigation buttons to move among drivers or to move among the customers of the driver currently displayed on the screen. By clicking the driver's Web Page field, you can display the driver's Web page. As soon as you close the window containing the Web page, Access returns to the form.

Perform the steps on the next page to display data using the form.

Form Headers

You may wish to add more than just a title to a form header. For example, you may wish to add a picture such as a company logo. To do so, click the Image tool in the toolbox, click the position where you want to place the picture, and then select the picture to insert.

Microsoft **Access 2002**

Steps **To View Data and Web Pages Using the Form**

1 **If necessary, click Forms on the Objects bar. Right-click Driver Master Form and then click Open on the shortcut menu. Be sure the window containing the form is maximized. Point to the Next Record button for the Driver table.**

The data from the first record displays in the form (Figure 5-63).

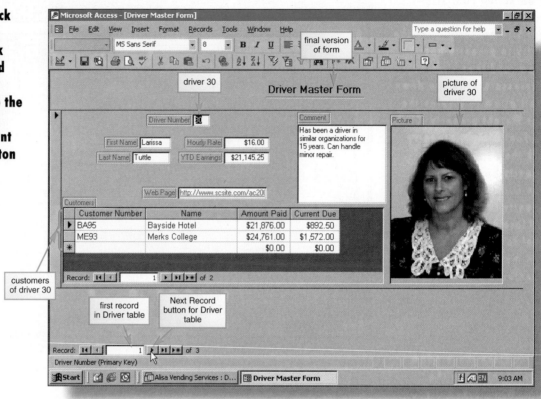

FIGURE 5-63

2 **Click the Next Record button to move to the second driver. Point to the Next Record button for the Customers subform (the Next Record button in the set of navigation buttons immediately below the subform).**

*The data from the second record displays (Figure 5-64). (The records in your form may display in a different order.) If more customers were included than would fit in the subform at a single time, Access would automatically add a **vertical scroll bar** to the Customers subform. You can use either a scroll bar or the navigation buttons to move among customers.*

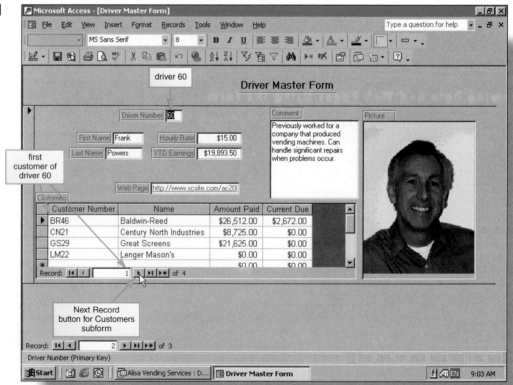

FIGURE 5-64

3 **Click the subform's Next Record button twice.**

The data from the third customer of driver 60 is selected (Figure 5-65).

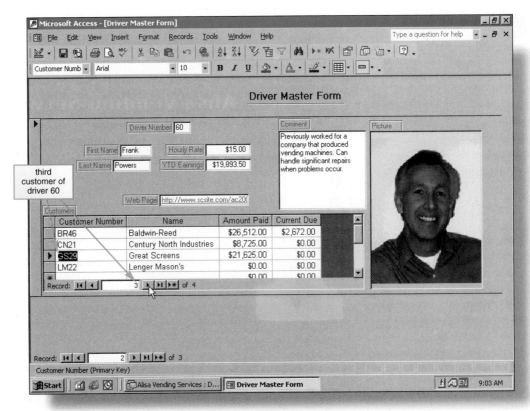

FIGURE 5-65

4 **Point to the Web Page control (Figure 5-66).**

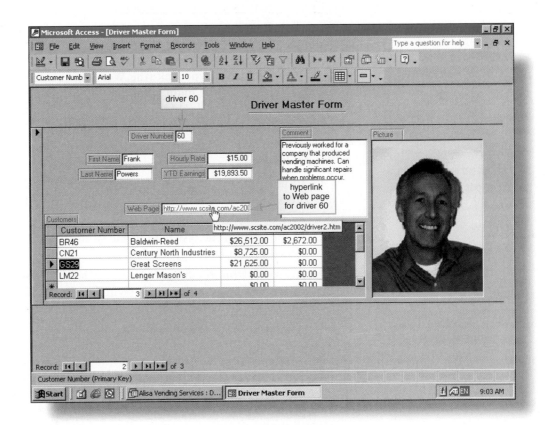

FIGURE 5-66

5 **Click the Web Page control. If a dialog box displays in either this step or the next, follow the directions given in the dialog box.**

The driver's Web page displays in the Microsoft Internet Explorer window (Figure 5-67).

6 **When you have finished viewing the driver's Web page, click the Close button for the Microsoft Internet Explorer window to return to the form. Click the Close Window button to close the form.**

The form no longer displays.

FIGURE 5-67

The previous steps illustrated the way you work with a main form and subform, as well as how to use a hyperlink (the Web Page control in this form). Clicking the navigation buttons for the main form moves to a different driver. Clicking the navigation buttons for the subform moves to a different customer of the driver whose photograph displays in the main form. Clicking a hyperlink moves to the corresponding document or Web page. The following are other actions you can take within the form:

1. To move from the last field in the main form to the first field in the subform, press the TAB key. To move back to the last field in the main form, press CTRL+SHIFT+TAB.

2. To move from the last field in the subform to the first field in the next record's main form, press CTRL+TAB.

3. To switch from the main form to the subform using the mouse, click anywhere in the subform. To switch back to the main form, click any control in the main form. Clicking the background of the main form will not cause the switch to occur.

More *About*

Date Fields in Queries: Using Date()

To test for the current date in a query, type Date() in the criteria row of the appropriate column. Placing <Date() in the criteria row for Start Date, for example, finds those drivers who started anytime before the date on which you run the query.

Using Date and Memo Fields in a Query

To use date fields in queries, you simply type the dates including the slashes. To search for records with a specific date, you must type the date. You also can use **comparison operators**. To find all the drivers whose start date is prior to June 1, 2001, for example, you type <6/1/2001 as the criterion.

You also can use memo fields in queries. Typically, you will want to find all the records on which the memo field contains a specific word or phrase. To do so, you use wildcards. For example, to find all the drivers who have the word, repair, somewhere in the Comment field, you type *repair* as the criterion.

Perform the following steps to create and run queries that use date and memo fields.

Date Fields in Queries: Using Expressions

Expressions have a special meaning in date fields in queries. Numbers that appear in expressions represent numbers of days. The expression <Date()-30 for Start Date finds drivers who started anytime up to 30 days before the day on which you run the query.

 ## To Use Date and Memo Fields in a Query

1 In the Database window, click Tables on the Objects bar and then, if necessary, select the Driver table. Click the New Object: AutoForm button arrow on the Database toolbar. Click Query. Be sure Design View is highlighted and then click the OK button.

2 If necessary, maximize the Microsoft Access - [Query1 : Select Query] window that displays. Resize the upper and lower panes and the Driver field list to the sizes shown in Figure 5-68. Double-click the Driver Number, First Name, Last Name, Start Date, and Comment fields to include them in the query. Click the criteria row under the Comment field and then type *repair* as the entry. Point to the Run button on the toolbar (Figure 5-68).

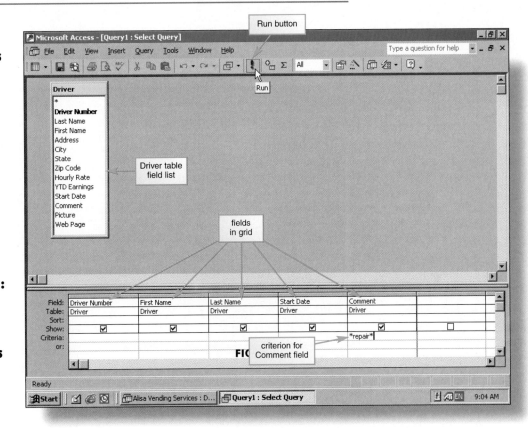

FIGURE 5-68

3 Click the Run button on the toolbar to run the query.

The results display in Datasheet view (Figure 5-69). Two records are included. Both records have the word, repair, contained within the comment.

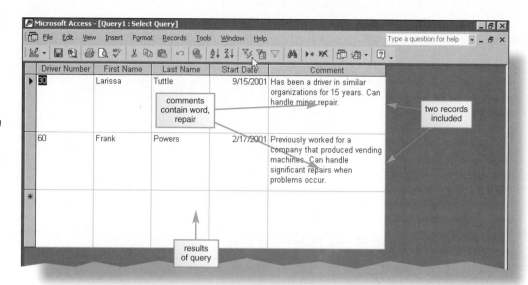

FIGURE 5-69

4 Click the View button to return to the Select Query window. Click the Criteria row under the Start Date field, and then type <6/1/2001 (Figure 5-70). Point to the Run button on the Query Design toolbar.

*The criterion for the Start Date field is entered. Access automatically adds the LIKE operator and quotation marks to criteria that use the * wildcard.*

5 Click the Run button to run the query.

The result contains only a single row, because only one driver was hired before June 1, 2001 and has a comment entry that contains the word, repair.

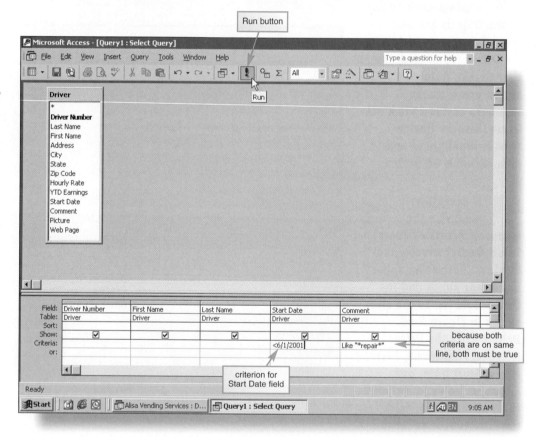

FIGURE 5-70

6 Close the Select Query window by clicking its Close Window button. When asked if you want to save the query, click the No button.

The results of the query are removed from the screen and the Database window again displays.

Closing the Database

The following step closes the database by closing its Database window.

TO CLOSE A DATABASE

1 Click the Close Window button for the Alisa Vending Services : Database window.

Compacting and Repairing a Database

As you add more data to a database, it naturally grows larger. Pictures will increase the size significantly. When you delete objects (for example, records, tables, forms, pictures), the space previously occupied by the object does not become available for additional objects. Instead, the additional objects are given new space, that is, space that was not already allocated. If you decide to change a picture, for example, the new picture will not occupy the same space as the previous picture, but instead it will be given space of its own.

In order to remove this wasted space from the database, you must **compact** the database. Compacting the database makes an additional copy of the database, one that contains the same data, but does not contain the wasted space that the original does. The original database still will exist in its unaltered form.

A typical three-step process for compacting a database is as follows:

1. Compact the original database (for example, Alisa Vending Services) and give the compacted database a different name (for example, Alisa Vending Services Compacted).

2. Assuming that the compacting operation completed successfully, delete the original database (Alisa Vending Services).

3. Also assuming that the compacting operation completed successfully, rename the compacted database (Alisa Vending Services Compacted) with the name of the original database (Alisa Vending Services).

Of course, if there is a problem in the compacting operation, you should continue to use the original database; that is, do not complete Steps 2 and 3.

The operation can be carried out on a floppy disk, provided there is sufficient space available. If the database to be compacted occupies more than half the floppy disk, however, there may not be enough room for Access to create the compacted database. In such a case, you first should copy the database to a hard disk or network drive. (You can use whatever Windows technique you prefer for copying files in order to do so.) You then can complete the process on the hard disk or network drive.

In addition to compacting the database, the same operation is used to **repair** the database in case there are problems. If Microsoft Access reports a problem with the database or if some aspect of the database seems to be behaving in an unpredictable fashion, you should run the Compact and Repair Database operation to attempt to correct the problem.

Perform the steps on the next page to compact the Alisa Vending Services database and repair any problems after you have copied the database to a hard disk. If you have not copied the database to a hard disk, check with your instructor before completing these steps.

More About

Microsoft Certification

The Microsoft Office User Specialist (MOUS) Certification program provides an opportunity for you to obtain a valuable industry credential — proof that you have the Access 2002 skills required by employers. For more information, see appendix E or visit the Shelly Cashman Series MOUS Web page at scsite.com/offxp/ cert.htm.

More About

Quick Reference

For a table that lists how to complete tasks covered in this book using the mouse, menu, shortcut menu, and keyboard, see the Quick Reference Summary at the back of this book, or visit the Shelly Cashman Series Office XP Web page (scsite.com/ offxp/qr.htm) and then click Microsoft Access 2002.

More About

Compacting a Database

You can copy the original database before you compact the database giving it a name such as Alisa Vending Services Uncompacted. Then, proceed with the compacting operation and name the compacted database, Alisa Vending Services. Assuming that the compacting operation was successful, you then could delete the uncompacted database.

Steps To Compact and Repair a Database

1 Be sure the database is closed. Click Tools on the menu bar, point to Database Utilities, and then point to Compact and Repair Database on the Database Utilities submenu (Figure 5-71).

2 Click Compact and Repair Database. In the Database to Compact From dialog box, select the folder containing the Alisa Vending Services database on the hard disk, select the Alisa Vending Services database, and then click the Compact button.

3 In the Compact Database Into dialog box, type Alisa Vending Services Compacted as the name of the database and then click the Save button.

The compacted database is stored with the name Alisa Vending Services Compacted.

4 Assuming the operation is completed successfully, delete the original database (Alisa Vending Services) and rename Alisa Vending Services Compacted as Alisa Vending Services.

The Alisa Vending Services database now is the compacted form of the original.

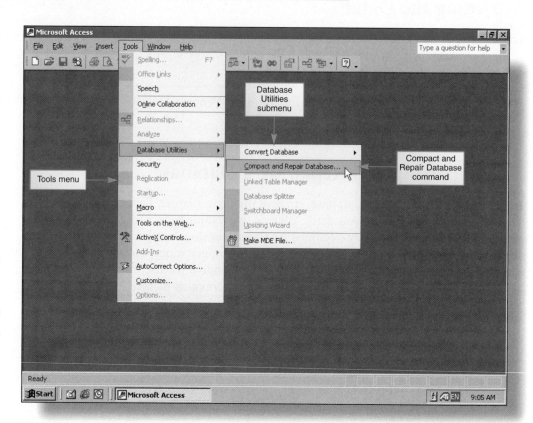

FIGURE 5-71

CASE PERSPECTIVE SUMMARY

You have added the new fields requested by Alisa Vending Services to the Driver table in its database. You have updated the new fields and created a form incorporating some of the new fields. You also have included data about the customers of the driver on this new form. In addition, you included a link to the driver's Web page on the form. You created queries for Alisa Vending Services that included criteria based on the new fields. Finally, you compacted and repaired the database to remove any wasted space and correct any potential problems.

Project Summary

Project 5 introduced you to some additional field types. To maintain the additional data required at Alisa Vending Services, you needed to learn how to create and work with date, memo, OLE, and Hyperlink fields. You also learned how to use such fields in a form. You then learned how to build a form on a one-to-many relationship in which you had several records from one of the tables displaying on the screen at the same time in order to create the form required for Alisa Vending Services. You learned how to use the form to view driver and customer data as well as to view the driver's Web page. You saw how to use date and memo fields in queries to answer two important questions for the organization. Finally, you learned how to compact and repair a database.

What You Should Know

Having completed this project, you now should be able to perform the following tasks:

▶ Add a Form Title (A 5.38)
▶ Add Fields to a Table (A 5.06)
▶ Change Label Alignment (A 5.32)
▶ Change Special Effects and Colors of Labels (A 5.36)
▶ Change the Row and Column Size (A 5.13)
▶ Change the Size Mode of a Picture (A 5.35)
▶ Close a Database (A 5.47)
▶ Close the Table and Save the Properties (A 5.20)
▶ Compact and Repair a Database (A 5.48)
▶ Create a Form with a Subform Using the Form Wizard (A 5.21)
▶ Enter Data in Date Fields (A 5.09)
▶ Enter Data in Hyperlink Fields (A 5.18)

▶ Enter Data in Memo Fields (A 5.11)
▶ Enter Data in OLE Fields and Convert the Data to Pictures (A 5.15)
▶ Modify the Form Design (A 5.28)
▶ Modify the Subform Design (A 5.26)
▶ Move Fields (A 5.31)
▶ Move and Resize Fields (A 5.29)
▶ Move a Label (A 5.31)
▶ Open a Database (A 5.05)
▶ Resize a Label (A 5.34)
▶ Use Date and Memo Fields in a Query (A 5.45)
▶ View Data and Web Pages Using the Form (A 5.42)

Learn It Online

Instructions: To complete the Learn It Online exercises, start your browser, click the Address bar, and then enter scsite.com/offxp/exs.htm. When the Office XP Learn It Online page displays, follow the instructions in the exercises below.

1 Project Reinforcement TF, MC, and SA

Below Access Project 5, click the Project Reinforcement link. Print the quiz by clicking Print on the File menu. Answer each question. Write your first and last name at the top of each page, and then hand in the printout to your instructor.

2 Flash Cards

Below Access Project 5, click the Flash Cards link. When Flash Cards displays, read the instructions. Type 20 (or a number specified by your instructor) in the Number of Playing Cards text box, type your name in the Name text box, and then click the Flip Card button. When the flash card displays, read the question and then click the Answer box arrow to select an answer. Flip through Flash Cards. Click Print on the File menu to print the last flash card if your score is 15 (75%) correct or greater and then hand it in to your instructor. If your score is less than 15 (75%) correct, then redo this exercise by clicking the Replay button.

3 Practice Test

Below Access Project 5, click the Practice Test link. Answer each question, enter your first and last name at the bottom of the page, and then click the Grade Test button. When the graded practice test displays on your screen, click Print on the File menu to print a hard copy. Continue to take practice tests until you score 80% or better. Hand in a printout of the final practice test to your instructor.

4 Who Wants to Be a Computer Genius?

Below Access Project 5, click the Computer Genius link. Read the instructions, enter your first and last name at the bottom of the page, and then click the Play button. Hand in your score to your instructor.

5 Wheel of Terms

Below Access Project 5, click the Wheel of Terms link. Read the instructions, and then enter your first and last name and your school name. Click the Play button. Hand in your score to your instructor.

6 Crossword Puzzle Challenge

Below Access Project 5, click the Crossword Puzzle Challenge link. Read the instructions, and then enter your first and last name. Click the Play button. Work the crossword puzzle. When you are finished, click the Submit button. When the crossword puzzle redisplays, click the Print button. Hand in the printout.

7 Tips and Tricks

Below Access Project 5, click the Tips and Tricks link. Click a topic that pertains to Project 5. Right-click the information and then click Print on the shortcut menu. Construct a brief example of what the information relates to in Access to confirm you understand how to use the tip or trick. Hand in the example and printed information.

8 Newsgroups

Below Access Project 5, click the Newsgroups link. Click a topic that pertains to Project 5. Print three comments. Hand in the comments to your instructor.

9 Expanding Your Horizons

Below Access Project 5, click the Articles for Microsoft Access link. Click a topic that pertains to Project 5. Print the information. Construct a brief example of what the information relates to in Access to confirm you understand the contents of the article. Hand in the example and printed information to your instructor.

10 Search Sleuth

Below Access Project 5, click the Search Sleuth link. To search for a term that pertains to this project, select a term below the Project 5 title and then use the Google search engine at google.com (or any major search engine) to display and print two Web pages that present information on the term. Hand in the printouts to your instructor.

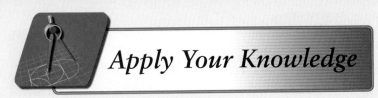

Apply Your Knowledge

1 **Enhancing the Beyond Clean Database**

Instructions: Start Access. If you are using the Microsoft Access 2002 Complete or the Microsoft Access 2002 Comprehensive text, open the Beyond Clean database that you used in Project 4. Otherwise, see the inside back cover for instructions for downloading the Data Disk or see your instructor for information about accessing the files required for this book. Perform the following tasks.

1. Add the fields, Start Date and Comment, to the Custodian table structure as shown in Figure 5-72.

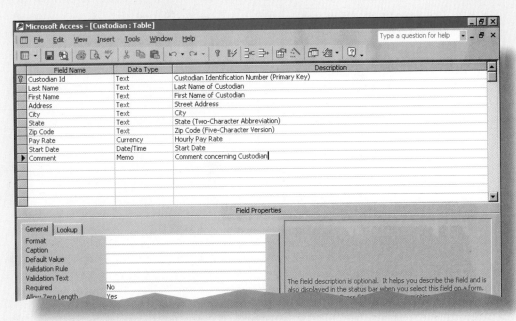

FIGURE 5-72

2. Save the changes to the structure.
3. Add the data shown in Figure 5-73 to the Custodian table. Adjust the row and column spacing for the table.
4. Print and then close the table.
5. Query the Custodian table to find all custodians who can do maintenance work. Print the results. Do not save the query.
6. Use the Form Wizard to create a form with a subform for the Custodian table. Include the Custodian Id, First Name, Last Name, Pay Rate, Start Date, and Comment fields from the Custodian table. Include the Client Number, Name, Telephone Number, and Balance fields from the Client table.

Data for Custodian Table		
CUSTODIAN ID	**START DATE**	**COMMENT**
002	11/12/2001	Can work nights and weekends only. Cannot do work that requires using a ladder.
009	12/02/2002	Has good mechanical skills. Enjoys maintenance work.
011	10/16/2002	Prefers to work during school hours only.
013	01/06/2003	Enjoys maintenance work.

FIGURE 5-73

(continued)

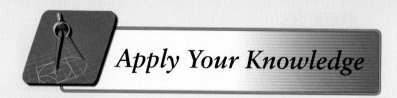

Apply Your Knowledge

Enhancing the Beyond Clean Database *(continued)*

7. Modify the form design to create the form shown in Figure 5-74.

8. Print the form. To print the form, open the form, click File on the menu bar, click Print, and then click Selected Record(s) as the Print Range. Click the OK button.

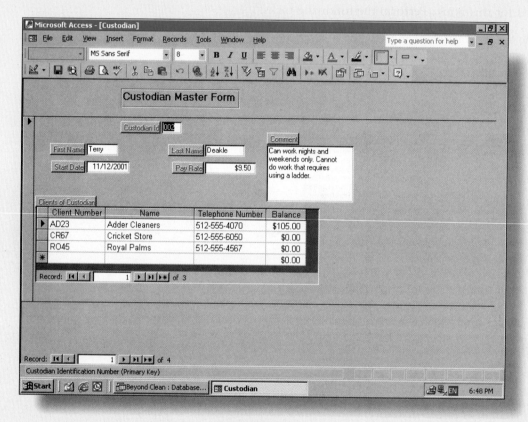

FIGURE 5-74

In the Lab

1 Enhancing the Wooden Crafts Database

Problem: Jan Merchant has found that the Wooden Crafts database needs to maintain additional data on suppliers. She needs to know the last date she placed an order with a supplier. She also would like to store some notes about each supplier's special order policy as well as store the Web page address of each supplier's Web page. Jan requires a form that displays information about the supplier as well as the products that she purchases from the supplier.

Instructions: If you are using the Microsoft Access 2002 Complete or the Microsoft Access 2002 Comprehensive text, open the Wooden Crafts database that you used in Project 4. Otherwise, see the inside back cover for instructions for downloading the Data Disk or see your instructor for information about accessing the files required for this book. Perform the following tasks.

1. Add the fields, Last Order Date, Note, and Web Page, to the Supplier table structure as shown in Figure 5-75 and then save the changes to the structure.

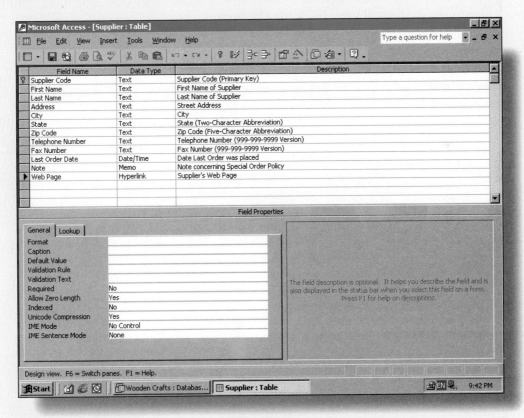

FIGURE 5-75

(continued)

In the Lab

Enhancing the Wooden Crafts Database *(continued)*

2. Add the data shown in Figure 5-76 to the Supplier table. Use the same hyperlink files that you used for the Driver table in this project. Adjust the row and column spacing for the table.

3. Print the table.

4. Create the form shown in Figure 5-77 for the Supplier table. Use Supplier Master Form as the name of the form and Products of Supplier as the name of the subform.

Data for Supplier Table

SUPPLIER CODE	LAST ORDER DATE	NOTE
AP	07/10/2003	Will accept special orders from customers but only through Jan.
BH	08/18/2003	Will not accept special orders from customers.
PL	08/25/2003	Will accept special orders directly from customers.

FIGURE 5-76

5. Print the form. To print the form, open the form, click File on the menu bar, click Print, and then click Selected Record(s) as the Print Range. Click the OK button.

6. Query the Supplier table to find all suppliers that accept special orders. Include the Supplier Code, First Name, and Last Name in the query. Print the results. Do not save the query.

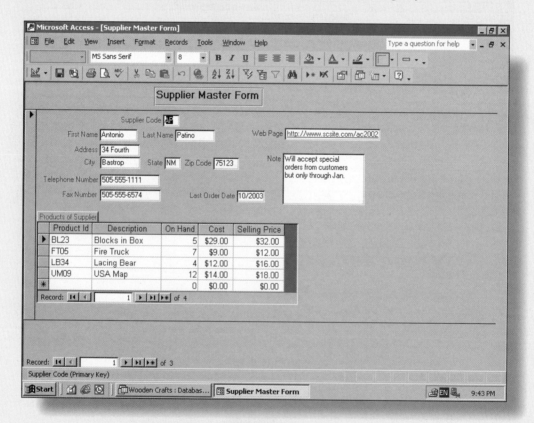

FIGURE 5-77

In the Lab

2 Enhancing the Restaurant Supply Database

Problem: The restaurant supply company needs to maintain additional data on the sales representatives. The company needs to maintain the date a sales rep started as well as some notes concerning the representative's training and abilities. They also would like to store a picture of the representative as well as a link to each representative's Web page. The company wants a form that displays sales representative information and the restaurants for which they are responsible.

Instructions: If you are using the Microsoft Access 2002 Complete or the Microsoft Access 2002 Comprehensive text, open the Restaurant Supply database that you used in Project 4. Otherwise, see the inside back cover for instructions for downloading the Data Disk or see your instructor for information about accessing the files required for this book. Perform the following tasks.

1. Add the Start Date, Notes, Picture, and Web Page fields to the Sales Rep table as shown in Figure 5-78. Save the changes to the structure.

2. Add the data shown in Figure 5-79 to the Sales Rep table. Add pictures and hyperlinks for each representative. Use the same picture and hyperlink files that you used for the Driver table in this project. Pict2.bmp and pict3.bmp are pictures of males; pict1.bmp is of a female. Adjust the row and column spacing for the table.

3. Print the table.

4. Create the form shown in Figure 5-80 on the next page for the Sales Rep table. Use Sales Rep Master Form as the name of the form and Restaurant Accounts as the name of the subform.

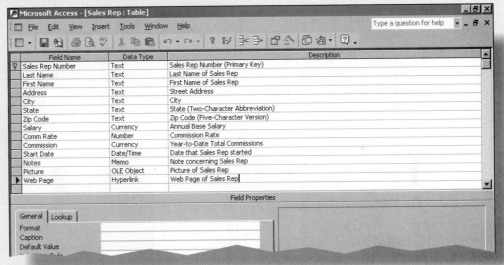

FIGURE 5-78

Data for Sales Rep Table		
SALES REP NUMBER	**START DATE**	**NOTE**
44	05/01/2002	Has had first aid training. Some background in food preparation.
49	09/09/2002	Previous experience as a restaurant waitperson.
51	12/03/2001	Has had first aid training.

FIGURE 5-79

(continued)

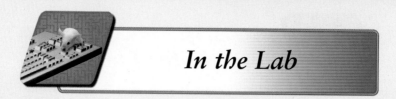

In the Lab

Enhancing the Restaurant Supply Database *(continued)*

5. Add the current date to the form. (*Hint:* use Microsoft Access Help to solve this problem.)
6. Print the form. To print the form, open the form, click File on the menu bar, and then click Print. Click Selected Record(s) as the Print Range. Click the OK button.
7. Compact the database.
8. Query the Sales Rep table to find all sales reps who have had first aid training. Include the Sales Rep Number, First Name, and Last Name in the query. Print the query results. Do not save the query.
9. Query the Sales Rep table to find all sales reps who started before 2002. Include the Sales Rep Number, First Name, Last Name, Commission, and Comm Rate in the query. Print the query results. Do not save the query.

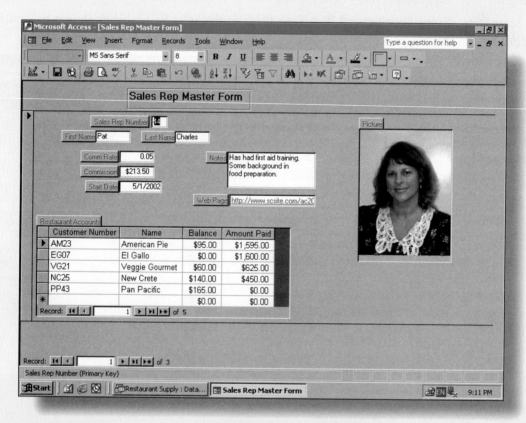

FIGURE 5-80

In the Lab

3 Enhancing the Condo Management Database

Problem: The condo management company needs to maintain additional data on the owners. The company needs to store pictures of the owners as well as some notes concerning the owner's rental policies. The company wants a form that displays owner information and the rental properties they own.

Instructions: If you are using the Microsoft Access 2002 Complete or the Microsoft Access 2002 Comprehensive text, open the Condo Management database that you used in Project 4. Otherwise, see the inside back cover for instructions for downloading the Data Disk or see your instructor for information about accessing the files required for this book. Perform the following tasks.

1. Add the fields, Notes and Picture, to the Owner table structure as shown in Figure 5-81. Save the changes to the structure.
2. Add the data shown in Figure 5-82 to the Owner table. Adjust the row and column spacing for the table, if necessary.
3. Print the table.

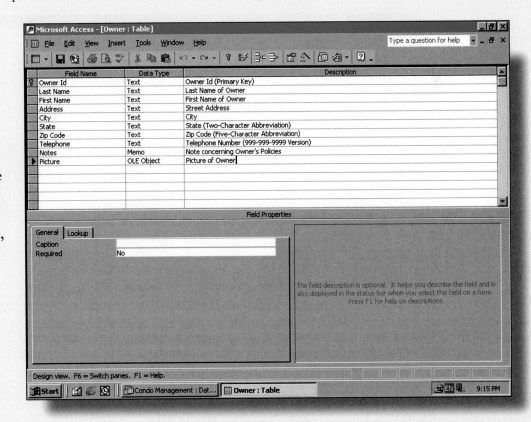

FIGURE 5-81

Data for Owner Table	
OWNER ID	**NOTES**
AB10	Has no smoking policy. Will not rent to families with children under 18.
BR18	Will rent to families with children.
GM50	Has no smoking policy.
HJ05	Will not rent during the month of February.

FIGURE 5-82

(continued)

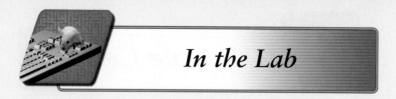

In the Lab

Enhancing the Condo Management Database *(continued)*

4. Create the form shown in Figure 5-83. Use Owner Master Form as the name of the form and Rental Properties as the name of the subform.
5. Print the form. To print the form, open the form, click File on the menu bar, and then click Print. Click Selected Record(s) as the Print Range. Click the OK button.
6. Compact the database.
7. Query the Owner table to find all owners who have a no smoking policy. Include the Owner Id, First Name, and Last Name in the query. Print the results. Do not save the query.

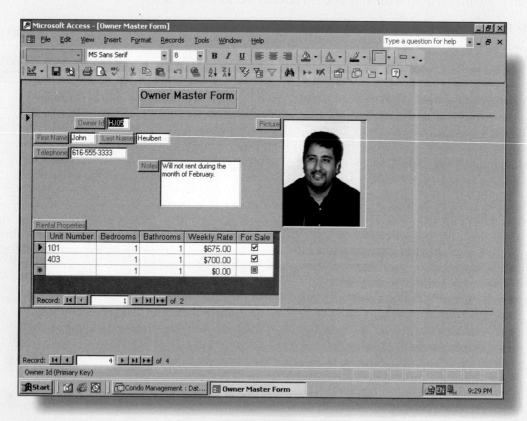

FIGURE 5-83

Cases and Places

The difficulty of these case studies varies:
▶ are the least difficult; ▶▶ are more difficult; and ▶▶▶ are the most difficult.

1 ▶ Use the CompuWhiz database that you used in Project 4 for this assignment or see your instructor for information on accessing the files required for this book. The CompuWhiz database needs to store additional data on the technicians. Add the fields and data shown in Figure 5-84 to the Technician table. Adjust the row and column spacing so the complete notes about the technician display. Print the Technician table. Query the Technician table to find all technicians that have MOUS certification in Access.

Data for Technician Table		
TECHNICIAN ID	**START DATE**	**NOTES**
78	09/16/2002	Has MOUS Certification in Access and Excel.
82	09/23/2002	Extensive network experience. Has a good rapport with clients.
89	01/06/2001	Excellent diagnostic skills. Prefers to handle hardware problems.

FIGURE 5-84

2 ▶ Create and print a Technician Master Form for the Technician table that you modified in Cases and Places 1. The form should be similar in format to Figure 5-85. Compact the database.

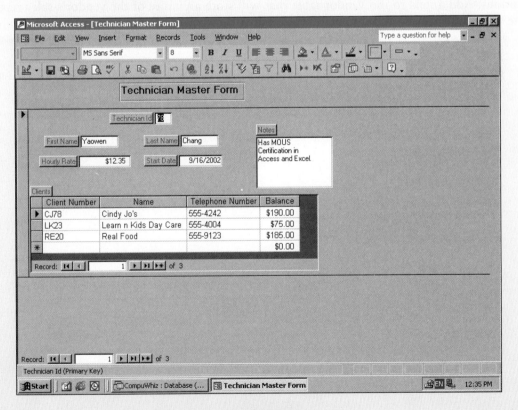

FIGURE 5-85

Cases and Places

3 Use the Hockey Shop database that you used in Project 4 for this assignment or see your instructor for information on accessing the files required for this book. The Hockey Shop needs additional information on vendors. Add the fields and data shown in Figure 5-86 to the Vendor table. Adjust the row and column spacing so the complete notes about the vendor display. Print the Vendor table. Query the database to find all vendors that offer volume discounts.

Data for Vendor Table		
VENDOR CODE	LAST ORDER DATE	NOTES
AC	07/17/2003	Offers volume discount when more than 12 items are ordered.
BH	08/25/2003	No discounts.
LG	09/01/2003	Discounts tee shirts when more than 12 of the same color and size are ordered.

FIGURE 5-86

4 Create and print a Vendor Master Form for the Vendor table that you modified in Cases and Places 3. The form should be similar in format to Figure 5-77 on page A 5.54 and include all fields in the Vendor table. The subform that displays should include all fields in the Item table except Selling Price and Vendor Code. Be sure to include a form header and change the special effects and colors of the labels.

5 ▶▶▶ Enhance the Hockey Shop database by adding a description for each item. Make up your own descriptions. Add a field to the Vendor table that will store a picture of the vendor's sales representative. Use the same picture files used for the Driver table in the project. Compact the database.

Microsoft Access 2002

PROJECT

Creating an Application System Using Macros, Wizards, and the Switchboard Manager

You will have mastered the material in this project when you can:

O B J E C T I V E S

- Create and use lookup fields
- Create and use input masks
- Add single-field controls to reports and forms
- Add calculated controls to reports
- Create, modify, and run macros
- Create a copy of a macro
- Create and use a switchboard
- Modify switchboard pages and items

Legal Hotlines

Professional Advice for a Fraction of the Cost

L ast week you paid a rather large sum for repairs to your car's radiator, but this week while driving to work your car overheated and stalled in traffic. Because your car is old and in poor condition the mechanic warned you that the repairs might not prevent your car from overheating. Despite his warning, you believe you should be reimbursed for the cost of the repairs. Is your position justified? Do you have the legal right to be reimbursed? An experienced lawyer could provide the answers to your questions, but you fear that hiring a lawyer would cost more than you paid for the repairs in the first place.

The American Bar Association, a voluntary professional association composed of more than 400,000 lawyers, paralegals, and others involved in the legal profession, indicates that minor issues such as this one often can be resolved when people represent their own interests, which is known as pro se litigation. Legal hotlines are one resource you can turn to for quick, inexpensive assistance. Knowledgeable advice provided by an experienced lawyer or paralegal over the telephone sometimes can help a person resolve an issue or, at the very least, make an informed decision that hiring a lawyer is the better option. To provide more efficient hotline services, attorneys and paralegals make use of powerful database application systems such as Access 2002 that help organize client information using forms and macros as you will do in this project.

A potential client calling the hotline provides basic information about the legal matter. The hotline staff member answering the telephone selects the client registration form in the database system and begins interviewing the client while simultaneously entering the answers in fields on the form.

Usually, the first field is the client's name. When the name is entered, the database system executes a macro, which is a series of actions designed to carry out a specific task. In this case, the macro searches the client table for a matching name. If a match is found, remaining fields in the registration form are filled in automatically with personal data from the client's previous record. If a match is not found, the hotline staff member interviews the client to obtain the required data.

A second macro is performed when the Social Security number is entered. While a client's last name may change, the Social Security number remains the same. Therefore, the last name macro might not retrieve the client's record if the client has used the hotline service previously using a different name, whereas the Social Security macro would find the client's record regardless.

After this basic client data has been entered in the registration form, the database application system retrieves another form that includes a field for the name of the person or company causing the conflict. An attorney cannot represent a client if he or she previously has represented the opposing party in a similar case. A third macro verifies that no such conflicts of interest exist for the attorney who is providing assistance to the caller.

If no conflict is found, the hotline worker continues to interview the caller about the case and record the facts and issues in memo fields. Many database application systems integrate with word processing applications, so the attorney can generate a form letter that merges data from this initial client conversation with prewritten text that confirms the results of this telephone conversation.

Although a legal hotline cannot provide a practical substitute for a lawyer in every situation, hotlines do provide an important resource for people who need a knowledgeable and experienced guide to help them respond to a legal dilemma. Lawyers and paralegals who staff hotlines are bound by the same code of ethics as lawyers working in more traditional settings. Callers thus can receive valuable advice at a fraction of the cost of traditional legal representation, while remaining fully confident that the answers they receive are every bit as valuable.

Microsoft Access 2002

Creating an Application System Using Macros, Wizards, and the Switchboard Manager

PROJECT

6

CASE PERSPECTIVE

The management of Alisa Vending Services is pleased with the tables, forms, and reports created thus far. They have additional requests, however. They now realize they need telephone numbers for customers in the database. They want you to add the Phone Number field to the Customer table, the Customer Amount Report, and the Customer Update Form. They want to be able to type only the digits in the telephone number and then have Access format the number appropriately. If the user enters the 10-digit number, 7275554625, for example, Access will format the number as (727) 555-4625. The management is pleased with the Customer Type combo box you placed in the Customer Update Form, which allows users to select a customer type from a list. They realized, however, that this combo box is not visible in Datasheet view. They want you to incorporate a similar feature in Datasheet view. Finally, they have heard about switchboard systems that enable users to click a button or two to open any form or table, preview any report, or print any report. They want you to create such a system for them because they believe this will increase employee productivity.

Introduction

In previous projects, you created tables, forms, and reports. Each time you wanted to use any of these, however, you had to follow the correct series of steps. To open the Customer Update Form in a maximized window, for example, first you must click Forms on the Objects bar in the Database window, and then right-click the correct form. Next, you had to click Open on the shortcut menu, and then finally click the Maximize button for the window containing the form.

All these steps are unnecessary if you create your own switchboard system, such as the one shown in Figure 6-1a. A **switchboard** is a form that includes buttons to perform a variety of actions. In this system, you click just one button — View Form, View Table, View Report, Print Report, or Exit Application — to indicate the desired action. Except for the Exit Application button, clicking a button leads to another switchboard. For example, clicking the View Form button leads to the View Form switchboard shown in Figure 6-1b. You then click the button that identifies the form to view. Similarly, clicking the View Table button would lead to a switchboard on which you would click a button to indicate the table to view. Thus, viewing any form, table, or report, or printing any report requires clicking only two buttons.

In this project, you will create the switchboard system represented in Figures 6-1a and 6-1b. The first step is to create **macros,** which are collections of actions designed to carry out specific tasks, such as opening a form and maximizing the window containing the form. You can run the macros directly from the Database window. When you do, Access will execute the various steps, called **actions,** in the macro. You also can use the macros in the switchboard system. Clicking certain buttons in the switchboard system you create will cause the appropriate macros to be run.

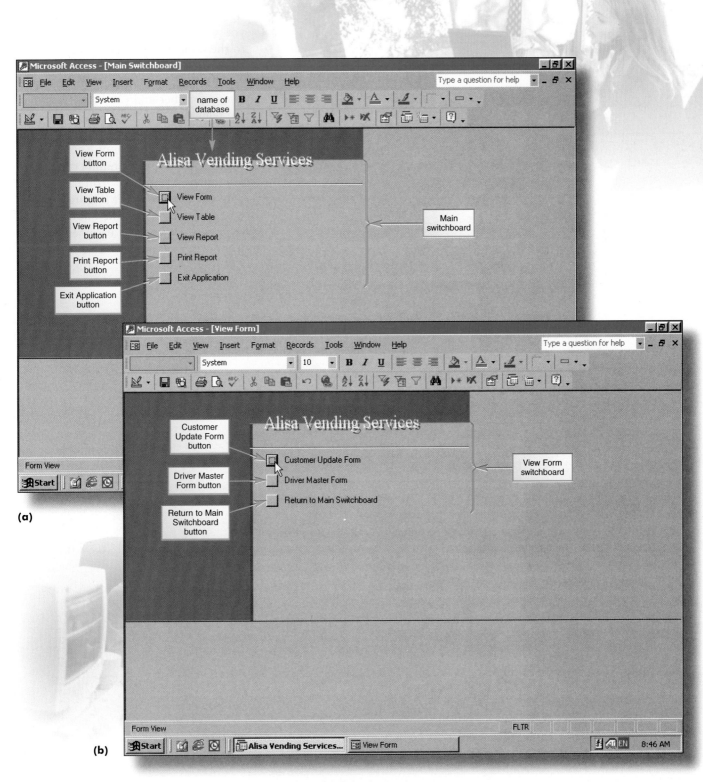

FIGURE 6-1

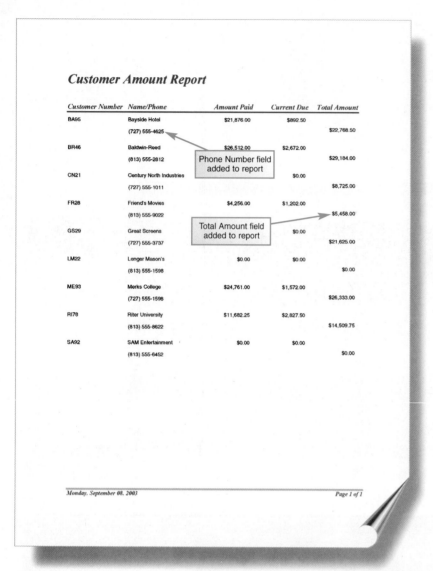

Before creating the switchboard system, two changes are required to the Customer table. You will convert the data type of the Customer Type field to Lookup Wizard. This change allows users to select a customer type from a list just as they do when using the combo box on a form. Then, you will add the Phone Number field to the table and use the Input Mask Wizard to ensure that (1) users need to enter only the digits in the telephone number and (2) Access formats the telephone numbers appropriately. The next step is to make the changes to the Customer Amount Report by adding the telephone number and the total amount (amount paid plus current due) to the report (Figure 6-2a). Finally, you will add the Phone Number field to the Customer Update Form (Figure 6-2b).

(a)

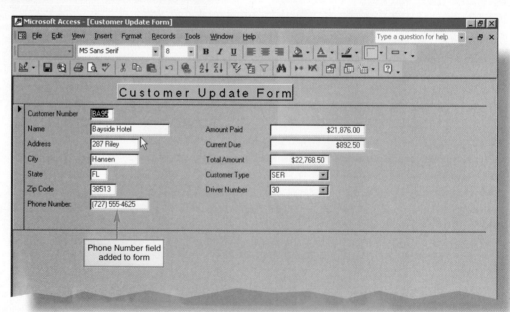

(b)

FIGURE 6-2

Project Six — Creating an Application System for Alisa Vending Services

You will begin this project by changing the data type of the Customer Type field to Lookup Wizard. You then will add the Phone Number field and use the Input Mask Wizard to specify the special format that telephone numbers must follow. Next, you will add the telephone number to the Customer Amount Report. You also will add the total amount (amount paid plus current due) to this report. You will add the telephone number to the Customer Update Form. Before creating the switchboard system required by the management of Alisa Vending Services, you will create and test the macros that will be used in the system. Finally, you will create the switchboard system that will allow users to access any form, table, or report simply by clicking the appropriate buttons.

Opening the Database

Before completing the tasks in this project, you must open the database. Perform the following steps to complete this task.

TO OPEN A DATABASE

1 Click the Start button, click Programs on the Start menu, and then click Microsoft Access on the Programs submenu.

2 Click Open on the Database toolbar, and then click 3½ Floppy (A:) in the Look in box. If necessary, click the Alisa Vending Services database name.

3 Click the Open button.

The database opens and the Alisa Vending Services : Database window displays.

Lookup and Input Mask Wizards

Before you add the new data in this project, you will need to change the data type for certain fields. You also will need to be able to specify how the data is to be entered and how it will display. To accomplish these tasks, you will use the Lookup Wizard and the Input Mask Wizard.

Using the Lookup Wizard

Currently, the data type for the Customer Type field is text. You need to change the data type to Lookup Wizard. A **Lookup Wizard** field allows the user to select from a list of values.

To change a data type, click the Data Type column for the field, and then select the desired data type. For many data type changes, no additional action would be required. If the selected type is Lookup Wizard, however, a wizard will guide you through the necessary additional steps. After you complete the wizard, Microsoft Access sets the data type based on the values selected in the wizard. Perform the steps on the next page to change the data type for the Customer Type field.

Steps **To Use the Lookup Wizard**

1 **If necessary, click the Tables object. Right-click Customer, and then point to Design View on the shortcut menu.**

The shortcut menu for the Customer table displays, and the Design View command is highlighted (Figure 6-3).

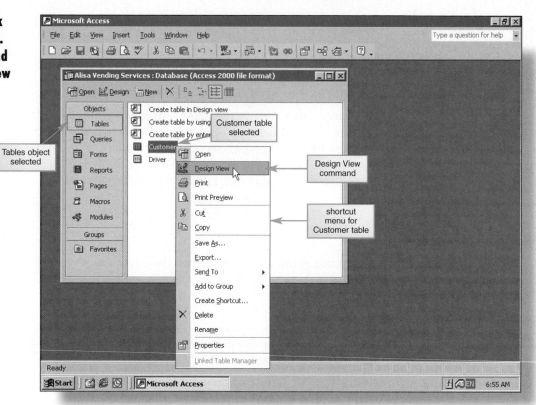

FIGURE 6-3

2 **Click Design View. Make sure the window containing the table design is maximized. Click the Data Type column for the Customer Type field, click the arrow, and then point to Lookup Wizard.**

The list of available data types displays (Figure 6-4).

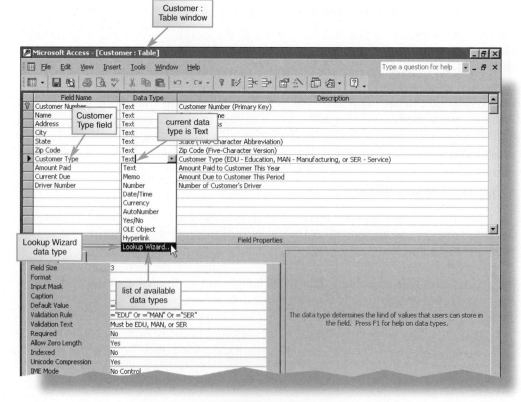

FIGURE 6-4

3 Click Lookup Wizard, and then point to the I will type in the values that I want option button.

The Lookup Wizard dialog box displays (Figure 6-5).

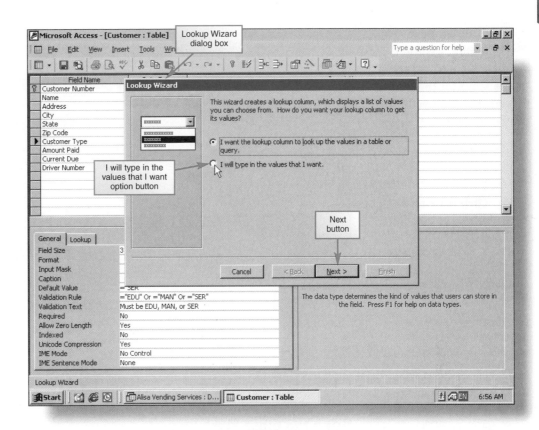

FIGURE 6-5

4 Click the I will type in the values that I want option button, click the Next button in the Lookup Wizard dialog box, click the first row of the table (under Col1), and then type EDU as the entry. Press the DOWN ARROW key and then type MAN in the second row. Press the DOWN ARROW key and then type SER in the third row. Point to the Next button.

The list of values for the combo box is entered (Figure 6-6).

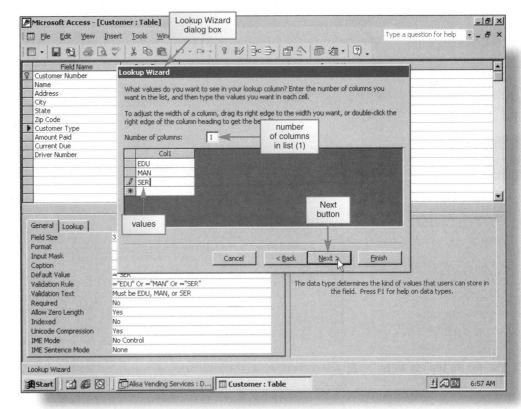

FIGURE 6-6

5 **Click the Next button. Ensure Customer Type is entered as the label for the lookup column and then point to the Finish button.**

The label is entered (Figure 6-7).

6 **Click the Finish button to complete the definition of the Lookup Wizard field.**

Customer Type is now a Lookup Wizard field, but the data type still is text because the values entered in the wizard were entered as text.

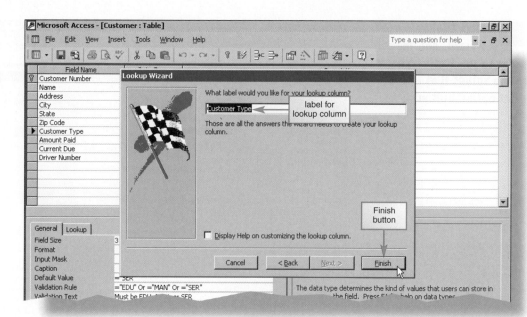

FIGURE 6-7

More *About*

Input Masks

When you construct an input mask, there are many built-in input masks from which to choose. Otherwise, you can construct your own. For more information, visit the Access 2002 More About page (scsite.com/ac2002/more.htm) and then click Input Mask.

Using the Input Mask Wizard

An **input mask** specifies how the data is to be entered and how it will display. You can enter an input mask directly or you can use the **Input Mask Wizard**. The wizard assists you in the creation of the input mask by allowing you to select from a list of input masks you are most likely to want.

To use the Input Mask Wizard, select the Input Mask property and then click the Build button. The following steps add the Phone Number field and then specify how the telephone number is to appear by using the Input Mask Wizard.

Steps **To Use the Input Mask Wizard**

1 **Point to the row selector for the Customer Type field.**

The mouse pointer changes to a right-pointing arrow (Figure 6-8).

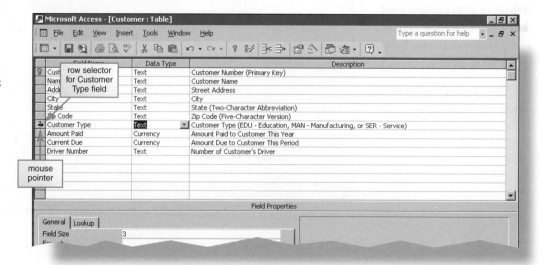

FIGURE 6-8

2 Click the row selector for the Customer Type field, and then press the INSERT key to insert a blank row. Click the Field Name column for the new field. Type Phone Number as the field name and then press the TAB key. Select the Text data type by pressing the TAB key. Type Phone Number as the description. Click the Input Mask property box, and then point to the Build button (the button containing three dots).

The data is entered for the field and the Build button displays (Figure 6-9).

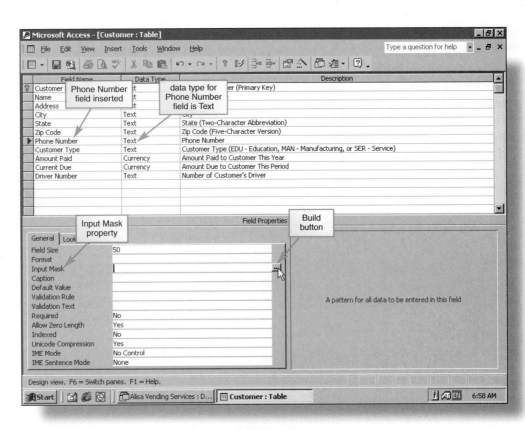

FIGURE 6-9

3 Click the Build button. If a dialog box displays asking you to save the table, click the Yes button. (If a dialog box displays a message that the Input Mask Wizard is not installed, check with your instructor before proceeding with the following steps.) Ensure that Phone Number is selected and then point to the Next button.

The Input Mask Wizard dialog box displays (Figure 6-10). The dialog box contains several common input masks. The Phone Number input mask is highlighted.

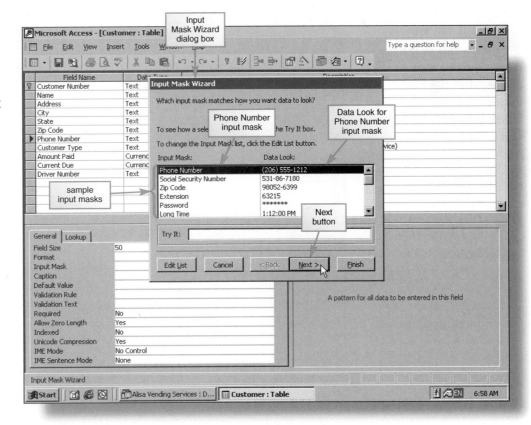

FIGURE 6-10

Microsoft **Access 2002**

4 **Click the Next button. You then are given the opportunity to change the input mask. Because you do not need to change it, click the Next button a second time. Point to the With the symbols in the mask, like this option button.**

The Input Mask Wizard dialog box displays (Figure 6-11). You are asked to indicate whether the symbols in the mask (the parentheses and the hyphen) are to be stored in the database or not. Your dialog box may display different numbers in the examples.

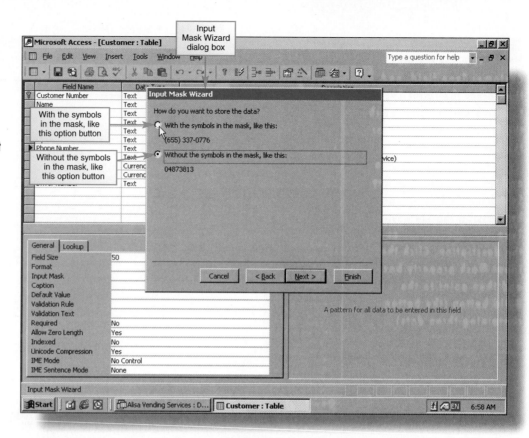

FIGURE 6-11

5 **Click the With the symbols in the mask, like this option button, click the Next button, and then click the Finish button. Point to the Close Window button.**

The input mask displays (Figure 6-12).

6 **Click the Close Window button on the Customer : Table window title bar to close the window. When the Microsoft Access dialog box displays, click the Yes button to save your changes.**

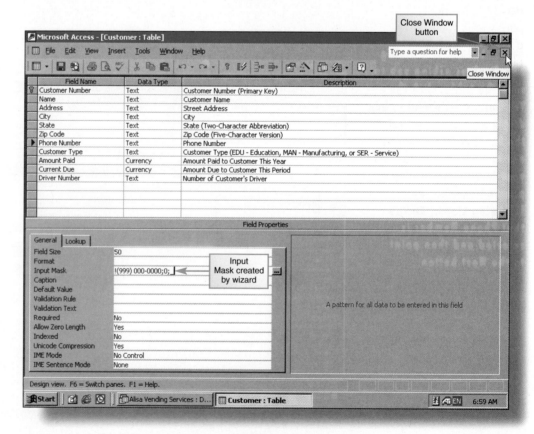

FIGURE 6-12

Entering Data Using an Input Mask

When entering data in a field that has an input mask, Access will insert the appropriate special characters in the proper positions. This means Access will insert the parentheses around the area code, the space following the second parenthesis, and the hyphen automatically in the Phone Number field. Perform the following steps to add the telephone numbers.

Steps To Enter Data Using an Input Mask

1 If necessary, click the Tables object on the Objects bar. Right-click Customer and then click Open on the shortcut menu. Make sure the window is maximized. Point to and then click the Phone Number field on the first record.

The table displays in Datasheet view (Figure 6-13). Access automatically inserts parentheses, a space, and a hyphen. Underscores are placeholders for the data to be entered.

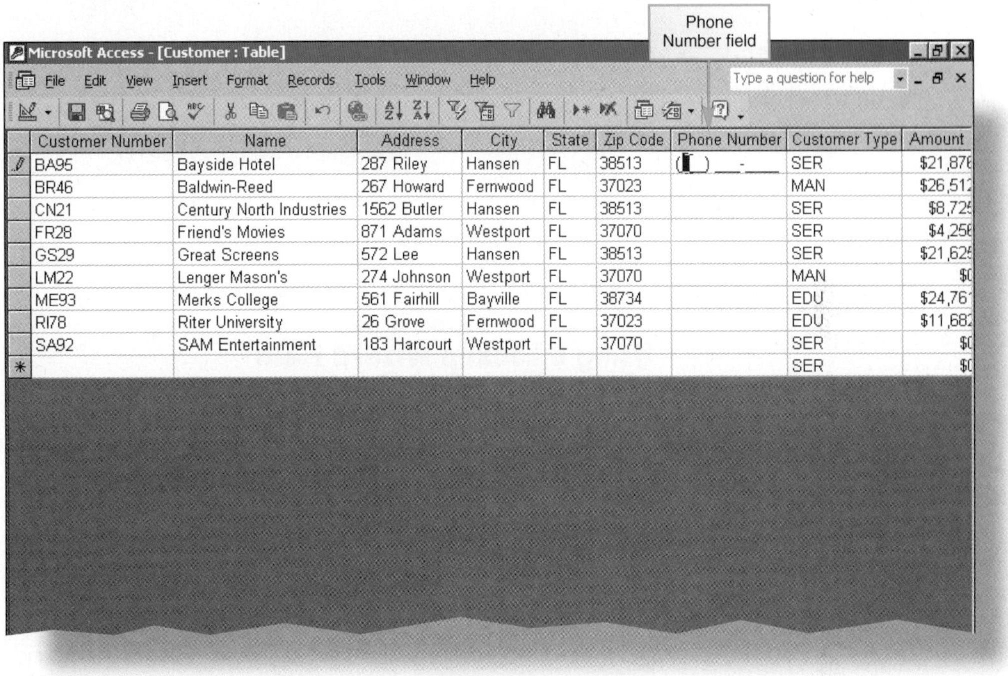

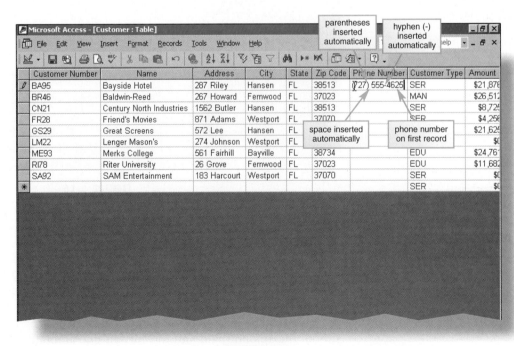

FIGURE 6-13

2 If necessary, use the BACKSPACE key to move the insertion point to the beginning of the Phone Number field, and then type 7275554625 as the telephone number.

The data is inserted in its proper location and the telephone number displays with the appropriate symbols (Figure 6-14).

FIGURE 6-14

3 Use the same technique to enter the remaining telephone numbers as shown in Figure 6-15.

4 Close the window containing the datasheet by clicking its Close Window button.

The datasheet no longer displays. The telephone numbers are entered.

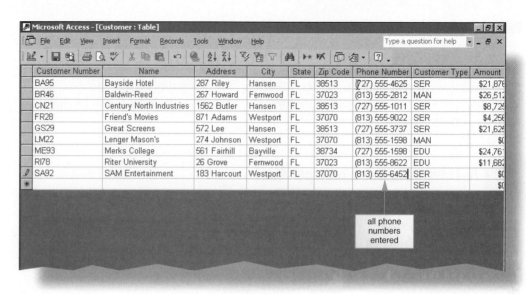

FIGURE 6-15

Using a Lookup Wizard Field

You use a Lookup Wizard field just as you use a combo box in a form. Click the arrow to display a list of available selections (see Figure 6-16). You then can click one of the items to select it from the list.

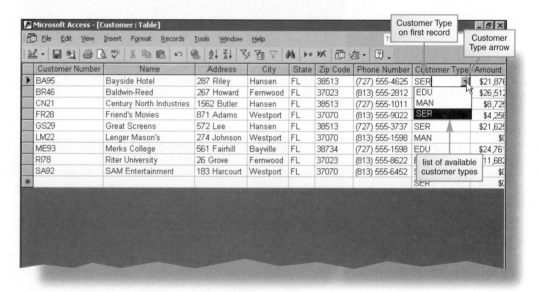

FIGURE 6-16

Modifying a Report

The Customer Amount Report shown in Figure 6-2a on page A 6.06 has two additional controls not present in the original version of the report. One of the additional controls is the Phone Number field that you just added to the Customer table. The other is a calculated control. It displays the total amount, which is the sum of the amount paid and the current due amount.

Resizing and Moving Controls in a Report

Before adding the additional fields, you need to make changes to the size of the control for the Name field because currently it is not long enough to display all the names. This is due to the fact that the Name field was expanded after this report first was created. You also need to resize and move the controls for the Amount Paid and Current Due fields to allow space to add the Total Amount field. Perform the following steps to resize and move the controls in the Customer Amount Report.

Steps **To Resize and Move Controls in a Report**

1 **Click the Reports object in the Database window, right-click Customer Amount Report, and then point to Design View on the shortcut menu.**

The Design View command on the shortcut menu is highlighted (Figure 6-17).

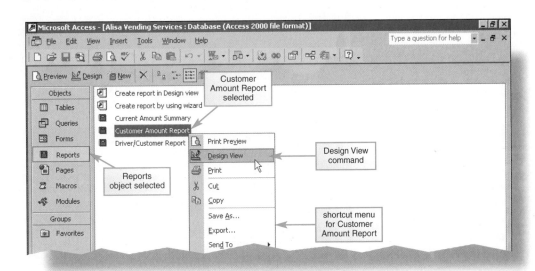

FIGURE 6-17

2 **Click Design View. Be sure that the Customer Amount Report : Report window is maximized. Click the Amount Paid control in the Page Header section to select the control. Hold down the SHIFT key, and then click the Current Due control in the Page Header section, the Amount Paid control in the Detail section, and the Current Due control in the Detail section to select all four controls simultaneously. Point to the left sizing handle for the Amount Paid control in the Page Header section.**

The report design displays (Figure 6-18).

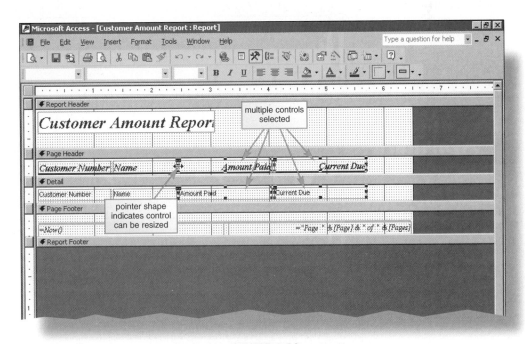

FIGURE 6-18

3 Drag the handle to the right to resize the controls to the approximate sizes shown in Figure 6-19.

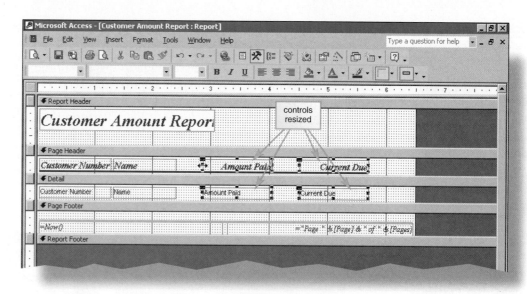

FIGURE 6-19

4 Click the Name control in the Page Header section. Hold down the SHIFT key, and then click the Name control in the Detail section to select both controls simultaneously. Point to the right sizing handle for the Name control in the Detail section.

The Name control in both the Page Header and Detail sections is selected (Figure 6-20).

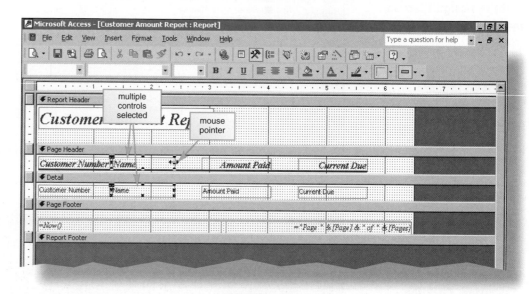

FIGURE 6-20

5 Drag the handle to the right to resize the controls to the approximate sizes shown in Figure 6-21.

The controls are resized.

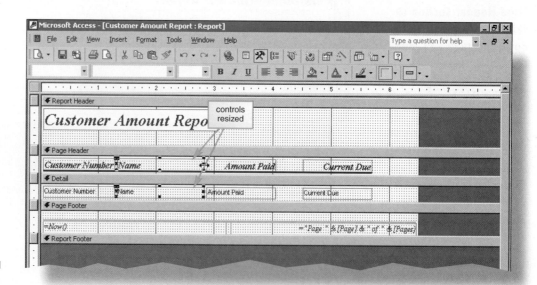

FIGURE 6-21

6 Select the Current Due controls in the Page Header and Detail sections. Point to the border of either control so the mouse pointer changes shape to a hand and then drag the controls to the approximate position shown in Figure 6-22.

The Current Due controls in the Page Header and Detail sections have been repositioned.

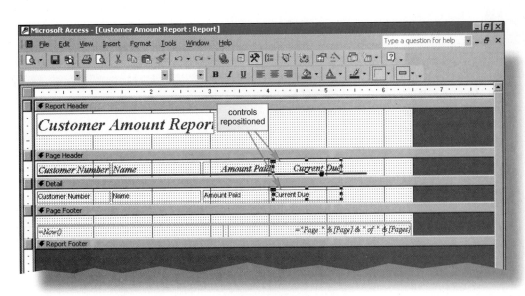

FIGURE 6-22

7 Drag the lower boundary of the Detail section to the position shown in Figure 6-23.

The Detail section is resized.

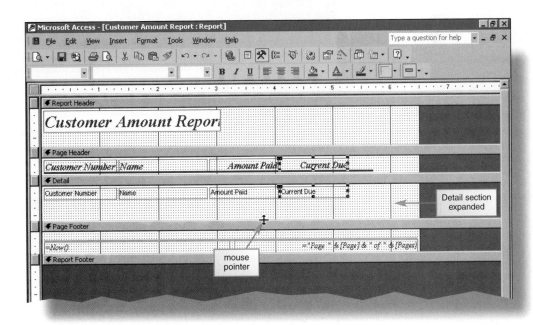

FIGURE 6-23

Adding Controls to a Report

You can add controls to a report just as you added them to a form in Project 4 (pages A 4.37 through A 4.40). You can use either the toolbox or a field list to add various types of controls. If the control is for a single field, using the field list is usually an easier way to add the control. In this section you will add a control for the Phone Number field. You also will add a control that will display the total amount (amount paid plus current due). Perform the steps on the next page to add the controls and also to make appropriate changes to the column headings.

More About

Adding Controls

Even though a control is for a single field, you do not have to use a field list. You also can click the Text Box tool in the toolbox, place the text box in the desired location on the report or form, and then type the name of the field in square brackets ([ ]).

Steps **To Add Controls to a Report**

1 If the field list
does not display
already, point to the
Field List button on the
Report Design toolbar
(Figure 6-24).

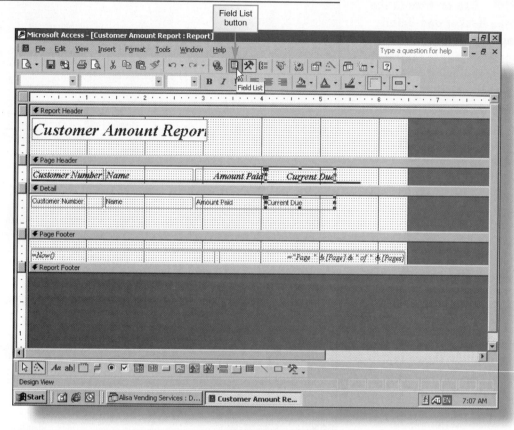

FIGURE 6-24

2 Click the Field
List button. Point
to Phone Number in the
field list. You may need
to scroll down the field
list to display the Phone
Number field.

*The field list displays
(Figure 6-25).*

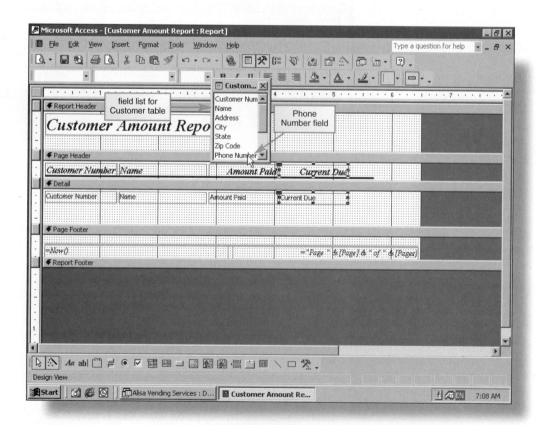

FIGURE 6-25

3 Drag the Phone Number field to the approximate position shown in Figure 6-26.

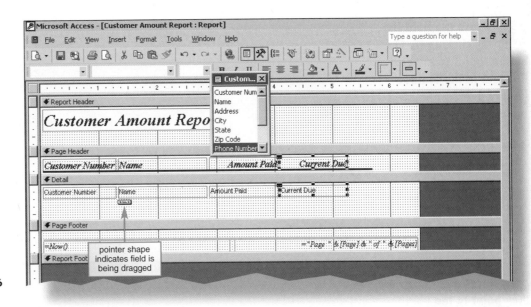

FIGURE 6-26

4 Release the mouse button to complete the placement of the field. Point to the label of the newly placed control (Figure 6-27).

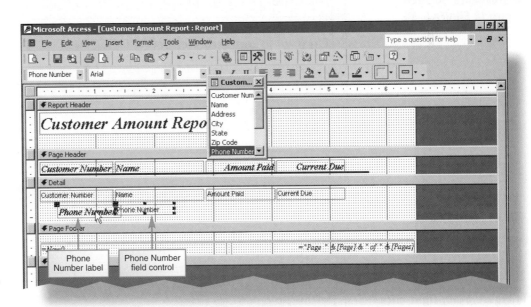

FIGURE 6-27

5 Click the label and then press the DELETE key to delete it. Click the Name control in the Page Header section to select it and then click immediately following the letter e to display an insertion point. Type /Phone to change the contents of the control to Name/Phone.

The contents of the control are changed (Figure 6-28).

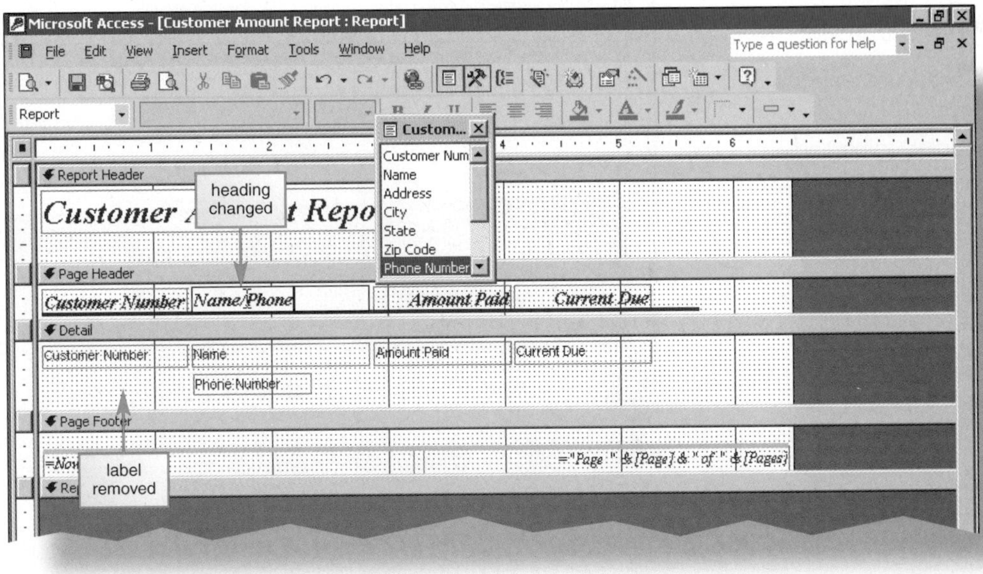

FIGURE 6-28

Microsoft **Access 2002**

6 Close the field list by clicking its Close button. Point to the Text Box tool in the toolbox (Figure 6-29).

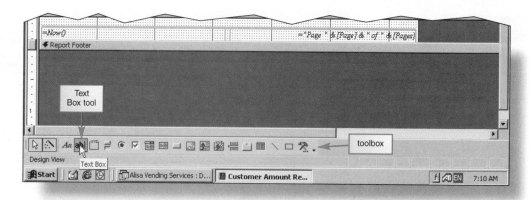

FIGURE 6-29

7 Click the Text Box tool and then point to the approximate position shown in Figure 6-30.

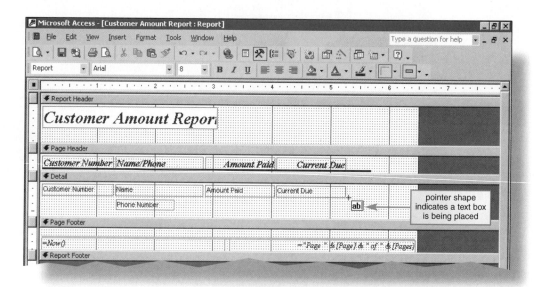

FIGURE 6-30

8 Click the position shown in Figure 6-30, right-click the control, and then point to Properties on the shortcut menu.

The shortcut menu for the control displays, and the Properties command is highlighted (Figure 6-31).

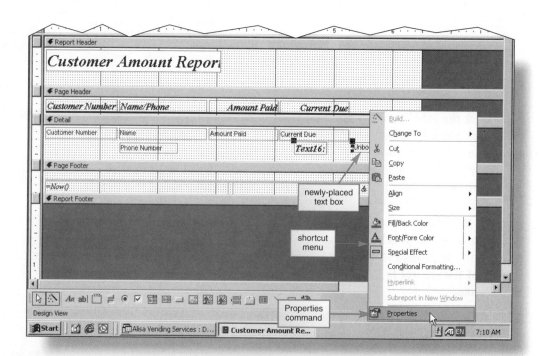

FIGURE 6-31

9 Click Properties, click the Control Source property, and then type =[Amount Paid]+[Current Due] in the Control Source property box.

The final portion of the expression displays in the Control Source property box (Figure 6-32).

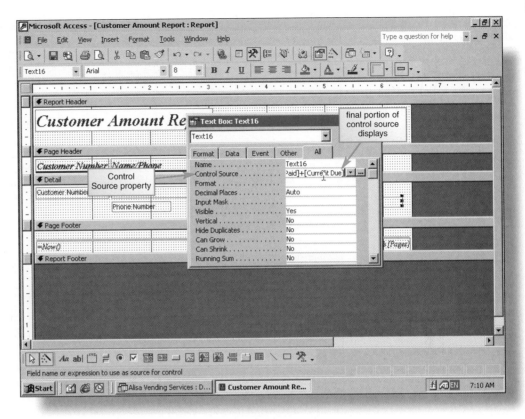

FIGURE 6-32

10 Click the Format property, click the Format property box arrow, scroll down so Currency displays, and then point to Currency (Figure 6-33).

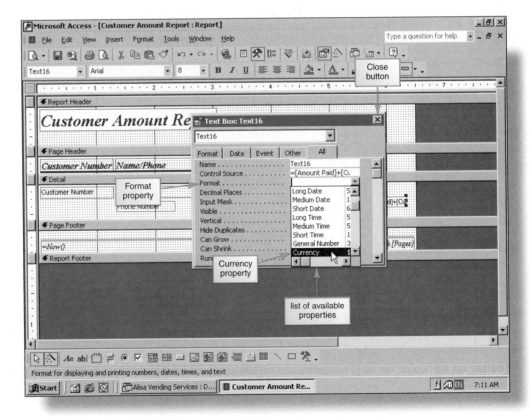

FIGURE 6-33

11 Click Currency to change the Format property. Close the property sheet, and then point to the label for the text box (Figure 6-34).

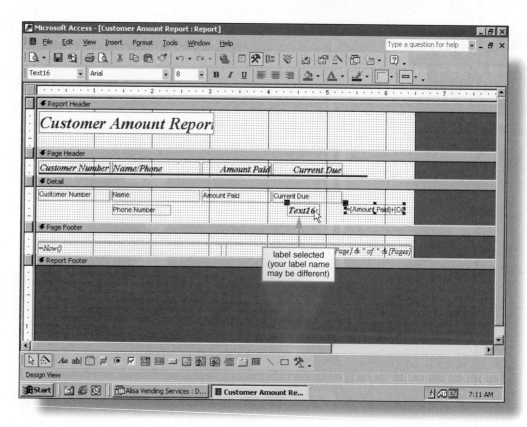

FIGURE 6-34

12 Click the label for the text box (your label name may be different) to select it, press the DELETE key to delete the label, and then point to the Label tool in the toolbox (Figure 6-35).

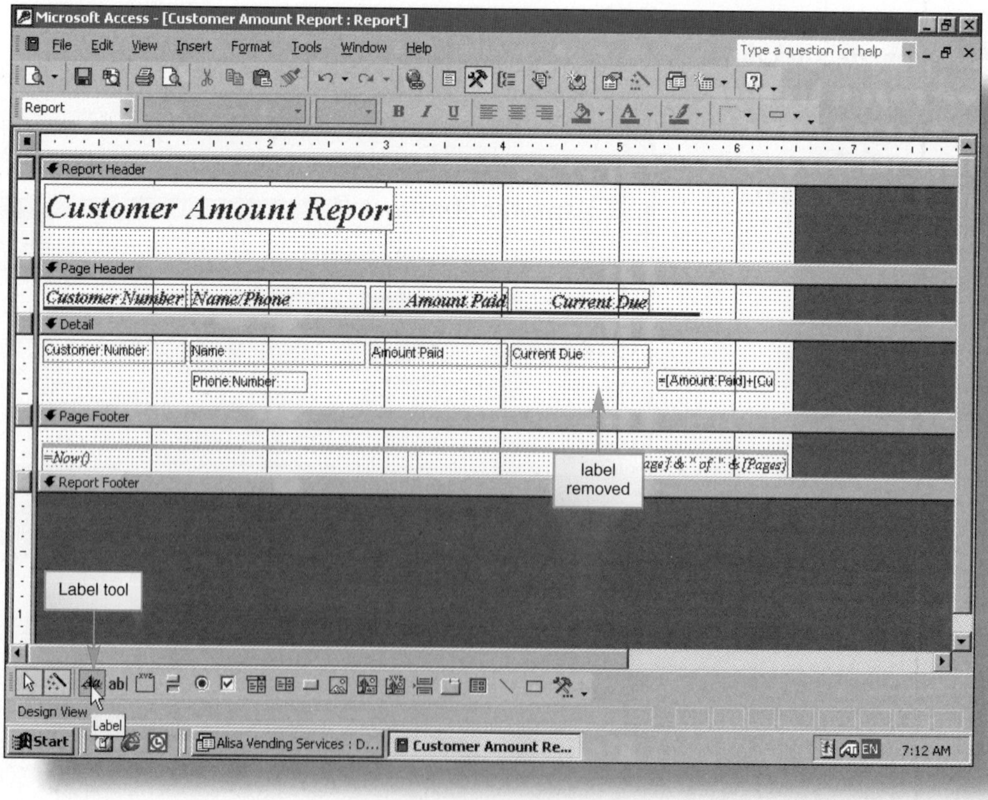

FIGURE 6-35

13 Click the Label tool, and then move the pointer, whose shape changes to a small plus sign and label, to the approximate position shown in Figure 6-36.

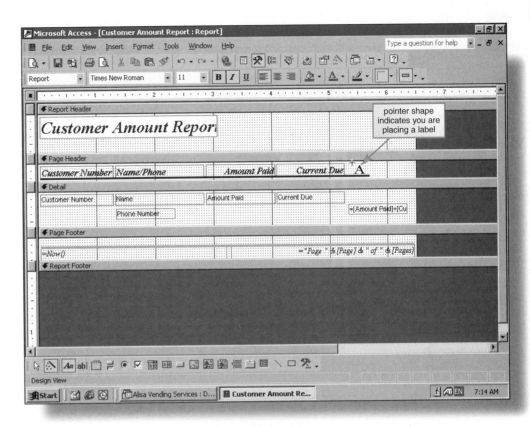

FIGURE 6-36

14 Click the position and then type Total Amount as the entry in the label.

The label displays (Figure 6-37).

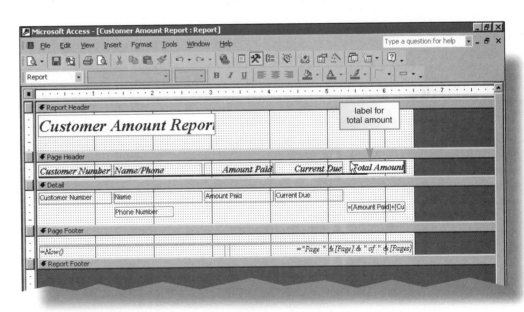

FIGURE 6-37

Resizing a Line

With the addition of the Total Amount label, the bold line in the Page Header section is too short. To lengthen it, click it and then drag its right sizing handle as in the step on the next page.

Steps **To Resize a Line**

1 **Click the bold line in the Page Header section to select it and then drag the right sizing handle to the position shown in Figure 6-38.**

The line is resized.

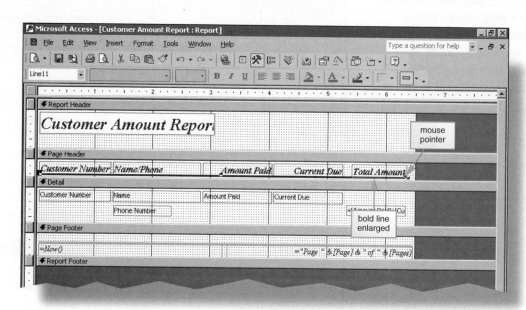

FIGURE 6-38

Previewing a Report

To view the report with sample data, preview the report by clicking the View button on the Report Design toolbar as illustrated in the following steps.

Steps **To Preview a Report**

1 **Point to the View button on the Report Design toolbar (Figure 6-39).**

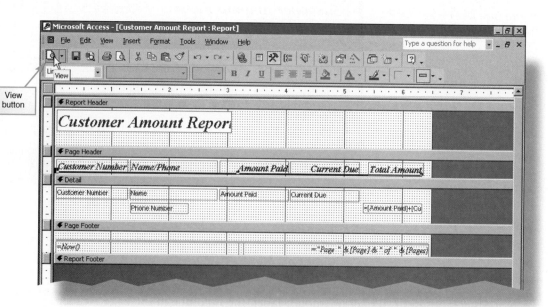

FIGURE 6-39

2 **Click the View button to view the report. Point to the Close Window button for the window containing the report.**

The report displays (Figure 6-40). It looks similar to the one illustrated in Figure 6-2a on page A 6.06.

3 **Click the Close Window button to close the report. Click the Yes button in the Microsoft Access dialog box to save the changes to the report.**

The report is closed, and the changes to the report are saved.

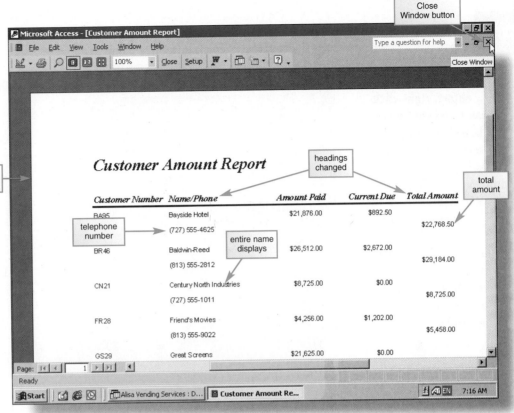

FIGURE 6-40

Other Ways

1. Click Print Preview button on Report Design toolbar
2. On View menu click Print Preview
3. In Voice Command mode, say "Print Preview"

Modifying the Form

The Customer Update Form does not contain the telephone number because there was no Phone Number field when the form was created. To incorporate this field in the form, you must perform the necessary steps to add it to the form.

Adding Controls to a Form

You can add a control to a form by using the toolbox. If the control is for a single field, however, the easiest way to add the control is to use the field list, just as you did with the report. Perform the steps on the next page to add a control for the Phone Number field.

More About

The Access Help System

Need Help? It is no further than the Ask a Question box in the upper-right corner of the window. Click the box that contains the text, Type a question for help (Figure 6-40), type help and then press the ENTER key. Access will respond with a list of items you can click to learn about obtaining help on any Access-related topic. To find out what is new is Access 2002, type what's new in Access in the Ask a Question box.

Steps To Add a Control to a Form

1 **Click the Forms object, right-click Customer Update Form, and then click Design View on the shortcut menu. If necessary, maximize the window. If the field list does not display, click the Field List button on the Form Design toolbar. Point to Phone Number in the field list. You may need to scroll down the field list to display the Phone Number field.**

The Microsoft Access - [Customer Update Form : Form] window displays (Figure 6-41).

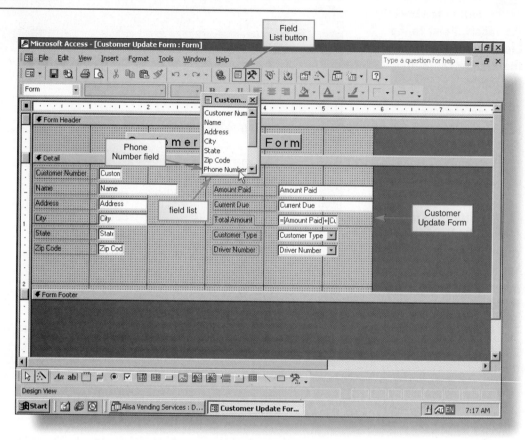

FIGURE 6-41

2 **Drag the Phone Number control to the position shown in Figure 6-42.**

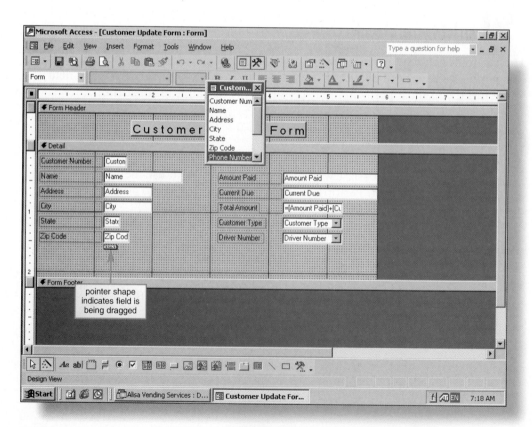

FIGURE 6-42

3 Release the mouse button to place the control. Point to the Move handle of the label for the Phone Number control.

The mouse pointer changes to a pointing finger with hand mouse pointer indicating the label can be moved (Figure 6-43).

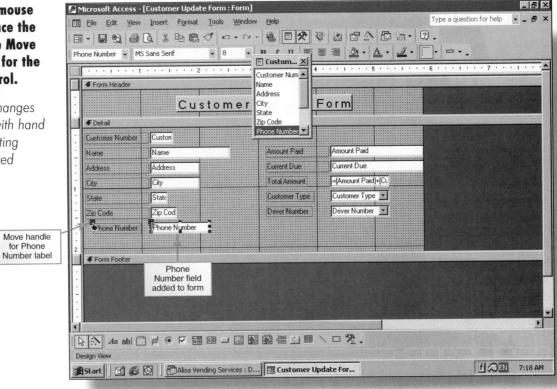

Move handle for Phone Number label

Phone Number field added to form

FIGURE 6-43

4 Drag the label so it lines up with the labels above it.

The label is repositioned (Figure 6-44).

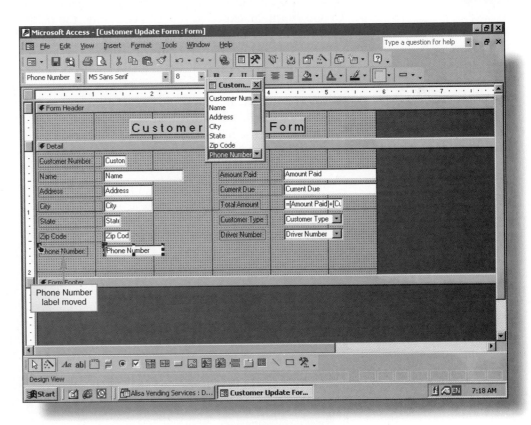

Phone Number label moved

FIGURE 6-44

5 Point to the View button on the Form Design toolbar (Figure 6-45).

6 Click the View button to view the form.

The form displays. It looks similar to the one illustrated in Figure 6-2b on page A 6.06.

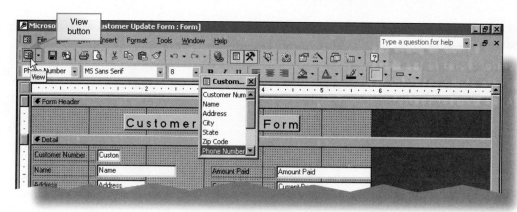

FIGURE 6-45

7 Click the Close Window button to close the form. Click the Yes button in the Microsoft Access dialog box to save the changes.

The form is closed and the changes are saved.

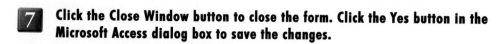

More About

Adding Calculated Controls

You also can type the expression for the calculated control in the text box. To do so, click the text box to select it, click again to place the insertion point inside the text box, and then type the expression. Then, use the property sheet to change the format for the control.

Changing the Tab Order

Users can repeatedly press the TAB key to move through the fields on a form. When you add new fields to a form, the resulting order in which the fields are encountered in this process may not be the most logical sequence. For example, on the Customer Update Form, an expected order to encounter the fields would be Customer Number, Name, Address, City, State, Zip Code, Phone Number, Amount Paid, Current Due, Customer Type, and Driver Number. This order skips the Total Amount field, because the total amount is calculated automatically from other fields. Because the Phone Number field was just added, however, it will not be encountered between Zip Code and Amount Paid, as you would like, but instead will be the last field encountered.

To change the **tab order**, that is, the order in which fields are encountered when tabbing through a form, ensure you are in Design view, and then use the Tab Order command on the View menu. When the Tab Order dialog box displays (Figure 6-46), click and drag the selected row(s) to change the tab order.

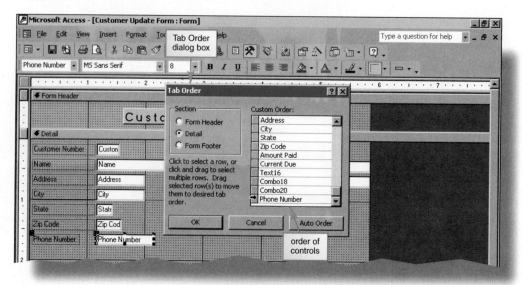

FIGURE 6-46

Creating and Using Macros

A **macro** consists of a series of actions that Access performs when the macro is run; therefore, you will need to specify the actions when you create the macro. The actions are entered in a special window called a **Macro window**. Once a macro is created, you can run it from the Database window by right-clicking the macro and then clicking Run on the shortcut menu. Macros also can be associated with items on switchboards. When you click the corresponding button on the switchboard, Access will run the macro. Whether a macro is run from the Database window or from a switchboard, the effect is the same: Access will execute the actions in the macro in the order in which they are entered.

In this project, you will create macros to open forms and maximize the windows; open tables in Datasheet view; open reports in preview windows; and print reports. As you enter actions, you will select them from a list box. The names of the actions are self-explanatory. The action to open a form, for example, is OpenForm. Thus, it is not necessary to memorize the specific actions that are available.

Perform the following steps to create a macro.

More About

Macros

The actions in a macro are executed when a particular event occurs. The event may be a user clicking Run on the macro's shortcut menu. It also may be clicking a button on a form or switchboard when the macro is associated with the button.

Steps **To Create a Macro**

1 **Click the Macros object and then point to the New button.**

The list of previously created macros displays (Figure 6-47). Currently, no macros exist.

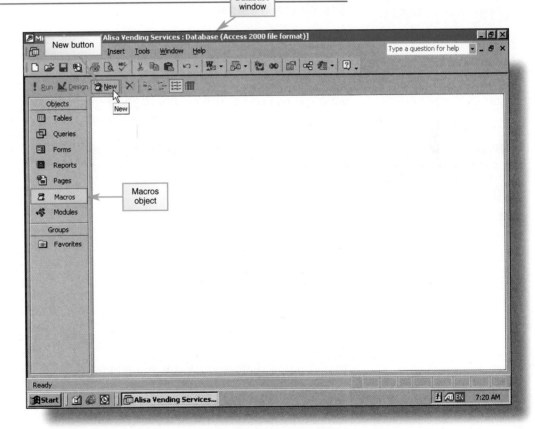

FIGURE 6-47

2 **Click the New button.**

The Microsoft Access – [Macro1: Macro] window displays (Figure 6-48).

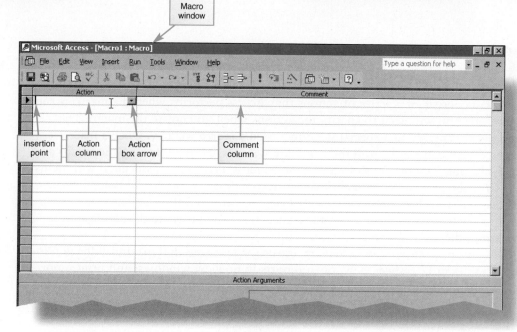

FIGURE 6-48

Other **Ways**

1. Click New Object: AutoForm button arrow on Database toolbar, click Macro
2. On Insert menu click Macro
3. In Voice Command mode, say "Macros, New"

The Macro Window

The first column in the Macro window is the **Action column**. You enter the **actions** you want the macro to perform in this column (Figure 6-48). To enter an action, click the arrow in the Action column and then select the action from the list that displays. Many actions require additional information, called the **arguments** of the action. If you select such an action, the arguments will display in the lower portion of the Macro window and you can make any necessary changes to them.

The second column in the Macro window is the **Comment column**. In this column, you enter **comments**, which are brief descriptions of the purpose of the corresponding action. The actions, the arguments requiring changes, and the comments for the first macro you will create are illustrated in Table 6-1.

The macro begins by turning off the echo. This will eliminate the screen flicker that can be present when a form is being opened. The second action changes the shape of the mouse pointer to an hourglass to indicate that some process is taking place. The third action opens the form called Customer Update Form. The fourth action turns off the hourglass, and the fifth action turns the echo back on so the Customer Update Form will display.

Turning on and off the echo and the hourglass are not absolutely necessary. On computers with faster processors, you may not notice a difference between running a macro that includes these actions and one that does not. For computers with slower processors, however, these actions can make a noticeable difference, so they are included here.

Table 6-1	Specifications for First Macro		
ACTION	**ARGUMENT TO CHANGE**	**NEW VALUE FOR ARGUMENT**	**COMMENT**
Echo	Echo On	No	Turn echo off to avoid screen flicker
Hourglass			Turn on hourglass
OpenForm	Form Name	Customer Update Form	Open Customer Update Form
Hourglass	Hourglass On	No	Turn off hourglass
Echo			Turn echo on

Adding Actions to and Saving a Macro

To continue creating this macro, enter the actions. For each action, enter the action and comment in the appropriate text boxes, and then make the necessary changes to any arguments. When all the actions have been entered, close the macro, click the Yes button to save the changes, and then assign the macro a name. Perform the following steps to add the actions to, and save, the macro.

Steps **To Add Actions to and Save a Macro**

1 **Click the box arrow in the first row of the Action column to display a list of available actions. Scroll down until Echo displays, and then point to Echo.**

The list of available actions displays, and the Echo action is highlighted (Figure 6-49).

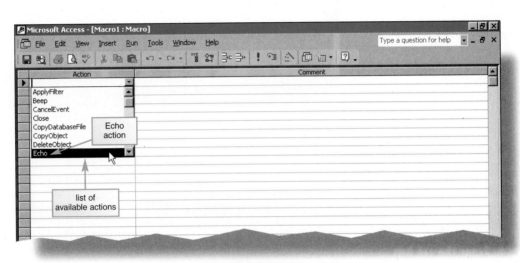

FIGURE 6-49

2 **Click Echo. Press the F6 key to move to the Action Arguments for the Echo action. Click the Echo On box arrow. Point to No.**

The arguments for the Echo action display (Figure 6-50). The list of values for the Echo On argument displays, and the No value is highlighted. Pressing the F6 key switches panes.

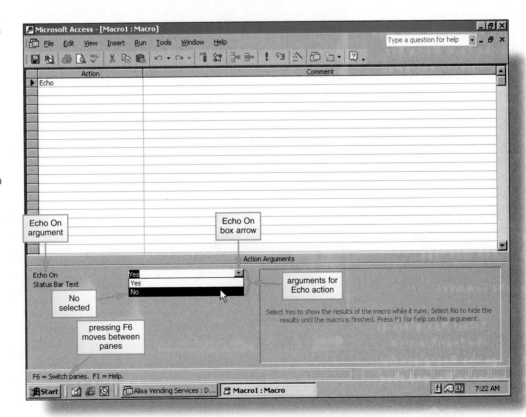

FIGURE 6-50

Microsoft **Access** 2002

3 Click No. Press the F6 key to move back to Echo in the Action column. Press the TAB key. Type Turn echo off to avoid screen flicker in the Comment column and then press the TAB key.

The first action and comment are entered (Figure 6-51). The insertion point has moved to the second row.

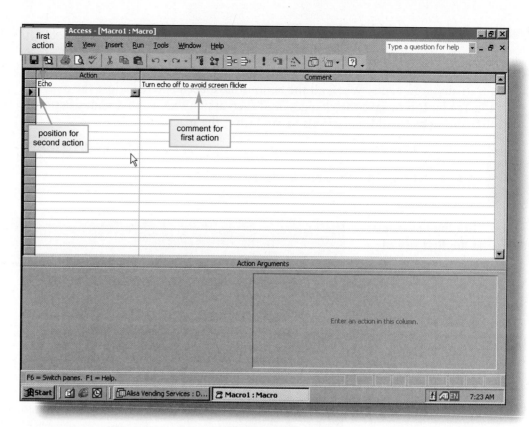

FIGURE 6-51

4 Select Hourglass as the action in the second row. Press the TAB key and then type Turn on hourglass as the comment in the second row. Press the TAB key and then select OpenForm as the third action. Press the F6 key to move to the Action Arguments and then click the Form Name box arrow. Point to Customer Update Form.

A list of available forms displays, and Customer Update Form is highlighted (Figure 6-52).

5 Click Customer Update Form, press the F6 key, press the TAB key, and then type Open Customer Update Form as the comment.

6 Select Hourglass as the fourth action. Change the Hourglass On argument to No, and then type Turn off hourglass as the comment.

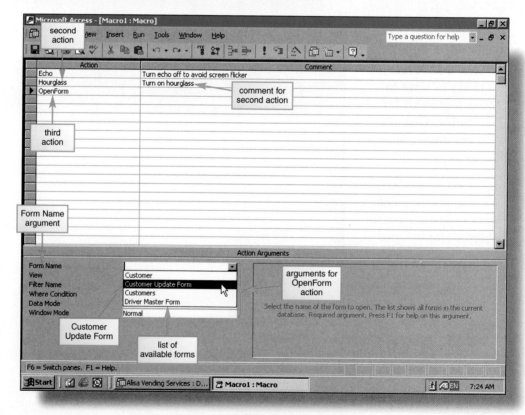

FIGURE 6-52

7 Select Echo as the fifth action. Type *Turn echo on* as the comment. Point to the Close Window button for the Macro1: Macro window.

The actions and comments are entered (Figure 6-53).

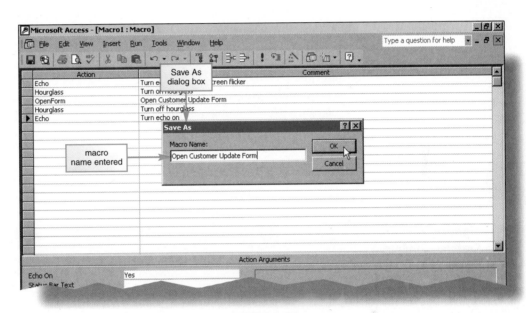

FIGURE 6-53

8 Click the Close Window button to close the macro, click the Yes button to save the macro, type *Open Customer Update Form* as the name of the macro, and then point to the OK button.

The Save As dialog box displays (Figure 6-54).

9 Click the OK button.

The actions and comments have been added to the macro, and the macro is saved.

FIGURE 6-54

Running a Macro

To **run a macro**, click the Macros object in the Database window, right-click the macro, and then click Run on the shortcut menu. The actions in the macro will execute. Perform the following steps to run the macro you just created.

TO RUN A MACRO

1 Right-click the Open Customer Update Form macro and then click Run on the shortcut menu.

2 Click the Close Window button on the Customer Update Form window title bar.

The macro runs and the Customer Update Form displays. The window containing the form is maximized because the previous windows were maximized. The form no longer displays.

If previous windows had not been maximized, the window containing the form also would not be maximized. In order to ensure that the window containing the form is maximized automatically, you can include the Maximize action in your macro.

More About

Running a Macro

You can run a macro from any window within Access. To do so, click Macro on the Tools menu, click Run Macro, and then select the macro from the Macro Name list.

More About

Inserting an Action

If you inadvertently press the DELETE key instead of the INSERT key when you are inserting a new line in a macro, you will delete the selected action from the macro. To return the deleted action to the macro, click the Undo button on the toolbar.

Modifying a Macro

To modify a macro, right-click the macro in the Database window, click Design View on the shortcut menu, and then make the necessary changes. To insert a new action, click the position for the action, or press the INSERT key to insert a new blank row if the new action is to be placed between two actions. Enter the new action, change the values for any necessary arguments, and then enter a comment.

When modifying a macro, two additional columns may display: the Macro Name column and the Condition column. It is possible to group multiple macros into a single macro group. When doing so, the Macro Name column is used to identify the particular macro within the group. It also is possible to have an action be contingent on a certain condition being true. If so, the condition is entered in the Condition column. Because the macros you are creating are not combined into a macro group and the actions are not dependent on any conditions, you will not need these columns. You can remove these unneeded columns from the screen by clicking the appropriate toolbar buttons.

The following steps modify the macro just created, adding a new step to maximize the form automatically. The steps remove both the Macro Name and the Condition column from the screen.

Steps To Modify a Macro

1 Right-click the Open Customer Update Form macro, and then point to Design View on the shortcut menu.

The shortcut menu displays, and the Design View command is highlighted (Figure 6-55).

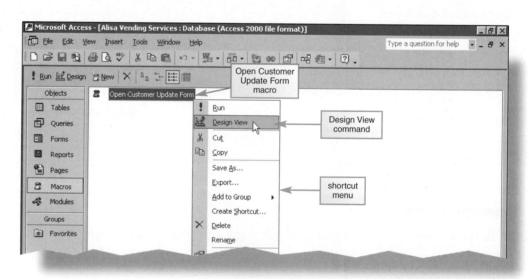

FIGURE 6-55

2 Click Design View. If the Macro Name column displays, point to the Macro Names button on the Macro Design toolbar (Figure 6-56).

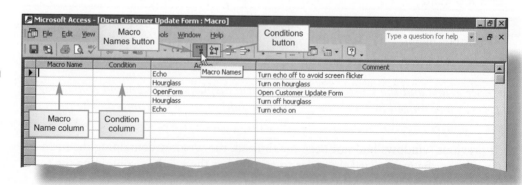

FIGURE 6-56

3 If the Macro name column displays, click the Macro Names button on the Macro Design toolbar. If the Condition column displays, click the Conditions button on the Macro Design toolbar. Point to the row selector in the fourth row, which is directly to the left of the second Hourglass action.

The Microsoft Access - [Open Customer Update Form : Macro] window displays (Figure 6-57). The Macro Name and Condition columns do not display.

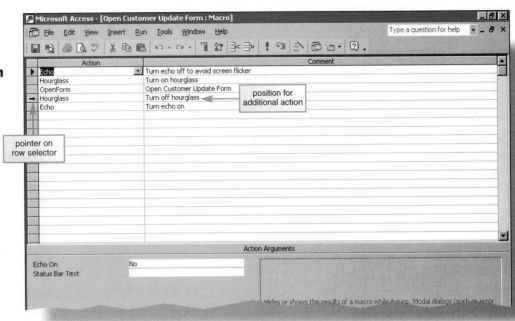

FIGURE 6-57

4 Click the row selector to select the row, and then press the INSERT key to insert a new row. Click the Action column on the new row, select Maximize as the action, and then type Maximize the window as the comment.

The new action is entered (Figure 6-58).

5 Click the Close Window button, and then click the Yes button to save the changes.

The macro has been changed and saved.

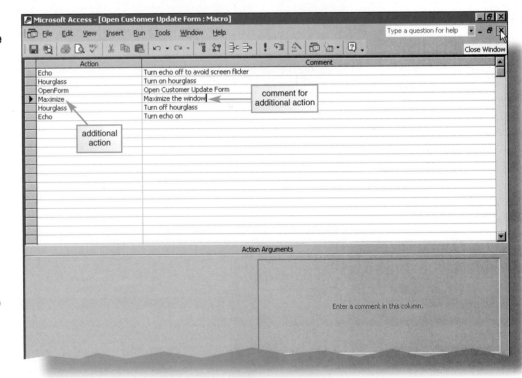

FIGURE 6-58

The next time the macro is run, the form not only will be opened, but the window containing the form also will be maximized automatically.

Other Ways

1. Click Macros on Objects bar, click Macro name, click Design on Macro Design toolbar
2. In Voice Command mode, say "Macros, [click macro name], Design"

Errors in Macros

There are times when the order of the actions in a macro is incorrect. You can move an action by clicking the row selector to the left of the action name to highlight the row. Then click the highlighted row again and drag it to the correct location.

Errors in Macros

Macros can contain errors. For example, if you type the name of the form in the Form Name argument of the OpenForm action instead of selecting it from the list, you may type it incorrectly. Access then will not be able to execute the desired action. In that case, a Microsoft Access message box will display, indicating the error and solution as shown in Figure 6-59.

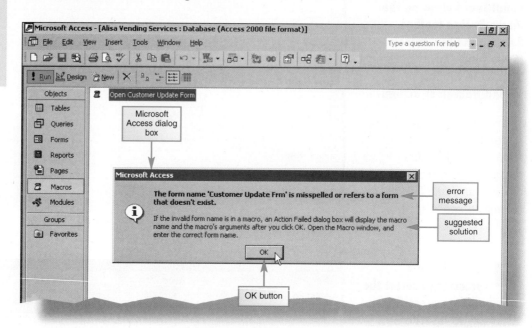

FIGURE 6-59

If such a message box displays, click the OK button. The Action Failed dialog box then displays (Figure 6-60). It indicates the macro that was being run, the action that Access was attempting to execute, and the arguments for the action. This information tells you which action needs to be corrected. To make the correction, click the Halt button, and then modify the design of the macro.

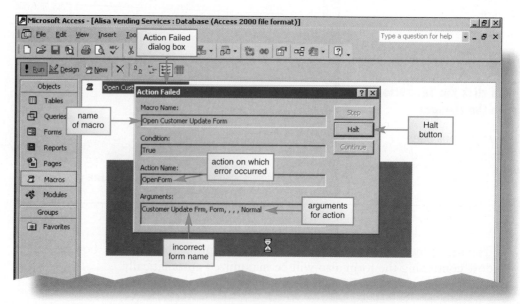

FIGURE 6-60

Additional Macros

The additional macros to be created are shown in Table 6-2. The first column gives the name of the macro, and the second column indicates the actions for the macro. The third column contains the values of those arguments that may need to be changed, and the fourth column contains the comments. (Any arguments not listed can be left as they are.)

Copying a Macro

When you wish to create a new macro, you often find there is an existing macro that is very similar to the one you wish to create. If this is the case, it often is simpler to use a copy of the existing macro and modify it instead of creating a new macro from scratch. The Open Driver Master Form macro you wish to create, for example, is very similar to the existing Open Customer Update Form macro. Thus, you can make a copy of the Open Customer Update Form macro, call it Open Driver Master Form, and then modify it to the new requirements by changing only the portion that differs from the original macro.

To make a copy of a macro, you use the clipboard. First copy the existing macro to the clipboard and then paste the contents of the clipboard. At that point, assign the new name to the macro.

Incidentally, these same techniques will work for other objects as well. If you wish to create a new report that is similar to an existing report, for example, use the clipboard to make a copy of the original report, paste the contents, rename it, and then modify the copied report in whatever way you wish.

Perform the steps on the next page to use the clipboard to copy the Open Customer Update Form macro.

Table 6-2	Specifications for Additional Macros		
MACRO NAME	ACTION	ARGUMENT(S)	COMMENT
Open Driver Master Form	Echo	Echo on: No	Turn echo off to avoid screen flicker
	Hourglass	Hourglass On: Yes	Turn on hourglass
	OpenForm	Form Name: Driver Master Form	Open Driver Master Form
	Maximize		Maximize the window
	Hourglass	Hourglass On: No	Turn off hourglass
	Echo	Echo on: Yes	Turn echo on
Open Customer Table	OpenTable	Table Name: Customer	Open Customer Table
		View: Datasheet	
	Maximize		Maximize the window
Open Driver Table	OpenTable	Table Name: Driver	Open Driver Table
		View: Datasheet	
	Maximize		Maximize the window
Preview Customer Amount Report	OpenReport	Report Name: Customer Amount Report	Preview Customer Amount Report
		View: Print Preview	
	Maximize		Maximize the window
Print Customer Amount Report	OpenReport	Report Name: Customer Amount Report	Print Customer Amount Report
		View: Print	
Preview Current Amount Summary	OpenReport	Report Name: Current Amount Summary	Preview Current Amount Summary
		View: Print Preview	
	Maximize		Maximize the window
Print Current Amount Summary	OpenReport	Report Name: Current Amount Summary	Print Current Amount Summary
		View: Print	
Preview Driver/ Customer Report	OpenReport	Report Name: Driver/ Customer Report	Preview Driver/ Customer Report
		View: Print Preview	
	Maximize		Maximize the window
Print Driver/ Customer Report	OpenReport	Report Name: Driver/ Customer Report	Print Driver/ Customer Report
		View: Print	

Steps **To Copy a Macro**

1 **Ensure the Macros object is selected, right-click the Open Customer Update Form macro, and then point to Copy on the shortcut menu.**

The shortcut menu for the Open Customer Update Form macro displays, and the Copy command is highlighted (Figure 6-61).

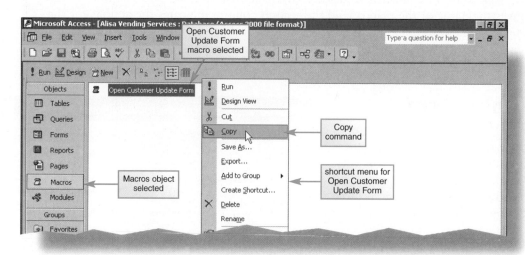

FIGURE 6-61

2 **Click Copy to copy the macro to the clipboard. Right-click any open area of the Database window, and then point to Paste on the shortcut menu.**

The shortcut menu displays, and the Paste command is highlighted (Figure 6-62).

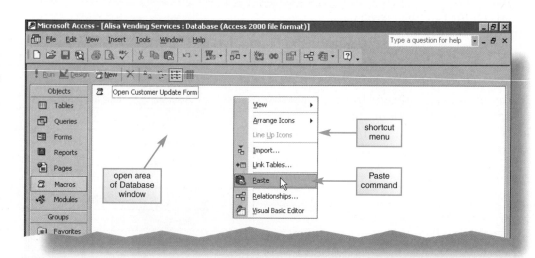

FIGURE 6-62

3 **Click Paste, type** Open Driver Master Form **in the Macro Name text box in the Paste As dialog box, and then point to the OK button.**

The Paste As dialog box displays, and the new macro name is entered in the text box (Figure 6-63).

4 **Click the OK button.**

The new macro is copied and saved.

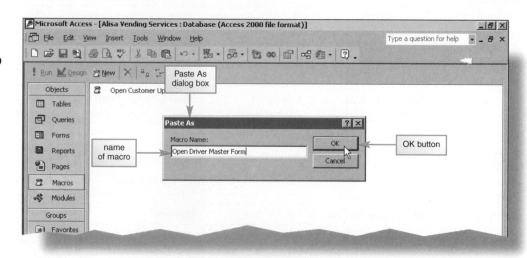

FIGURE 6-63

Modifying the Copied Macro

Once you have copied the macro, you can modify the copy to make any needed changes. The following steps modify the macro just copied by changing the Form Name argument for the OpenForm action to Driver Master Form.

Steps To Modify the Copied Macro

1 **Right-click the Open Driver Master Form macro, and then point to Design View on the shortcut menu (Figure 6-64).**

2 **Click Design View. Click the row selector for the OpenForm action, click the Form Name argument, click the Form Name box arrow, and then point to the Driver Master Form.**

The macro displays in Design view. The OpenForm action is selected, the list of available forms displays, and Driver Master Form is highlighted (Figure 6-65).

3 **Click Driver Master Form to change the Form Name argument. Click the Comment text box for the OpenForm action, delete the comment, and then type** Open Driver Master Form **as the new comment. Click the Close Window button for the Open Driver Master Form : Macro window and then click the Yes button to save the changes.**

The changes to the macro have been saved.

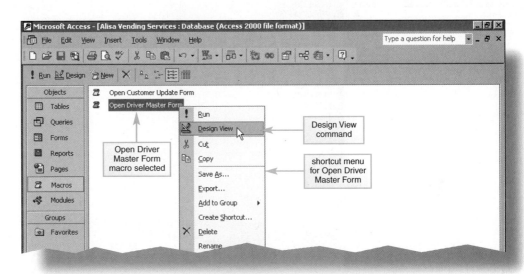

FIGURE 6-64

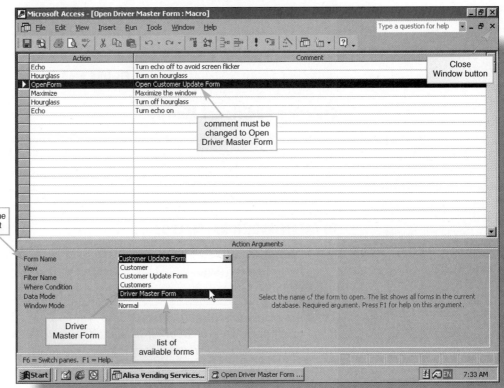

FIGURE 6-65

Macro Arguments

Some macros require a change to more than one argument. For example, to create a macro to preview or print a report requires a change to the Report Name argument and a change to the View argument. In Figure 6-66, the OpenReport action displays Customer Amount Report in the Report Name argument text box and Print Preview is highlighted in the View text box.

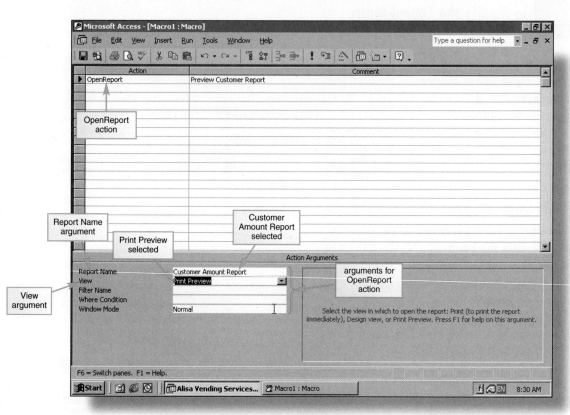

FIGURE 6-66

Creating Additional Macros

You can create additional macros using the same steps you used to create the first macro. You copy an existing macro and then modify the copied macro as needed. Perform the following step to create the additional macros illustrated in Table 6-2 on page A 6.37.

TO CREATE ADDITIONAL MACROS

 Using the same techniques you used to create the Open Customer Update Form macro (page A 6.31), create each of the macros described in Table 6-2 on page A 6.37.

The Open Customer Table, Open Driver Table, Preview Customer Amount Report, Print Customer Amount Report, Preview Current Amount Summary, Print Current Amount Summary, Preview Driver/Customer Report, and Print Driver/Customer Report macros are created.

Application Systems

An application system is simply an easy-to-use collection of forms, reports, and queries designed to satisfy the needs of some specific user or group of users, such as the users at Alisa Vending Services. A switchboard system is one type of application system that has found widespread acceptance in the Windows environment. For more information about application systems, visit the Access 2002 More About page (scsite.com/ac2002/more.htm) and then click Application Systems.

Running the Macros

To run any of the other macros just as you ran the first macro, right-click the appropriate macro in the Database window and then click Run on the shortcut menu. The appropriate actions then are carried out. Running the Preview Customer Amount Report macro, for example, displays the Customer Amount Report in a maximized preview window.

Creating and Using a Switchboard

A **switchboard** (see Figures 6-1a and 6-1b on page A 6.05) is a special type of form. It contains buttons you can click to perform a variety of actions. Buttons on the main switchboard can lead to other switchboards. Clicking the View Form button, for example, causes Access to display the View Form switchboard. Buttons also can be used to open forms or tables. Clicking the Customer Update Form button on the View Form switchboard opens the Customer Update Form. Still other buttons cause reports to display in a preview window or print reports.

Creating a Switchboard

To create a switchboard, you use the Database Utilities command on the Tools menu and then click **Switchboard Manager**, which is an Access tool that allows you to create, edit, and delete switchboard forms for an application. If you have not previously created a switchboard, you will be asked if you wish to create one. Clicking the Yes button causes Access to create the switchboard. Perform the following steps to create a switchboard for the Alisa Vending Services database.

More About

Switchboards

A switchboard is considered a form and is run like any other form. A special tool is used to create it, however, called the Switchboard Manager. Although you can modify the design of the form by clicking Design View on its shortcut menu, it is easier to use the Switchboard Manager for modifications.

Steps To Create a Switchboard

1 **With the Database window displaying, click Tools on the menu bar, click Database Utilities on the Tools menu, and then point to Switchboard Manager.**

The Tools menu displays (Figure 6-67). The Database Utilities submenu displays, and the Switchboard Manager command is highlighted. If the Database Utilities command does not display immediately, wait a few seconds for the full menu to display.

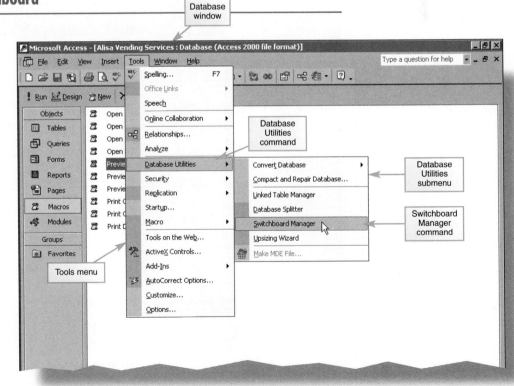

FIGURE 6-67

2 Click Switchboard Manager and then point to the Yes button.

The Switchboard Manager dialog box displays (Figure 6-68). The message indicates that no switchboard currently exists for this database and asks whether to create one.

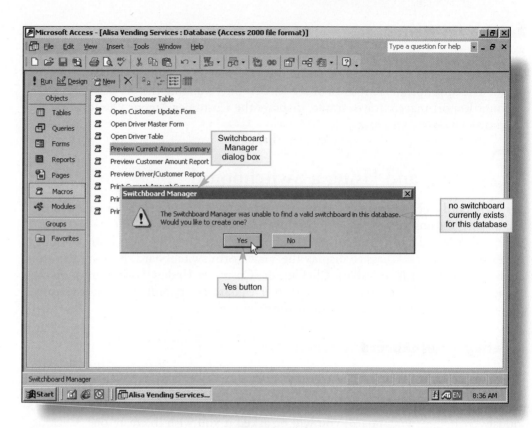

FIGURE 6-68

3 Click the Yes button to create a new switchboard, and then point to the New button.

The Switchboard Manager dialog box displays and indicates there is only the Main Switchboard at this time (Figure 6-69).

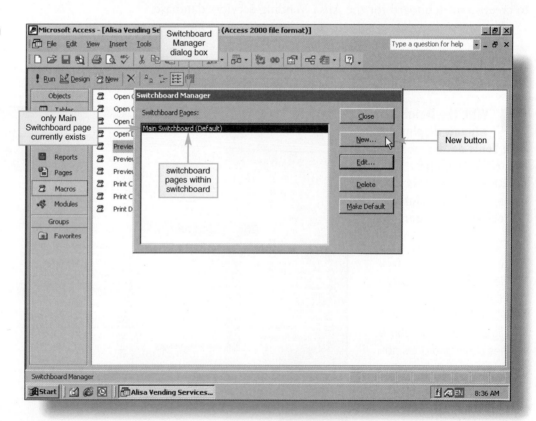

FIGURE 6-69

Creating Switchboard Pages

The next step in creating the switchboard system is to create the individual switchboards within the system. These individual switchboards are called the **switchboard pages**. The switchboard pages to be created are listed in the first column of Table 6-3. You do not have to create the Main Switchboard page because Access has created it automatically (Figure 6-69). To create each of the other pages, click the New button in the Switchboard Manager dialog box, and then type the name of the page.

Table 6-3 Specifications for Switchboard Pages and Items

SWITCHBOARD PAGE	SWITCHBOARD ITEM	COMMAND	ARGUMENT
Main Switchboard	View Form	Go to Switchboard	Switchboard: View Form
	View Table	Go to Switchboard	Switchboard: View Table
	View Report	Go to Switchboard	Switchboard: View Report
	Print Report	Go to Switchboard	Switchboard: Print Report
	Exit Application	Exit Application	None
View Form	Customer Update Form	Run Macro	Macro: Open Customer Update Form
	Driver Master Form	Run Macro	Macro: Open Driver Master Form
	Return to Main Switchboard	Go to Switchboard	Switchboard: Main Switchboard
View Table	Customer Table	Run Macro	Macro: Open Customer Table
	Driver Table	Run Macro	Macro: Open Driver Table
	Return to Main Switchboard	Go to Switchboard	Switchboard: Main Switchboard
View Report	View Customer Amount Report	Run Macro	Macro: Preview Customer Amount Report
	View Current Amount Summary	Run Macro	Macro: Preview Current Amount Summary
	View Driver/ Customer Report	Run Macro	Macro: Preview Driver/ Customer Report
	Return to Main Switchboard	Go to Switchboard	Switchboard: Main Switchboard
Print Report	Print Customer Amount Report	Run Macro	Macro: Print Customer Amount Report
	Print Current Amount Summary	Run Macro	Macro: Print Current Amount Summary
	Print Driver/ Customer Report	Run Macro	Macro: Print Driver/ Customer Report
	Return to Main Switchboard	Go to Switchboard	Switchboard: Main Switchboard

Perform the steps on the next page to create the switchboard pages.

Steps | To Create Switchboard Pages

1 **Click the New button in the Switchboard Manager dialog box. Type** View Form **as the name of the new switchboard page. Point to the OK button.**

The Create New dialog box displays (Figure 6-70). The name of the new page is entered in the Switchboard Page Name text box.

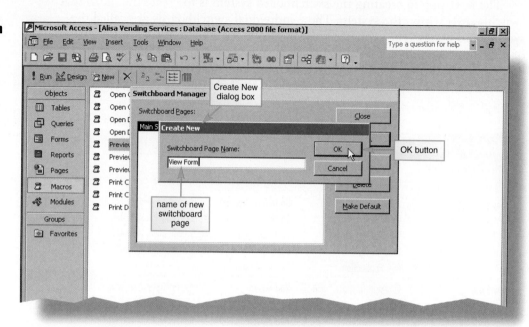

FIGURE 6-70

2 **Click the OK button to create the View Form switchboard page. Use the technique described in Steps 1 and 2 to create the View Table, View Report, and Print Report switchboard pages.**

The newly-created switchboard pages display in the Switchboard Manager dialog box in alphabetical order (Figure 6-71).

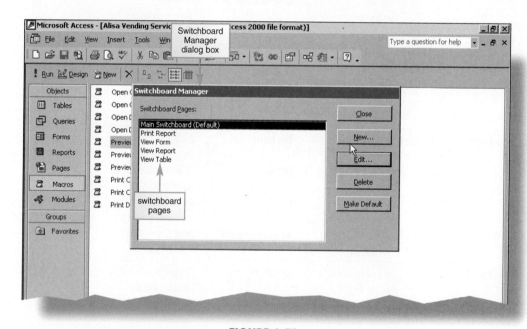

FIGURE 6-71

Modifying Switchboard Pages

You can modify a switchboard page by using the following procedure. Select the page in the Switchboard Manager dialog box, click the Edit button, and then add new items to the page, move existing items to a different position in the list of items, or delete items. For each item, you can indicate the command to be executed when the item is selected.

Perform the following steps to modify the Main Switchboard page.

To Modify the Main Switchboard Page

1 **With the Main Switchboard (Default) page selected, point to the Edit button (Figure 6-72).**

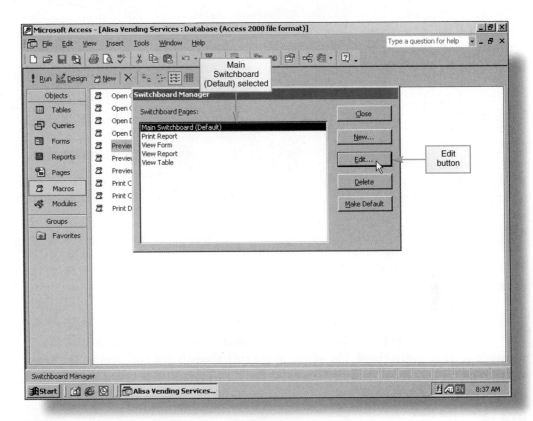

FIGURE 6-72

2 **Click the Edit button, and then point to the New button in the Edit Switchboard Page dialog box.**

The Edit Switchboard Page dialog box displays (Figure 6-73).

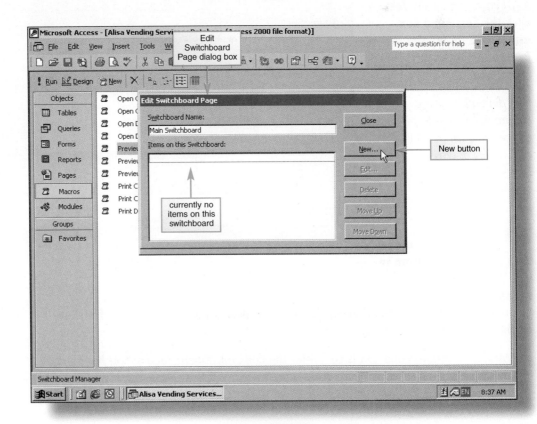

FIGURE 6-73

3 Click the New button, type View Form as the text, click the Switchboard box arrow, and then point to View Form.

The Edit Switchboard Item dialog box displays (Figure 6-74). The text is entered, the command is Go to Switchboard, the list of available switchboards displays, and the View Form switchboard is highlighted.

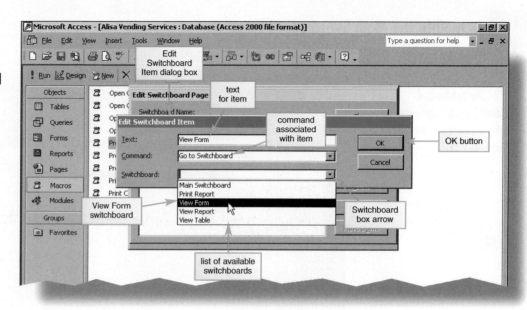

FIGURE 6-74

4 Click View Form, and then click the OK button to add the item to the switchboard.

5 Using the techniques illustrated in Steps 3 and 4, add the View Table, View Report, and Print Report items to the Main Switchboard page. In each case, the command is Go to Switchboard. The names of the switchboards are the same as the name of the items. For example, the switchboard for the View Table item is called View Table.

6 Click the New button, type Exit Application as the text, click the Command box arrow, and then point to Exit Application.

The Edit Switchboard Item dialog box displays (Figure 6-75). The text is entered, the list of available commands displays, and the Exit Application command is highlighted.

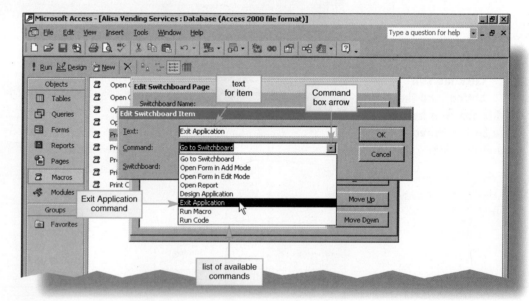

FIGURE 6-75

7 Click Exit Application, and then click the OK button to add the item to the switchboard. Click the Close button in the Edit Switchboard Page dialog box to indicate you have finished editing the Main Switchboard.

The Main Switchboard page now is complete. The Edit Switchboard Page dialog box closes, and the Switchboard Manager dialog box displays.

Modifying the Other Switchboard Pages

The other switchboard pages from Table 6-3 on page A 6.43 are modified in exactly the same manner you modified the Main Switchboard page. Perform the following steps to modify the other switchboard pages.

 To Modify the Other Switchboard Pages

1 Click the View Form switchboard page, and then point to the Edit button.

The View Form page is selected (Figure 6-76).

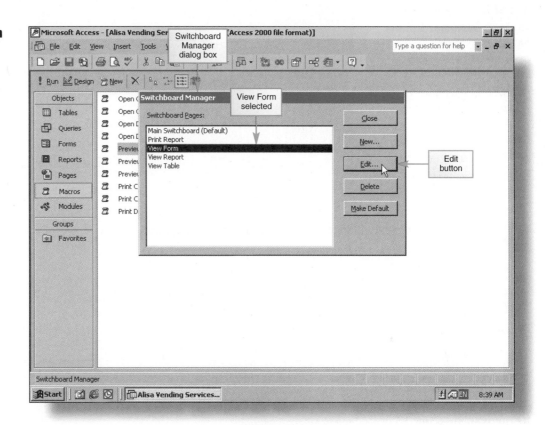

FIGURE 6-76

2 Click the Edit button, click the New button to add a new item, type `Customer Update Form` as the text, click the Command box arrow, and then click Run Macro. Click the Macro box arrow, and then point to Open Customer Update Form.

The Edit Switchboard Item dialog box displays (Figure 6-77). The text is entered and the command selected. The list of available macros displays, and the Open Customer Update Form macro is highlighted.

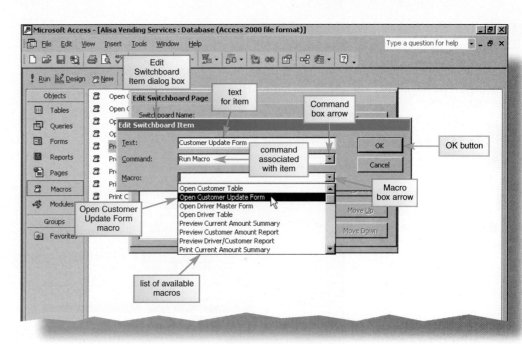

FIGURE 6-77

3 Click Open Customer Update Form, and then click the OK button.

The Customer Update Form item is added to the View Form switchboard.

4 Click the New button, type `Driver Master Form` as the text, click the Command box arrow, and then click Run Macro. Click the Macro box arrow, click Open Driver Master Form, and then click the OK button.

5 Click the New button, type `Return to Main Switchboard` as the text, click the Command box arrow, and then click Go to Switchboard. Click the Switchboard box arrow, and then point to Main Switchboard.

The text is entered, the command is selected, the list of available switchboards displays, and the Main Switchboard is highlighted (Figure 6-78).

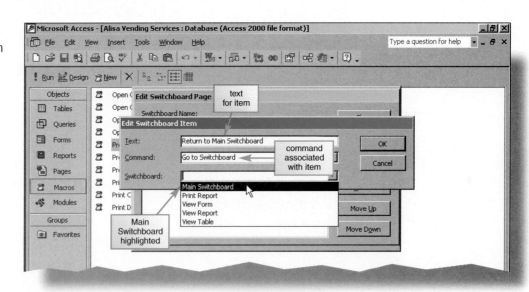

FIGURE 6-78

6 Click Main Switchboard, and then click the OK button. Click the Close button in the Edit Switchboard Page dialog box to indicate you have finished editing the View Form switchboard.

Use the techniques illustrated in Steps 1 through 6 to add the items indicated in Table 6-3 on page A 6.43 to the other switchboards. When you have finished, point to the Close button in the Switchboard Manager dialog box (Figure 6-79).

 **Click the Close button.**

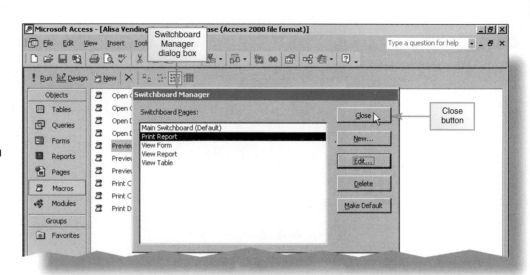

FIGURE 6-79

The switchboard is complete and ready for use. Access has created a form called Switchboard that you will run to use the switchboard. It also has created a table called Switchboard Items. *DO NOT modify this table.* It is used by the Switchboard Manager to keep track of the various switchboard pages and items.

Using a Switchboard

To use the switchboard, click the Forms object, right-click the switchboard, and then click Open on the shortcut menu. The Main Switchboard then will display. To take any action, click the appropriate buttons. When you have finished, click the Exit Application button. The switchboard will be removed from the screen, and the database will be closed. The following steps illustrate opening a switchboard system for use.

More About

Displaying Switchboards

It is possible to have the switchboard display automatically when the database is opened. To do so, click Tools on the menu bar, and then click Startup. Click the Display Form/Page box arrow, select the Switchboard form, and then click the OK button.

Steps **To Use a Switchboard**

Click the Forms object, and then right-click Switchboard. Point to Open on the shortcut menu.

The shortcut menu for Switchboard displays (Figure 6-80).

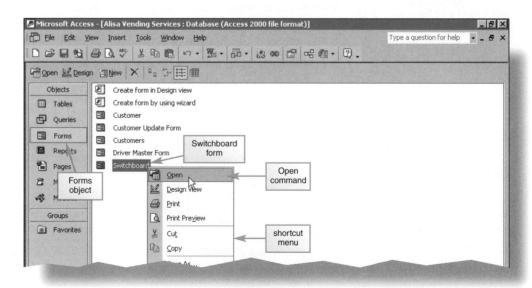

FIGURE 6-80

2 **Click Open.**

The Main Switchboard displays (Figure 6-81).

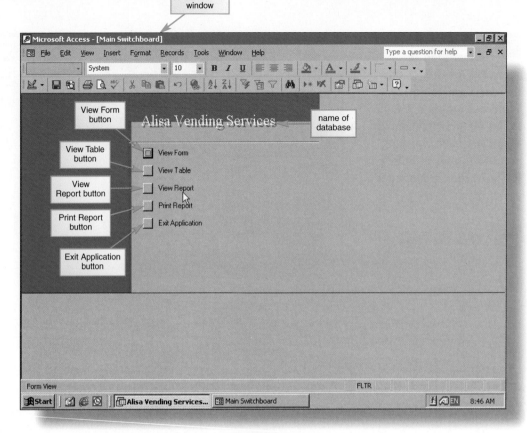

FIGURE 6-81

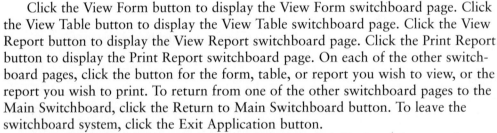

More *About*

Quick Reference

For a table that lists how to complete tasks covered in this book using the mouse, menu, shortcut menu, and keyboard, see the Quick Reference Summary at the back of this book or visit the Shelly Cashman Series Office XP Web page (scsite.com/offxp/qr.htm) and then click Microsoft Access 2002.

Click the View Form button to display the View Form switchboard page. Click the View Table button to display the View Table switchboard page. Click the View Report button to display the View Report switchboard page. Click the Print Report button to display the Print Report switchboard page. On each of the other switchboard pages, click the button for the form, table, or report you wish to view, or the report you wish to print. To return from one of the other switchboard pages to the Main Switchboard, click the Return to Main Switchboard button. To leave the switchboard system, click the Exit Application button.

If you discover a problem with the switchboard, click Tools on the menu bar, click Database Utilities, and then click Switchboard Manager. You can modify the switchboard system using the same techniques you used to create it.

Closing the Switchboard and Database

To close the switchboard and the database, click the Exit Application button. Perform the following step to close the switchboard.

More *About*

Closing a Switchboard

The button to close a switchboard is usually labeled Exit Application because a switchboard system is just a special type of application system.

TO CLOSE THE SWITCHBOARD AND DATABASE

1 Click the Exit Application button.

The switchboard is removed from the screen. The database closes.

CASE PERSPECTIVE SUMMARY

In Project 6, you modified the Customer Type field, and you added the Phone Number field to the Customer table. You also added the Phone Number field to the Customer Amount Report and to the Customer Update Form. You added the total amount (amount paid plus current due) to the Customer Amount Report, and then you created the macros to be used in the switchboard system. Finally, you created a switchboard system for Alisa Vending Services.

Project Summary

In Project 6, you learned how to use the Lookup Wizard and the Input Mask Wizard. You added controls to both a report and a form. You created and used macros. Using Switchboard Manager, you created the switchboard, the switchboard pages, and the switchboard items. You also used the Switchboard Manager to assign actions to the buttons on the switchboard pages.

What You Should Know

Having completed this project, you now should be able to perform the following tasks:

▶ Add a Control to a Form *(A 6.26)*
▶ Add Actions to and Save a Macro *(A 6.31)*
▶ Add Controls to a Report *(A 6.18)*
▶ Close the Switchboard and Database *(A 6.50)*
▶ Create Additional Macros *(A 6.40)*
▶ Create a Macro *(A 6.29)*
▶ Create a Switchboard *(A 6.41)*
▶ Create Switchboard Pages *(A 6.44)*
▶ Copy a Macro *(A 6.38)*
▶ Enter Data Using an Input Mask *(A 6.13)*
▶ Modify the Copied Macro *(A 6.39)*

▶ Modify a Macro *(A 6.34)*
▶ Modify the Main Switchboard Page *(A 6.45)*
▶ Modify the Other Switchboard Pages *(A 6.47)*
▶ Open a Database *(A 6.07)*
▶ Preview a Report *(A 6.24)*
▶ Resize a Line *(A 6.24)*
▶ Resize and Move Controls in a Report *(A 6.15)*
▶ Run a Macro *(A 6.33)*
▶ Use a Switchboard *(A 6.49)*
▶ Use the Lookup Wizard *(A 6.08)*
▶ Use the Input Mask Wizard *(A 6.10)*

More *About*

Microsoft Certification

The Microsoft User Specialist (MOUS) Certification program provides an opportunity for you to obtain a valuable industry credential — proof that you have the Access 2002 skills required by employers. For more information, see Appendix E or visit the Shelly Cashman Series MOUS Web page at scsite.com/offxp/cert.htm.

Learn It Online

Instructions: To complete the Learn It Online exercises, start your browser, click the Address bar, and then enter scsite.com/offxp/exs.htm. When the Office XP Learn It Online page displays, follow the instructions in the exercises below.

1 Project Reinforcement TF, MC, and SA

Below Access Project 6, click the Project Reinforcement link. Print the quiz by clicking Print on the File menu. Answer each question. Write your first and last name at the top of each page, and then hand in the printout to your instructor.

2 Flash Cards

Below Access Project 6, click the Flash Cards link. When Flash Cards displays, read the instructions. Type 20 (or a number specified by your instructor) in the Number of Playing Cards text box, type your name in the Name text box, and then click the Flip Card button. When the flash card displays, read the question and then click the Answer box arrow to select an answer. Flip through Flash Cards. Click Print on the File menu to print the last flash card if your score is 15 (75%) correct or greater and then hand it in to your instructor. If your score is less than 15 (75%) correct, then redo this exercise by clicking the Replay button.

3 Practice Test

Below Access Project 6, click the Practice Test link. Answer each question, enter your first and last name at the bottom of the page, and then click the Grade Test button. When the graded practice test displays on your screen, click Print on the File menu to print a hard copy. Continue to take practice tests until you score 80% or better. Hand in a printout of the final practice test to your instructor.

4 Who Wants to Be a Computer Genius?

Below Access Project 6, click the Computer Genius link. Read the instructions, enter your first and last name at the bottom of the page, and then click the Play button. Hand in your score to your instructor.

5 Wheel of Terms

Below Access Project 6, click the Wheel of Terms link. Read the instructions, and then enter your first and last name and your school name. Click the Play button. Hand in your score to your instructor.

6 Crossword Puzzle Challenge

Below Access Project 6, click the Crossword Puzzle Challenge link. Read the instructions, and then enter your first and last name. Click the Play button. Work the crossword puzzle. When you are finished, click the Submit button. When the crossword puzzle redisplays, click the Print button. Hand in the printout.

7 Tips and Tricks

Below Access Project 6, click the Tips and Tricks link. Click a topic that pertains to Project 6. Right-click the information and then click Print on the shortcut menu. Construct a brief example of what the information relates to in Access to confirm you understand how to use the tip or trick. Hand in the example and printed information.

8 Newsgroups

Below Access Project 6, click the Newsgroups link. Click a topic that pertains to Project 6. Print three comments. Hand in the comments to your instructor.

9 Expanding Your Horizons

Below Access Project 6, click the Articles for Microsoft Access link. Click a topic that pertains to Project 6. Print the information. Construct a brief example of what the information relates to in Access to confirm you understand the contents of the article. Hand in the example and printed information to your instructor.

10 Search Sleuth

Below Access Project 6, click the Search Sleuth link. To search for a term that pertains to this project, select a term below the Project 6 title and then use the Google search engine at google.com (or any major search engine) to display and print two Web pages that present information on the term. Hand in the printouts to your instructor.

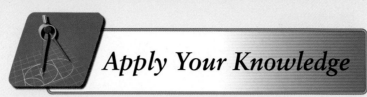

Apply Your Knowledge

1 Creating Macros and Modifying a Report for the Beyond Clean Database

Instructions: Start Access. If you are using the Microsoft Access 2002 Complete or the Microsoft Access 2002 Comprehensive text, open the Beyond Clean database that you used in Project 5 or see your instructor for information on accessing the files required for this book. Perform the following tasks.

1. Create a macro to open the Client Update Form you created in Project 4. The macro should maximize the form automatically when it is opened.
2. Save the macro as Open Client Update Form.
3. Create a macro to print the Custodian/Client Report you created in Project 4.
4. Save the macro as Print Custodian/Client Report.
5. Run the Print Custodian/Client Report macro, and then print the report.
6. Modify the Balance Due Report to include the telephone number as shown in Figure 6-82.
7. Print the report.

Balance Due Report

Client Number	Name	Telephone Number	Balance
AD23	Adder Cleaners	512-555-4070	$105.00
AR76	The Artshop	510-555-0200	$80.00
CR67	Cricket Store	512-555-6050	$0.00
DL61	Del Sol	513-555-1231	$135.00
GR36	Great Foods	513-555-5431	$104.00
HA09	Halyards Manufacturing	512-555-6895	$145.00
ME17	Merry Café	513-555-9780	$168.00
RO45	Royal Palms	512-555-4567	$0.00
ST21	Steed's	510-555-9080	$123.00

Monday, September 08, 2003   Page 1 of 1

FIGURE 6-82

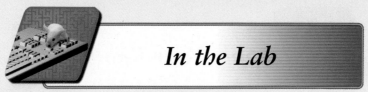

In the Lab

1 Creating an Application System for the Wooden Crafts Database

Problem: Jan Merchant is pleased with the tables, forms, and reports you have created. She has some additional requests, however. First, she would like to be able to type only the digits in the Last Order Date field. She also would like to display the profit (selling price - cost) for a product on the Product Update Form. Finally, she would like an easy way to access the various tables, forms, and reports, by simply clicking a button or two. This would make the database much easier to maintain and update.

Instructions: If you are using the Microsoft Access 2002 Complete or the Microsoft Access 2002 Comprehensive text, open the Wooden Crafts database that you used in Project 5 or see your instructor for information on accessing the files required for this book. Perform the following tasks.

1. Open the Supplier table in Design view and create an input mask for the Last Order Date field. Use the Short Date input mask. Save the change.
2. Modify the Product Update Form to create the form shown in Figure 6-83. The form includes a calculated control to display the profit (selling price - cost) on the product. Format the control as currency.

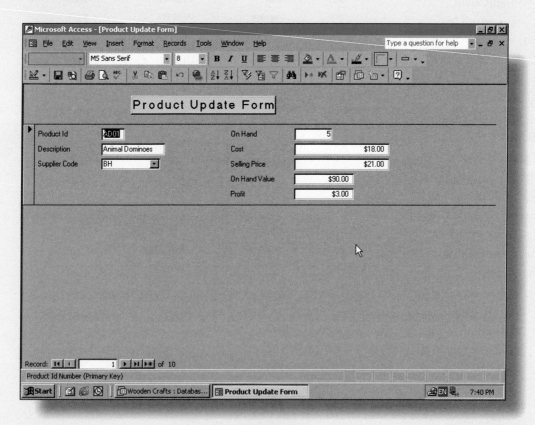

FIGURE 6-83

3. Save and print the form. To print the form, open the form, click File on the menu bar, click Print, and then click Selected Record(s) as the Print Range. Click the OK button.

In the Lab

4. Create macros that will perform the following tasks:
   a. Open the Product Update Form
   b. Open the Supplier Master Form
   c. Open the Product Table
   d. Open the Supplier Table
   e. Preview the Inventory Report
   f. Preview the Supplier/Products Report
   g. Preview the On Hand Value Report
   h. Print the Inventory Report
   i. Print the Supplier/Products Report
   j. Print the On Hand Value Report

5. Create the switchboard for the Wooden Crafts database shown in Figure 6-84. Use the same design for your switchboard pages as the one illustrated in this project. For example, the View Form switchboard page should have three choices: Open Product Update Form, Open Supplier Master Form, and Return to Main Switchboard. Include all the forms, tables, and reports for which you created macros in Step 4.

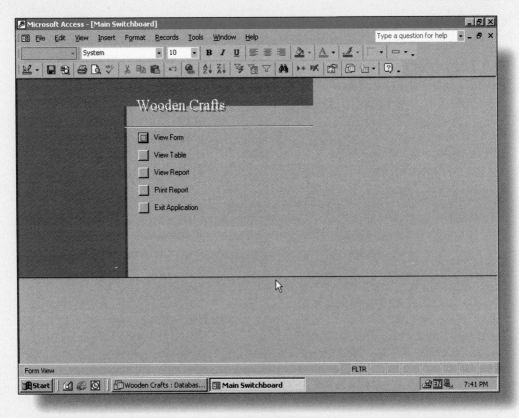

FIGURE 6-84

6. Run the switchboard and correct any errors.

In the Lab

2 Creating an Application System for the Restaurant Supply Database

Problem: The restaurant supply company is pleased with the tables, forms, and reports you have created. They have some additional requests, however. The company is pleased with the Dining Type combo box you placed in the Customer Update Form and would like to incorporate a similar feature in Datasheet view. They also would like an easy way to access the various tables, forms, and reports by simply clicking a button or two.

Instructions: If you are using the Microsoft Access 2002 Complete or the Microsoft Access 2002 Comprehensive text, open the Restaurant Supply database that you used in Project 5 or see your instructor for information on accessing the files required for this book. Perform the following tasks.

1. Change the data type for the Dining Type field to a Lookup Wizard field. The values for the Dining Type field are: FAM, FFT, and FIN.
2. Save the changes to the Customer table.
3. Modify the Customer Status Report to include the Telephone field as shown in Figure 6-85.
4. Print the report.
5. Change the tab order for the Customer Update Form so the Dining Type field follows the Telephone field. (**Hint:** Dining Type is a combo box control.) Be sure that the Customer Income control is bypassed when you press the TAB key to move through the controls. See page A 4.51 for instructions on changing tab stops.

Customer Status Report

Customer Number	Name/Telephone	Balance	Amount Paid
AM23	American Pie 555-2150	$95.00	$1,595.00
BI15	Bavarian Inn 555-7510	$445.00	$1,250.00
CB12	China Buffet 555-0804	$45.00	$610.00
CM09	Curry and More 555-0604	$195.00	$980.00
EG07	El Gallo 555-1404	$0.00	$1,600.00
JS34	Joe's Seafood 555-0313	$260.00	$600.00
LV20	Little Venice 555-5161	$100.00	$1,150.00
NC25	New Crete 555-4210	$140.00	$450.00
PP43	Pan Pacific 555-3470	$165.00	$0.00
RD03	Reuben's Deli 555-7657	$0.00	$875.00
TD01	Texas Diner 555-1673	$280.00	$0.00
VG21	Veggie Gourmet 555-6554	$60.00	$625.00

Monday, September 08, 2003   *Page 1 of 1*

FIGURE 6-85

In the Lab

6. Save the changes to the form.
7. Create macros that will perform the following tasks:
    a. Open the Customer Update Form
    b. Open the Sales Rep Master Form
    c. Open the Customer Table
    d. Open the Sales Rep Table
    e. Preview the Customer Status Report
    f. Preview the Customer Income Report
    g. Preview the Sales Rep/Customers Report
    h. Print the Customer Status Report
    i. Print the Customer Income Report
    j. Print the Sales Rep/Customers Report
8. Create the switchboard for the Restaurant Supply database shown in Figure 6-86. Use the same design for your switchboard pages as the one illustrated in this project. For example, the View Form switchboard page should have three choices: Open Customer Update Form, Open Sales Rep Master Form, and Return to Main Switchboard. Include all the forms, tables, and reports for which you created macros in Step 7.

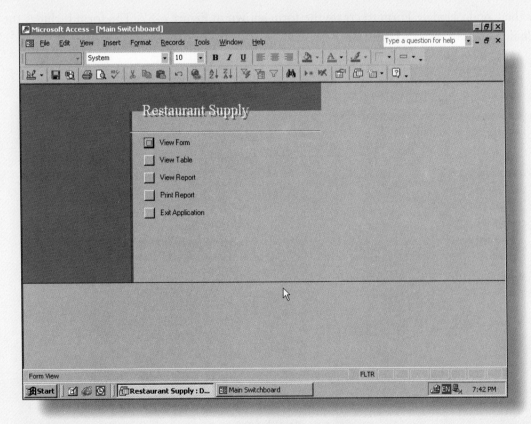

FIGURE 6-86

9. Run the switchboard and correct any errors.

In the Lab

3 Creating an Application System for the Condo Management Database

Problem: The condo management company is pleased with the tables, forms, and reports that you have created. The company has some additional requests, however. First, they want to add the sales price to the database. Then, they want an easy way to access the various tables, form, and reports by simply clicking a button or two.

Instructions: If you are using the Microsoft Access 2002 Complete or the Microsoft Access 2002 Comprehensive text, open the Condo Management database that you used in Project 5 or see your instructor for information on accessing the files required for this book. Perform the following tasks.

1. Add a Sales Price field to the Condo table. Place the field after the For Sale field. Use Currency as the data type. Save these changes.
2. Open the Condo table in Datasheet view, and then add the following data to the Sales Price field:

UNIT NUMBER	SALES PRICE
101	$90,000
300	$150,000
403	$105,000

3. Modify the Condo Update Form to create the form shown in Figure 6-87. The form includes the Sales Price field. Change the tab order so the Sales Price field follows the For Sale field.

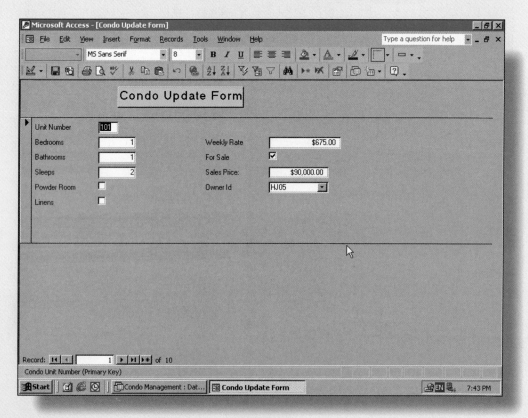

FIGURE 6-87

In the Lab

4. Save and print the form. To print the form, open the form, click File on the menu bar, and then click Print. Click Selected Record(s) as the Print Range. Click the OK button.

5. Add the Sales Price field to the Rental Properties subform you created in Project 5. If necessary, modify the Owner Master Form to ensure that the complete Sales Price field displays on the subform.

6. Save and print the form.

7. Create macros that will perform the following tasks:
   a. Open the Condo Update Form
   b. Open the Owner Master Form
   c. Open the Condo Table
   d. Open the Owner Table
   e. Preview the Available Condo Rentals Report
   f. Preview the Owner/Rental Units Report
   g. Print the Available Condo Rentals Report
   h. Print the Owner/Rental Units Report

8. Create the switchboard for the Condo Management database shown in Figure 6-88. Use the same design for your switchboard pages as the one illustrated in this project. For example, the View Form switchboard page should have three choices: Open Condo Update Form, Open Owner Master Form, and Return to Main Switchboard. Include all the forms, tables, and reports for which you created macros in Step 7.

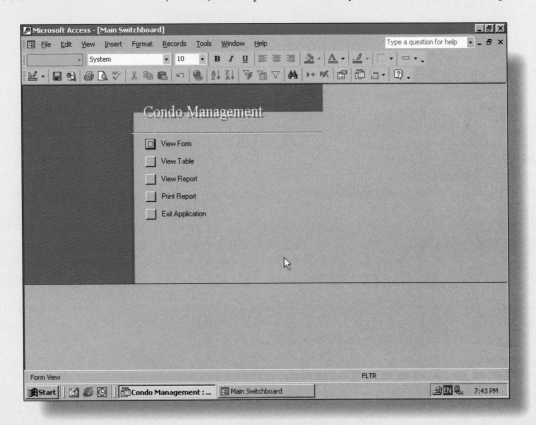

FIGURE 6-88

9. Run the switchboard and correct any errors.

Cases and Places

The difficulty of these case studies varies:
▶ are the least difficult; ▶▶ are more difficult; and ▶▶▶ are the most difficult.

1 ▶ Use the CompuWhiz database that you used in Project 5 for this assignment or see your instructor for information on accessing the files required for this book. Change the data type for the Client Type field and Technician Id field to Lookup Wizard. (*Hint:* See More About Lookup Wizard Fields on page A 6.07 to solve this problem.) The database includes a report, Client Status Report. Modify this report to include the Telephone Number field. Place the telephone number below the name as shown in Figure 6-2a on page A 6.06.

2 ▶ Use the CompuWhiz database and create macros that will perform the following tasks:

    a. Open the Client Update Form created in Project 4
    b. Open the Technician Master Form created in Project 5
    c. Open the Client table
    d. Open the Technician table
    e. Preview the Client Status Report
    f. Preview the Technicians/Clients Report created in Project 4
    g. Print the Client Status Report
    h. Print the Technicians/Clients Report

Create and run a switchboard that uses these macros.

3 ▶▶ Use the Hockey Shop database that you used in Project 5 for this assignment or see your instructor for information about accessing the files required for this book. Modify the Item Update Form and the Inventory Value Report that you created in Project 4 to include a calculated control called Profit. Profit is the result of subtracting Cost from Selling Price. Place the calculated control below the Vendor Code field on the form. Be sure to format Profit as currency. Change the tab order on the form so you tab through the fields in the following order: Item Id, Description, Vendor Code, On Hand, Cost, and Selling Price. The Profit and Inventory Value control should be bypassed.

4 ▶▶ Add a Fax Number field to the Vendor table in the Hockey Shop database. Place the field after the Telephone field. Create an input mask for the Telephone field, the Fax Number field, and the Last Order Date field. In Datasheet view, enter the following fax numbers:

VENDOR CODE	FAX NUMBER		
AC	616-555-7654	BH	317-555-9854
		LG	517-555-3201

Create a Lookup field for Vendor Code in the Item table by changing the Display Control property. (*Hint:* See More About Lookup Fields on page A 6.07 to solve this problem.) Add the Fax Number field to the Vendor Master Form that you created in Project 5.

5 ▶▶▶ Create the appropriate macros to open all forms and tables in the Hockey Shop database. Create macros to preview and print all reports in the database. Create a switchboard system for the database that uses these macros.

Microsoft Access 2002

Sharing Data among Applications

CASE PERSPECTIVE

Lebond Industries is a company offering equipment repair and maintenance. Lebond has been using Microsoft Excel to automate a variety of tasks for several years.

When Lebond decided it needed to maintain client data, the familiarity with Excel led to the decision to maintain the data as an Excel worksheet. Later, they discovered that other organizations were using Microsoft Access to maintain similar data. Officials at Lebond decided to follow the lead of other organizations and convert their data from Excel to Access. Your task is to help Lebond in this effort.

Alisa Vending Services also needs your help in sharing data among applications. Alisa users proficient in Excel, for example, want to use its powerful what-if features to analyze the financial data. Other users want the financial data to be placed in a Microsoft Word document. Alisa also wants to e-mail one of the Access reports to several users. To accomplish this, they need to create a snapshot of the database. The snapshot then can be sent to anyone who has the Snapshot Viewer. Your task is to help Alisa Vending Services export the data to Excel and to Word as well as to create a snapshot of the report.

Introduction

It is not uncommon for people to use an application for some specific purpose, only to find later that another application may be better suited. For example, an organization such as Lebond Industries might initially keep data in an Excel worksheet, only to discover later that the data would be better maintained in an Access database. Some common reasons for using a database instead of a worksheet are:

1. The worksheet contains a great deal of redundant data. As discussed in Project 1 on pages A 1.49 through A 1.51, databases can be designed to eliminate redundant data.

2. The worksheet would need to be larger than Excel can handle. Excel has a limit of 16,384 rows. In Access, no such limit exists.

3. The data to be maintained consists of multiple interrelated items. For example, at Alisa Vending Services, they need to maintain data on two items, customers and drivers, and these items are interrelated. A customer has a single driver and each driver is responsible for several customers. The Alisa Vending Services database is a very simple one. Databases easily can contain 30 or more interrelated items.

4. You want to use the extremely powerful query and report capabilities of Microsoft Access.

Regardless of the reasons for making the change from a worksheet to a database, it is important to be able to make the change easily. In the not-too-distant past, converting data from one tool to another often could be a very difficult, time-consuming task. Fortunately, an easy way of converting data from Excel to Access is available.

Figures 1a and 1b illustrate the conversion process. The type of worksheet that can be converted is one in which the data is stored as a **list**, that is, a labeled series of rows in which each row contains the same type of data. For example, in the worksheet in Figure 1, the first row contains the labels, which are entries indicating the type of data found in the column. The entry in the first column, for example, is Client Number, indicating that all the other values in the column are client numbers. The entry in the second column is Name, indicating that all the other values in the column are names. Other than the first row, which contains the labels, all the rows contain precisely the same type of data: a client number in the first column, a name in the second column, an address in the third column, and so on.

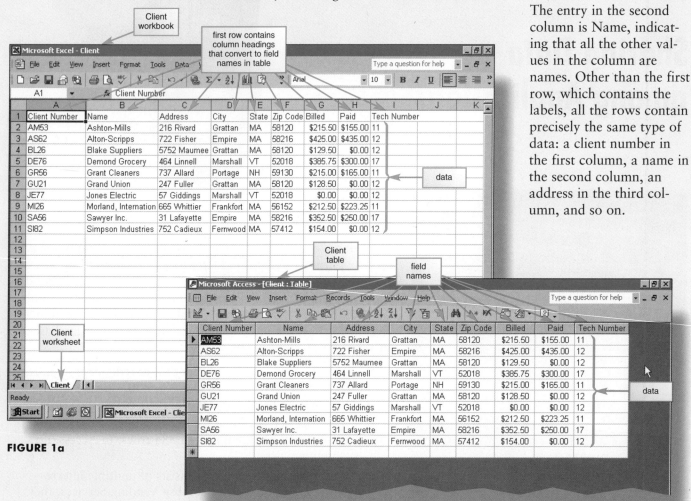

FIGURE 1a

FIGURE 1b

More *About*

Microsoft Certification

The Microsoft User Specialist (MOUS) Certification program provides an opportunity for you to obtain a valuable industry credential — proof that you have the Access 2002 skills required by employers. For more information, see Appendix E or visit the Shelly Cashman Series MOUS Web page at scsite.com/offxp/cert.htm.

As the figures illustrate, the worksheet, shown in Figure 1a, is copied to a database table, shown in Figure 1b. The columns in the worksheet become the fields. The column headings in the first row of the worksheet become the field names. The rows of the worksheet, other than the first row, which contains the labels, become the records in the table. In the process, each field will be assigned the data type that seems the most reasonable, given the data currently in the worksheet.

The process of copying data to an Access database, referred to as **importing**, uses an Import Wizard. Specifically, if the data is copied from an Excel worksheet, the process will use the Import Spreadsheet Wizard. The wizard takes you through some basic steps, asking a few simple questions. Once you have answered the questions, the wizard will perform the conversion, creating an appropriate table in the database and filling it with the data from the worksheet.

Conversely, **exporting** is the process of copying database objects to another database, to a spreadsheet, or to some other format so another application (for example, Excel) can use the data. There are different ways to export data. The two most common are to use the Export command on the File menu, which you will use to export a query to an Excel worksheet (Figure 2a), and to use drag-and-drop, which you will use to export the query to a Word document (Figure 2b).

There are occasions when you would like to send a report to a user via e-mail. It would be prohibitive to send the whole database to the other user, just so the user could print or view the report. In addition, doing so would require the other user to have Microsoft Access installed. A better way is to create a snapshot of the report. A **snapshot** is a special file that contains the report exactly as it appears when printed (Figure 2c on the next page). The other user then can use the Snapshot Viewer to view or print the report.

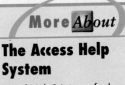

The Access Help System

Need Help? It is no further than the Ask a Question box in the upper-right corner of the window. Click the box that contains the text, Type a question for help (Figure 2b), type help, and then press the ENTER key. Access will respond with a list of items you can click to learn about obtaining help on any Access-related topic. To find out what is new in Access 2002, type what's new in Access in the Ask a Question box.

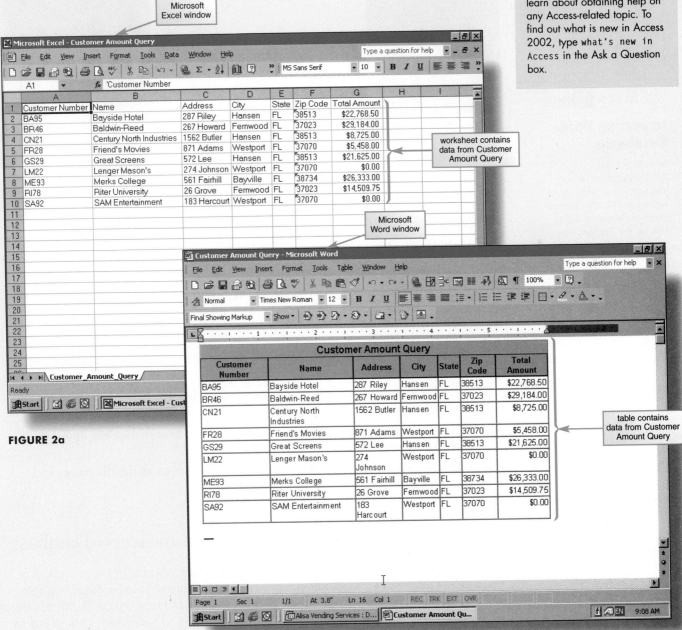

FIGURE 2a

FIGURE 2b

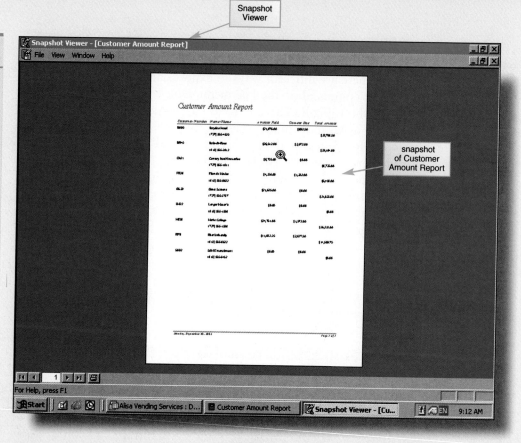

FIGURE 2c

Creating an Access Database

Before converting the data, you need to create the database that will contain the data. Perform the following steps to create the Lebond Industries database.

TO CREATE A NEW DATABASE

1 Click the Start button, click Programs on the Start menu, and then click Microsoft Access on the Programs submenu.

2 Click New on the Database toolbar, and then click the Blank Database option in the task pane.

3 Click the Save in box arrow in the File New Database dialog box and then click 3½ Floppy (A:).

4 Delete the current file name, type Lebond Industries as the file name, and then click the Create button.

Converting an Excel Worksheet to an Access Database

To convert the data, you will use the Import Spreadsheet Wizard. In the process, you will indicate that the first row contains the column headings. These column headings then will become the field names in the Access table. In addition, you will indicate the primary key for the table. As part of the process, you can, if you desire, choose not to include all the fields from the worksheet in the resulting table. You should be aware that some of the steps might take a significant amount of time for Access to execute.

Steps **To Convert an Excel Worksheet to an Access Database**

1 With the Lebond Industries database open, right-click in the open area of the Database window, and then point to Import on the shortcut menu.

The shortcut menu displays (Figure 3).

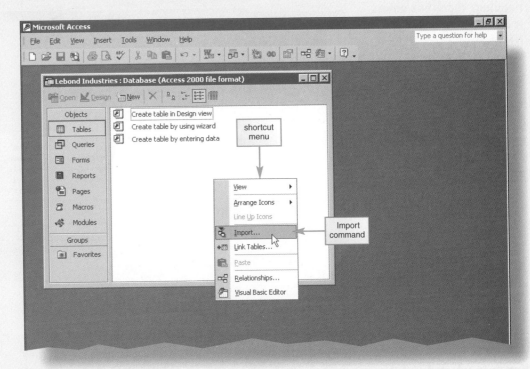

FIGURE 3

2 Click Import. Click the Files of type box arrow in the Import dialog box and then click Microsoft Excel. If necessary, select 3½ Floppy (A:) in the Look in box. Make sure the Client workbook is selected, and then click the Import button. If you are asked which worksheet or range you would like, be sure Client is selected and then click the Next button. Point to the First Row Contains Column Headings check box in the Import Spreadsheet Wizard dialog box.

The Import Spreadsheet Wizard dialog box displays (Figure 4).

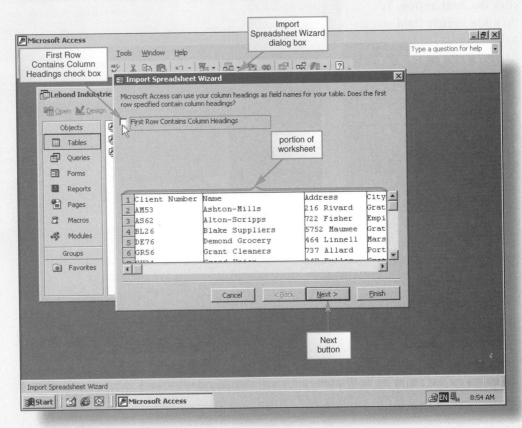

FIGURE 4

3 **Click the First Row Contains Column Headings check box unless it already is selected (check mark in check box). Click the Next button.**

The Import Spreadsheet Wizard dialog box displays asking whether the data is to be placed in a new table or in an existing table (Figure 5).

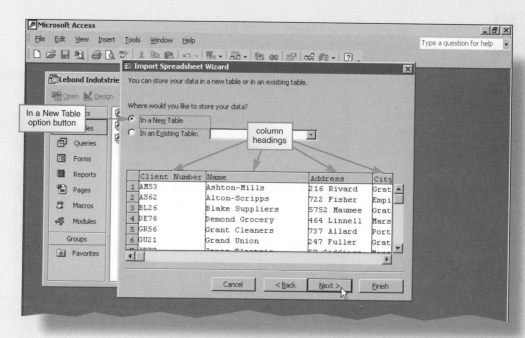

FIGURE 5

4 **Be sure that the In a New Table option button is selected and then click the Next button. You then can specify field options and/or indexes. Because you do not need to specify any field options, click the Next button a second time. Point to the Choose my own primary key option button.**

The Import Spreadsheet Wizard dialog box displays (Figure 6). Use this dialog box to indicate the primary key of the Access table. You can allow Access to add a special field to serve as the primary key as illustrated in the figure. You can choose an existing field to serve as the primary key. You also can indicate no primary key. Most of the time, one of the existing fields will serve as the primary key. In this worksheet, for example, the Client Number serves as the primary key.

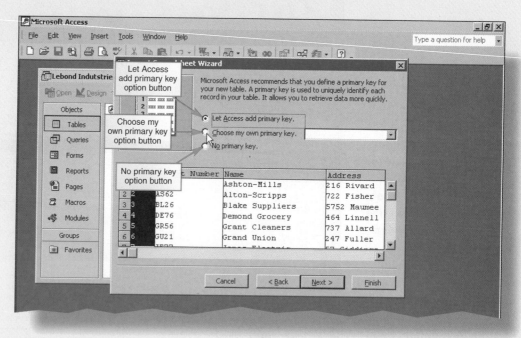

FIGURE 6

5 **Click the Choose my own primary key option button.**

The Client Number field, which is the correct field, will be the primary key. If some other field were to be the primary key, you could click the down arrow and select the other field from the list of available fields.

6 **Click the Next button. Be sure Client displays in the Import to Table text box. Click the Finish button.**

The worksheet is converted into an Access table named Client. When the process is completed the Import Spreadsheet Wizard dialog box displays (Figure 7).

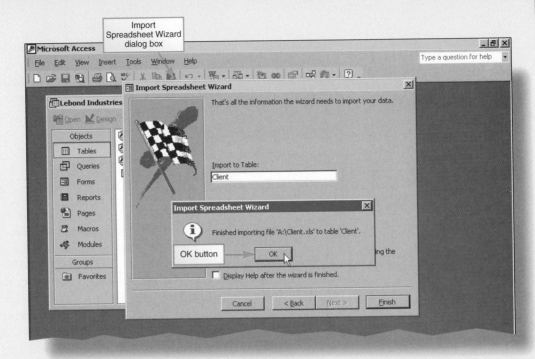

FIGURE 7

7 **Click the OK button.**

The table now has been created (Figure 8).

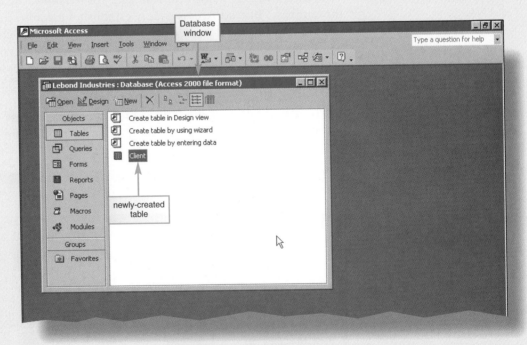

FIGURE 8

Using the Access Table

Once the Access version of the table has been created, you can treat it as you would any other table. After first opening the database containing the table, you can open the table in Datasheet view (Figure 1b on page AI 1.02). You can make changes to the data. You can create queries that use the data in the table.

By clicking Design View on the table's shortcut menu, you can view the table's structure and make any necessary changes to the structure. The changes may include changing field sizes and types, creating indexes, or adding additional fields. To accomplish any of these tasks, use the same steps you used in Project 3. In the Client table shown in Figure 1b on page AI 1.03, for example, the columns have been resized to best fit the data.

Linking Versus Importing

When an external table or worksheet is imported, or converted, into an Access database, a copy of the data is placed as a table in the database. The original data still exists, just as it did before, but there is no further connection between it and the data in the database. Changes to the original data do not affect the data in the database. Likewise, changes in the database do not affect the original data.

It also is possible to **link** data stored in a variety of formats to Access databases by selecting Link Tables instead of Import on the shortcut menu. (The available formats include several other database management systems as well as a variety of non-database formats, including Excel worksheets.) With linking, the connection is maintained.

When an Excel worksheet is linked, for example, the worksheet is not stored in the database. Instead Access simply establishes a connection to the worksheet so you can view or edit the data in either Access or Excel. Any change made in either one will be visible immediately in the other. For example, if you would change an address in Access and then view the worksheet in Excel, you would see the new address. If you add a new row in Excel and then view the table in Access, the row would appear as a new record.

To identify that a table is linked to other data, Access places an arrow in front of the table (Figure 9). In addition, the Excel icon in front of the name identifies the fact that the data is linked to an Excel worksheet.

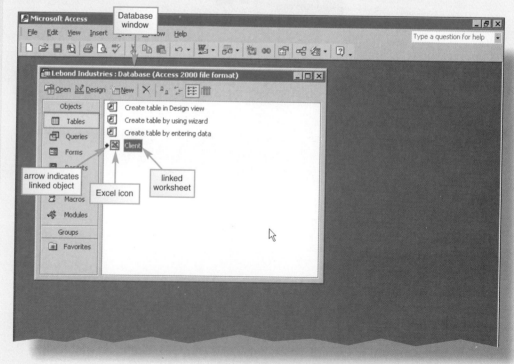

FIGURE 9

Closing the Database

The following step closes the database by closing its Database window.

TO CLOSE A DATABASE

1 Click the Close button for the Lebond Industries : Database window.

Opening the Database

Before exporting the Alisa Vending Services data, you first must open the database. To do so, perform the following steps.

TO OPEN A DATABASE

1 Click the Open button on the Database toolbar.

2 If necessary, click 3½ Floppy (A:) in the Look in box. Click the Alisa Vending Services database name.

3 Click the Open button in the Open dialog box.

The database opens and the Alisa Vending Services : Database window displays.

Using the Export Command to Export Data to Excel

One way to export data to Excel, as well as to a variety of other formats, is to select the data to be exported and then select the Export command on the shortcut menu. Once you have selected the command, indicate the file type (for example, Microsoft Excel 97-2002) and then click the Save button. For some of the formats, including Excel, you can select Save formatted, in which case the export process will attempt to preserve as much of the Access formatting of the data as possible. You also can select Autostart in which case, the application receiving the data will be started automatically once the data is exported. The resulting data then will display in the application.

Perform the steps on the next page to use the Export command to export the Customer Amount Query to Excel.

More About

Linking: Linked Table Manager

After you link tables between a spreadsheet and a database or between two databases, you can modify many of the linked table's features. For example, you can rename the linked table, set view properties, and set links between tables in queries. If you move, rename, or modify linked tables, you can use the Linked Table Manager to update the links. To do so, click Tools on the menu bar, click Database Utilities, and then click Linked Table Manager. When the Linked Table Manager dialog box displays, select the table or tables to be updated and then click the OK button.

More About

Exporting

The process of exporting records from a table is identical to that of exporting records from a query. Simply select the Tables object and then the table containing the records to be exported before selecting the Export command. All records and all fields from the table then will be exported.

To Use the Export Command to Export Data to Excel

1 **Click Queries on the Objects bar, right-click Customer Amount Query, and then point to Export on the shortcut menu.**

The shortcut menu displays (Figure 10).

2 **Click Export. If necessary, click the Save in box arrow and then click 3½ Floppy (A:). Click the Save as type box arrow and then select Microsoft Excel 97-2002 in the Save as type list. Be sure the file name is Customer Amount Query, and then click the Export button.**

The worksheet is created.

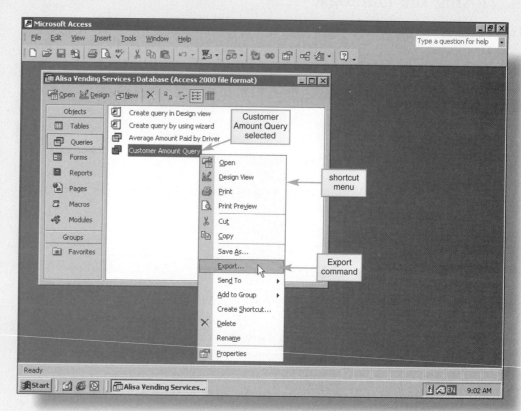

FIGURE 10

To view the worksheet, you could open it in Excel. You then could make any changes to it. For example, you could resize the columns to best fit the data by double-clicking the right-hand edge of the column heading. Figure 2a on page AI 1.03 shows the worksheet displayed in Excel with the columns resized.

Using Drag-and-Drop to Export Data to Word

When using the Export command, Microsoft Word is not one of the available file types. You would need to select one of the file types that can be imported into Word, export from Access to the selected file type, and then import the file that is created into Word. A simpler way to export to Word is to use the drag-and-drop method. In this method, both Access and Word must be open simultaneously. You then drag the object to be imported from Access to the Word document. Perform the following steps to export the Customer Amount Query to Word using the drag-and-drop method.

Steps **To Use Drag-and-Drop to Export Data to Word**

1 **Click the Start button, click Programs, and then click Microsoft Word. Click the Alisa Vending Services button on the taskbar. Point to the Restore Down button for the Microsoft Access window.**

Microsoft Access displays (Figure 11). Microsoft Word also is open.

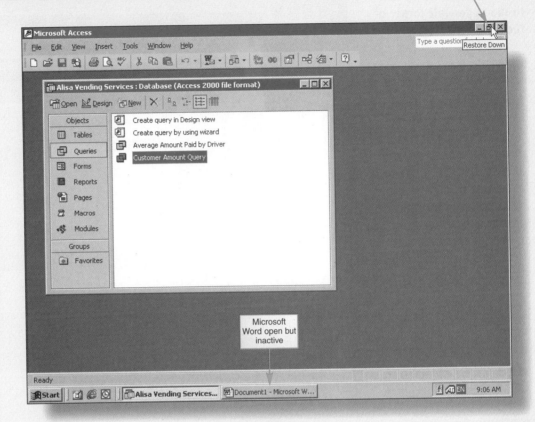

FIGURE 11

2 **Click the Restore Down button so Microsoft Access does not occupy the full screen. Be sure the Queries object is selected. Point to the icon for the Customer Amount Query.**

Both Microsoft Word and Microsoft Access display (Figure 12).

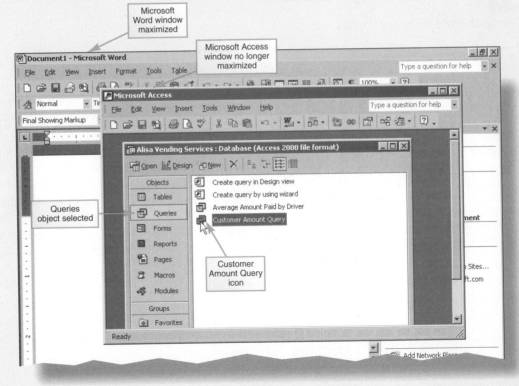

FIGURE 12

3 Drag the Customer Amount query icon to the upper-left corner of the document (Figure 13).

4 Click the Save button on the Standard toolbar. Be sure 3½ Floppy (A:) is selected in the Save in box and the name entered is Customer Amount Query in the File name text box. Then click the Save button in the Save As dialog box.

The data from the query is inserted in the Word document. The title of the query displays in boldface at the top of the document. The data is inserted as a Word table. The document is saved. It looks like the one shown in Figure 2b on page AI 1.03.

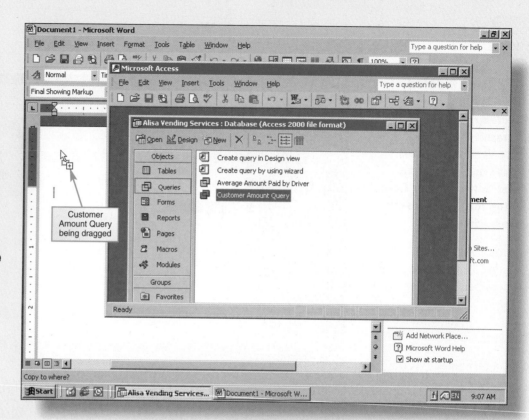

FIGURE 13

5 Quit Word by clicking its Close button.

Microsoft Word no longer displays.

Using the Export Command to Create a Snapshot

If you want to send a report to someone via e-mail, the simplest way is to create a snapshot of the report. The snapshot is stored in a separate file with an extension of snp. This file contains all the details of the report, including fonts, effects (for example, bold or italic), and graphics. In other words, the contents of the snapshot file look precisely like the report. The snapshot file can be viewed by anyone having the Snapshot Viewer; Microsoft Access is *not* required. You can use the Snapshot Viewer to e-mail the snapshot; the recipient can use the Snapshot Viewer to view or print the snapshot.

To create a snapshot, use the Export command on the File menu as in the following steps.

Steps To Use the Export Command to Create a Snapshot

1 **Click the Maximize button on the Microsoft Access window title bar. Click the Reports object, right-click the Customer Amount Report, and then click Print Preview on the shortcut menu. Maximize the window, right-click the preview of the report, and then point to Export on the shortcut menu.**

A preview of the Customer Amount Report displays (Figure 14). The date on your report may be different.

2 **Click Export. If necessary, click the Save in box arrow and then click 3½ Floppy (A:). Click the Save as type box arrow, select Snapshot Format, be sure the Autostart check box is checked, and then click the Export button.**

The snapshot of the report displays in the Snapshot Viewer. It looks similar to the one in Figure 2c on page AI 1.04. If a Microsoft Access dialog box displays asking if you want to install Snapshot Viewer, click the No button and see your instructor.

3 **Close the Snapshot Viewer by clicking its Close button. Close the Print Preview window for the Customer Amount Report.**

The Snapshot Viewer and the Customer Amount Report no longer display.

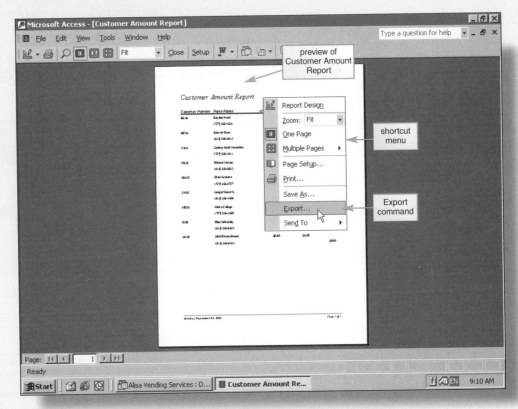

FIGURE 14

You can e-mail the snapshot file to other users. The other users can use the Snapshot Viewer to view the report or to print the report.

More About

Exporting XML Documents

You can export a table, query, form, or report as an XML document. You also can use a schema to specify the structure of the XML document. To export a table, query, form, or report as an XML document, right-click the database object, and then click Export on the shortcut menu. Click XML Documents as the Save as type file. When the Export XML dialog box displays, use the check boxes to indicate whether you want to export only the data, or the data and schema. You also can export the format of your data by checking Presentation in the dialog box. Click the OK button.

Closing the Database

The following step closes the database by closing its Database window.

TO CLOSE A DATABASE

 Click the Close button for the Microsoft Access [Alisa Vending Services : Database] window.

CASE PERSPECTIVE SUMMARY

You now have created a table in an Access database containing the same data that the users at Lebond Industries had placed previously in an Excel worksheet. To do so, you used the Import Spreadsheet Wizard. Now that the data has been converted, the users at Lebond can take advantage of any of the features of Access that they wish.

You also have assisted the management of Alisa Vending Services by exporting financial data to a Microsoft Excel worksheet and to a Microsoft Word document. You also created a snapshot of the Customer Amount Report that can be viewed by anyone who has the Snapshot Viewer installed.

Integration Feature Summary

The Integration Feature covered the process of integrating an Excel worksheet into an Access database. To convert a worksheet to an Access table, you learned to use the Import Spreadsheet Wizard. Working with the wizard, you identified the first row of the worksheet as the row containing the column headings and you indicated the primary key. The wizard then created the table for you and placed it in a new database. You also saw how you could link data instead of importing it.

You learned to use the Export command and used it to export data to an Excel worksheet. You also learned to use the drag-and-drop feature and used it to export data to a Word document. Finally, you learned to use the Export command to create a snapshot of a report.

What You Should Know

Having completed this Integration Feature, you now should be able to perform the following tasks:

▶ Create a New Database *(AI 1.04)*
▶ Convert an Excel Worksheet to an Access Database *(AI 1.05)*
▶ Close a Database *(AI 1.08, AI 1.14)*
▶ Open a Database *(AI 1.08)*
▶ Use Drag-and-Drop to Export Data to Word *(AI 1.11)*
▶ Use the Export Command to Create a Snapshot *(AI 1.13)*
▶ Use the Export Command to Export Data to Excel *(AI 1.10)*

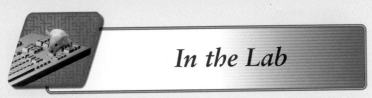

In the Lab

1 Importing Data to an Access Database

Problem: JMZ Computer Supply has been using Excel for a number of tasks. JMZ uses several worksheets to keep track of inventory, customers, and sales reps. The company realizes that the customer and sales rep data would be better handled by Access. Previously, JMZ had experimented with sharing sales rep data between computer applications and the company has sales rep data in XML format. The company wants to maintain the computer items inventory in Excel worksheets but also would like to be able to use the query and report features of Access.

Instructions: For this assignment, you will need four files: Customer.xls, Sales Rep.xml, Sales Rep.xsd, and Computer Items.xls. These files are on the Data Disk. See the inside back cover of this book for instructions for downloading the Data Disk or see your instructor for information about accessing the files required for this book. Perform the following tasks.

1. Start Access and create a new database in which to store all the objects for JMZ Computer Supply. Call the database JMZ Computer Supply.
2. Import the Customer worksheet shown in Figure 15 into Access. The worksheet is in the Customer workbook on the Data Disk.

	A	B	C	D	E	F	G	H	I
1	Customer Number	Name	Address	City	State	Zip Code	Balance	Credit Limit	Sales Rep Number
2	BA91	Baywater Inc.	215 Ratkins	Oakwood	IN	48101	$3,478.50	$8,000.00	04
3	BE52	Better Foods	266 Walston	Benwood	IN	48102	$492.20	$5,000.00	07
4	CT22	Certified Temps	542 Meadow	Oakwood	IN	48101	$57.00	$5,000.00	07
5	DE76	Derben Enterprise	96 Magee	Cardinal	MI	61354	$4,125.00	$10,000.00	11
6	GU63	Gump Co.	85 Tracking	Fergus	OH	48902	$7,822.00	$8,000.00	04
7	GY16	Gylder-Yansen	198 Ruby	Oakwood	IN	48101	$3,912.00	$8,000.00	07
8	MN72	Manross, Inc.	195 Grayling	Cardinal	MI	61354	$0.00	$8,000.00	07
9	NG19	Norton Ghent	867 Medford	Acme	MI	62127	$1,867.50	$8,000.00	04
10	SO22	Southwest, Inc.	682 Ohio	Benwood	IN	48102	$2,336.25	$10,000.00	11
11	SP92	Samuel A. Port	872 Eastham	Benson	OH	49246	$6,420.00	$10,000.00	07

FIGURE 15

(continued)

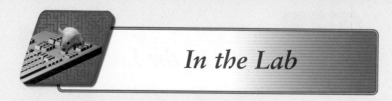

In the Lab

Importing Data to an Access Database *(continued)*

3. Use Customer as the name of the Access table and Customer Number as the primary key.
4. Open the Customer table in Datasheet view and resize the columns to best fit the data. Print the table.
5. Import the Sales Rep XML document into Access. The XML document is on the Data Disk.
6. Open the Sales Rep table in Datasheet view and resize the columns to best fit the data. Print the table.
7. Link the Computer Items worksheet shown in Figure 16 to the database. The worksheet is in the Computer Items workbook on the Data Disk.

	A	B	C	D	E	F
1	Item Id	Description	Units On Hand	Cost	Selling Price	Supplier Code
2	1663	Antistatic Wipes	30	$0.15	$0.25	ER
3	1683	CD Wallet	8	$3.45	$4.00	HI
4	2563	Desktop Holder	4	$3.85	$4.75	ER
5	2593	Disks	145	$0.20	$0.75	HI
6	3923	Disk Cases	12	$2.20	$2.75	HI
7	3953	Mouse Holder	10	$0.80	$1.00	MT
8	4343	Mouse Pad-Plain	16	$2.25	$3.00	MT
9	5810	Mouse Pad-Logo	25	$3.45	$5.00	MT
10	6140	Zip DiskWallet	3	$11.90	$14.00	HI

FIGURE 16

8. Open the linked Computer Items table in Datasheet view and resize the columns to best fit the data. Print the table.
9. Rename the linked Computer Items table as Items. Then, use the Linked Table Manager to update the link between the Excel spreadsheet and the Access table. (*Hint:* See More About Linking on page AI 1.09. If the Linked Table Manager wizard is not installed on your machine, see your instructor before continuing.)
10. Print the Items table.
11. Link the Client table in the Lebond Industries database to the database. Clients of Lebond are potentials customers for JMZ Computer Supply.
12. Rename the Client table as Potential Customers. Then, use the Linked Table Manager to update the link between the two tables. (*Hint:* See More About Linking on page AI 1.09. If the Linked Table Manager wizard is not installed on your machine, see your instructor before continuing.)
13. Print the Potential Customers table.

In the Lab

2 Exporting Data to Other Applications

Problem: Wooden Crafts wants to be able to export some of the data in the Access database to other applications. Jan wants to export the On Hand Value query for further processing in Excel. She also wants to use the Supplier and Products query in a Word document. She has corresponded with other entrepreneurs with similar businesses and they have agreed to share supplier information. She also wants to be able to e-mail a report to her accountant.

Instructions: Start Access and open the Wooden Crafts database you used in Project 6 or see your instructor for information about accessing the files required for this book. Perform the following tasks.

1. Export the On Hand Value query to Excel as shown in Figure 17.

Product Id	Description	On Hand	Cost	On Hand Value
AD01	Animal Dominoes	5	$18.00	$90.00
BF01	Barnyard Friends	3	$54.00	$162.00
BL23	Blocks in Box	5	$29.00	$145.00
CC14	Coal Car	8	$14.00	$112.00
FT05	Fire Truck	7	$9.00	$63.00
LB34	Lacing Bear	4	$12.00	$48.00
MR06	Midget Railroad	3	$31.00	$93.00
PJ12	Pets Jigsaw	10	$8.00	$80.00
SK10	Skyscraper	6	$25.00	$150.00
UM09	USA Map	12	$14.00	$168.00

FIGURE 17

2. Resize the columns to best fit the data as shown in Figure 17.
3. Print the Excel worksheet.
4. Use drag-and-drop to place the Supplier and Products query in a Word document.
5. Print the Word document.
6. Preview the On Hand Value Report shown in Figure 18 on the next page and then export the report as a snapshot.

(continued)

In the Lab

Exporting Data to Other Applications *(continued)*

On Hand Value Report

Product Id	Description	On Hand	Cost	On Hand Value
AD01	Animal Dominoes	5	$18.00	$90.00
BF01	Barnyard Friends	3	$54.00	$162.00
BL23	Blocks in Box	5	$29.00	$145.00
CC14	Coal Car	8	$14.00	$112.00
FT05	Fire Truck	7	$9.00	$63.00
LB34	Lacing Bear	4	$12.00	$48.00
MR06	Midget Railroad	3	$31.00	$93.00
PJ12	Pets Jigsaw	10	$8.00	$80.00
SK10	Skyscraper	6	$25.00	$150.00
UM09	USA Map	12	$14.00	$168.00

Monday, September 08, 2003   Page 1 of 1

FIGURE 18

7. Open the report in the Snapshot Viewer and print it.
8. Export the Supplier table as an XML document. When the Export XML dialog box displays, click OK.
9. Print the Supplier XML document. To print the document, open Internet Explorer, type A:\Supplier.XML in the Address text box (if your document is not located on drive A, you will need to change the path), and then click Print on the Standard Buttons toolbar.

APPENDIX A
Microsoft Access Help System

Using the Microsoft Access Help System

This appendix shows you how to use the Microsoft Access Help system. At anytime while you are using Access, you can interact with its Help system and display information on any Access topic. It is a complete reference manual at your fingertips.

As shown in Figure A-1, you can access Access's Help system in four primary ways:

1. Ask a Question box on the menu bar
2. Function key F1 on the keyboard
3. Microsoft Access Help command on the Help menu
4. Microsoft Access Help button on the Database toolbar

If you use the Ask a Question box on the menu bar, Access responds by opening the Microsoft Access Help window, which gives you direct access to its Help system. If you use one of the other three ways to access Access's Help system, Access responds in one of two ways:

1. If the Office Assistant is turned on, then the Office Assistant displays with a balloon (lower-right side in Figure A-1).
2. If the Office Assistant is turned off, then the Microsoft Access Help window opens (lower-left side in Figure A-1).

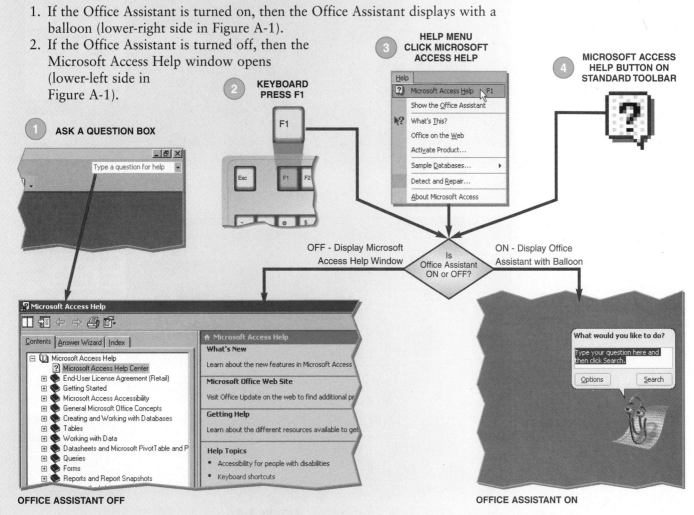

FIGURE A-1

Microsoft **Access 2002**

The best way to familiarize yourself with the Access Help system is to use it. The next several pages show examples of how to use the Help system. Following the examples is a set of exercises titled Use Help that will sharpen your Access Help system skills.

Ask a Question Box

The **Ask a Question box** on the right side of the menu bar lets you type questions in your own words, or you can type terms, such as query, edit, or relationships window. Access responds by displaying a list of topics related to the term(s) you entered. The following steps show how to use the Ask a Question box to obtain information on data types.

Steps To Obtain Help Using the Ask a Question Box

1 **Type** Data types **in the Ask a Question box on the right side of the menu bar and then press the ENTER key. When the Ask a Question list displays, point to the See more link.**

The Ask a Question list displays (Figure A-2).

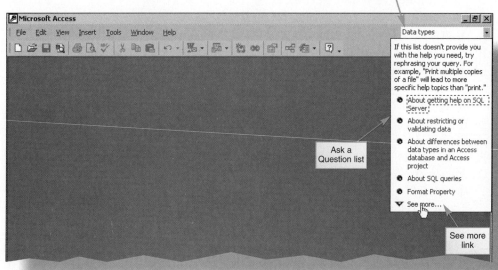

FIGURE A-2

2 **Click See more. Point to Set the default control type for a field.**

A new Ask a Question list displays (Figure A-3).

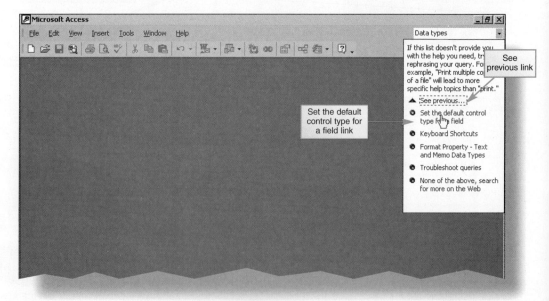

FIGURE A-3

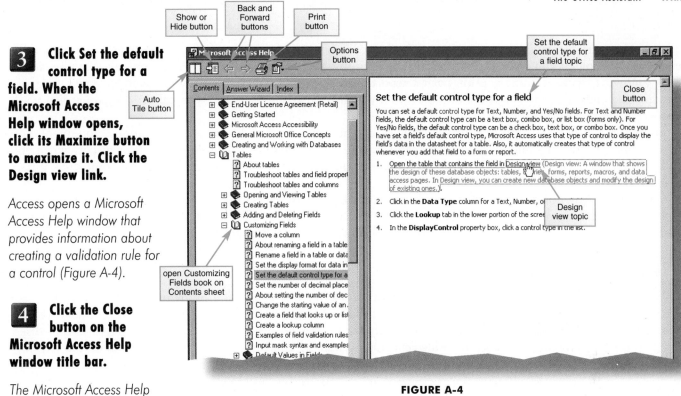

3 **Click Set the default control type for a field. When the Microsoft Access Help window opens, click its Maximize button to maximize it. Click the Design view link.**

Access opens a Microsoft Access Help window that provides information about creating a validation rule for a control (Figure A-4).

4 **Click the Close button on the Microsoft Access Help window title bar.**

The Microsoft Access Help window closes.

FIGURE A-4

If the Contents sheet is active on the left side of the Microsoft Access Help window, then Access opens the book that pertains to the topic for which you are requesting help. In this case, Access opens the Tables book and the Customizing Fields book, which includes a list of topics related to customizing fields. If the information on the right side is not satisfactory, you can click one of the topics in the Contents sheet to display alternative information related to customizing fields.

As you enter questions and terms in the Ask a Question box, Access adds them to its list. Thus, if you click the Ask a Question box arrow, a list of previously asked questions and terms will display.

Use the six buttons in the upper-left corner of the Microsoft Access Help window (Figure A-4) to navigate through the Help system, change the display, and print the contents of the window. Table A-1 lists the function of each of these buttons.

Table A-1	Microsoft Access Help Toolbar Buttons	
BUTTON	**NAME**	**FUNCTION**
	Auto Tile	Tiles the Microsoft Access Help window and Microsoft Access window when the Microsoft Access Help window is maximized
or	Show or Hide	Displays or hides the Contents, Answer Wizard, and Index tabs
	Back	Displays the previous Help topic
	Forward	Displays the next Help topic
	Print	Prints the current Help topic
	Options	Displays a list of commands

The Office Assistant

The **Office Assistant** is an icon (lower-right side of Figure A-1 on page A A.01) that displays in the Access window when it is turned on and not hidden. It has dual functions. First, it will respond in the same way the Ask a Question box does with a list of topics that relate to the entry you make in the text box at the bottom of the balloon. The entry can be in the form of a word, phrase, or question written as if you were talking to a human being. For example, if you want to learn more about printing a report, in the balloon text box, you can type any of the following terms or phrases: print, print a report, how do i print a report, or anything similar. The Office Assistant responds by displaying a list of topics from which you can choose. Once you choose a topic, it displays the corresponding information.

Second, the Office Assistant monitors your work and accumulates tips during a session on how you might increase your productivity and efficiency. You can view the tips at anytime. The accumulated tips display when you activate the Office Assistant balloon. Also, if at anytime you see a lightbulb above the Office Assistant, click it to display the most recent tip.

You may or may not want the Office Assistant to display on the screen at all times. You can hide it and then show it at a later time. You may prefer not to use the Office Assistant at all. Thus, not only do you need to know how to show and hide the Office Assistant, but you also need to know how to turn the Office Assistant on and off.

Showing and Hiding the Office Assistant

When Access initially is installed, the Office Assistant may be off. You turn it on by invoking the **Show the Office Assistant command** on the Help menu. If the Office Assistant is on the screen and you want to hide it, you click the **Hide the Office Assistant command** on the Help menu. You also can right-click the Office Assistant to display its shortcut menu and then click the **Hide command** to hide it. You can move it to any location on the screen. You can click it to display the Office Assistant balloon, which allows you to request Help.

Turning the Office Assistant On and Off

The fact that the Office Assistant is hidden does not mean it is turned off. To turn the Office Assistant off, it must be displayed in the Access window. You right-click it to display its shortcut menu (right-side of Figure A-5). Next, click Options on the shortcut menu. Invoking the **Options command** causes the **Office Assistant dialog box** to display (left-side of Figure A-5).

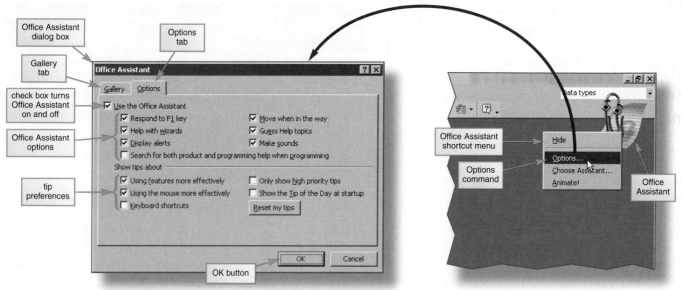

FIGURE A-5

The top check box in the **Options sheet** determines whether the Office Assistant is on or off. To turn the Office Assistant off, remove the check mark from the **Use the Office Assistant check box** and then click the OK button. As shown in Figure A-1 on page A A.01, if the Office Assistant is off when you invoke Help, then Access opens the Microsoft Access Help window instead of displaying the Office Assistant. To turn the Office Assistant on at a later date, click the Show the Office Assistant command on the Help menu.

Through the Options command on the Office Assistant shortcut menu, you can change the look and feel of the Office Assistant. For example, you can hide the Office Assistant, turn the Office Assistant off, change the way it works, choose a different Office Assistant icon, or view an animation of the current one. These options also are available by clicking the **Options button** that displays in the Office Assistant balloon (Figure A-6).

The **Gallery sheet** (Figure A-5) in the **Office Assistant dialog box** allows you to change the appearance of the Office Assistant. The default is the paper clip (Clippit). You can change it to a bouncing red happy face (The Dot), a robot (F1), the Microsoft Office logo (Office Logo), the wizard (Merlin), the earth (Mother Nature), a cat (Links), or a dog (Rocky).

Using the Office Assistant

As indicated earlier, the Office Assistant allows you to enter a word, phrase, or question and then responds by displaying a list of topics from which you can choose to display Help. The following steps show how to use the Office Assistant to obtain Help on calculating a total.

Steps To Use the Office Assistant

1 If the Office Assistant is not turned on, click Help on the menu bar and then click Show the Office Assistant. Click the Office Assistant. When the Office Assistant balloon displays, type how do I calculate a total in the text box immediately above the Options button. Point to the Search button.

The Office Assistant balloon displays (Figure A-6).

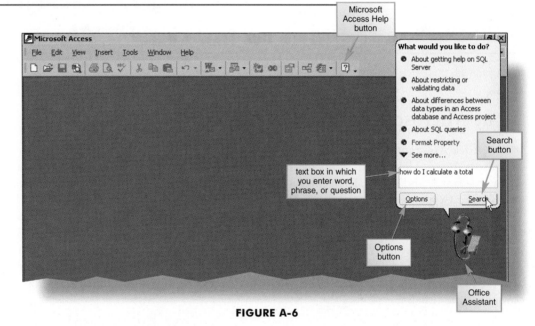

FIGURE A-6

2 Click the Search button. When the Office Assistant balloon redisplays, point to the Calculate a total or other aggregate values topic (Figure A-7).

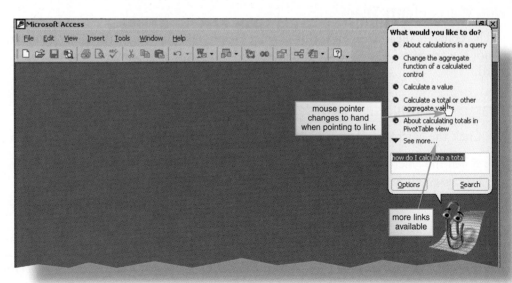

FIGURE A-7

3 **Click the Calculate a total or other aggregate values topic and then click the Maximize button. If necessary, move or hide the Office Assistant so you can view all of the text in the Microsoft Access Help window. Click the Calculate a total or average on a form or report link.**

The Microsoft Access Help window displays the information on how to calculate a total or average on a form or report (Figure A-8).

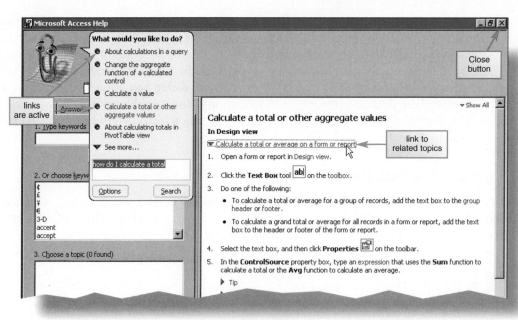

FIGURE A-8

The Microsoft Access Help Window

If the Office Assistant is turned off and you click the Microsoft Access Help button on the Database toolbar, the Microsoft Access Help window opens (Figure A-9). The left side of this window contains three tabs: Contents, Answer Wizard, and Index. Each tab displays a sheet with powerful look-up capabilities.

Use the Contents sheet as you would a table of contents at the front of a book to look up Help. The Answer Wizard sheet answers your queries the same as the Office Assistant. You use the Index sheet in the same fashion as an index in a book to look up Help. Click the tabs to move from sheet to sheet.

Besides clicking the Microsoft Access Help button on the Database toolbar, you also can click the Microsoft Access Help command on the Help menu, or press the F1 key to display the Microsoft Access Help window to gain access to the three sheets. To close the Microsoft Access Help window, click the Close button in the upper-right corner on the title bar.

Using the Contents Sheet

The **Contents sheet** is useful for displaying Help when you know the general category of the topic in question, but not the specifics. The following steps show how to use the Contents sheet to obtain information on saving a record.

TO OBTAIN HELP USING THE CONTENTS SHEET

1 Click the Microsoft Access Help button on the Database toolbar (see Figure A-6 on the previous page).

2 When the Microsoft Access Help window opens, click the Maximize button to maximize the window. If necessary, click the Show button to display the tabs.

3 Click the Contents tab. Double-click the Working with Data book on the left side of the window. Double-click the Adding, Editing, or Deleting Data book.

4 Double-click the Save a record subtopic, and then click the Save a record in a datasheet or form link.

Access displays help on the Save a record subtopic (Figure A-9). Access displays specific help on saving a record in a datasheet or a form.

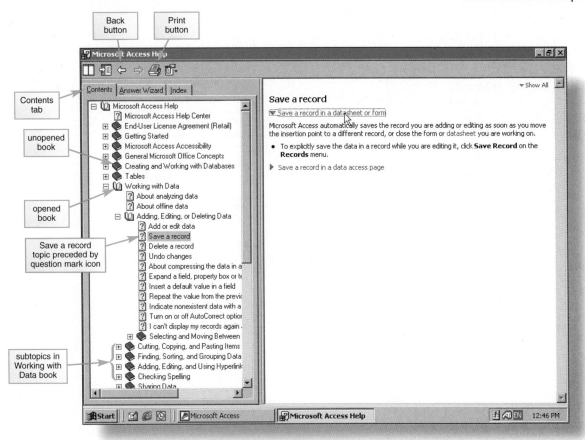

FIGURE A-9

Once the information on the subtopic displays, you can scroll through and read it or you can click the Print button to obtain a printed copy. If you decide to click another subtopic on the left or a link on the right, you can get back to the Help page shown in Figure A-9 by clicking the Back button.

Each topic in the Contents list is preceded by a book icon or question mark icon. A **book icon** indicates subtopics are available. A **question mark icon** means information on the topic will display if you double-click the title. The book icon opens when you double-click the book (or its title) or click the plus sign (+) to the left of the book icon.

Using the Answer Wizard Sheet

The **Answer Wizard sheet** works like the Office Assistant in that you enter a word, phrase, or question and it responds by listing topics from which you can choose to display Help. The following steps show how to use the Answer Wizard sheet to obtain Help on adding a picture.

TO OBTAIN HELP USING THE ANSWER WIZARD SHEET

1 With the Office Assistant turned off, click the Microsoft Access Help button on the Database toolbar (see Figure A-6 on page A A.05).

2 When the Microsoft Access Help window opens, double-click the title bar to maximize the window. If necessary, click the Show button to display the tabs.

3 Click the Answer Wizard tab. Type add a picture in the What would you like to do text box on the left side of the window and then click the Search button.

4 When a list of topics displays in the Select topic to display list box, click the About adding a picture or object topic.

Access displays help about adding a picture or object (Figure A-10 on the next page).

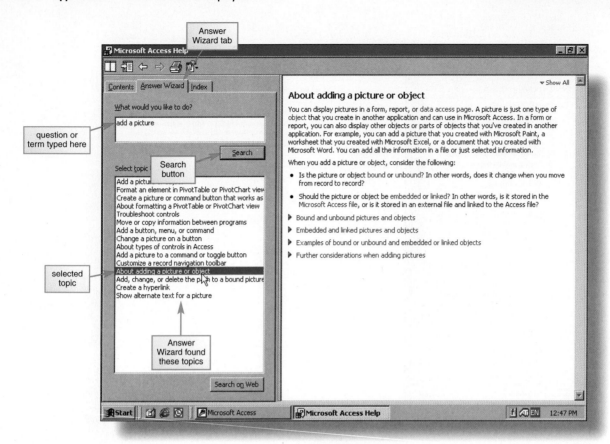

FIGURE A-10

If the About adding a picture or object topic does not include the information you are seeking, click another topic in the list. Continue to click topics until you find the desired information.

Using the Index Sheet

The third sheet in the Microsoft Access Help window is the Index sheet. Use the **Index sheet** to display Help when you know the keyword or the first few letters of the keyword you want to look up. The following steps show how to use the Index sheet to obtain Help on printing the Relationships window.

TO OBTAIN HELP USING THE INDEX SHEET

1 With the Office Assistant turned off, click the Microsoft Access Help button on the Database toolbar (see Figure A-6 on page A A.05).

2 When the Microsoft Access Help window opens, double-click the title bar to maximize the window. If necessary, click the Show button to display the tabs.

3 Click the Index tab. Type print in the Type keywords text box on the left side of the window. Click the Search button.

4 When a list of topics displays in the Choose a topic list, click the down scroll arrow three times, and then click Print the design of a database or a database object. Click the Print the Relationships window link.

Access displays help on printing the Relationships window (Figure A-11). When you click the Search button, Access automatically appends a semicolon to the keyword in the Type keywords text box.

What's This? Command and Question Mark Button • A A.09

APPENDIX A

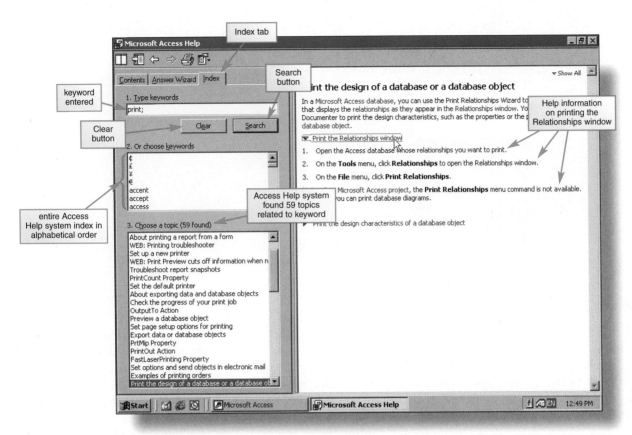

FIGURE A-11

An alternative to typing a keyword in the Type keywords text box is to scroll through the Or choose keywords list (the middle list on the left side of the window). When you locate the keyword you are searching for, double-click it to display Help on the topic. Also in the Or choose keywords list, the Access Help system displays other topics that relate to the new keyword. As you begin typing a new keyword in the Type keywords text box, Access jumps to that point in the middle list box. To begin a new search, click the Clear button.

What's This? Command and Question Mark Button

Use the What's This? command on the Help menu or the Question Mark button in a dialog box when you are not sure what an object on the screen is or what it does.

What's This? Command

You use the **What's This? command** on the Help menu to display a detailed ScreenTip. When you invoke this command, the mouse pointer changes to an arrow with a question mark. You then click any object on the screen, such as a button, to display the ScreenTip. For example, after you click the What's This? command on the Help menu and then click the Print button on the Database toolbar, a description of the Print button displays (Figure A-12 on the next page). You can print the ScreenTip by right-clicking it and then clicking Print Topic on the shortcut menu.

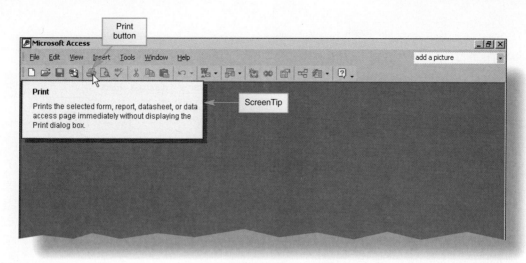

FIGURE A-12

Question Mark Button

In a fashion similar to the What's This? command, the **Question Mark button** displays a ScreenTip. You use the Question Mark button with dialog boxes. It is located in the upper-right corner on the title bar of dialog boxes, next to the Close button. For example, in Figure A-13, the Options dialog box displays on the screen. If you click the Question Mark button in the upper-right corner of the dialog box and then click one item in the dialog box (for example, Hidden objects), an explanation displays. You can print the ScreenTip by right-clicking it and then clicking Print Topic on the shortcut menu.

If a dialog box does not include a Question Mark button, press SHIFT+F1. This combination of keys displays an explanation or changes the mouse pointer to an arrow with a question mark. You then can click any object in the dialog box to display the ScreenTip.

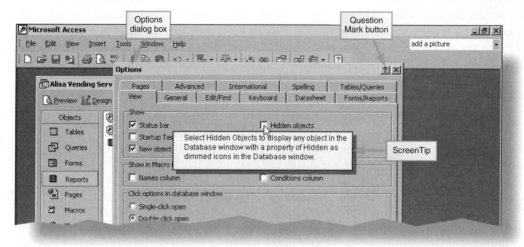

FIGURE A-13

Office on the Web Command

The **Office on the Web command** on the Help menu displays a Microsoft Web page containing up-to-date information on a variety of Office-related topics. To use this command, you must be connected to the Internet. When you invoke the Office on the Web command, the Assistance Center Home page displays. Read through the links that in general pertain to topics that relate to all Office XP topics. Scroll down and click the Access link in the Help By Product area to display the Assistance Center Access Help Articles Web page (Figure A-14). This Web page contains numerous helpful links related to Access.

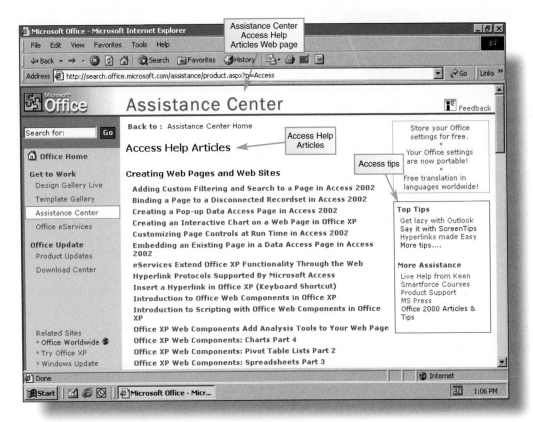

FIGURE A-14

Other Help Commands

Four additional commands available on the Help menu are Activate Product, Sample Databases, Detect and Repair, and About Microsoft Access. The Sample Databases command is available only if the sample databases are installed.

Activate Product Command

The **Activate Product command** on the Help menu lets you activate your Access subscription if you selected the Office Subscription mode.

Sample Databases Command

The **Sample Databases command** on the Help menu lets you open the sample databases that come with Access.

Detect and Repair Command

Use the **Detect and Repair command** on the Help menu if Access is not running properly or if it is generating errors. When you invoke this command, the Detect and Repair dialog box displays. Click the Start button in the dialog box to initiate the detect and repair process.

About Microsoft Access Command

The **About Microsoft Access command** on the Help menu displays the About Microsoft Access dialog box. The dialog box lists the owner of the software and the product identification. You need to know the product identification if you call Microsoft for assistance. The two buttons below the OK button are the System Info button and the Tech Support button. The **System Info button** displays system information, including hardware resources, components, software environment, and applications. The **Tech Support button** displays technical assistance information.

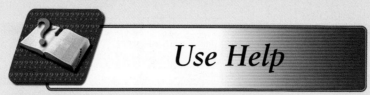

Use Help

1 Using the Ask a Question Box

Instructions: Perform the following tasks using the Access Help system.

1. Type how do I order records in the Ask a Question box on the menu bar. Press the ENTER key.
2. Click the See More link, and then, click Sort records in the Ask a Question list. Double-click the Microsoft Access Help window title bar. Click the Sort records in Form view or Datasheet view link. Read and print the information. Hand in the printout to your instructor.
3. If necessary, click the Show button to display the tabs. Click the Contents tab to prepare for the next step. Click the Close button in the Microsoft Access Help window.
4. Click the Ask a Question box and then type creating indexes. Press the ENTER key. Click the See More link, and then click Create an index to find and sort records faster in the Ask a Question list. When the Microsoft Access Help window displays, maximize the window. One at a time, click the two links on the right side of the window to learn more about creating indexes. Read and print the information. Click each of the remaining eight subtopics in the Primary Keys and Indexes book in the Contents sheet. Print the information for each. Close the Microsoft Access Help window.

2 Expanding on the Access Help System Basics

Instructions: Use the Access Help system to understand the topics better and answer the questions listed below. Answer the questions on your own paper, or hand in the printed Help information to your instructor.

1. Right-click the Office Assistant. If it is not turned on, click Show the Office Assistant on the Help menu. When the shortcut menu displays, click Options. Click Use the Office Assistant to remove the check mark, and then click the OK button.
2. Click the Microsoft Access Help button on the Database toolbar. Maximize the Microsoft Access Help window. If the tabs are hidden on the left side, click the Show button. Click the Index tab. Type resize in the Type keywords text box. Click the Search button. Click Resize a column or row. Click the Hide and then Show buttons. One at a time, click the two links below step 2 on the right side of the window to learn about resizing columns and rows. Read and print the information. Close the Microsoft Access Help window. Hand in the printout to your instructor.
3. Press the F1 key. Click the Answer Wizard tab. Type join in the What would you like to do? text box, and then click the Search button. Click Join tables and queries in a query. Read through the information that displays. Print the information. Click the two links. Read and print the information for both.
4. Click the Contents tab. Double-click the Creating and Working with Databases book, and then double-click the Working with Database Objects book that displays. One at a time, click the first three topics below the Working with Database Objects book. Read and print each one. Close the Microsoft Access Help window. Hand in the printouts to your instructor.
5. Click Help on the menu bar and then click the What's This? command. Click the Search button on the Database toolbar. Right-click the ScreenTip and then click Print Topic on the shortcut menu. Click the Customize command on the Tools menu. When the Customize dialog box displays, click the Question Mark button on the title bar. Click the Reset button. Right-click the ScreenTip and then click Print Topic. Hand in the printouts to your instructor.

APPENDIX B
Speech and Handwriting Recognition

Introduction

This appendix discusses how you can create and modify databases using Office XP's new input technologies. Office XP provides a variety of **text services**, which enable you to speak commands and enter text in an application. The most common text service is the keyboard. Two new text services included with Office XP are speech recognition and handwriting recognition.

When Windows was installed on your computer, you specified a default language. For example, most users in the United States select English (United States) as the default language. Through text services, you can add more than 90 additional languages and varying dialects such as Basque, English (Zimbabwe), French (France), French (Canada), German (Germany), German (Austria), and Swahili. With multiple languages available, you can switch from one language to another while working in Access. If you change the language or dialect, then text services may change the functions of the keys on the keyboard, adjust speech recognition, and alter handwriting recognition.

The Language Bar

You know that text services are installed properly when the Language Indicator button displays by the clock in the tray status area on the Windows taskbar (Figure B-1a) or the Language bar displays on the screen (Figure B-1b or B-1c). If the Language Indicator button displays in the tray status area, click it, and then click the **Show the Language bar command** (Figure B-1a). The Language bar displays on the screen in the same location it displayed last time.

You can drag the Language bar to any location in the window by pointing to its move handle, which is the vertical line on its left side (Figure B-1b). When the mouse pointer changes to a four-headed arrow, drag the Language bar to the desired location.

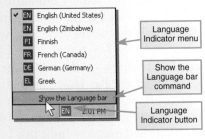

(a) Language Indicator Button in Tray Status Area on Windows Taskbar and Its Menu

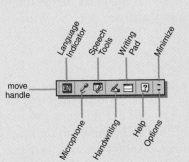

(b) Language Bar with Text Labels Disabled

(c) Language Bar with Text Labels Enabled

FIGURE B-1

If you are sure that one of the services was installed and neither the Language Indicator button nor the Language bar displays, then do the following:

1. Click Start on the Windows taskbar, point to Settings, click Control Panel, and then double-click the Text Services icon in the Control Panel window.
2. When the Text Services dialog box displays, click the Language Bar button, click the Show the Language bar on the desktop check box to select it, and then click the OK button in the Language Bar Settings dialog box.
3. Click the OK button in the Text Services dialog box.
4. Close the Control Panel window.

You can perform tasks related to text services by using the **Language bar**. The Language bar may display with just the icon on each button (Figure B-1b on the previous page) or it may display with text labels to the right of the icon on each button (Figure B-1c on the previous page). Changing the appearance of the Language bar will be discussed shortly.

Buttons on the Language Bar

The Language bar shown in Figure B-2a contains eight buttons. The number of buttons on your Language bar may be different. These buttons are used to select the language, customize the Language bar, control the microphone, control handwriting, and obtain help.

When you click the **Language Indicator button** on the far left side of the Language bar, the Language Indicator menu displays a list of the active languages (Figure B-2b) from which you can choose. The **Microphone button**, the second button from the left, enables and disables the microphone. When the microphone is enabled, text services adds two buttons and a balloon to the Language bar (Figure B-2c). These additional buttons and the balloon will be discussed shortly.

The third button from the left on the Language bar is the Speech Tools button. The **Speech Tools button** displays a menu of commands (Figure B-2d) that allow you to hide or show the balloon on the Language bar; train the Speech Recognition service so that it can better interpret your voice; add and delete words from its dictionary, such as names and other words not understood easily; and change the user profile so more than one person can use the microphone on the same computer.

The fourth button from the left on the Language bar is the Handwriting button. The **Handwriting button** displays the **Handwriting menu** (Figure B-2e), which lets you choose the Writing Pad (Figure B-2f), Write Anywhere (Figure B-2g), or the on-screen keyboard (Figure B-2h). The **On-Screen Symbol Keyboard command** on the Handwriting menu displays an on-screen keyboard that allows you to enter special symbols that are not available on a standard keyboard. You can choose only one form of handwriting at a time.

The fifth button indicates which one of the handwriting forms is active. For example, in Figure B-1a on the previous page the Writing Pad is active. The handwriting recognition capabilities of text services will be discussed shortly.

The sixth button from the left on the Language bar is the Help button. The **Help button** displays the Help menu. If you click the Language Bar Help command on the Help menu, the Language Bar Help window displays (Figure B-2i). On the far right of the Language bar are two buttons stacked above and below each other. The top button is the Minimize button and the bottom button is the Options button. The **Minimize button** minimizes (hides) the Language bar so that the Language Indicator button displays in the tray status area on the Windows taskbar. The next section discusses the Options button.

Customizing the Language Bar

The down arrow icon immediately below the Minimize button in Figure B-2a is called the Options button. The **Options button** displays a menu of text services options (Figure B-2j). You can use this menu to hide the Speech Tools, Handwriting, and Help buttons on the Language bar by clicking their names to remove the check mark to the left of each button. The Settings command on the Options menu displays a dialog box that lets you customize the Language bar. This command will be discussed shortly. The Restore Defaults command redisplays hidden buttons on the Language bar.

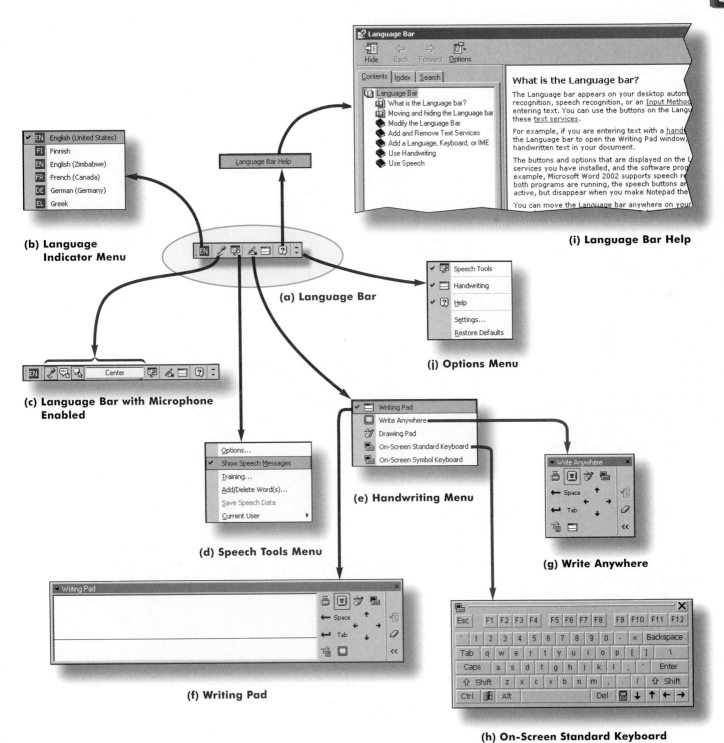

FIGURE B-2

If you right-click the Language bar, a shortcut menu displays (Figure B-3a on the next page). This shortcut menu lets you further customize the Language bar. The **Minimize command** on the shortcut menu minimizes the Language bar the same as the Minimize button on the Language bar. The **Transparency command** toggles the Language bar between being solid and transparent. You can see through a transparent Language bar (Figure B-3b). The **Text Labels command** toggles text labels on the Language bar on (Figure B-3c) and off (Figure B-3a). The **Additional icons in taskbar command** toggles between only showing the Language Indicator button in the tray status area and showing icons that represent the text services that are active (Figure B-3d).

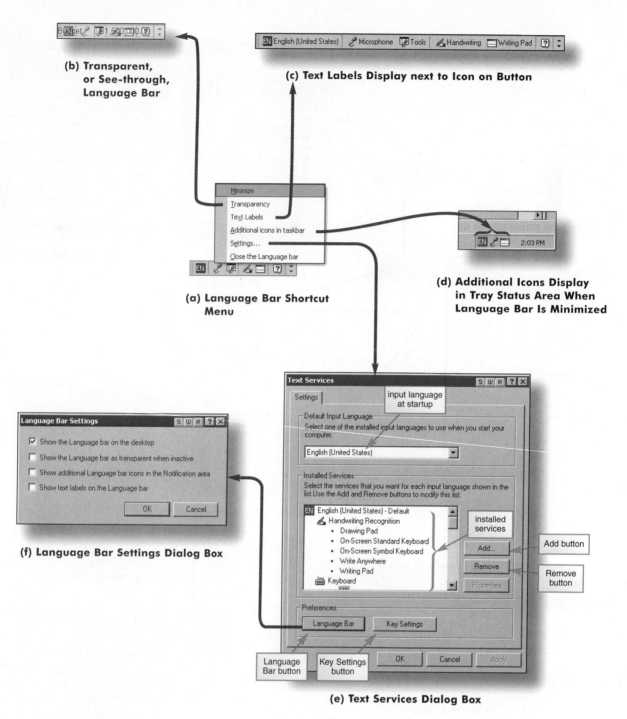

(b) Transparent, or See-through, Language Bar

(c) Text Labels Display next to Icon on Button

(a) Language Bar Shortcut Menu

(d) Additional Icons Display in Tray Status Area When Language Bar Is Minimized

(f) Language Bar Settings Dialog Box

(e) Text Services Dialog Box

FIGURE B-3

The **Settings command** displays the Text Services dialog box (Figure B-3e). The **Text Services dialog box** allows you to select the language at startup; add and remove text services; modify keys on the keyboard; and modify the Language bar. If you want to remove any one of the entries in the Installed Services list, select the entry, and then click the Remove button. If you want to add a service, click the Add button. The Key Settings button allows you to modify the keyboard. If you click the **Language Bar button** in the Text Services dialog box, the **Language Bar Settings dialog box** displays (Figure B-3f). This dialog box contains Language bar options, some of which are the same as the commands on the Language bar shortcut menu described earlier.

The **Close the Language bar command** on the shortcut menu shown in Figure B-3a closes the Language bar and hides the Language Indicator button in the tray status area on the Windows taskbar. If you close the Language bar and want to redisplay it, follow the instructions at the top of page A B.02.

Speech Recognition

The **Speech Recognition service** available with Office XP enables your computer to recognize human speech through a microphone. The microphone has two modes: dictation and voice command (Figure B-4). You switch between the two modes by clicking the Dictation button and the Voice Command button on the Language bar. These buttons display only when you turn on Speech Recognition by clicking the **Microphone button** on the Language bar (Figure B-5 on the next page). If you are using the Microphone button for the very first time in Access, it will require that you check your microphone settings and step through voice training before activating the Speech Recognition service.

The **Dictation button** places the microphone in Dictation mode. In **Dictation mode**, whatever you speak is entered as text in the table. The **Voice Command button** places the microphone in Voice Command mode. In **Voice Command mode**, whatever you speak is interpreted as a command. If you want to turn off the microphone, click the Microphone button on the Language bar or in Voice Command mode say, "Mic off" (pronounced mike off). It is important to remember that minimizing the Language bar does not turn off the microphone.

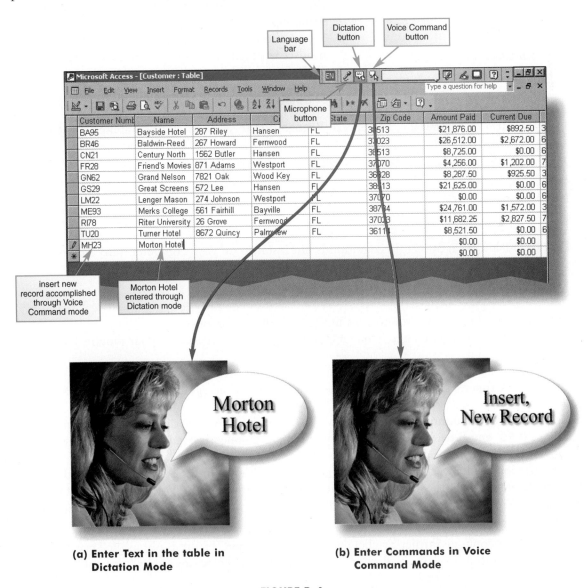

(a) Enter Text in the table in
Dictation Mode

(b) Enter Commands in Voice
Command Mode

FIGURE B-4

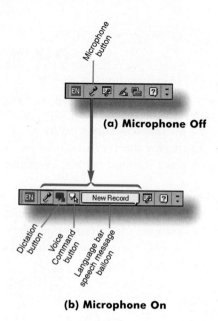

(a) Microphone Off

(b) Microphone On

FIGURE B-5

The **Language bar speech message balloon** shown in Figure B-5b displays messages that may offer help or hints. In Voice Command mode, the name of the last recognized command you said displays. If you use the mouse or keyboard instead of the microphone, a message will appear in the Language bar speech message balloon indicating the word you could say. In Dictation mode, the message, Dictating, usually displays. The Speech Recognition service, however, will display messages to inform you that you are talking too soft, too loud, too fast, or to ask you to repeat what you said by displaying, What was that?

Getting Started with Speech Recognition

For the microphone to function properly, you should follow these steps:

1. Make sure your computer meets the minimum requirements.
2. Install Speech Recognition.
3. Set up and position your microphone, preferably a close-talk headset with gain adjustment support.
4. Train Speech Recognition.

The following sections describe these steps in more detail.

SPEECH RECOGNITION SYSTEM REQUIREMENTS   For Speech Recognition to work on your computer, it needs the following:

1. Microsoft Windows 98 or later or Microsoft Windows NT 4.0 or later
2. At least 128 MB RAM
3. 400 MHz or faster processor
4. Microphone and sound card

INSTALLING SPEECH RECOGNITION   If Speech Recognition is not installed on your computer, start Microsoft Word and then click Speech on the Tools menu.

SETUP AND POSITION YOUR MICROPHONE   Set up your microphone as follows:

1. Connect your microphone to the sound card in the back of the computer.
2. Position the microphone approximately one inch out from and to the side of your mouth. Position it so you are not breathing into it.
3. On the Language bar, click the Speech Tools button, and then click Options (Figure B-6a).
4. When the Speech Properties dialog box displays (Figure B-6b), if necessary, click the Speech Recognition tab.
5. Click the Configure Microphone button. Follow the Microphone Wizard directions as shown in Figures B-6c, B-6d, and B-6e. The Next button will remain dimmed in Figure B-6d until the volume meter consistently stays in the green area.
6. If someone else installed Speech Recognition, click the New button in the Speech Properties dialog box and enter your name. Click the Train Profile button and step through the Voice Training Wizard. The Voice Training Wizard will require that you enter your gender and age group. It then will step you through voice training.

You can adjust the microphone further by clicking the **Settings button** (Figure B-6b) in the Speech Properties dialog box. The Settings button displays the **Recognition Profile Settings dialog box** that allows you to adjust the pronunciation sensitivity and accuracy versus recognition response time.

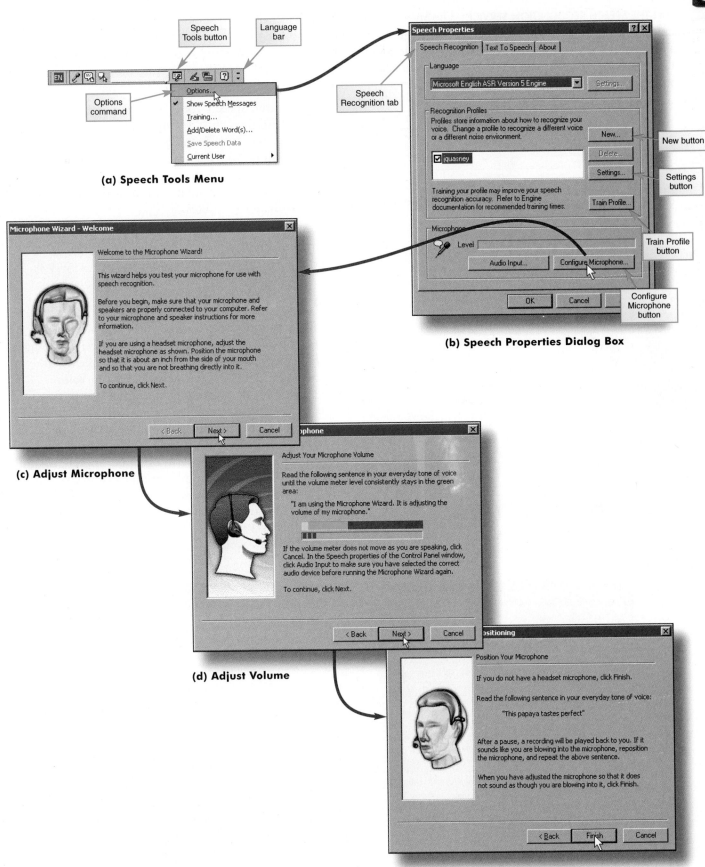

(a) Speech Tools Menu

(b) Speech Properties Dialog Box

(c) Adjust Microphone

(d) Adjust Volume

(e) Test Microphone

FIGURE B-6

TRAIN THE SPEECH RECOGNITION SERVICE The Speech Recognition service will understand most commands and some dictation without any training at all. It will recognize much more of what you speak, however, if you take the time to train it. After one training session, it will recognize 85 to 90 percent of your words. As you do more training, accuracy will rise to 95 percent. If you feel that too many mistakes are being made, then continue to train the service. The more training you do, the more accurately it will work for you. Follow these steps to train the Speech Recognition service:

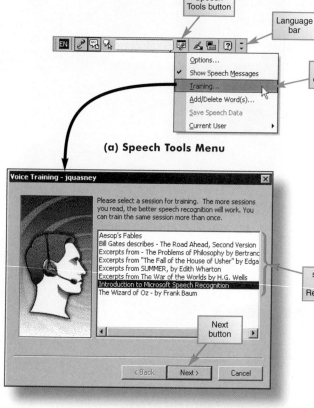

1. Click the Speech Tools button on the Language bar and then click Training (Figure B-7a).
2. When the **Voice Training dialog box** displays (Figure B-7b), click one of the sessions and then click the Next button.
3. Complete the training session, which should take less than 15 minutes.

If you are serious about using a microphone to speak to your computer, you need to take the time to go through at least three of the eight training sessions listed in Figure B-7b.

(a) Speech Tools Menu

(b) Voice Training Dialog Box

FIGURE B-7

Using Speech Recognition

Speech recognition lets you enter text into a table similarly to speaking into a tape recorder. Instead of typing, you can dictate text that you want to assign to fields, and you can issue voice commands. In **Voice Command mode**, you can speak menu names, commands on menus, toolbar button names, and dialog box option buttons, check boxes, list boxes, and button names. Speech Recognition, however, is not a completely hands-free form of input. Speech recognition works best if you use a combination of your voice, the keyboard, and the mouse. You soon will discover that Dictation mode is far less accurate than Voice Command mode. Table B-1 lists some tips that will improve the Speech Recognition service's accuracy considerably.

Table B-1	Tips to Improve Speech Recognition
NUMBER	**TIP**
1	The microphone hears everything. Though the Speech Recognition service filters out background noise, it is recommended that you work in a quiet environment.
2	Try not to move the microphone around once it is adjusted.
3	Speak in a steady tone and speak clearly.
4	In Dictation mode, do not pause between words. A phrase is easier to interpret than a word. Sounding out syllables in a word will make it more difficult for the Speech Recognition service to interpret what you are saying.
5	If you speak too loudly or too softly, it makes it difficult for the Speech Recognition service to interpret what you said. Check the Language bar speech message balloon for an indication that you may be speaking too loudly or too softly.
6	If you experience problems after training, adjust the recognition options that control accuracy and rejection by clicking the Settings button shown in Figure B-6b on the previous page.
7	When you are finished using the microphone, turn it off by clicking the Microphone button on the Language bar or in Voice Command mode say, "Mic off." Leaving the microphone on is the same as leaning on the keyboard.
8	If the Speech Recognition service is having difficulty with unusual words, then add the words to its dictionary by using the Add/Delete Word(s) command on the Speech Tools menu (Figure B-8a). The last names of individuals and the names of companies are good examples of the types of words you should add to the dictionary.
9	Training will improve accuracy; practice will improve confidence.

The last command on the Speech Tools menu is the Current User command (Figure B-8a). The **Current User command** is useful for multiple users who share a computer. It allows them to configure their own individual profiles, and then switch between users as they use the computer.

For additional information on the Speech Recognition service, click the Help button on the toolbar, click the Answer Wizard tab, and search for the phrase, Speech Recognition.

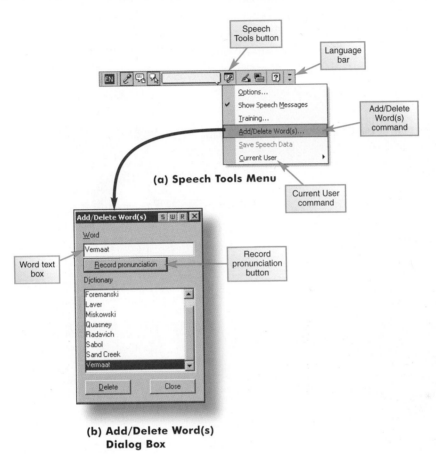

(a) Speech Tools Menu

(b) Add/Delete Word(s)
Dialog Box

FIGURE B-8

Handwriting Recognition

Using the Office XP handwriting recognition capabilities, you can enter text and numbers into Access by writing instead of typing. You can write using a special handwriting device that connects to your computer or you can write on the screen using your mouse. Four basic methods of handwriting are available by clicking the **Handwriting button** on the Language bar: Writing Pad; Write Anywhere; Drawing Pad; and On-Screen Keyboard. The Drawing Pad button is dimmed, which means it is not available in Access. Although the on-screen keyboard does not involve handwriting recognition, it is part of the Handwriting menu and, therefore, will be discussed in this section.

If your Language bar does not include the Handwriting button (Figures B-1b or B-1c on page A B.01), then for installation instructions click the Help button on the toolbar, click the Answer Wizard tab, and search for the phrase Install Handwriting Recognition.

Writing Pad

To display the Writing Pad, click the Handwriting button on the Language bar and then click Writing Pad (Figure B-9). The **Writing Pad** resembles a note pad with one or more lines on which you can use freehand to print or write in cursive. With the **Text button** enabled, you can form letters on the line by moving the mouse while holding down the mouse button. To the right of the note pad is a rectangular toolbar. Use the buttons on this toolbar to adjust the Writing Pad, select cells, and activate other handwriting applications.

Consider the example in Figure B-9. The word, Westport, is written in cursive on the **Pen line** in the Writing Pad. As soon as the word is complete, the Handwriting Recognition service automatically assigns the word to the City field.

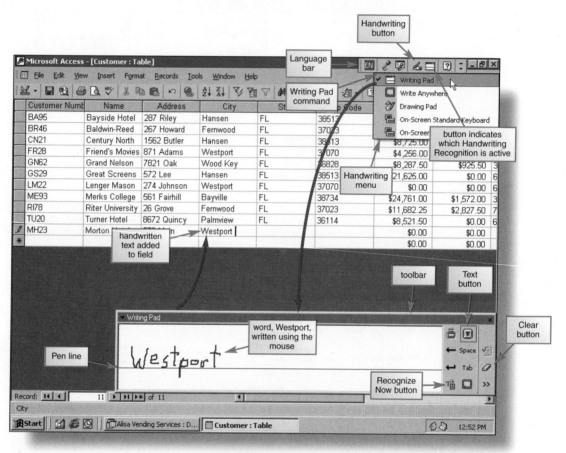

FIGURE B-9

You can customize the Writing Pad by clicking the **Options button** on the left side of the title bar and then clicking the Options command (Figure B-10a). Invoking the **Options command** causes the Handwriting Options dialog box to display. The **Handwriting Options dialog box** contains two sheets: Common and Writing Pad. The **Common sheet** lets you change the pen color and pen width, adjust recognition, and customize the toolbar area of the Writing Pad. The **Writing Pad sheet** allows you to change the background color and the number of lines that display in the Writing Pad. Both sheets contain a **Restore Default button** to restore the settings to what they were when the software was installed initially.

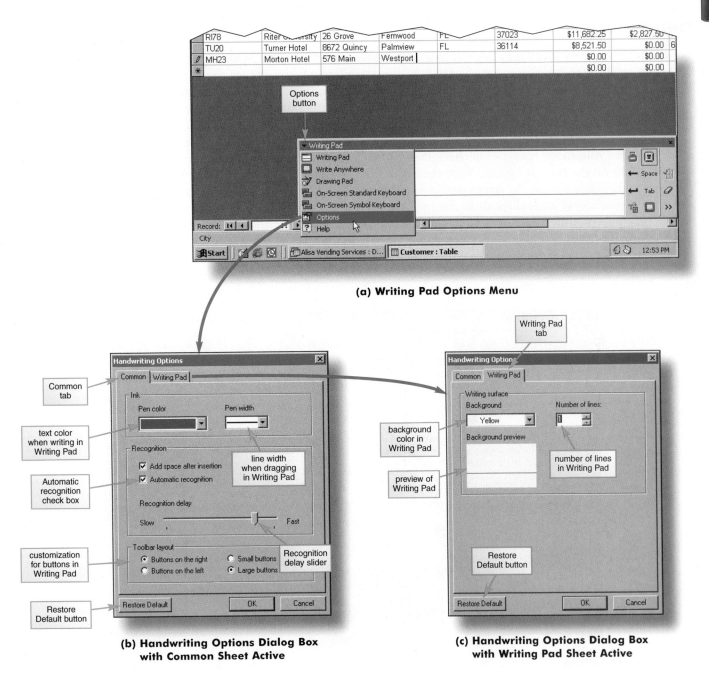

FIGURE B-10

When you first start using the Writing Pad, you may want to remove the check mark from the **Automatic recognition check box** on the Common sheet in the Handwriting Options dialog box (Figure B-10b). With the check mark removed, the Handwriting Recognition service will not interpret what you write in the Writing Pad until you click the **Recognize Now button** on the toolbar (Figure B-9). This allows you to pause and adjust your writing.

The best way to learn how to use the Writing Pad is to practice with it. Also, for more information, click the Help button on the toolbar, click the Answer Wizard tab, and search for the phrase, Handwriting Recognition.

Write Anywhere

Rather than use a Writing Pad, you can write anywhere on the screen by invoking the **Write Anywhere command** on the Handwriting menu (Figure B-11) that displays when you click the Handwriting button on the Language bar. In this case, the entire window is your writing pad.

In Figure B-11, the state abbreviation, FL, is written using the mouse button. Shortly after you finish writing the word, the Handwriting Recognition service interprets it, assigns it to the State field, and erases what you wrote.

It is recommended that when you first start using the Writing Anywhere service that you remove the check mark from the Automatic recognition check box in the Common sheet in the Handwriting Options dialog box (Figure B-10b on the previous page). With the check mark removed, the Handwriting Recognition service will not interpret what you write on the screen until you click the Recognize Now button on the toolbar (Figure B-11).

Write Anywhere is more difficult to use than the Writing Pad, because when you click the mouse button, Access may interpret the action as selecting a field rather than starting to write. For this reason, it is recommended that you use the Writing Pad.

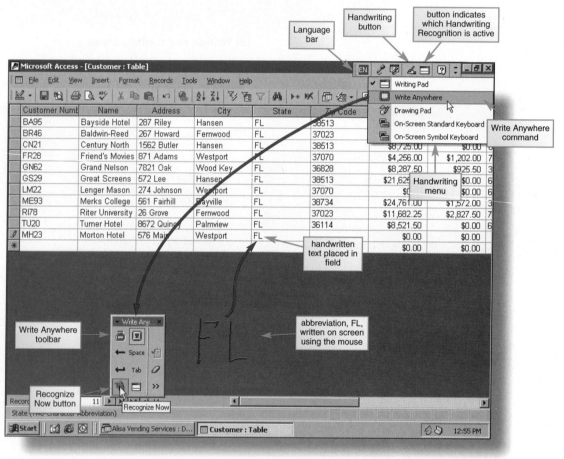

FIGURE B-11

On-Screen Keyboard

The **On-Screen Standard Keyboard command** on the Handwriting menu (Figure B-12) displays an on-screen keyboard. The **on-screen keyboard** lets you enter data into a field by using your mouse to click the keys. The on-screen keyboard is similar to the type found on handheld computers.

The **On-Screen Symbol Keyboard command** on the Handwriting menu (Figure B-12) displays a special on-screen keyboard that allows you to enter symbols that are not on your keyboard, as well as Unicode characters. **Unicode characters** use a coding scheme capable of representing all the world's current languages.

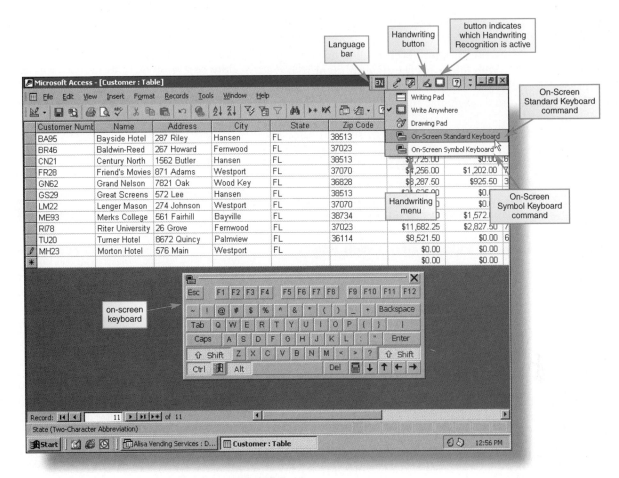

FIGURE B-12

APPENDIX C
Publishing Office Web Pages to a Web Server

With the Office applications, you use the Save as Web Page command on the File menu to save the Web page to a Web server using one of two techniques: Web folders or File Transfer Protocol. A **Web folder** is an Office shortcut to a Web server. **File Transfer Protocol (FTP)** is an Internet standard that allows computers to exchange files with other computers on the Internet.

You should contact your network system administrator or technical support staff at your ISP to determine if their Web server supports Web folders, FTP, or both, and to obtain necessary permissions to access the Web server. If you decide to publish Web pages using a Web folder, you must have the Office Server Extensions (OSE) installed on your computer.

Using Web Folders to Publish Office Web Pages

When publishing to a Web folder, someone first must create the Web folder before you can save to it. If you are granted permission to create a Web folder, you must obtain the URL of the Web server, a user name, and possibly a password that allows you to access the Web server. You also must decide on a name for the Web folder. Table C-1 explains how to create a Web folder.

Office adds the name of the Web folder to the list of current Web folders. You can save to this folder, open files in the folder, rename the folder, or perform any operations you would to a folder on your hard disk. You can use your Office program or Windows Explorer to access this folder. Table C-2 explains how to save to a Web folder.

Using FTP to Publish Office Web Pages

When publishing a Web page using FTP, you first must add the FTP location to your computer before you can save to it. An **FTP location**, also called an **FTP site**, is a collection of files that reside on an FTP server. In this case, the FTP server is the Web server.

To add an FTP location, you must obtain the name of the FTP site, which usually is the address (URL) of the FTP server, and a user name and a password that allows you to access the FTP server. You save and open the Web pages on the FTP server using the name of the FTP site. Table C-3 explains how to add an FTP site.

Office adds the name of the FTP site to the FTP locations list in the Save As and Open dialog boxes. You can open and save files using this list. Table C-4 explains how to save to an FTP location.

Table C-1 Creating a Web Folder
1. Click File on the menu bar and then click Save As (or Open).
2. When the Save As dialog box (or Open dialog box) displays, click My Network Places (or Web Folders) on the Places Bar. Double-click Add Network Place (or Add Web Folder).
3. When the Add Network Place Wizard dialog box displays, click the Create a new Network Place option button and then click the Next button. Type the URL of the Web server in the Folder location text box, enter the folder name you want to call the Web folder in the Folder name text box, and then click the Next button. Click Empty Web and then click the Finish button.
4. When the Enter Network Password dialog box displays, type the user name and, if necessary, the password in the respective text boxes and then click the OK button.
5. Close the Save As or the Open dialog box.

Table C-2 Saving to a Web Folder
1. Click File on the menu bar and then click Save As.
2. When the Save As dialog box displays, type the Web page file name in the File name text box. Do not press the ENTER key.
3. Click My Network Places on the Places Bar.
4. Double-click the Web folder name in the Save in list.
5. If the Enter Network Password dialog box displays, type the user name and password in the respective text boxes and then click the OK button.
6. Click the Save button in the Save As dialog box.

Table C-3 Adding an FTP Location
1. Click File on the menu bar and then click Save As (or Open).
2. In the Save As dialog box, click the Save in box arrow and then click Add/Modify FTP Locations in the Save in list; or in the Open dialog box, click the Look in box arrow and then click Add/Modify FTP Locations in the Look in list.
3. When the Add/Modify FTP Locations dialog box displays, type the name of the FTP site in the Name of FTP site text box. If the site allows anonymous logon, click Anonymous in the Log on as area; if you have a user name for the site, click User in the Log on as area and then enter the user name. Enter the password in the Password text box. Click the OK button.
4. Close the Save As or the Open dialog box.

Table C-4 Saving to an FTP Location
1. Click File on the menu bar and then click Save As.
2. When the Save As dialog box displays, type the Web page file name in the File name text box. Do not press the ENTER key.
3. Click the Save in box arrow and then click FTP Locations.
4. Double-click the name of the FTP site to which you wish to save.
5. When the FTP Log On dialog box displays, enter your user name and password and then click the OK button.
6. Click the Save button in the Save As dialog box.

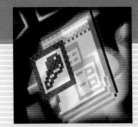

APPENDIX D
Resetting the Access Toolbars and Menus

In Microsoft Access, you can personalize toolbars and menus. You can change the toolbar or toolbars that display by clicking View on the menu bar, clicking Toolbars, and then clicking the toolbar name you want to display. You also can change the buttons that display on a particular toolbar by clicking the Toolbar Options button (see Figure D-1). In addition, Access personalizes the commands on the menus based on their usage. Each time you start Access, the toolbars and menus display in the same settings as the last time you used the application. This appendix shows you how to reset usage data, that is, clear menu and toolbar settings. Resetting usage data does not affect the location of the toolbars, nor does it change any buttons you might have added using the Customize dialog box. To reverse these changes, you need to reset the toolbar. The following steps reset the usage data and also the Database toolbar.

Steps To Reset My Usage Data and Toolbars

1 **Click View on the menu bar, point to Toolbars on the View menu, and then point to Customize on the Toolbars submenu. If the full View menu does not display, wait a few seconds to view the entire menu.**

The View menu and the Toolbars submenu display (Figure D-1).

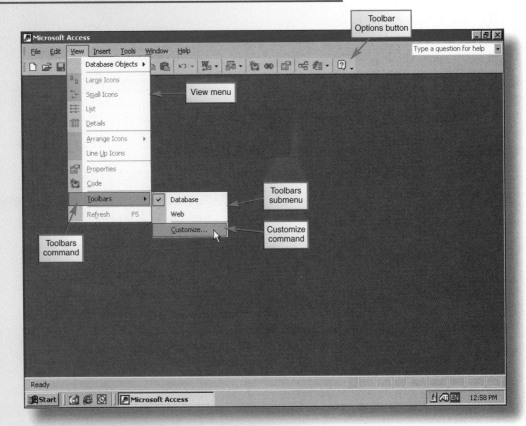

FIGURE D-1

2 **Click Customize on the Toolbars submenu. If necessary, click the Options tab in the Customize dialog box and then point to the Reset my usage data button.**

The Customize dialog box displays (Figure D-2).

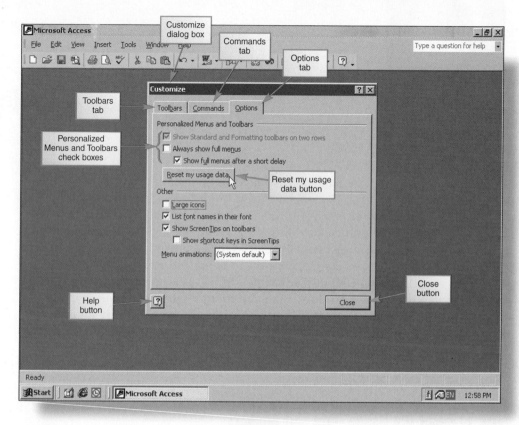

FIGURE D-2

3 **Click the Reset my usage data button. When the Microsoft Access dialog box displays explaining the function of the Reset my usage data button, point to the Yes button.**

The Microsoft Access dialog box displays (Figure D-3). The message indicates the actions that will be taken and asks if you are sure you wish to proceed.

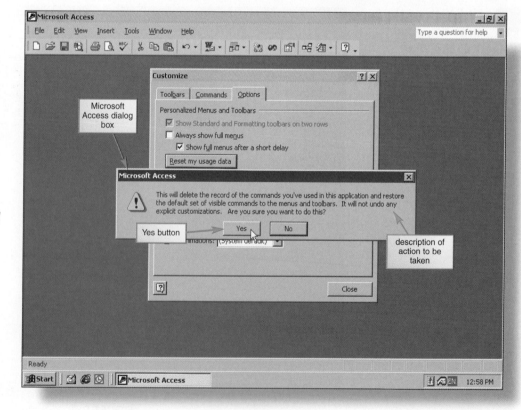

FIGURE D-3

Click the Yes button in the Microsoft Access dialog box. Click the Toolbars tab in the Customize dialog box and then point to Database in the Toolbars list box.

The Customize dialog box displays (Figure D-4).

 Click Database (the word Database and not the check box in front of the toolbar name) in the Toolbars list box, and then click the Reset button. When the Microsoft Access dialog box displays asking if you are sure you want to reset the changes made to the Database toolbar, click the OK button. Repeat the process for any other toolbar you want to reset.

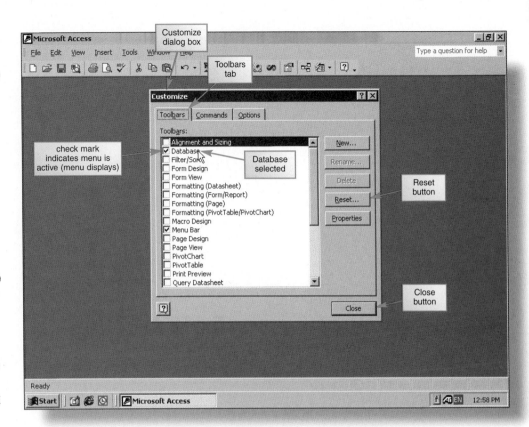

FIGURE D-4

 Click the Close button in the Customize dialog box.

Access resets the Database toolbar to its installation settings.

You can turn off short menus by placing a check mark in the Always show full menus check box in the Customize dialog box (see Figure D-2).

One other task you can complete using the Customize dialog box shown in Figure D-2 is to add buttons to toolbars and commands to menus. To add buttons, click the Commands tab in the Customize dialog box and drag the commands to a toolbar. To add commands to a menu, click the Commands tab in the Customize dialog box and drag the commands to the menu name. When the menu displays, you then can drag the commands to the desired menu location.

Access considers the menu at the top of the Access window to be a toolbar. If you add commands to menus as described in the previous paragraph and want to reset them to their installation settings, do the following: (1) click Toolbars on the View menu; (2) click Customize; (3) click the Toolbars tab; (4) scroll down in the Toolbars list and click Menu Bar; (5) click the Reset button; (6) click the OK button; and (7) then click the Close button.

1. On View menu click Toolbars, click Customize, click Toolbars tab, click toolbar name, click Reset button, click OK button, click Close button

2. Right-click toolbar, click Customize, click Toolbars tab, click toolbar name, click Reset button, click OK button, click Close button

APPENDIX E
Microsoft Office User Specialist Certification Program

What Is MOUS Certification?

The Microsoft Office User Specialist (MOUS) Certification Program provides a framework for measuring your proficiency with the Microsoft Office XP applications, such as Word 2002, Excel 2002, Access 2002, PowerPoint 2002, Outlook 2002, and FrontPage 2002. The levels of certification are described in Table E-1.

Table E-1 Levels of MOUS Certification			
LEVEL	*DESCRIPTION*	*REQUIREMENTS*	*CREDENTIAL AWARDED*
Expert	Indicates that you have a comprehensive understanding of the advanced features in a specific Microsoft Office XP application	Pass any ONE of the Expert exams: Microsoft Word 2002 Expert Microsoft Excel 2002 Expert Microsoft Access 2002 Expert Microsoft Outlook 2002 Expert Microsoft FrontPage 2002 Expert	Candidates will be awarded one certificate for each of the Expert exams they have passed: Microsoft Office User Specialist: Microsoft Word 2002 Expert Microsoft Office User Specialist: Microsoft Excel 2002 Expert Microsoft Office User Specialist: Microsoft Access 2002 Expert Microsoft Office User Specialist: Microsoft Outlook 2002 Expert Microsoft Office User Specialist: Microsoft FrontPage 2002 Expert
Core	Indicates that you have a comprehensive understanding of the core features in a specific Microsoft Office 2002 application	Pass any ONE of the Core exams: Microsoft Word 2002 Core Microsoft Excel 2002 Core Microsoft Access 2002 Core Microsoft Outlook 2002 Core Microsoft FrontPage 2002 Core	Candidates will be awarded one certificate for each of the Core exams they have passed: Microsoft Office User Specialist: Microsoft Word 2002 Microsoft Office User Specialist: Microsoft Excel 2002 Microsoft Office User Specialist: Microsoft Access 2002 Microsoft Office User Specialist: Microsoft Outlook 2002 Microsoft Office User Specialist: Microsoft FrontPage 2002
Comprehensive	Indicates that you have a comprehensive understanding of the features in Microsoft PowerPoint 2002	Pass the Microsoft PowerPoint 2002 Comprehensive Exam	Candidates will be awarded one certificate for the Microsoft PowerPoint 2002 Comprehensive exam passed.

Why Should You Get Certified?

Being a Microsoft Office User Specialist provides a valuable industry credential — proof that you have the Office XP applications skills required by employers. By passing one or more MOUS certification exams, you demonstrate your proficiency in a given Office XP application to employers. With over 100 million copies of Office in use around the world, Microsoft is targeting Office XP certification to a wide variety of companies. These companies include temporary employment agencies that want to prove the expertise of their workers, large corporations looking for a way to measure the skill set of employees, and training companies and educational institutions seeking Microsoft Office XP teachers with appropriate credentials.

The MOUS Exams

You pay $50 to $100 each time you take an exam, whether you pass or fail. The fee varies among testing centers. The Expert exams, which you can take up to 60 minutes to complete, consists of between 40 and 60 tasks that you perform online. The tasks require you to use the application just as you would in doing your job. The Core exams contain fewer tasks, and you will have slightly less time to complete them. The tasks you will perform differ on the two types of exams.

How Can You Prepare for the MOUS Exams?

The Shelly Cashman Series® offers several Microsoft-approved textbooks that cover the required objectives on the MOUS exams. For a listing of the textbooks, visit the Shelly Cashman Series MOUS site at scsite.com/offxp/cert.htm and click the link Shelly Cashman Series Office XP Microsoft-Approved MOUS Textbooks (Figure E-1). After using any of the books listed in an instructor-led course, you will be prepared to take the MOUS exam indicated.

How to Find an Authorized Testing Center

You can locate a testing center by calling 1-800-933-4493 in North America or visiting the Shelly Cashman Series MOUS site at scsite.com/offxp/cert.htm and then clicking the link Locate an Authorized Testing Center Near You (Figure E-1). At this Web site, you can look for testing centers around the world.

Shelly Cashman Series MOUS Web Page

The Shelly Cashman Series MOUS Web page (Figure E-1) has more than fifteen Web sites you can visit to obtain additional information on the MOUS Certification Program. The Web page (scsite.com/offxp/cert.htm) includes links to general information on certification, choosing an application for certification, preparing for the certification exam, and taking and passing the certification exam.

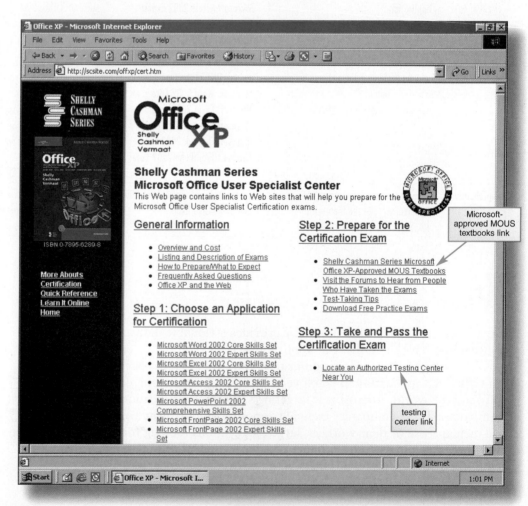

FIGURE E-1

Microsoft Access 2002 User Specialist Certification Core and Expert Maps

This book has been approved by Microsoft as courseware for the Microsoft Office User Specialist (MOUS) program. After completing the projects and exercises in this book, students will be prepared to take the Core-level Microsoft Office User Specialist Exam for Microsoft Access 2002. Table E-2 lists the Microsoft Access 2002 Core Exam skill sets, activities, page numbers where the activities are demonstrated, and page numbers where the activities can be practiced.

Table E-3 lists the Microsoft Access 2002 Expert Exam skill sets, activities, page numbers where the activities are demonstrated, and page numbers where the activities can be practiced. COMP in the rightmost two columns means that the activity is demonstrated in the companion textbook *Microsoft Access 2002: Comprehensive Concepts and Techniques* (0-7895-6282-0).

Table E-2 Microsoft Access 2002 MOUS Core Skill Sets, Activities, and Locations in the Book			
SKILL SET	*ACTIVITY*	*ACTIVITY DEMONSTRATED IN BOOK*	*ACTIVITY EXERCISE IN BOOK*
I. Creating and Using Databases	A. Create Access databases	A 1.11	A 1.64 (Cases & Places 6)
	B. Open database objects in multiple views	A 1.21, A 1.38, A 1.39, A 3.16, A 4.18, A 4.19, A 4.36, A 4.52	A 1.58-61 (In the Lab 2, In the Lab 3), A 3.51-57 (Apply Your Knowledge, In the Lab 1-3), A 4.56-60 (Apply Your Knowledge, In the Lab 1-3)
	C. Move among records	A 1.26, A 1.38, A 5.42	A 1.55 (Apply Your Knowledge Step 5), A 1.59 (In the Lab 2 Steps 9-10), A 1.61 (In the Lab 3 Step 10)
	D. Format datasheets	A 3.21, A 5.13, A 5.14	A 3.51 (Apply Your Knowledge Step 10), A 3.53 (In the Lab 1 Step 3), A 3.55 (In the Lab 2 Step 11), A 5.51-57 (Apply Your Knowledge, In the Lab 1-3)
II. Creating and Modifying Tables	A. Create and modify tables	A 1.13, A 1.15	A 1.63 (Cases & Places 3)
	B. Add a pre-defined input mask to a field	A 6.10	A 6.54 (In the Lab 1 Step 1), A 6.60 (Cases & Places 4)
	C. Create Lookup fields	A 6.07, A 6.08	A 6.56 (In the Lab 2 Step 1), A 6.60 (Cases & Places 1)
	D. Modify field properties	A 3.16, A 3.28, A 3.30, A 3.31, A 3.46, A 6.10	A 3.51-59 (Apply Your Knowledge Steps 2-6, In the Lab 1 Steps 2-3, 11, In the Lab 2 Steps 9, 12, In the Lab 3 Steps 2, 5, 9, Cases & Places 1-5), A 6.54 (In the Lab 1 Step 1), A 6.60 (Cases & Places 4)
III. Creating and Modifying Queries	A. Create and modify Select queries	A 2.06	A 2.44 (In the Lab 1 Step 2)
	B. Add calculated fields to Select queries	A 2.33	A 2.45 (In the Lab 1 Step 13), A 2.46 (In the Lab 2 Step 12), A 2.47 (In the Lab 3 Step 12), A 2.48 (Cases & Places 2 Part c)
IV. Creating and Modifying Forms	A. Create and display forms	A 1.38, A 4.34, A 5.21	A 1.56 (In the Lab 1 Step 8), A 1.58 (In the Lab 2 Step 8), A 1.61 (In the Lab 3 Step 12), A 4.56-62 (Apply Your Knowledge Step 3, In the Lab 1-3, Cases & Places 2, 4), A 5.51-58 (Apply Your Knowledge, In the Lab 1-3, Cases & Places 2, 4)
	B. Modify form properties	A 4.40, A 4.48, A 4.51, A 5.35	A 4.56-62 (Apply Your Knowledge, In the Lab 1-3, Cases & Places 2, 4), A 5.52-58 , (In the Lab 1-3, Cases & Places 2, 4)
V. Viewing and Organizing Information	A. Enter, edit, and delete records	A 1.21, A 1.27, A 3.06, A 3.14, A 3.20	A 1.54-64 (Apply Your Knowledge Step 1, In the Lab 1-3, Cases & Places 1-6), A 3.53 (In the Lab 1 Step 5), A 3.55 (In the Lab 2 Step 13), A 3.57 (In the Lab 3 Step 10), A 1.55 (Apply Your Knowledge Step 5), A 1.59 (In the Lab 2 Steps 9, 10), A 1.61 (In the Lab 3 Step 10), A 3.51 (Apply Your Knowledge Step 9), A 3.53 (In the Lab 1 Step 12), A 3.54 (In the Lab 2 Steps 7, 13), A 3.57 (In the Lab 3 Step 7), A 3.58 (Cases & Places 1-2)

Table E-2 Microsoft Access 2002 MOUS Core Skill Sets, Activities, and Locations in the Book *(continued)*

SKILL SET	ACTIVITY	ACTIVITY DEMONSTRATED IN BOOK	ACTIVITY EXERCISE IN BOOK
	B. Create queries	A 2.06, A 3.39, A 3.45	A 2.44 (In the Lab 1 Step 2), A 3.59 (Cases & Places 5 Parts a, e)
	C. Sort records	A 2.25, A 3.41, A 3.42	A 3.51 (Apply Your Knowledge Step 15), A 3.53 (In the Lab 2 Step 6), A 3.56 (In the Lab 3 Step 3), A 2.44 (Apply Your Knowledge Step 14), A 2.46 (In the Lab 2 Step 12), A 2.47 (In the Lab 3 Steps 8-9) A 2.48 (Cases & Places 1 Part c, Cases & Places 2 Part e, Cases & Places 4 Part c)
	D. Filter records	A 3.13	A 3.51 (Apply Your Knowledge Step 13), A 3.55 (In the Lab 2 Step 16)
VI. Defining Relationships	A. Create one-to-many relationships	A 3.36-38	A 3.51 (Apply Your Knowledge Step 17), A 3.53 (In the Lab 1 Step 15), A 3.55 (In the Lab 2 Step 18), A 3.57 (In the Lab 3 Step 15), A 3.58-59 (Cases & Places 1-2, 4-5)
	B. Enforce referential integrity	A 3.36-38	A 3.51 (Apply Your Knowledge Step 17), A 3.53 (In the Lab 1 Step 15), A 3.55 (In the Lab 2 Step 18), A 3.57 (In the Lab 3 Step 15), A 3.58-59 (Cases & Places 1-2, 4-5)
VII. Producing Reports	A. Create and format reports	A 1.41, A 4.09, A 4.21	A 1.55 (Apply Your Knowledge Step 7), A 1.57 (In the Lab Step 9) A 1.59 (In the Lab 2 Step 12), A 1.61 (In the Lab 3 Step 12), A 4.56-62 (Apply Your Knowledge Step 1, In the Lab 1 Step 1, In the Lab 2 Steps 1, 3, In the Lab 3 Steps 1, 3, Cases & Places 1, 3, 5)
	B. Add calculated controls to reports	A 4.33, A 6.20-21	A 4.57 (In the Lab 1, Steps 1, 3), A 4.62 (Cases & Places 3), A 6.60 (Cases & Places 3)
	C. Preview and print reports	A 1.46, A 4.20, A 4.33	A 1.55 (Apply Your Knowledge Step 7), A 1.57 (In the Lab Step 9) A 1.59 (In the Lab 2 Step 12), A 1.61 (In the Lab 3 Step 12), A 4.56-62 (Apply Your Knowledge Step 1, In the Lab 1 Step 1, In the Lab 2 Steps 1, 3, In the Lab 3 Steps 1 and 3, Cases & Places 1, 3, 5)
VIII. Integrating with Other Applications	A. Import data to Access	AI 1.05	AI 1.15 (In the Lab 1 Step 2), AI 1.16 (In the Lab 1 Step 5, In the Lab 1 Step 8)
	B. Export data from Access	AI 1.09, AI 1.11, AI 1.13	AI 1.17 (In the Lab 2 Step 1, In the Lab 2 Step 4), AI 1.18 (In the Lab 2 Step 7, In the Lab 2 Step 8)
	C. Create a simple data Access page	AW 1.02	AW 1.10 (In the Lab 1)

Table E-3 Microsoft Access 2002 MOUS Expert Skill Sets, Activities, and Locations in Book

SKILL SET	ACTIVITY	ACTIVITY DEMONSTRATED IN BOOK	ACTIVITY EXERCISE IN BOOK
I. Creating and Modifying Tables	A. Use data validation	A 3.29, A 3.31	A 3.51-59 (Apply Your Knowledge Steps 2-6, In the Lab 1 Steps 2-3, 11, In the Lab 2 Steps 9, 12, In the Lab 3 Steps 2, 5, 9, Cases & Places 1-5)
	B. Link tables	AI 1.08	AI 1.16 (In the Lab 1 Step 8)
	C. Create lookup fields and modify Lookup field properties	A 6.07, A 6.08, A 6.14	A 6.56 (In the Lab 2 Step 1), A 6.60 (Cases & Places 1)
	D. Create and modify input masks	COMP	COMP
II. Creating and Modifying Forms	A. Create a form in Design View	COMP	COMP
	B. Create a Switchboard and set startup options	A 6.41, COMP	A 6.54-60 (In the Lab 1-3, Cases & Places 2, 5), COMP
	C. Add Subform controls to Access forms	A 5.21, COMP	A 5.51-58 (Apply Your Knowledge, In the Lab 1-3, Cases & Places 2, 4), COMP

Table E-3   Microsoft Access 2002 MOUS Expert Skill Sets, Activities, and Locations in Book

SKILL SET	ACTIVITY	ACTIVITY DEMONSTRATED IN BOOK	ACTIVITY EXERCISE IN BOOK
III. Refining Queries	A. Specify multiple query criteria	A 2.23, A 2.24	A 2.45 (In the Lab 1 Steps 8-9), A 2.46 (In the Lab 2 Steps 5, 7, 9), A 2.47 (In the Lab 3 Steps 4-5, 7)
	B. Create and apply advanced filters	COMP	COMP
	C. Create and run parameter queries	COMP	COMP
	D. Create and run Action queries	A 3.23, A 3.25, A 3.27	A 3.54 (In the Lab 2 Steps 3, 4, 5)
	E. Use aggregate functions in queries	A 2.36	A 2.45 (In the Lab 1 Steps 14-15), A 2.46 (In the Lab 2 Step 13), A 2.47 (In the Lab 3 Step 13, Cases & Places 1 Parts d, e, f, Cases & Places 2 Part f, Cases & Places 4 Parts d, e, f, g)
IV. Producing Reports	A. Create and modify reports	COMP	COMP
	B. Add Subreport controls to Access reports	COMP	COMP
	C. Sort and group data in reports	COMP	COMP
V. Defining Relationships	A. Establish one-to-many relationships	A 3.36, COMP	A 3.51-58 (Apply Your Knowledge, In the Lab 1-3, Cases & Places 1-2)
	B. Establish many-to-many relationships	COMP	COMP
VI. Operating Access on the Web	A. Create and Modify a Data Access Page	COMP	COMP
	B. Save PivotTables and PivotCharts views to Data Access Pages	COMP	COMP
VII. Using Access tools	A. Import XML documents into Access	AI 1.08	AI 1.16 (In the Lab 1 Step 5)
	B. Export Access data to XML documents	AI 1.09	AI 1.18 (In the Lab 2 Step 8)
	C. Encrypt and decrypt databases	COMP	COMP
	D. Compact and repair databases	A 5.48	A 5.55 (In the Lab 2 Step 7), A 5.57 (In the Lab 3 Step 6), A 5.58 (Cases & Places 2, 5)
	E. Assign database security	COMP	COMP
	F. Replicate a database	COMP	COMP
VIII. Creating Database Applications	A. Create Access Modules	COMP	COMP
	B. Use the Database Splitter	COMP	COMP
	C. Create an MDE file	COMP	COMP

Index

Microsoft
ACCESS 2002
Quick Reference Summary

In Microsoft Access 2002, you can accomplish a task in a number of ways. The following table provides a quick reference to each task presented in this textbook. The first column identifies the task. The second column indicates the page number on which the task is discussed in the book. The subsequent four columns list the different ways the task in column one can be carried out. You can invoke the commands listed in the MOUSE, MENU BAR, and SHORTCUT MENU columns using Voice commands.

Microsoft Access 2002 Quick Reference Summary

TASK	PAGE NUMBER	MOUSE	MENU BAR	SHORTCUT MENU	KEYBOARD SHORTCUT
Add Combo Box	A 4.41, A 4.43	Combo Box tool			
Add Field	A 3.17	Insert Rows button	Insert	Rows	Insert Rows	INSERT
Add Group of Records	A 3.25	Query Type button arrow	Append Query	Query	Append Query	Query Type	Append Query	
Add Label	A 4.46	Label tool			
Add Record	A 1.21, A 1.27	New Record button	Insert	New Record		
Add Switchboard Item	A 6.46	New button			
Add Switchboard Page	A 6.44	New button			
Add Table to Query	A 2.30	Show Table button	Query	Show Table	Show Table	
Add Text Box	A 4.38	Text Box tool			
Apply Filter	A 3.13	Filter By Selection or Filter By Form button	Records	Filter		
Calculate Statistics	A 2.36	Totals button	View	Totals	Totals	
Change Group of Records	A 3.23	Query Type button arrow	Update Query	Query	Update Query	Query Type	Update Query	
Change Property	A 4.16	Properties button	View	Properties	Properties	F4
Change Tab Order	A 6.28		View	Tab Order	Tab Order	
Clear Query	A 2.15		Edit	Clear Grid		
Close Database	A 1.25	Close Window button	File	Close		
Close Form	A 1.36	Close Window button	File	Close		
Close Query	A 2.13	Close Window button	File	Close		
Close Table	A 1.25	Close Window button	File	Close		
Compact a Database	A 5.48		Tools	Database Utilities	Compact and Repair		
Collapse Subdatasheet	A 3.40	Expand indicator (-)			
Create Calculated Field	A 2.34			Zoom	SHIFT+F2
Create Data Access Page	AW 1.02	New Object: AutoForm button arrow	Page	Insert	Page		
Create Database	A 1.11	New button	File	New		CTRL+N

Microsoft Access 2002 Quick Reference Summary *(continued)*

TASK	PAGE NUMBER	MOUSE	MENU BAR	SHORTCUT MENU	KEYBOARD SHORTCUT
Create Form	A 1.35, A 4.34	New Object: AutoForm button arrow | AutoForm	Insert | AutoForm		
Create Input Mask	A 6.10	Input Mask property box			
Create Index	A 3.47	Indexes button	View | Indexes		
Create Lookup Wizard Field	A 6.08	Text arrow | Lookup Wizard			
Create Macro	A 6.29	New Object button arrow | Macro	Insert | Macro		
Create Query	A 2.06	New Object: AutoForm button arrow | Query	Insert | Query		
Create Snapshot	AI 1.13		File | Export	Export	
Create Switchboard	A 6.41		Tools | Database Utilities | Switchboard Manager		
Create Report	A 1.41	New Object AutoForm button arrow | Report	Insert | Report		
Create Table	A 1.15	Tables object | Create table in Design view or Create table by using wizard	Insert | Table		
Default Value	A 3.30	Default Value property box			
Delete Field	A 1.19, A 3.19	Delete Rows button	Edit | Delete	Delete Rows	DELETE
Delete Group of Records	A 3.26	Query Type button arrow | Delete Query	Query | Delete Query	Query Type | Delete Query	
Delete Record	A 3.14	Delete Record button	Edit | Delete Record	Delete Record	DELETE
Exclude Duplicates	A 2.26	Properties button	View | Properties | Unique Values Only	Properties | Unique Values Only	
Exclude Field from Query Results	A 2.19	Show check box			
Expand Subdatasheet	A 3.40	Expand indicator (+)			
Export Data Using Drag and Drop	AI 1.11	Drag object to desired application			
Export Data Using Export Command	AI 1.10		File | Export	Export	
Field Size	A 1.18, A 3.16	Field Size property box			
Field Type	A 1.19	Data Type box arrow | appropriate type			Appropriate letter
Filter Records	A 3.13	Filter By Selection or Filter By Form button	Records | Filter		
Format	A 3.32	Format property box			
Format a Calculated Field	A 2.33	Properties button	View | Properties	Properties	
Import Worksheet	AI 1.05		File | Get External Data | Import	Import	
Include All Fields in Query	A 2.14	Double-click asterisk in field list			
Include Field in Query	A 2.10	Double-click field in field list			
Key Field	A 1.18	Primary Key button	Edit | Primary Key	Primary Key	
Link Worksheet	AI 1.08		File | Get External Data | Link Tables	Link Tables	
Modify Switchboard Page	A 6.45, A 6.47	Edit button			
Move Control	A 4.36	Drag control			

Microsoft Access 2002 Quick Reference Summary

TASK	PAGE NUMBER	MOUSE	MENU BAR	SHORTCUT MENU	KEYBOARD SHORTCUT
Move to Design View	A 5.38	View button	View | Design View	Design View	
Move to First Record	A 1.26	First Record button			CTRL+UP ARROW
Move to Last Record	A 1.26	Last Record button			CTRL+DOWN ARROW
Move to Next Record	A 1.26	Next Record button			DOWN ARROW
Move to Previous Record	A 1.26	Previous Record button			UP ARROW
Open Database	A 1.25	Open button	File | Open		CTRL+O
Open Form	A 3.06	Forms object | Open button		Open	Use ARROW keys to move highlight to name, then press ENTER key
Open Table	A 1.21	Tables object | Open button		Open	Use ARROW keys to move highlight to name, then press ENTER key
Preview Table	A 1.29	Print Preview button	File | Print Preview	Print Preview	
Print Relationships	A 3.39		File | Print Relationships		
Print Report	A 1.46	Print button	File | Print	Print	CTRL+P
Print Results of Query	A 2.11	Print button	File | Print	Print	CTRL+P
Print Table	A 1.29	Print button	File | Print	Print	CTRL+P
Quit Access	A 1.49	Close button	File | Exit		ALT+F4
Relationships (Referential Integrity)	A 3.36	Relationships button	Tools | Relationships		
Remove Control	A 4.26	Cut button	Edit | Cut	Cut	DELETE
Remove Filter	A 3.14	Remove Filter button	Records | Remove Filter/Sort		
Resize Column	A 3.21, A 5.13	Drag right boundary of field selector	Format | Column Width	Column Width	
Resize Control	A 5.29	Drag sizing handle			
Resize Row	A 5.13	Drag lower boundary of row selector	Format | Row Height	Row Height	
Resize Section	A 4.46	Drag section boundary			
Restructure Table	A 3.16	Tables object | Design button		Design View	
Return to Design View	A 2.12	View button arrow	View | Design View		
Run Query	A 2.11	Run button	Query | Run		
Save Form	A 1.36	Save button	File | Save		CTRL+S
Save Query	A 2.41	Save button	File | Save		CTRL+S
Save Table	A 1.20	Save button	File | Save		CTRL+S
Search for Record	A 3.09	Find button	Edit | Find		CTRL+F
Select Fields for Report	A 1.43	Add Field button or Add All Fields button			
Sort Data in Query	A 2.25	Sort row | Sort row arrow | type of sort			
Sort Records	A 3.41	Sort Ascending or Sort Descending button	Records | Sort | Sort Ascending or Sort Descending	Sort Ascending or Sort Descending	
Switch Between Form and Datasheet Views	A 1.39, A 3.11	View button arrow	View | Datasheet View		
Update Hyperlink Field	A 5.18	Insert Hyperlink	Insert | Hyperlink	Hyperlink | Edit Hyperlink	CTRL+K
Update OLE Field	A 5.15		Insert | Object	Insert Object	
Use AND Criterion	A 2.23				Place criteria on same line
Use OR Criterion	A 2.24				Place criteria on separate lines
Validation Rule	A 3.29	Validation Rule property box			
Validation Text	A 3.29	Validation Text property box			